Once a Cigar Maker

Once a Cigar Maker

Men, Women, and Work Culture in American Cigar Factories, 1900–1919

Patricia A. Cooper

University of Illinois Press

Urbana and Chicago

Publication of this work was supported in part by a grant
from the Andrew W. Mellon Foundation.

Illini Books edition, 1992

This book is printed on acid-free paper

Library of Congress Cataloging-in-Publication Data

Cooper, Patricia, 1949-
    Once a cigar maker.

    (The Working class in American history)
    Bibliography: p.
    Includes index.
    1. Cigar makers—United States—History—20th century.
2. Trade-unions—Tobacco workers—United States—
History—20th century.   3. Cigar industry—United States—
History—20th century.   I. Title.   II. Series.
    HD8039.C542U63   1987   331.7′67972′0973   86–11207
    ISBN 0–252–01333–6 (cloth: alk. paper). ISBN 0–252–06257–4
(paper: alk. paper)

To my mother, Elizabeth Doyne Cooper,
and in memory of my father, Byron Nelson Cooper

We were really . . . more like a brotherhood. . . . Once a cigar maker, always a cigar maker. That means that you may get away from the trade for a couple of years, but you always have in your mind the cigar makers. And if something go wrong when you are working somewhere else, you will go back to the cigar shop. They were so congenial one with the other that you enjoy. . . . You are working for a couple of years out of the shop, at something else, and then for some reason you come back to the cigar shop they welcome you. No animosity or nothing like it. But what they used to say, once a cigar maker, always a cigar maker.

—José Santana

Mr. José Concepción Santana in his shop, Chicago, 1979. Photo courtesy of the Chicago *Sun-Times*.

Contents

Preface

I always thought that writing the acknowledgments would be one of the sweet pleasures of this book. Now I know I was right. The people I have met in the course of doing it and friends who have been beside me all along the way not only made it possible for me to undertake and complete the project, they enriched my experience of being a historian. Acknowledging them here is only the barest expression of my appreciation and thanks.

I hope that my intellectual debts will be clear from the notes, but there are some I absolutely could not bury there. Reading the work of David Montgomery inspired a young first-year graduate student fresh from a miserable clerk-typist job in Cleveland to imagine that she could write about life inside the workplace. The feminist movement, part of my life since 1969, not only shaped the way I look at the world, it bestowed both a community of women upon whom I could depend and the self-confidence to write about what matters to me. My advisor at the University of Maryland, Stuart Kaufman, a colleague rather than a mentor, encouraged me to trust my own judgment and take the study in whatever direction felt right, while his work as editor of the Samuel Gompers' papers strengthened the project at every turn. Others at Maryland, particularly Martha Ross (who taught me the trade of oral history and lent me a tape recorder to do my first interview), Ira Berlin, David Grimsted, and Hilda Smith generously offered their ideas and criticism.

It is hard to imagine having written this book without the wonderful work space and resources the Library of Congress provides to scholars. My special appreciation goes to Bruce Martin of Reader Services. It's impossible to list and name all of the other librarians and archivists who guided me through the maze of research, but I especially want to thank Joseph Howerton and Jerry Hess at the National Archives, Sara Dunlap

Jackson of the National Historical Publications and Records Commission, Pablo Calvan of the Library of Congress, Mary Boccaccio formerly of the University of Maryland Archives, and Phyllis Frey at the Kaltreider Memorial Library in Red Lion, Pennsylvania, for the time they spent helping me find material on the cigar makers.

Several colleagues faithfully read the manuscript in part or whole and offered invaluable insights and suggestions, including Cindy Aron, Susan Porter Benson, John Bukowczyk, Cynthia Costello, Pete Daniel, Maurine Greenwald, Cynthia Harrison, Dolores Janiewski, Barbara Melosh, Bill Pretzer, Glenn Westfall, and Nan Woodruff. As professionals they made me a better historian; as friends they cheered my spirits and renewed my enthusiasm. I was extremely fortunate in having David Montgomery as the reader for this manuscript, for his comments and incisive critique both energized and challenged me. Alice Kessler-Harris also generously agreed to read the manuscript and made numerous suggestions for improvement.

My resident expert on cigar makers, Dorothee Schneider, deepened my understanding of the CMIU through her research on the union in New York City during the late nineteenth century and in the process we've shared many good times, especially over a glass of Weissbier. Ava Baron sharpened my thinking and prodded me to just say what I mean. Micaela di Leonardo introduced me not only to cultural anthropology but to the variety and complexity of the field of women's studies. Her friendship and her feminism sustained me through some grim and discouraged days. My former neighbor and fellow historian, Grace Palladino, may not have read much beyond the introduction of this study, but her high standards of scholarship and her sense of humor helped carry me along to the finish line. Besides, it is refreshing to find someone else who actually likes Samuel Gompers. There are some friends who keep you going, make you laugh, or lure you away from work even though they have few direct connections to the project itself. Michael Blim, Julia Epstein, Harry Liebersohn, Julie Mostov, Dave Noble, Mary Ann O'Connor, Ellen Rose, Amy Saldinger, Judy Silver, Don Stevens, Michelle Trahan, and Jim Taylor performed these essential services for me more than once.

Few could ask for a more supportive work environment than the one I have at Drexel University. For that I warmly thank Thomas L. Canavan, dean of the College of Social Sciences and Humanities, and Bernard P. Sagik, vice-president for Academic Affairs. On a day-to-day basis, two Drexel colleagues made special contributions to this book. Philip V. Cannistraro and Gilbert Ware were always ready to offer assistance and invariably provided just the right amounts of prodding and encouragement. Without the patient efforts of Ted Fry, Julia McDonald, and Lettitia Dolores, I would still be trying to type the manuscript and get it in the mail, so my debt to them is more than obvious. The production process is never a simple matter. Richard Wentworth, director of the University of Illinois Press, and Pat Hollahan, my copyeditor, deserve a great deal of credit for bringing the book to fruition.

The heart of this study lies in oral history. The men and women who invited me into their living rooms, often shared a meal, and helped me learn about their lives, their work, and their industry deserve much more than an acknowledgment. I was truly touched by their reception. The pleasures and satisfactions of meeting people who had so much to teach me and who did so with such patience and grace made this study worth all its moments of doubt and anxiety. While it is tempting to write about each of them here, there is one cigar maker I especially want to thank, José Santana. We met almost by chance. In the fall of 1975, I wrote the Forest Home Cemetery in Chicago trying to get more information on the burial of Adolph Strasser there in 1939. The reply I received offered little about Strasser, but mentioned an old man who came to the cemetery faithfully every few weeks. Cigar makers of Local 14 had a section of ground and this gentleman came to pay his respects to them and to his wife who had died only a few years before. Would I be interested in writing him? We began a correspondence which turned into telephone interviews and then finally my first visit to Chicago in the summer of 1976. Through our long hours of conversation both on the phone and in person the four summers I visited him, he was able to transport me back into the cigar factories of eighty years ago. He became more than a respondent: he was a sincere and committed friend. Two of his daughters, Lillian Santana Dresmal and Conchita Santana Goldberg, kindly entertained this yearly visitor and made me feel forever welcome at Roscoe Street. José Santana died just shy of ninety years old in the spring of 1980, but somehow he has never been very far away from this study. It is my deep regret that he did not live to see the completed book.

Don Ritchie was unflagging in his support and unstinting in his praise. He endured much in the course of my writing this book and read parts of it so many times that I began to suspect he could recite the first three lines of some chapters by heart. He helped me smoke the free cigars I collected and celebrated each bench mark I reached. His humor, affection, and belief in me and my work sustained me throughout this project.

Once a Cigar Maker

Introduction

Little remains of the once-vibrant trade that produced both Samuel Gompers, the founder of the American Federation of Labor, and the Cigar Makers' International Union of America (CMIU), often labeled the model for craft unionism in the United States. When I began my research nearly a decade ago, I found mostly vacant buildings with dusty ledges and the thick smell of tobacco still hanging in the air, but few signs of life. At the turn of the century, however, hardly a town or city neighborhood throughout the East and Midwest, and even parts of the West, was without at least a tiny cigar workshop—perhaps with a show window so passersby could watch the lightning hands of the experienced craftsman. Not far away there might be a larger factory employing hundreds or in some cases close to a thousand workers, usually women. But by my day, the industry had just about vanished. At first, the life inside a turn-of-the-century cigar factory seemed elusive, much like the cigar's own swirl of smoke that lingers for a while and finally disappears without a trace.

The task I saw before me then was simply to reenter the workplace of eighty years ago and describe the work and activity of the men and women who spent their days there. Along the way, though, the cigar makers taught me much about relationships of power and domination in terms of class and gender. I learned by poring over newspapers and the CMIU's journal, sifting through union records, tracking down state, local, and federal investigations and reports and ferreting out studies of women's work—the usual stuff of our own craft. But mostly I learned from listening to the cigar makers I was fortunate enough to meet and visit. Oral history proved an unexpected but essential resource for this project and I have included a longer discussion of my approach to it in the Note on Sources. The everyday contours of life and work that emerged from the interviews and documentary sources helped me to reconstruct the cigar makers'

1

world as it existed during the first two decades of the twentieth century and to analyze the twists and turns of work relations in the industry.

I have termed the system of occupational customs I discerned in my research *work culture*.[1] By this I mean first the patterns of daily work into which any newcomer would become initiated after a time—the unwritten rules, the ways of doing the job, and how one thought about his or her work. But work culture is not simply a collection of interesting traditions. I found a coherent system of ideas and practices, forged in the context of the work process itself, through which workers modified, mediated, and resisted the limits of their jobs. Fundamentally the study of work culture involved examining power. Capitalist structures of production created and sustained a very specific set of human relationships. Work culture revealed the clashing and conflicting class interests of workers' shop-floor struggles with employers and expressed workers' own oppositional values and outlook. Just as important, the study of work culture exposed the contours of another form of domination—one based on gender, the socially constructed definition of what it means to be a man or a woman.[2] In a patriarchal gender system the sexual hierarchy makes women, with some exceptions, subordinate to men. The ideology of male dominance defines women as "sexual dependents, as mothers, and as housewives," whose primary function revolves around household and child-care duties.[3] Thus work culture provided an especially appropriate vehicle for viewing the intersection of class and gender in a small, competitive industry typical of hundreds of others at the turn of the century.

Two groups of workers occupy center stage of this project, male unionists who belonged to the CMIU and nonunion women who came to outnumber men in the industry during the second decade of the century. Other categories of workers are present, but play only supporting roles. These include workers in the similar-but-separate stogie industry; male cigar makers who did not belong to the union; Cuban, Spanish, and Italian workers of the Clear Havana industry in Tampa, Florida, and other factory operatives, such as tobacco stemmers, who did not roll cigars.[4] At the turn of the century, somewhere between one-third and one-half of the cigar makers in the country were members of the CMIU. Through a combination of skill and boldness, unionists maintained a higher wage level and superior working conditions for the medium-priced (ten cents and up) cigars they produced. During this period, the CMIU's influence also extended beyond its numbers because its most famous son, Samuel Gompers, headed the American Federation of Labor.

Yet at the very time the CMIU seemed to be enjoying its peak of success, shifts in the nature and organization of production were taking place which would forever alter the industry's configuration. Five-cent-cigar output expanded as large manufacturers hoped to maximize profits by using cheaper tobaccos, dividing the labor process, and hiring less skilled young immigrant women. New firms tended to enter this branch of the trade, seeing it as the expanding and more lucrative sector and the ideal way to avoid dealing with the union. Although these manufacturers divided the labor process into two steps which might be performed by hand or with the aid of simple machines, the method of production for most of the period changed little from the nineteenth century. Indeed cigar manufacturing remained so competitive and decentralized in part because of its labor intensive character. No inventor had been able to design a machine which could mass-produce the idiosyncratic cigar. Yet the industry's changing structure, evident by 1910 or so, spelled trouble for the CMIU. Union men were not only being pushed out of the cheaper grades of production, their own more expensive cigars increasingly suffered from the competition. Signs of concentration grew more ominous by the century's second decade as several large nonunion firms opened numerous branch factories, adopted elementary machinery, and began claiming a larger and larger share of production. By 1920 women accounted for 58 percent of the labor force and the CMIU was visibly in retreat.

I confess I began this project with a distinct prejudice against the CMIU and its members. I assumed that the wooden cigar mold introduced in the 1870s had completely "bastardized"[5] the work process, transformed the industry, and rendered the union helpless. Besides, the CMIU and its leaders represented what was worst about the American labor movement in general: its essentially narrow, conservative, selfish, and patriarchal perspective. But I soon discovered a rather different picture. I had written the epitaph prematurely, because the CMIU was alive and well in the early twentieth century and continued to exert a great deal of influence not only in the industry but throughout the labor movement. More surprising, I came to recognize that this was not simply a business union whose members cared only about their own immediate needs in bread-and-butter terms. Even if Sam Gompers had consciously aimed in that direction, and there is much to suggest that his own outlook was much more complex,[6] his reorganization of the CMIU in 1879 had not given him and his friends a blank check. Rank-and-file cigar makers continued to shape their organization and to argue matters of class and union with each other and with their leaders long after the ink was dry on the new constitution.

To understand the CMIU's members, it was necessary to steer between two simplistic conceptions of craft unionists—that they were little more than racist, sexist, white male labor aristocrats and class collaborationists, or alternatively that they were the exclusive standard-bearers of anti-capitalist thought during the late nineteenth and early twentieth centuries.[7] Certainly the consciousness of cigar makers and other skilled union members of the day was infected with racism and a sense of ethnic superiority, and was rooted in a belief in male supremacy. Their labor militancy must not be mistaken for a committed radicalism and there were clear limitations in their outlook. Yet we have not fully unlocked the puzzle of craft unionism and the crisis it faced in the early twentieth century simply by exposing its faults. I tried to avoid rigid standards of class consciousness and terms such as "false consciousness" or "craft consciousness," because I wanted most of all to take these cigar makers seriously and view them on their own terms.[8]

What I found was a work culture which stressed autonomy, collective identity, and mutual aid, a fierce independence, pride, and self-worth, control over work, respect for manliness, a sense of both adventure and humor, duty to the trade, and loyalty to each other. Cigar makers asserted their class interests vis à vis employers through both shop-floor customs and, when the occasion demanded it, collective action in the form of strikes. One of their work culture's key features was a tradition of geographic mobility which initiated newcomers to the trade by sending them on the road to test their skills and scout out the cigar-making landscape. But the tradition of travel was more than simply an element of work culture—it made that work culture national. It reinforced shared values and helped to weave members together into a brotherhood, a community which cut across ethnic, neighborhood, and geographic lines. To underscore this important aspect of their work culture, I decided to treat unionists in a national rather than local context and interviewed surviving members wherever I could find them—in Denver, New Haven, Chicago, Boston, and several places in New Hampshire and Pennsylvania. Each locale had its own special ethnic character and history, but what I wanted to capture is the way in which their work culture bound them together despite these distances. Certainly their work culture had its limitations, as we shall see. But to understand it we must view it as whole cloth. It embodied values that were at once egalitarian and exclusivistic, generous and reactionary, anticapitalist and accommodationist. To us these seem oddly contradictory, but at the time they had a logic all their own.[9] Tragically, the very strength of cigar makers' work culture proved to be their downfall, for it rested on members' solidarity and manliness, whose other side was exclusivity and male supremacy. Unable to open their doors to women team workers or to confront the vast changes in the industry, union cigar makers guaranteed their own demise and the consequent collapse of their work culture.

Not surprisingly, manufacturers at the turn of the century wanted to avoid this troublesome union. Those who led the way in large-scale, five-cent-cigar manufacture expected that their reorganization of the production process and their choice of women as workers would yield higher profits and a pliable labor force. They did not necessarily get what they wanted. The women they hired, who primarily worked in factories with other women rather than alongside men, developed their own work culture quite apart from the CMIU or craft traditions. To examine their workplace patterns, I focused on two specific geographic areas. I did so in part because women lacked a national framework and had no meaningful links to each other beyond the immediate community. By viewing them more firmly in a community context, I was also able to highlight some of the ways gender defined their association with both work and home. I chose Detroit, Michigan, and the towns of southeastern Pennsylvania because both were expanding centers of women's employment and five-cent-cigar production and because they permitted some comparison between rural and urban settings.[10]

The work culture of women was distinctive in several respects, but it also paralleled that of men in many ways. Both developed a cohesiveness and solidarity which served them well in their workplace struggles. Both sought to maximize their freedom to determine work conditions and assert control on the shop floor. These were no passive female victims. They too assaulted and challenged managerial authority and took part in dramatic strikes often over the same grievances as male unionists. Their actions demonstrated that workers did not need a craft tradition in order to create an assertive, dynamic work culture, one which revealed a consciousness of differing class interests. Thus while nonunion manufacturers achieved some of the advantages they had sought, ultimately their solution to the labor problem proved unsatisfactory.

The study of work culture revealed much about the social relations of production at the turn of the century, but it also offered important insights about the social division of the sexes.[11] (I might add that it obviously also revealed something about race since almost all workers in the industry were white throughout this period.) The patriarchal system of gender relations meant that men's and women's experiences would not be the same. Employers organized the workplace according to their assumptions regarding gender: it was no accident that they hired women for deskilled, low-paying jobs. Men's and women's resources as workers, while meager, were different and for the most part unequal. Union men had access to forms of power less available to women.[12] Their mobility, for example, diminished the ignorance and isolation of the lone shop, bound them together over great distances, and provided them with an added basis for challenging managerial authority. They also had the advantage of a union and the financial benefits and resources it bestowed.

While gender was not the only factor shaping women's working lives during these years, it was a central one. In contrast to men, women remained more isolated from each other and burdened by their second jobs in the home. Throughout their daily lives, women encountered a sexual hierarchy in which men were more privileged. At home they held a lower status than male kinsmen, who benefited from their unpaid household labor, and at work they experienced subordination both as workers and as women. Sexual harassment, too, reminded them of their place. Gender complicated the efforts of CMIU members to organize women cigar makers, since male unionists tended to characterize them either as helpless victims or as exploited workers and potential prostitutes. Women were not part of a community of insiders not only because they posed an economic threat, but also because they were women.

Yet women's separate sphere did not always mean weakness and victimization—indeed at times it worked as a resource for them, fostering a form of solidarity out of separateness. Analysis of women's work culture reveals this cohesiveness. Paid employment did not miraculously liberate working women during the early twentieth century; the structures of work frequently duplicated the patriarchal authority structure in the home. Yet as several scholars have recently demonstrated, the experience of paid work was central to working women's consciousness because the workplace created a special set of circumstances not duplicated elsewhere. Without discounting the significance of neighborhood and ethnic ties, it is important to recognize that work itself forged identities at least as strong.[13] In contrast to the isolation of the home, work provided a place for women to associate and to talk about common experiences and needs.[14]

In all-female workplaces, it additionally provided the possibility of some autonomy from men. Cigar making itself required a degree of cooperation which helped cement a recognition of group rather than individual interests. While they may not have developed a feminist outlook, women had clear notions regarding what treatment they were entitled to based on traditional notions of womanhood. This "female consciousness,"[15] as one scholar has termed it, provided them with a basis for acting collectively to preserve their rights. The workplace thus facilitated the recognition of women's collective interests both as workers and as women.

The work cultures of male unionists and women cigar makers converged under the special conditions prevailing during World War I, which provided cigar makers with opportunities to win wage increases and shop demands. They briefly joined together, united by goals relating to both work cultures. This massive strike movement, which demanded shop control in the form of a grievance committee, suggested the possibility of an alliance across skill and gender lines. The threat of labor militancy and the specter of a united labor force stunned union and nonunion manufacturers alike. Yet the dramatic entrance of new and revolutionary technology in 1919 signified manufacturers' superior power and paved the way for the introduction of a new group of workers with no previous ties to the industry.

In treating these workers and their work cultures, one discerns elements of "consent"[16] along with resistance, and limitations as well as possibilities. Union men failed to face up to the changes around them and labor militancy never was transformed into a unified revolutionary vision of a truly classless, feminist, nonracist society. Wartime solidarity was fleeting, and gender continued to divide workers in the industry. Yet the story of these men and women constitutes an honorable chapter in the history of "struggles for human recognition"[17] which still require our attention and energy.

Notes

1. Barbara Melosh, *"The Physician's Hand": Work Culture and Conflict in American Nursing* (Philadelphia, 1982), pp. 5–6. My ideas about work culture have been influenced most by Barbara Melosh and Susan Porter Benson. See Benson, *Counter Cultures: Saleswomen, Managers, and Customers in American Department Stores, 1890–1940* (Urbana, Ill., 1986). See also Ken Kusterer, *Know-How on the Job: The Important Working Knowledge of "Unskilled" Workers* (Boulder, Colo., 1978).

2. See Gayle Rubin, "The Traffic in Women: Notes on the 'Political Economy' of Sex," in Rayna Reiter, ed., *Towards an Anthropology of Women* (New York, 1975), pp. 157–210 and n. 2, chap. 8. While I do not fully agree with his provocative analysis, see also Isaac Balbus, *Marxism and Domination: A Neo-Hegelian, Feminist, Psychoanalytic Theory of Sexual, Political and Technological Liberation* (Princeton, N.J., 1982).

3. Cynthia Costello, "Working Women's Consciousness and Collective Action: The Case of the Strike at the Wisconsin Educational Association Insurance Trust," paper presented at the meetings of the American Sociological Society, Aug. 1983, Detroit, Mich. Regarding patriarchy and the sex/gender system see Rubin, "Traffic in Women," and Heidi Hartmann, "The Unhappy Marriage of Marxism and Feminism: Towards a More Progressive Union," in Lydia Sargent, ed., *Women and Revolution: A Discussion of the Unhappy Marriage of Marxism and Feminism* (Boston, 1981), pp. 1–12, along with the other essays in the volume.

4. I found the least information on nonunion men and therefore have been unwilling to make many generalizations about them here.

5. With apologies to Sean Wilentz, *Chants Democratic: New York City and the Rise of the American Working Class, 1788–1850* (New York, 1984), pp. 107–42.

6. See Stuart Kaufman, *Samuel Gompers and the Origins of the American Federation of Labor, 1848–1896* (Westport, Conn., 1973) and forthcoming research on Gompers by Grace Palladino.

7. David Montgomery, *Workers' Control in America: Studies in the History of Work, Technology and Labor Struggles* (Cambridge, 1979); Jim Green, "Culture, Politics and Workers' Response to Industrialization in the U.S.," *Radical America*, 16 (Jan.–Mar. 1982), 122–26; Jean Monds, "Workers' Control and the Historians: A New Economism," *New Left Review*, 97 (May-June 1976), 81–99; Harold Benanson, "The Community and Family Bases of U.S. Working Class Protest, 1880–1920: A Critique of the 'Skill Degradation' and 'Ecological' Perspectives," in Louis Kriesberg, ed., *Research in Social Movements, Conflicts and Change*, vol. 8 (Greenwich, Conn., 1985); Lawrence T. McDonnell, "'You Are Too Sentimental': Problems and Suggestions for a New Labor History," *Journal of Social History*, 17 (Summer 1984), 629–54.

8. See Sean Wilentz, "Against Exceptionalism: Class Consciousness and the American Labor Movement," *International Labor and Working Class History*, no. 26 (Fall 1984), 1–24; Eric Foner, "Why Is There No Socialism in the United States?" *History Workshop Journal*, 17 (Spring 1984), 57–80.

9. Andrew Dawson, "History and Ideology: Fifty Years of 'Job Consciousness,'" *Literature and History*, 8 (Autumn 1978), 223–41; Andrew Dawson, "The Paradox of Dynamic Technological Change and the Labor Aristocracy in the United States, 1880–1914," *Labor History*, 20 (Summer 1979), 345–48; Andrew Dawson, "The Parameters of Craft Consciousness: The Social Outlook of the Skilled Worker, 1890–1920," in Dirk Hoerder, ed., *American Labor and Immigration History, 1877–1920s: Recent European Research* (Urbana, Ill., 1983), pp. 135–55.

10. This approach did not come out of my conviction that such a compartmentalization of work and home is preferable or that work is somehow more important than home for either men or women. In large part it is a function of the limitations

of space in any single study and the history of this particular project, based as it was on oral history interviews and the difficulties of reinterviewing informants. See Roslyn L. Feldberg and Evelyn Nakano Glenn, "Male and Female: Job versus Gender Models in the Sociology of Work," *Social Problems,* 26 (June 1979), 524–38, for a critical view of separating work and home.

11. See, for example, the essays in Lydia Sargent, *Women and Revolution,* and Zillah Eisenstein, *Capitalist Patriarchy and the Case for Socialist Feminism* (New York, 1979).

12. Sarah Eisenstein, *Give Us Bread but Give Us Roses: Working Women's Consciousness in the United States, 1890 to the First World War* (London, 1983), pp. 40–43; Thomas Dublin, *Women at Work: The Transformation of Work and Community in Lowell, Massachusetts, 1826–1860* (New York, 1979); Ruth Milkman, "Organizing the Sexual Division of Labor: Historical Perspectives on 'Women's Work' and the American Labor Movement," *Socialist Review,* 49 (1980), 110.

13. See Louise A. Tilly, "Paths of Proletarianization: Organization of Production, Sexual Division of Labor, and Women's Collective Action," *Signs,* 7 (Winter 1981), 400–417; Melosh, *"Physician's Hand,"* p. 219.

14. Eisenstein, *Give Us Bread,* passim. See Benson's study of department-store clerks, *Counter Cultures,* and her handling of their identities as workers, as women, and as consumers. It is especially important to view women in terms of work because too often scholars have assumed the primacy of home and family for women and of the public sphere for men. See Feldberg and Glenn, "Male and Female."

15. See Temma Kaplan, "Female Consciousness and Collective Action: The Case of Barcelona, 1910–1918," *Signs,* 7 (Spring 1982), 545–66.

16. Michael Burawoy, *Manufacturing Consent: Changes in the Labor Process under Monopoly Capitalism* (Chicago, 1979).

17. Balbus, *Marxism and Domination,* pp. 3–8.

"Keep on Rolling Them"
The Nineteenth-Century Setting

When thirteen-year-old Samuel Gompers arrived in New York City from London in July 1863, cigar manufacturing was a tiny U.S. industry, producing only about two hundred million cigars yearly and employing fewer than five thousand cigar makers. Small craft shops with only one to four workers dominated the cigar-making landscape, although there were a few larger establishments with twenty workers or more. Most smokers in the U.S. preferred snuff, chewing, and pipe tobacco, but even those who enjoyed cigars generally bought imported brands—the cheapest from Germany and Belgium and the finer, fancy grades from Cuba.[1]

Before the 1830s and 1840s, most domestic production had rested in the hands of tobacco-growing farm families, who rolled cigars for their own use or bartered them to nearby storekeepers. They in turn traded to local or regional wholesale dealers, who sold and resold the cigars up and down the coast. But when Dutch, English, and especially German immigrants began settling in eastern cities before the Civil War, they brought their cigar-making skills with them and set up craft shops producing a finer quality domestic cigar. For them, cigar making was a full-time occupation. On the eve of the Civil War, the trade could be found in Baltimore, Cincinnati, Detroit, Richmond, St. Louis, several places in Connecticut, upstate New York, and Massachusetts. The weed's popularity had started to inch upward as well: per capita cigar consumption rose from ten in 1850 to twenty-six ten years later. In 1862 Congress imposed a tax on manufactured cigars and two years later required manufacturers to place a bond on their factories. Both actions increased the cost of opening one's own shop and stimulated the growth of larger-scale production, despite the protests of many cigar makers who rightly claimed that they were quickly becoming wage earners instead of craftsmen. The tariffs of the 1860s, together with the disruption of the Civil War, virtually eliminated German and Belgian imports and further stimulated domestic industry.[2]

So Samuel Gompers arrived in New York just as cigar making was becoming a true industry. Gompers initially worked in his father's craft shop in the house the family rented on the East Side near the shipyards. But, symbolic of the changes occurring, he soon went to work in a small factory, as a wage earner, not an independent craftsman. While still with his father he had joined Local 15 of the Cigar Makers' International Union (CMIU), although both the local and the parent body were new and weak. When he decided to look for an outside job, he and a friend walked from shop to shop until they got a chance at M. Stachelberg's on Pearl Street. As was the custom, Gompers was given the opportunity to show his skill. He began forming the loose filler tobacco in his hand, then deftly rolled it up in the coarse binder leaf to form a bunch. Next he added the delicate outer wrapper, making sure to taper the tuck (the lighting end) and perfectly round and finish the opposite end, called the head. Having made two such finely crafted smokes, Gompers won a place at the bench as a journeyman.[3] He thus became part of a small industry where all the work was done by hand, where each year a few more cigar makers worked in factories, where a tiny union struggled to survive, and where craft traditions in such a new industry were just then in the making.

In April 1909, nearly fifty years later, another cigar maker disembarked in New York City after a long voyage. Nineteen-year-old José Santana had left his home in Mayagüez, Puerto Rico, hoping to support his wish to travel by making cigars. He had learned to make them by hand—the finest, known as Clear Havanas—first in a small shop and later in a large factory near his hometown. Arriving in New York with $20 in his pocket and knowing only a few words of English, he quickly began walking the streets looking for a job. The cigar industry he encountered jolted him. The large factories and small shops seemed familiar enough, but here so many of the cigar makers were women, and they frequently worked under a division of labor known as the team system. Instead of working alone by hand, three people worked in a team to make only half a cigar, using wooden shaping blocks called molds or sometimes even machinery in parts of the process. He finally walked into one factory run by and filled with Bohemians who, along with Germans, dominated the trade in the

city. Despite the language barrier, Santana understood that the company
had just received a special order for high-grade cigars—all handwork. He
nervously sat down with the sample, knowing that his money was dwindling and that he desperately needed a job. "So I start by working, trying
to make really artistic work and I look at the sample . . . I try to put more
knowledge or ability" into it. He passed the test and won the job. In a few
weeks he joined CMIU Local 90, a large union of about sixteen hundred
members, hoping to secure a better position. When it became clear in
a couple of months that there were no union jobs available, he left the
city and went to London, Ontario, where he had heard about plenty of
openings.[4]

Both men arrived as craftsmen, with patiently learned skills in con-
structing a fine cigar, but in the fifty years which had elapsed between
their separate arrivals, the industry and the CMIU had changed dramatically. In 1909, Manhattan had hundreds of manufactures—from huge
firms employing over one thousand workers to small shops with only a
handful of people working. Cigars by the early twentieth century were
America's most popular tobacco product—6.7 billion were produced in
the U.S. that year (representing about 350,000 different brands!) and per
capita consumption had risen to nearly seventy-five. Somewhere between
120,000 and about 150,000 people found employment in the industry generally and perhaps about 90,000 to 110,000 of them were cigar makers.
The industry had spread into nearly every state, although 90 percent of
U.S. cigars came from Pennsylvania, New York, Ohio, New Jersey, Florida, Illinois, Michigan, Virginia, and Massachusetts respectively. Samuel
Gompers no longer worked at the cigar maker's bench, but headed the
American Federation of Labor, and the once-insignificant CMIU now
reached its zenith with 44,000 members, probably about 40 to 48 percent
of the country's cigar makers.[5]

The full story of these changes and exactly how they unfolded must be
left to another historian, but the life of a cigar maker—man or woman,
union or nonunion—in the early twentieth century, the focus of this
study, had a great deal to do with the history that had passed before.
The industry witnessed a transition to factory production, a separation
into branches from the grandest Clear Havana to the meanest, cheapest
stogie. Workers had also been sorted into categories with different skills,
pay, and working conditions. More women entered the trade, and molds
and machines altered the work process. The CMIU had evolved into a
model for the American labor movement; and while it sustained repeated

setbacks in the midst of industrial change and depression, it did not die with the introduction of the mold or bunching machines. Nor was it simply a narrow craft union which perfectly reflected the goals and ideology of its most famous son, Samuel Gompers. Over the course of the 1870s and 1880s it was molded into a complex organization full of contradictions and encompassing people who sometimes had conflicting goals and ideas. A survey of the outlines of these changes provides the background necessary for understanding the two primary groups of workers in the industry by the early twentieth century, union members and non-union women, and offers some important clues about the work cultures they created.

What happened between the arrivals of Gompers and Santana? Certainly part of the answer lies in the changing landscape of America in general in the late nineteenth century. Industrial capitalism entered a new and expansive phase after the Civil War, and the great trusts began their quest for centralization and monopoly. The whole fabric of life seemed to stand on its head. Cigars fit the times. They had become the ubiquitous symbol of the gaudy, freewheeling Gilded Age and a familiar prop in male culture. In the homes of the well-to-do, gentlemen withdrew from the ladies after dinner to enjoy fine cigars and brandy while they discussed matters they regarded as important. In other neighborhoods, working men gathered at a popular saloon after work to talk and enjoy a smoke and a stein of beer. Politicians crowded into proverbial smoke-filled rooms to cut deals and make the choices voters could not.

Cigars soared in popularity in the 1870s and 1880s. The industry experienced an explosion of growth as consumption jumped a mighty 107 percent during the ten years after 1870, while the population grew by just 30 percent. By 1890 the industry turned out four billion cigars a year. The number of factories rose from 4,631 in 1869 to 14,522 in 1899. The expansion took place independent of other tobacco industries: cigar manufacturers were a new group of entrepreneurs with no connections to snuff, pipe, or chewing tobacco producers. Cigar leaf was also unique, grown outside the South and much of it imported, and the whole process of production had completely different requirements from any other tobacco product.[6]

Before the Civil War, makers of cigars integrated every phase, from buying leaf from the farmer to making the cigars to distribution. By the time Gompers arrived, however, parts of the industry were breaking off and specializing in specific functions. During the 1860s, the process of preparing and marketing cigar tobacco became the province of packers and dealers. They purchased the tobacco from farmers, treated and packed it, and then sold it locally or regionally. Leaf was no simple matter in an industry where standards of quality were rising. It took three different types of tobacco to make a cigar: filler provided the taste, binder held together the distinctive shape and form, and the thin, pliable outer wrapper leaf gave the cigar its color and appearance. The best tobaccos were imported, and the world's finest were grown in the Vuelta Abajo region of Cuba, an area which had a unique blend of soil and climate. By the 1890s, Sumatra wrappers, cheaper than Cuban, had come into vogue. Good U.S. leaf was grown in Connecticut and Wisconsin, while a lower grade came from Ohio and Pennsylvania. By the end of the century the leaf business became fairly concentrated and several large companies ruled the field. They established the industry's first trade papers—*Tobacco Leaf* (1865), *U.S. Tobacco Journal* (1874), and *Tobacco* (1886)—which circulated widely throughout the entire industry by the 1890s, treating everything from the tobacco itself to the retail counter.[7]

Distribution had also developed into a separate business by the second half of the nineteenth century. A few wholesale tobacco dealers operated before the Civil War, but a permanent group of cigar jobbers and dealers became firmly established in the 1870s. Some specialized in imported cigars, while the rest handled those produced domestically. Jobbers and wholesale grocers coordinated regional distribution and supplied retail outlets such as drug stores, tobacconists, and grocery stores. Few cigars were marketed nationally during these years and there were no national brand names. Small firms and shops continued to take custom orders and sell in the neighborhood, relying on the street trade, local saloons, and barber shops for sales.[8]

Manufacturing itself underwent vast changes during the late nineteenth century. As Gompers' own family illustrated, cigar manufacturing moved from the independent producer to precorporate forms (firms that were owned and managed by the same person) of large-scale factory production during these years. From the late nineteenth century on, a majority of cigar manufactures were always small shops with only a handful of workers, but during the 1870s an increasing proportion of cigars were being made in larger-sized firms of twenty to fifty workers, where the manufacturer himself no longer worked alongside his employees. The adoption of the mold in the 1870s had operated to boost factory size. By the 1890s, several large companies in various cities had factories employing several hundred and a few employed over one thousand workers. The small and the large grew together during the late nineteenth century, however, and in 1900, according to one estimate, 25 percent of U.S. production still came from shops with only one to three workers.[9]

The smallest shops continued to integrate the entire manufacturing process from preparing the raw tobacco to packing the finished cigars for shipping. Once more than ten or so workers were employed, however, the steps were divided into separate departments and work was often sex-segregated. Male casers wet and sorted the tobacco while female stemmers stripped away the midrib of the leaf. Stripping had initially been a boy's occupation, a stepping-stone to a cigar-making job. By the 1870s, it was becoming a separate occupation and manufacturers hired women for this dirty, dead-end, low-wage work. By the turn of the century stemming was primarily done by women. As one of the industry's least desirable jobs, stemming was one of the few places one might find black workers in a cigar factory during the period. Unlike much of the rest of the U.S. tobacco industry, which centered in the South and often depended on black labor, cigar factories hired few black workers—a result both of racist hiring policies and the industry's location away from black population centers. Cigar making itself had for some time been confined to male craftsmen, but during the 1870s manufacturers began dividing the labor process and hiring women. After the cigars were made, packers, whose ranks had traditionally been men but now increasingly included more women as the century drew to a close, carefully sorted the cigars by colors and packed them into brightly decorated cedar boxes.[10]

Cigars were not all alike. Indeed, one of the chief characteristics of cigar production during the late nineteenth century was the importance of product differentiation. In general, cigars broke into four large groupings: Clear Havanas, Seed and Havanas, five-cent cigars, and stogies. Each group was defined by the types of tobacco used, the methods of production, the nature of the work force, and a rather rigid graduated scale of retail prices. The latter moved from stogies selling at two for five cents to nickel cigars to ten-cent brands to those retailing at two for a quarter, fifteen or twenty cents each, and up. Prices in the cigar industry could not be raised. The five-cent cigar was an institution, and a six-cent cigar would be simply unthinkable. Profits came from volume selling or reducing labor, handling, and tobacco costs. Although there were some exceptions, manufacturers tended to concentrate on only one type of cigar so that each group developed somewhat distinctly from the others.[11]

Foremost were the Clear Havana cigars, made in the U.S. just as they were in Havana, using all Cuban tobaccos. These were the country's grandest smokes and, not surprisingly, its most expensive. Prices started at fifteen cents and went up from there. They were made using only the most expert workmanship, and they came in hundreds of different sizes, shapes, styles, and colors. The most discriminating smokers willingly paid high prices for exactly the cigar they preferred. About twenty general styles were widely recognized, some with tapered tucks or other special contours, and they carried Spanish names known as "front marks," suggestive of the cigar's appearance: corona, coquetta, brevas, perfecto, favorita, etc. It took years to learn to make these intricate shapes by hand. Their high price arose not only from the expensive labor required, but also the high quality leaf used.[12]

The Clear Havana had first been produced, of course, in Cuba in the eighteenth century. The cigar industry there grew after tobacco replaced coffee as Cuba's most lucrative export in the 1840s. Spaniards owned most of the factories, but Cubans outnumbered them in the labor force. During the 1860s, a number of manufacturers left the island and moved to Key West, Florida, and New York City to bypass steep U.S. import duties and to escape the instability created by the Ten Years' War with Spain. Vicente Ybor, a Spaniard who had emigrated to Cuba in 1832, strongly sympathized with his adopted country in its war with Spain. He moved his factory first to Key West in 1869 and then to New York in 1878. Plagued in both places by labor problems, Ybor in 1886 founded his own company town, Ybor City, just two miles west of the quiet village of Tampa on Florida's western cost. By the end of the century, while some Clear Havanas were made in New York City, Chicago, Denver, San Francisco, New Orleans, and Key West, the undisputed capital of the North American Clear Havana industry was Tampa. Indeed, it rivaled Havana itself.[13]

Tampa cigar makers were a special group of workers who had little connection to the rest of the North American industry. Cubans from Havana, a small percentage of whom were black, and Spaniards, recently from Havana but originally from the Spanish provinces of Galicia and Asturias, dominated the labor force initially. During the 1890s, Sicilians from the province of Agrigento began emigrating to Tampa and working in the industry. By the turn of the century about 60 percent of cigar workers were Cuban, 23 percent Italian, and the rest Spanish. A majority were men, but some women also made cigars. In Ybor City cigar makers recreated much of the life of Havana, with small groceries and taverns positioned on every corner and coffee vendors walking the streets and the aisles of cigar factories. Ties with Havana remained strong and cigar makers moved freely back and forth between the two cities throughout the late nineteenth and early twentieth centuries.[14]

Radical politics was a central part of life in Ybor City. Within a year after Vicente Ybor opened his factory there, the cigar workers, led by anarchists, conducted their first strike. Cuban cigar makers had long traditions of labor militancy, concern with class issues, and participation in various workers' associations. They had played an important role in working-class struggles in Cuba in the nineteenth century. Spaniards too had often been exposed to various socialist and anarchist ideologies in Spain before arriving in Cuba. Both groups of cigar makers set up numerous political clubs and newspapers in Tampa which reflected several streams of radical thought. The Italians contributed to this ideological mix from their experiences in various peasant uprisings in the early 1890s in Italy. They joined existing associations in Tampa and formed their own anarchist and socialist organizations and publications.[15]

At the other end of the cigar-making spectrum stood the cheapest cigars and stogies. Although the latter were sometimes referred to as cigars, they were viewed in the trade as a distinctively separate item manufactured by an altogether different set of producers. Cigars were usually made using long pieces of filler leaf, but stogies were made using domestically grown "short" (chopped-up) filler. Many were made without binders and no attention was paid to shape or contour. When the labor was divided, as it often was, machinery could easily be used in both the bunching and rolling stages. Although the industry was scattered throughout many communities in Ohio and Pennsylvania, the two primary centers of production were Wheeling, West Virginia, and Pittsburgh, Pennsylvania, the capital of the industry. Wheeling workers concentrated on handmade stogies and their union, the National Stogie Makers' League (formerly affiliated with the Knights of Labor), was formed in 1896. While some handwork remained in Pittsburgh, most stogies there were made under the team system with molds and machinery. Pittsburgh workers in the late nineteenth century were primarily Jewish, and women were replacing men in the trade, especially by the 1890s when bunching and rolling machines were introduced. In 1900 women outnumbered men by three to one.[16]

The last two categories of cigars, five-cent cigars and Seed and Havanas, were the largest groupings both in terms of cigars manufactured and in terms of numbers of cigar makers employed, and this study focuses on them. Manufactured primarily in larger eastern and midwestern cities, nickel cigars were made from domestic tobacco, possibly with some imported leaf, and came in only two or three different shapes. Manufacturers usually divided the labor process and often used machinery or at least molds. Bunch breakers shaped the long filler leaf and placed it in a binder. The bunch then went into the shaping mold and was pressed for twenty minutes or more.[17]

While men and women made five-cent cigars during the nineteenth century, the trend over the course of the last two decades moved toward hiring women exclusively. Manufacturers in New York City had been the first to hire women in the 1860s, but soon women found employment open to them in several cities including Detroit, Cincinnati, Baltimore, Chicago, and Philadelphia. Over the course of the late nineteenth century, manufacturers' interest in hiring women increased so that by 1910 when Edith Abbott studied the industry she concluded that it showed a definite "tendency to develop into a women's industry." Women workers and five-cent cigars were especially compatible, it seems. A manufacturer interviewed in New York City in 1886 commented that "men ought not to be engaged in cigar making at all. The vocation is fit only for women." If women became the industry's workers, "then the business will be pursued without these constant strikes and interruptions." The cheaper smoke meant that a division of labor and even some machinery could be used. In turn, hiring less skilled women workers lowered production costs and permitted manufacturers to sell a fairly good quality cigar for only five cents. By the turn of the century, one-third of the industry's labor force was female and a majority of five-cent-cigar makers were women.[18] With a few important exceptions, by 1900 women tended to work in all-female cigar-making departments in large factories which employed anywhere from twenty to several hundred or even one thousand workers.

The last category, the Seed and Havanas, was named for the tobaccos used to make the cigars—a blend of domestic tobaccos and Havana leaf. These generally came in three or four styles with several variations in shape and length. While a division of labor might be used and molds were quite common, one would not find them made by machinery. They sold principally for ten cents, although some were more expensive. Small shops tended to make ten-cent cigars, although these brands were sometimes manufactured in the largest factories. The latter, however, usually manufactured cheaper smokes. Most makers of ten-cent cigars were men and over the course of the period, as the CMIU grew and expanded, its members came to dominate this category. As they were being pushed out of five-cent cigar production, they sought to compensate by increasing their ranks not only in ten-cent cigars, but even in Clear Havanas, outside of Tampa. By 1900, a pattern had developed whereby union cigar makers had secured this niche for themselves in the Seed and Havana trade.[19] As nickel cigars improved in quality, however, they could increasingly hold their own in competition with ten-cent brands.

The picture for the CMIU, however, had begun quite differently. Sam Gompers arrived in New York just a year before a handful of small cigar makers' unions from Pennsylvania, New York, New Jersey, Ohio, Connecticut, Massachusetts, Rhode Island, and Michigan met in that city and formed the National Cigar Makers' Union. When Canadian locals joined in 1867, members changed the name to the Cigar Makers' International Union of America. Yet the new union was barely alive in the early 1870s. The introduction of the mold and the division of labor, along with the growth of factory employment, meant that cigar making was by no means a high-status occupation. The depression had only worsened conditions generally and weakened the CMIU. Membership fell from 5,900 in 1869 to 3,771 in 1873 and to 1,016 in 1877.[20]

Locals had little connection to each other and few resources upon which to draw. In the midst of the depression, they could do little about the degraded conditions under which members worked. In Kansas City, where cigar makers organized in 1871, most continued to work in shops until ten or eleven at night. There as elsewhere, cigar makers were always paid by the piece, so much money per thousand cigars. On payday, they received half their wages in cigars and spent half the weekend peddling them "the best way you could." Sometimes the pay came in vegetables rather than specie, a practice known in many trades as the "truck" system. Cigar makers who traveled to find work "were compelled to board where the boss sent them." Frequently cigar makers had to pay for the oil they used in lamps or they had to furnish their own candles. In some factories, cigar makers had to buy the molds and presses, "but a large majority of us balked on that," one cigar maker noted forty years later. The CMIU could do little to protect its members from such practices.[21]

To understand the development of the CMIU as a trade union, it is most useful to view it in the nineteenth century in New York City, the union's cradle and the industry's center during the period. Ethnicity, system of work, gender, and political ideology divided the cigar makers of

New York City in the 1870s and 1880s. The lines overlapped and conflicted with each other, producing a complex pattern of association and alliance and posing a formidable challenge to any serious effort at organization. In the early 1860s, when Gompers had first arrived, New York City cigar makers had been mostly native-born or German, but by the end of the decade, Bohemians, a majority of whom were women, had become a significant group in the labor force. They worked in an industry located on the lower East Side of Manhattan, which was changing in the 1870s. While small shops of only one to three workers still predominated, larger units of production were becoming more common. In 1877, four companies had over five hundred workers and half of the city's cigar makers went to work in factories with more than twenty employees. More women were entering the industry both in the factories and in the tenement house system. Here families of cigar makers, mostly Bohemians, made cigars by the piece in tenements they rented from manufacturers who supplied them with the tobacco.[22]

Up to the 1880s, immigrant cigar makers in New York preferred to affiliate with their own mutual aid and fraternal organizations and the New York CMIU union, Local 15, had little influence among them. Beginning in 1872, however, another nucleus of cigar makers entered the arena, the United Cigar Makers. Adolph Strasser, a German-speaking Hungarian, Samuel Gompers and a group of others, several of whom were also in the CMIU, stressed political activity, socialist principles, and organizing immigrant workers without regard to skill. Such an approach won many adherents, but as Gompers and Strasser consolidated their hold on the UC's leadership, their policies began to shift from this initial approach. When it affiliated with the CMIU in 1875 as Local 144, the union had already adopted a policy of high dues, a strong benefit package (including an out-of-work benefit, almost unheard-of at the time), and the elimination of separate language sections. These measures could only limit accessibility and keep out the very workers whom the union had initially targeted. Although the situation was still somewhat fluid at this point, differences had clearly developed among cigar makers regarding the goals and approaches of unions and organizing workers in general.[23]

The great strike of 1877 erupted in New York City in the midst of the union's reorganization and just as cigar makers throughout the city were reeling from the effects of the depression. Inspired perhaps by a nationwide railroad strike, cigar makers in several New York City shops successfully walked out and won major wage increases. Quickly the strike spread to other factories and to the tenement houses. By October 1877, about ten thousand men and women had left their benches. Despite initial reservations, Local 144 supported the strike. Assisted, but not dominated, by the union was the Central Committee which coordinated all strike activities. While it permitted no separate ethnic divisions, it admitted anyone in the industry and each shop in the city sent representatives to its deliberations. Efforts to continue the Central Committee after the strike failed in January 1878, however, were unsuccessful.[24]

In the wake of the strike, division among cigar makers sharpened, now based more on ideology than ethnicity, as Dorothee Schneider has demonstrated. Socialists criticized both Strasser and Gompers for their conduct of the strike and their opening of a cooperative-style factory. Criticism only multiplied as Gompers and Strasser proceeded with their plan to revamp completely the structure of the International. These men believed, and past experience confirmed, that the CMIU's initial structure doomed it as ineffectual, little more than a "collection of loosely federated locals." Their plan of reorganization roughly followed their previous prescription for Local 144. It included centralization of authority to place more power in the hands of International officers, high dues (ten cents a week in 1879, twenty-five cents soon after), increased discipline, and an array of benefits. Strasser took over the presidency of the International in 1877 and the duo's goals were basically realized by the early 1880s.[25]

"Equalization" gave the president the power to redistribute money from wealthier locals to those under more financial strain, placing all unions on an equal footing. Given the cigar makers' propensity to travel from one local to another to find work, particularly during depression times, equalization meant that their arrival would not create undue financial strain. Responding to the disastrous strikes of the 1870s, CMIU members voted in 1879 to restrict locals' authority to call strikes. This permitted the executive board to have some say over strikes and required a two-thirds positive vote by the entire CMIU membership before a strike could be supported financially by the International.[26]

By the 1880s, the CMIU could begin counting some real successes. It adopted the Blue Label in 1881 for cigars made by union cigar makers and packers and the label proved so popular that some jobbers specialized in union-made goods, while unscrupulous manufacturers stooped to counterfeiting the label. Membership had risen to between 11,000 and 13,000 as the decade opened, and though totals hedged upward haltingly and unevenly, membership topped 24,000 in 1890. The CMIU counted only sev-

enteen locals in 1878, but 276 ten years later. Strasser also enjoyed pointing out that between 1871 and 1875, the union had conducted seventy-
eight strikes and had won only twelve, while in the years between 1876
and 1881 the union had battled employers sixty-nine times and had won
fifty-eight.[27] The *Cigar Makers' Official Journal*, edited by President
Strasser, was established in 1875 and appeared monthly. In 1879, St. Louis
Local 44 became the first CMIU union to establish a citywide scale of
wages for union shops. This meant a uniform piece rate on each type of
cigar made by union workers. Before the end of the century this practice
had become standard in every town and city where a local existed. Slightly
more mixed was the union's achievement of the eight-hour day on May 1,
1886, given their piece rate form of payment. While many unionists won
the change with an accompanying increase in wages, others did not, and
for them the shortened workday represented a cut in pay. This was especially true for older workers whose speed had diminished. It also made
organizing in traditionally nonunion areas like Pennsylvania much more
difficult, as did the six dollars per thousand minimum wage requirement
in the union constitution.[28]

The changes in direction reflected in Gompers' and Strasser's policies
precipitated a secession movement in New York in 1882. While ideologically based, the split among the cigar makers was not easily defined: political disagreements were rooted in ethnic patterns and knotted with
issues of raw power. Beginning in 1880, a group of German-speaking
members of Local 144, supported by the Socialist Labor Party (SLP),
broke away and started their own organization. They soon added a Bohemian section and in 1882 tenement house workers began to affiliate. The
real break occurred that year in the context of 144's anti–tenement house
campaign. The Gompers/Strasser group intensified its efforts against the
system during 1880 and 1881, attempting to outlaw it rather than organize
its workers. After an attempt to use federal authority to ban it failed, the
union turned to the New York state legislature and supported a sympathetic Democratic candidate for election.[29]

Criticism of the legislative, reformist approach swelled within the
union and socialists attacked the open collusion with bourgeois politicians. They resented the domination of 144 by English-speaking cigar
makers and the resistance to separate language sections. They viewed
centralization as fundamentally undemocratic and called for more local
autonomy. The union, they said, should aggressively attempt to organize
tenement house and team workers, many of whom were women. The

union should be engaged not in mainstream politics, but in forging an independent labor party. These critics combined a blend of various socialist and other ideologies on the left, though no single one predominated. Strasser countered that the critics had only recently arrived in the country and wanted to turn trade unions into socialist clubs. Gompers' political differences with the opposition, their threat to his personal power, and his iron conviction that only he could successfully lead his fellow craftsmen further rent the union into camps.[30] When Strasser voided the results of local elections in 1882 after socialists won three of four seats, the rump group, composed of Germans and Bohemians, withdrew and formed the Cigar Makers' Progressive Union (CMPU). In 1882 it began publishing *Progress*, a newspaper which primarily covered events in New York City, but also gave attention to other Progressive locals which had formed elsewhere, including Buffalo, New Haven, Detroit, Chicago, Cincinnati, St. Louis, and Milwaukee.[31]

The split between Progressives and the CMIU, however, did not represent a clear divide between socialists and their pure and simple opponents, and socialists retained a strong presence in the CMIU. As the two sides negotiated at times on reunification, talks never foundered on the question of socialism. Dorothee Schneider and Richard Oestreicher have looked closely at Progressives and the CMIU in New York and Detroit respectively. Both found a kind of cultural split: Progressives tended to be less assimilated, more ethnically self-conscious than their English-speaking, more ethnically diverse CMIU counterparts. Leaders of both unions in Detroit were socialists, politically active, and assisted other trades and workers with generous aid. In Detroit and New York, Progressives set up benefit packages and strike restrictions. Ideological differences were real, but they developed in the context of the ethnic identities of these workers. The specific context also shaped patterns, and Progressives in Detroit and New York would probably not have agreed on all issues. In New York City, for example, they allied with the SLP, while in Detroit the SLP supported the CMIU and the International Working People's Association, more anarchist in nature, supported the Progressives.[32]

The CMIU continued its anti–tenement house campaign, but made some attempts to counter the secession movement. In 1882 it chartered Czech-speaking and German-speaking locals, reversing its policy on separate language locals. Initially its struggle over tenement house work brought success and some praise when the New York state legislature banned the system in March 1883. But a seesaw between the courts and the legislature during the next two years finally resulted in collapse of the movement in early 1885, when the courts ruled a revised law unconstitutional. The long and expensive battle had seemingly accomplished little, as critics only too readily pointed out.[33]

Complicating the configuration of cigar makers' organizations during these years in New York City and elsewhere was the Order of the Knights of Labor, first formed in 1869. Initially relations between the Knights and the CMIU were quite cordial in many cities and cigar makers frequently belonged to both organizations. In New York City, however, friction developed early since Socialist District 49 dominated the Order in the city and acted as the center of resistance to the Knights' national leadership. The Progressives affiliated with DA 49, while Gompers and Strasser formed their own Defiance Assembly to keep an eye on things.[34]

The struggle between the Progressives and the CMIU in New York grew especially bitter during 1885 and 1886, drawing the Knights into the fight. An attempted merger fell apart in 1885, although a group of New York Progressives did rejoin the International as Local 10 and elsewhere some Progressives returned to the fold.[35] In early 1886, after initial cooperation broke down, Progressives signed a new citywide scale of wages with the cigar bosses which raised most workers' wages slightly, but resulted in cuts for higher-paid cigar makers, especially CMIU members. At the same time, the Knights began pressuring Progressives to dissolve their separate organization and affiliate directly with the Order, and threatened to remove their popular white label if the CMPU failed to comply. Manufacturers, fearing loss of the label, stepped up the pressure and locked out all Progressives who were not Knights in the summer of 1886. Still DA 49 could not fill the places of the 5,000 locked out. In a puzzling move, the CMIU came to the Progressives' aid and assisted in fighting the Knights. Very quickly the two unions reached an agreement and the New York Progressives entered the CMIU as Local 90. Next, most Progressive locals elsewhere either merged with existing CMIU locals or entered the International as separate unions.[36]

By the 1890s, the CMIU had emerged as the major organization of cigar makers in the country. The Progressives had merged or disbanded and Knights' unions had faded into obscurity, especially after Knights' chief Terrence Powderly expelled CMIU members in 1887. Yet what kind of union had been forged by the 1890s? The CMIU had unquestionably become an organization whose vast material gains were reserved for those accepted into the union's craft fraternity, a select group of white men. It

organized only cigar makers and packers, not other cigar factory operatives, such as stemmers, and did not represent a cross section of cigar
makers in the country. Several groups remained outside its ranks. The
National Stogie Makers' League applied for affiliation during the 1890s
and again in 1907, but CMIU members turned down these overtures,
fearing competition from the cheap stogie and offended at the thought of
placing their label on such a lowly smoke. The CMIU also blocked the
league's membership in the American Federation of Labor.[37] While the
CMIU liked to point out that as early as 1867 the union had a black member, M. W. T. Jones of Mobile, Alabama, on its executive board, the subsequent record yielded no further examples. Few blacks belonged to the
CMIU and exceptions came primarily in the South. In 1884, for example,
black cigar makers in Charleston, South Carolina, formed the CMIU's first
black local. Most black members worked in New Orleans, but in 1894 a
white member there explained why the union had so much trouble organizing cigar makers in that city. White cigar makers, he wrote, "are
bitterly prejudiced against the colored ones."[38]

The CMIU's most blatant racism was perhaps reserved for Chinese in
California, who dominated the trade in San Francisco. Efforts by unorganized white cigar makers to boycott Chinese-made products began as
early as 1859 and a white label, to signify white labor, was introduced in
the 1860s. White cigar makers' organizations, especially the White Cigar
Makers' Association of the Pacific Coast, were not unions, but concentrated instead on working with manufacturers to oppose Chinese labor.
Beginning in 1885, the CMIU became actively involved through Local
228 in attempting to replace Chinese with white union cigar makers at the
same wages. Supported by the Knights of Labor, the CMIU initiated a
boycott of all cigars without the blue union label. Many manufacturers
settled with the union and about four hundred CMIU members from the
East moved to San Francisco to take jobs there. Only a few members objected to the campaign or the racist language which frequently found its
way into the *CMOJ*.[39]

Tampa cigar makers remained generally aloof from the CMIU during
the late nineteenth and early twentieth centuries, despite the latter's interest in organizing there. Labor organizations in Tampa in general were
notoriously short-lived. A black assembly of Knights apparently formed in
1886, although little is known of it. The CMIU managed to organize a tiny
union in 1892, but attracted few Ybor City cigar makers. Responding to
corporate ownership of the Tampa factories and manufacturers' efforts to

rationalize production, workers went out on strike in 1899. They succeeded in eliminating the new practice of allotting a particular weight of tobacco and requiring that a certain number of cigars be produced from it. Out of this strike, workers organized the Sociedad de Torcedores de Tampa y Sus Cercanías, popularly known as La Resistencia, a broad organization which included all cigar factory workers. Resistencia had many successes, but it also encountered problems. It tried to overcome ethnic conflicts among workers along with the rigid distinctions among occupations, but it also had to deal with the CMIU and for a short time with a third union. Difficulties among workers and with manufacturers continued and Resistencia was crushed in a major strike in 1901. Tampa workers remained embittered against the CMIU, which had undermined Resistencia after an initial plan of cooperation broke down. Periodically the International encountered success in Tampa and enrolled thousands of cigar makers, but for the most part Tampa's workers stood apart from the CMIU in the rest of the country.[40]

Perhaps the most difficult organizational question for the CMIU throughout its history related to the system of work of its members. In the nineteenth century the matter first arose with regard to the use of the mold and the inclusion of tenement house workers. Policy had developed unevenly, but by the 1880s Gompers and Strasser had both agreed to eliminate tenement house work altogether rather than try to organize it. Also, the 1877 strike had convinced CMIU leaders that "financial security and economic stability were paramount in the effort to build a strong union." The questions of the mold and a division of labor were not as simple, and the heated battles over both did not necessarily break down along ideological lines. All members carefully thought about the real economic threat such work presented and their own notions of craftmanship. Strasser called on members to put aside the "false pride of being something higher" and admit bunch breakers to the union.[41] Unable to agree on a uniform policy on the subject, however, members adopted a "local option" clause to the constitution in 1881 which basically permitted each local to reach its own conclusions. By the turn of the century some locals, such as those in New York City, Philadelphia, Binghamton, Baltimore, Harrisburg, and Cincinnati, permitted the team system, while Boston, Buffalo, Cleveland, Tampa, Chicago, St. Louis, and San Francisco locals did not. Complicating matters, an increasing proportion of team workers were women, so that gender became bound up with exclusivity, as we shall soon see. The questions of women members and system of work would continue to be explosive well into the twentieth century.[42]

The CMIU in 1900, however, was not simply a narrow craft union: it would prove much more complex and ambiguous. Certainly its members were not of one mind and voice. They continued to debate the goals of the labor movement, the tactics to be used, the role of independent politics, and questions of autonomy versus centralization throughout the early twentieth century. While the new groups of cigar makers joining the union may not have been as literate[43] as their predecessors in the 1870s in New York City, nevertheless they kept many of the same issues at the forefront. Strasser's and Gompers' restructuring of the CMIU had weakened democracy, but had not eliminated it. Using the rights of initiative and referendum within the union's constitution, union members frequently tinkered with the document in the twentieth century—often in ways that would perplex and aggravate its leaders.

Socialism remained very much alive within the CMIU. Many CMIU locals, including Detroit, New Haven, and various New York unions, included at least a minority of left-leaning critics of established leaders and conservative policies, and ethnicity declined as a force in many of these struggles. Several socialist locals had formerly been Progressive unions, such as Local 90 in New York, Local 15 in Chicago, Local 4 in Cincinnati, Local 100 in Philadelphia, Local 67 in New Haven, Local 128 in Boston, and Local 149 in Brooklyn. Other socialist locals doubtless included many former Progressives and Knights, such as Local 97 in Boston, Local 12 in Oneida, Local 44 in St. Louis, Local 25 in Milwaukee, and Local 236 in Reading, Pennsylvania. The most staunchly anarchist union was perhaps the small local in Jacksonville, Illinois.[44]

The membership as a whole remained drawn to socialist principles. In 1894, SLP supporters at the AFL convention in Denver submitted an eleven-plank proposal to govern the federation's future direction. Most called for traditional labor demands, but the tenth demanded the "collective ownership by the people of all the means of production and distribution." One of the leading proponents of the movement and involved in many of the AFL's political struggles of the early 1890s was J. Mahlon Barnes, a cigar maker from Philadelphia. Barnes stridently called for independent political action as essential to the class struggle. Not only did the CMIU's membership overwhelmingly support the platform in general, 68.4 percent of its members voted in favor of the tenth plank. By the early twentieth century Barnes had become a key figure in union politics. Every year members faithfully elected Samuel Gompers as one of the CMIU delegates to the AFL convention, but the other delegate they consistently chose was Barnes, who between 1904 and 1911 also served as secretary of the Socialist Party.[45]

Socialism meant different things to different people, of course. Clearly socialists within the CMIU, of whatever affiliation or philosophy, were those who could intellectually reconcile existing trade unionism and socialism. Even the radical Local 90 had increasing problems with the Socialist Labor Party in the 1890s and in 1895–96 withdrew from New York's Central Labor Federation, which the SLP supported, in part because of its growing hostility to the American Federation of Labor. It was not that 90 itself was without differences with the AFL, but its members believed strongly in working within labor organizations as well as on the political front to create an independent labor party.[46] Beyond a general agreement on the importance of trade unions, however, CMIU socialists did not share a coherent, consistent program. In any case, the radical milieu of the 1880s was by no means forgotten. Indeed, dissidents within the CMIU would repeatedly challenge the union's conservative leadership in the coming decades.

The CMIU's economic position at the turn of the century was complex. It had 33,955 members in 1900, about 37 percent of the national total, and about 414 locals. It tended to be strongest in smaller cities and towns in the Northeast and Midwest, where frequently it enrolled a majority of cigar makers. The union's real stronghold had become New England, where most factories carried the union label. In Boston, the CMIU organized every shop in the city and maintained the highest scale of wages in the country. In other cities, however, such as New York, Philadelphia, Chicago, and Detroit, the union was less successful in organizing a majority in the trade.[47]

Frequently, however, the CMIU held an important place in the local labor movement, such as in Philadelphia, New York, and Chicago. In St. Louis, for example, Local 44 not only provided a considerable number of leaders in the local central body, it led various city socialist organizations as well. Statewide, the cigar makers carried the "Socialist message" with them wherever they organized, and the historian of the Missouri labor movement, Gary Fink, has credited them with spreading socialist and labor organizing in the state and pointed to their leading role in the state labor movement itself.[48]

Still, the CMIU was losing ground at the turn of the century, as the number of large factories increased and the five-cent cigar became more popular. Given this trend, the union increasingly concentrated in the Seed and Havana trade, making ten-cent cigars. There machinery could not penetrate as yet and their blue label product sold well. The industry's diversity provided the union with a niche where seemingly it could prosper. In 1903, 24 percent of U.S. cigars were made by union members.[49]

At the close of the nineteenth century, the cigar industry was a mix of the old and the new. Thousands of small craft shops and a growing number of huge cigar companies, hand and machine methods of work, male and female, union and nonunion cigar makers—all coexisted in the same industry. While large firms held some advantages over small, the latter continued to compete successfully in the marketplace. In 1906, 98 percent of all factories employed no more than thirty employees, produced fewer than two million cigars a year, and accounted for 40 percent of U.S. output. Like the needle trades and other industries where goods could not be mass-produced through high-volume, continuous process technology, cigar making remained decentralized and competitive both in manufacturing and in retailing. The first signs of concentration began appearing between 1895 and 1905, when the number of factories dropped from 30,000 to 25,700 while production doubled. But even as late as 1912 the level of concentration remained relatively low: the ten largest companies in the industry accounted for only 22.6 percent of production.[50]

James B. Duke's efforts to monopolize the cigar industry perfectly illustrated the state of the trade at the turn of the century. His single-minded and often ruthless campaign was the last step in a systematic takeover of the country's tobacco industry. In 1881, Duke abandoned his faltering smoking tobacco business and decided to go into cigarettes, not yet a very popular smoke. Cigarette manufacturers then produced only a little over one-half billion cigarettes a year, yet even such a tiny industry was already concentrated in the hands of four large companies. They coolly dismissed young Duke and predicted that he would soon go under, but within a decade he had impressively demonstrated the consequences of such nonchalance.[51]

Duke began his factory in Durham using the skilled hand labor of Russian Jewish cigarette makers whom he had lured away from New York City. Each produced about three thousand cigarettes in a ten-hour day. In 1885, Duke signed a secret agreement with James Bonsack, who had recently perfected a continuous process automatic cigarette machine which in one day could turn out 70,000 cigarettes. By 1890, the improved model would make 120,000. His hand craftsmen were jettisoned: thereafter all of Duke's cigarettes would be made by Bonsack machines. The innovation gave him a considerable jump on competitors, for even after they mechanized their own operations, Duke retained exclusive use of the most efficient machine, the Bonsack. Taking the lead as well in marketing and distribution, he set up sales offices all over the country and began developing his own processing plants so he could buy tobacco directly from farmers. In 1890 the other four cigarette makers were ready to talk merger and the American Tobacco Company was born.[52]

Soon Duke set his sights on the entire tobacco industry and in 1900 the American Tobacco Company controlled 60 to 80 percent of production in twist, plug, smoking, snuff, and cigarettes—every tobacco product except cigars. In each case the branch he sought to claim was already consolidated among a few producers and he was also able to use machinery to give him an added competitive edge. Throughout the 1890s, he continued to expand and build his now-worldwide selling organization.[53]

Cigars were last, but not least. Smokers preferred the cigar to any other tobacco product and profits could be tremendous. Cigars represented 60 percent of the total value of all U.S. tobacco products at the turn of the century. To launch his cigar campaign, Duke organized the American Cigar Company in 1901. He used every tried and true technique he had ever learned, including extensive advertising, drastic price undercutting, "extravagant inducements" to jobbers to push his goods, and daring buy-outs. The latter included the purchase of the Havana-American Company, a consolidation of high-grade cigar companies formed in 1899, thus making American Cigar the largest single manufacturer in the U.S. Duke used his other companies to pay for short-term financial losses needed to gain a long-term controlling share of the market; in 1902 alone, American Cigar lost $3.5 million. Knowing that sophisticated continuous process machinery would clinch a takeover of the industry, he capitalized the formation of the American Machine and Foundry Company (AMF) in 1901. At its helm he placed a man from his own staff, Rufus Lenoir Patterson, and presented him with the mission of developing a cigar machine equivalent to the Bonsack. Finally, in 1901, Duke purchased United Cigar Stores, a retail chain with four hundred outlets centrally located in most U.S. cities so he could push his own products and not incidentally bar union-made goods from the counter.[54]

It was a formidable arsenal, but Duke gave up his campaign in defeat in 1904. True, he had succeeded in gaining control of Havana's already-concentrated Clear Havana industry, and his purchase of the Havana-American Company had given him several large factories in Tampa, but overall he gained only a modest foothold in the U.S. cigar industry. He never controlled more than 16.4 percent of production, and before the year was out he was back down to about 14 percent. Duke failed because cigar manufacture differed so fundamentally from the rest of the tobacco industry that he could not use any of the networks and systems he had already built. Tobacco came from not one but many different places, from the North not the South, and much of it was imported. Cigars were still sold in small lots to retailers and the jobbers who handled cigar distribution had no connections to those handling other products. Alone, Duke could not gain control of the distribution network, and his efforts to control distribution through United Cigar Stores proved fruitless. The industry he encountered was decentralized and spread among thousands of producers, large and small. Machinery was limited and too primitive to facilitate significant concentration. Besides, it could not yet be used on high-grade cigars. Because of the delicate and complicated nature of the work process, Patterson and his coterie of experts simply were unable to fashion a machine to mass-produce cigars. For all of these reasons, neither the use of mass advertising nor efficient, effective organization could achieve for one firm a dominating position within the industry.[55]

José Santana found a diverse and competitive trade when he reached the mainland in 1909. He knew little of its evolution or of the struggles which had taken place in the city among the cigar makers several decades earlier. Indeed, he knew nothing of the past history of the union he joined that year, but he did not need to in order to become a committed and loyal member. Just as Gompers had presided over the birth and dramatic growth of the cigar industry in the late nineteenth century, Santana would witness its maturity and eventual decline in the twentieth century. The two men met only once, at a CMIU convention in 1920. The grand old man, smiling and working his way among the delegates, shaking their hands, repeated a phrase over and over that Santana never forgot: "Keep on rolling them, boys. Keep on rolling them." He had no doubt that they always would.[56]

Notes

1. U.S. Department of Commerce, Bureau of the Census, *Census of Manufactures: 1900*, vol. 9, *Special Reports on Selected Industries* (Washington, D.C., 1902), pp. 669–71; Jack J. Gottsegen, *Tobacco: A Study of Its Consumption in the United States* (New York, 1940), pp. 11–29; Willis N. Baer, *The Economic Development of the Cigar Industry in the United States* (Lancaster, Pa., 1933), pp. 113–23, 30–31, 39–44; Joseph C. Robert, *The Story of Tobacco in America* (New York, 1952), p. 96; Edith Abbott, *Women in Industry: A Study in American Economic History* (New York, 1913), p. 190; *Cigar Makers' Official Journal* (*CMOJ*), Mar. 1888, p. 6; Dorothee Schneider, "The New York Cigarmakers Strike of 1877," *Labor History*, 26 (Summer 1985), 327.

2. Baer, *Economic Development of the Cigar Industry*, pp. 38–39, 40–42, 261–62; Gottsegen, *Tobacco*, pp. 1–2, 14; Abbott, *Women in Industry*, pp. 190–93; *CMOJ*, May 1878, p. 2; July 1930, p. 3; U.S. Congress, Senate, *Report on Condition of Woman and Child Wage-Earners in the United States*, vol. 9, *History of Women in Industry in the United States*, by Helen Sumner, S. Doc. 645, 61st Cong., 2d sess., 1911, pp. 195–200; Bureau of the Census, *Census of Manufactures: 1900*, vol. 9, *Special Reports*, p. 671; John P. Troxell, "Labor in the Tobacco Industry" (Ph.D. dissertation, University of Wisconsin, 1931), p. 2; Carl A. Werner, *Tobaccoland* (New York, 1922), pp. 44, 137; Robert, *Story of Tobacco*, p. 97; Robert K. Heiman, *Tobacco and Americans* (New York, 1960), pp. 88–91; *Workingman's Advocate*, 21 Aug. 1875; 4 Sept. 1875, Samuel Gompers Papers Collection, vol. 1, University of Maryland, College Park (hereafter SGP); Dorothee Schneider, "Trade Unions and Community: Three German Trade Unions in New York, 1870–1900," trans. Schneider and Harry Liebersohn (Ph.D. dissertation, University of Munich, 1983), chap. 2. Dorothee Schneider generously permitted me to read and use her unpublished manuscript. Because it is still being revised at this writing, I have cited it by chapter, rather than by page. In several cases, she has provided me with citations from her work which I have flagged with her initials (D. S.). Her reading of the present chapter in various drafts and our conversations about cigar makers in New York have fundamentally informed my understanding of the industry and its workers during the nineteenth century. Without her generosity and interest, this chapter really would not have been written. In addition, Stuart Kaufman, editor of the Papers of Samuel Gompers at the University of Maryland (being published by the University of Illinois Press), permitted me to use office files and the typescript of volume one. My sincere appreciation goes to both historians for their help.

3. Samuel Gompers, *Seventy Years of Life and Labor: An Autobiography*, vol. 1, ed. Philip Taft and John A. Sessions (New York, 1957 [1925]), pp. 53–59.

4. José Santana, interviews, 11 Jan. 1976 by telephone, 13–16 Aug. 1976; 6–11 July 1977; 15–17 Sept. 1978; 16–17, 20 May 1979, Chicago. I first learned of José Santana in late 1975 and began interviewing him early the next year. In addition to these formal interviews, we had innumerable telephone conversations in the years before his death in 1980. I located his membership records in the Cigar Makers' International Union of America Collection, McKeldin Library, Univ. of

Maryland, College Park (hereafter CMIU Papers). I used the card files of the union, but recently this material has been coded and the data base is available for use.

5. Lucy Winsor Killough, *The Tobacco Products Industry in New York and Its Environs: Present Trends and Probable Future Developments*, Regional Plan of New York and Its Environs, Monograph no. 5 (New York, 1924), pp. 22–24; U.S. Congress, Senate, *Report on Condition of Woman and Child Wage-Earners in the United States*, vol. 18, *Employment of Women and Children in Selected Industries*, S. Doc. 645, 61st Cong., 2d sess., 1913, pp. 88–91; U.S. Bureau of Corporations, *Report of the Commissioner of Corporations on the Tobacco Industry*, part I, *Position of the Tobacco Combination in the Industry* (Washington, D.C., 1909), p. 423; Gottsegen, *Tobacco*, p. 14; U.S. Industrial Commission, *Report of the Industrial Commission on the Relations and Conditions of Capital and Labor*, vol. 7 (Washington, D.C., 1901), pp. 191–98; vol. 15, pp. xxxii, xxxiii; *Tobacco Leaf*, 6 Mar. 1907, p. 6; 9 Sept. 1909, p. 11; 14 Oct. 1909, p. 11; *CMOJ*, Apr. 1920, p. 14; U.S. Office of Internal Revenue, *Annual Report of the Commissioner of Internal Revenue, 1909* (Washington, D.C., 1910), pp. 112–13.

6. Baer, *Economic Development of the Cigar Industry*, pp. 51–53, 58–59, 73–75, 104; Carl Avery Werner, *A Textbook on Tobacco* (New York, 1914), pp. 10–15, 36; Werner, *Tobaccoland*, p. 137; U.S. Department of Agriculture, *The Present Status of the Tobacco Industry*, by Wightman W. Garner (Washington, D.C., 1910), pp. 5–6; U.S. Industrial Commission, *Report*, vol. 7, pp. 194–97; U.S. Congress, Senate, *Report on Condition of Woman and Child Wage-Earners*, vol. 18, p. 90; Gottsegen, *Tobacco*, p. 16; Meyer Jacobstein, *The Tobacco Industry in the United States* (New York, 1907), p. 88; U.S. Bureau of Corporations, *Report*, part I, pp. 51–55.

7. Baer, *Economic Development of the Cigar Industry*, pp. 39–45, 51–53, 58–62, 71, 75, 104; Gottsegen, *Tobacco*, p. 14; Werner, *Textbook on Tobacco*, pp. 10–15, 36; U.S. Bureau of Corporations, *Report*, part I, pp. 45–49; U.S. Department of Agriculture, *Tobacco Industry*, pp. 5–6.

8. Troxell, "Labor in the Tobacco Industry," p. 24; Jacobstein, *Tobacco Industry*, p. 88; Baer, *Economic Development of the Cigar Industry*, pp. 261–62.

9. Schneider, "Trade Unions and Community," chap. 2; Jacobstein, *Tobacco Industry*, pp. 84–87, 90–91, 98–99; Baer, *Economic Development of the Cigar Industry*, pp. 13–50, 39, 81, 99, 104; Bureau of the Census, *Census of Manufactures: 1900*, vol. 9, p. 670; U.S. Bureau of Corporations, *Report*, part I, pp. 149, 423–24; Troxell, "Labor in the Tobacco Industry," p. 1–4, 46, 78; *U.S. Tobacco Journal*, 1 Nov. 1879 (D.S.); Schneider, "New York Strike," p. 329.

10. Schneider, "Trade Unions and Community," chap. 2; Troxell, "Labor in the Tobacco Industry," p. 79; Abbott, *Women in Industry*, p. 194; U.S. Commissioner of Labor, *Eleventh Special Report*, "Regulation and Restriction of Output" (Washington, D.C., 1904), p. 559; U.S. Congress, Senate, *Report on Woman and Child Wage-Earners*, vol. 18, pp. 95–102; Barbara Mary Klaczynska, "Working Women in Philadelphia, 1900–1930" (Ph.D. dissertation, Temple University, 1975), p. 57; Ruth F. Paul, "Negro Women in Industry" (M.A. thesis, Temple University, 1940), pp. 51–52; *New York Times*, 24 Apr. 1869 and 14 May 1872. My thanks to Leslie

Rowland for bringing these last two to my attention. On black workers in tobacco, see Peter Rachleff, *Black Labor in the South: Richmond, Virginia, 1865–1890* (Philadelphia, Pa., 1984).

11. Werner, *Textbook on Tobacco*, pp. 38–43; Baer, *Economic Development of the Cigar Industry*, pp. 85–87; *Tobacco Leaf*, 6 Mar. 1907, p. 6; 9 Sept. 1909, p. 11; 16 Sept. 1909, p. 11; 21 Oct. 1909, p. 20; U.S. Commissioner of Labor, "Regulation and Restriction of Output," p. 565; Troxell, "Labor in the Tobacco Industry," p. 78; U.S. Bureau of Corporations, *Report*, part I, p. 56; *CMOJ*, Mar. 1894, p. 8.

12. Werner, *Textbook on Tobacco*, p. 75–79; Santana, interviews, 1976–80. Snobbery played a role in the divisions. Clear Havana makers and manufacturers unquestionably saw themselves as superior and everyone looked down on the mean stogie. Smokers also observed the distinctions. One trade journal at the turn of the century reported on a dealer who decided to open a five-cent cigar shop on Broadway in New York City. Friends advised against it, however, because no one would want to be seen going into a cheap cigar store in such a prominent place. See *Tobacco*, 24 Aug. 1900, p. 2.

13. L. Glenn Westfall, "Don Vicent Martínez Ybor, the Man and His Empire: Development of the Clear Havana Industry in Cuba and Florida in the Nineteenth Century" (Ph.D. dissertation, University of Florida, 1977), pp. 6–7, 18, 21, 22, 24, 27, 31, 35, 39, and chaps. 2 and 3; Gary Mormino, "Tampa and the New Urban South: The Weight Strike of 1899," *Florida Historical Quarterly*, 60 (Jan. 1982), 338–42; Durward Long, "La Resistencia: Tampa's Immigrant Labor Union," *Labor History*, 6 (Fall 1965), 194; Durward Long, "The Historical Beginnings of Ybor City and Modern Tampa," *Florida Historical Quarterly*, 45 (July 1966), 31–44; Louis Pérez, "Cubans in Tampa: From Exiles to Immigrants, 1892–1901," *Florida Historical Quarterly*, 57 (Oct. 1978), 129–32; *CMOJ*, July 1895, p. 10.

14. George Pozzetta, "Italians and the Tampa General Strike of 1910," in George Pozzetta, ed., *Pane e Lavoro: The Italian American Working Class* (Toronto, 1980), p. 30; Gary Mormino, "We Worked Hard and Took Care of Our Own: Oral History and Italians in Tampa," *Labor History*, 23 (Summer 1982), 397–98, 401; Long, "La Resistencia," p. 211; Pérez, "Cubans in Tampa," pp. 131, 136; Westfall, "Don Vicente Martínez Ybor," pp. 20–24; *U.S. Tobacco Journal*, Mar. 1899, p. 5; Nancy Hewitt, "Women Cigar Makers in Tampa," paper presented at Oral History Association, Pensacola, Fla., Nov. 1985.

15. Pozzetta, "Italians and the Tampa General Strike of 1910," pp. 30–32, 36; George Pozzetta, "¡Alerta Tabaqueros! Tampa's Striking Cigar Workers," *Tampa Bay History*, 3 (Fall/Winter, 1981), 19; Pérez, "Cubans in Tampa," p. 131; Westfall, "Don Vicente Martínez Ybor," pp. 9–10.

16. *Pittsburgh Press*, 17 Dec. 1961; Eva Smill, "The Stogy Industry on the Hill in Pittsburgh, Pa." (M.A. thesis, Carnegie Institute, Pittsburgh, June 1920), pp. 6, 11, 21, 24; Elizabeth Butler, *Women and the Trades, Pittsburgh, 1907–1908* (New York, 1909), pp. 75–94; Patrick Lynch, "Pittsburgh, the I.W.W., and the Stogie Workers," in Joseph Conlin, ed., *At the Point of Production: The Local History of the I.W.W.* (Westport, Conn., 1981), pp. 79–94; U.S. Commissioner of

Labor, "Regulation and Restriction of Output," p. 558; *CMOJ*, Oct. 1887, p. 6; Dec. 1898, p. 4; Werner, *Textbook on Tobacco*, p. 13.

17. Troxell, "Labor in the Tobacco Industry," p. 46; Baer, *Economic Development of the Cigar Industry*, pp. 80–86; Jacobstein, *Tobacco Industry*, p. 99; Heiman, *Tobacco and Americans*, p. 104; Werner, *Textbook on Tobacco*, pp. 41–42.

18. U.S. Congress, Senate, *Report on Condition of Woman and Child Wage-Earners*, vol. 9, pp. 199–200; U.S. Industrial Commission, *Report*, vol. 15, p. 385; Abbott, *Women in Industry*, pp. 186, 194–95; *CMOJ*, 10 Mar. 1878, p. 1; *U.S. Tobacco Journal*, 9 Nov. 1886, p. 2, vol. 1, SGP; Werner, *Textbook on Tobacco*, pp. 40–41, 54; Bureau of the Census, *Census of Manufactures: 1900*, vol. 9, p. 653; Troxell, "Labor in the Tobacco Industry," p. 59; Elizabeth Faulkner Baker, *Technology and Women's Work* (New York, 1964), pp. 32–35, 162–68; U.S. Congress, Senate, *Report on Condition of Woman and Child Wage-Earners*, vol. 18, pp. 95–102. In 1881, Strasser estimated that about one-sixth of the industry's workers were women. See *CMOJ*, Oct. 1881, p. 3. Helen Sumner notes women working in the industry outside New York before the 1870s, but New York manufacturers were the first to employ women in great numbers. See U.S. Congress, Senate, *Report on Condition of Woman and Child Wage-Earners*, vol. 9, p. 198. Exceptions to the generalization that women tended to work primarily with other women were, for example, tenement house cigar making in New York City and the home and factory production common in southeastern Pennsylvania (see Chap. 7).

19. Werner, *Textbook on Tobacco*, pp. 40–41; U.S. Commissioner of Labor, "Regulation and Restriction of Output," pp. 557–85; Sumner H. Slichter, *Union Policies and Industrial Management* (New York, 1968 [1941]), p. 219; Abbott, *Women in Industry*, pp. 94–97; Lloyd Ulman, *The Rise of the National Trade Union: The Development and Significance of Its Structure, Governing Institutions and Economic Policies* (Cambridge, Mass., 1955), p. 304; Troxell, "Labor in the Tobacco Industry," p. 128; Irwin Yellowitz, *Industrialization and the American Labor Movement, 1850–1900* (New York, 1977), p. 64; U.S. Industrial Commission, *Report*, vol. 15, pp. 385–88; vol. 7., p. 197; *Tobacco Leaf*, 7 Oct. 1909, p. 6.

20. Schneider, "Trade Unions and Community," chap. 2; *CMOJ*, Sept. 1912, p. 8; Norman Ware, *The Labor Movement in the United States, 1860–1895* (New York, 1929), pp. 259–60; Bernard Mandel, *Samuel Gompers: A Biography* (Yellow Springs, Ohio, 1963), pp. 20–24; Adolph Strasser, "Cigar Makers' International Union," in George E. McNeil, ed., *The Labor Movement: The Problem of Today* (New York, 1971 [1887]), p. 597; Marie Hourwich, "Cigar Makers' Union History, 1851–1879," typescript, Research Files, Box 22, David Saposs Papers, State Historical Society of Wisconsin (SHSW), Madison, p. 4; Yellowitz, *Industrialization and the American Labor Movement*, p. 64.

21. *CMOJ*, Mar. 1876, p. 2; Aug. 1876, p. 3; Nov. 1876, p. 1; Feb. 1877, p. 2; May, 1877, pp. 2–3; Oct. 1878, p. 2; July 1910, pp. 2–3; Killough, *Tobacco Products Industry*, pp. 16, 20, 23.

22. Schneider, "Trade Unions and Community," chap. 2; Schneider, "New York Strike," pp. 329–30; *CMOJ*, Nov. 1877, p. 4; Abbott, *Women in Industry*, pp. 198–99; Hubert Perrier, "The Socialists and the Working Class in New York: 1890–1896," *Labor History*, 22 (Fall 1981), 485–511; Thomas Capek, *The Čech (Bohe-*

mian) Community of New York (New York, 1921), pp. 20–26, 38, 53, 80; Emily Greene Balch, *Our Slavic Fellow Citizens* (New York, 1910), pp. 663–76, 205, 257; Jane E. Robbins, "The Bohemian Women of New York," *Charities*, Dec. 1904, p. 195; *New York Times*, 26 Sept. 1874, SGP; Yellowitz, *Industrialization and the American Labor Movement*, p. 64; Hourwich, "Cigar Makers' Union History"; Ulman, *Rise of the National Trade Union*, p. 314; Slichter, *Union Policies and Industrial Management*, p. 21. See also Robert DeForest and Lawrence Veiller, *The Tenement House Problem* (New York, 1903). Schneider's work was essential for the entire section on the CMIU in New York City in the late nineteenth century. She is the first scholar to treat the subject since Norman Ware, Bernard Mandel, and Philip Taft did several decades ago. I have cited her work first and have added references to these earlier works in some cases, but in my view her research supersedes theirs.

23. Schneider, "Trade Unions and Community," chap. 2; Ware, *Labor Movement in the United States*, pp. 258–62; Mandel, *Samuel Gompers*, pp. 20–23; Stuart Kaufman, *Samuel Gompers and the Origins of the American Federation of Labor, 1848–1896* (Westport, Conn., 1973), pp. 37–39, 57, 92–98; *New York Sun*, 26 Sept. 1874; *Social-Demokrat*, 18 Oct. 1875, 24 Oct. 1875, 24 Nov. 1875; *Arbeiter-Zeitung*, 5 July 1873, vol. 1, SGP; Schneider, "New York Strike," p. 331.

24. Schneider, "Trade Unions and Community," chap. 3; *CMOJ*, July 1878, p. 1; Mandel, *Samuel Gompers*, pp. 23–26; *New York World*, 9 Dec. 1877; *New York Herald*, 15 Oct. 1877; *New York Tribune*, 7 Dec. 1877; *New York Sun*, 29 Dec. 1877, vol. 1, SGP; *CMOJ*, Oct. 1877, pp. 1–4; 10 Dec. 1877, pp. 1–4; 24 Dec. 1877, p. 1; 15 Jan. 1878, pp. 1–2; *Labor Standard*, 27 Jan. 1878; *New York Sun*, 20 Jan. 1878; *New York Tribune*, 18 Jan. 1878 (D.S.).

25. Schneider, "Trade Unions and Community," chap. 3; *CMOJ*, Oct. 1890, p. 5; Oct. 1896, p. 8; Strasser, "Cigar Makers' International Union," pp. 598–601; U.S. Industrial Commission, *Report*, vol. 7, p. 192; George M. Janes, *The Control of Strikes in American Trade Unions* (Baltimore, 1916), pp. 45, 51, 77, 92; Ware, *Labor Movement in the United States*, p. 262; F. E. Wolfe, *Admission to American Trade Unions* (Baltimore, Md., 1912), p. 18; Yellowitz, *Industrialization and the American Labor Movement*, p. 69; *Arbeiter-Stimme*, 27 Jan. 1878, vol. 1, SGP; Helen Sumner, "The Benefit System of the Cigar Makers' Union," in John R. Commons, ed., *Trade Unionism and Labor Problems* (New York, 1967 [1905]), pp. 527–28. See also on the need to reorganize, *CMOJ*, Feb. 1878, Jan. 1879, Apr. 1879, July 1879, Sept. 1879, Oct. 1879.

26. Theodore Glocker, "The Structure of the Cigar Makers' Union," in Jacob Hollander and George E. Barnet, eds., *Studies in American Trade Unionism* (New York, 1970 [1912]), pp. 59, 62; Theodore Glocker, *The Government of American Trade Unions* (New York, 1971 [1913]), pp. 196, 199, 288, 229; Troxell, "Labor in the Tobacco Industry," p. 136; *CMOJ*, Apr. 1903, p. 8.

27. *CMOJ*, Mar. 1881, p. 1; Jan. 1888, pp. 4, 5; May 1888, p. 9; Sept. 1912, pp. 8–9; Apr. 1920, p. 14; Strasser, "Cigar Makers' International Union," p. 605.

28. Hourwich, "Cigar Makers' Union History," p. 29; *CMOJ*, 10 Nov. 1879, p. 1; Apr. 1886, p. 4; Jan. 1888, pp. 5, 11; May 1888, p. 9.

29. Schneider, "Trade Unions and Community," chap. 4; *CMOJ*, May 1879,

p. 2; Jan. 1880, p. 1; Philip Taft, *Organized Labor in American History* (New York, 1964), pp. 108–9; Mandel, *Samuel Gompers*, pp. 30–33, 70–73; Ware, *Labor Movement in the United States*, pp. 258, 265; *New York Tribune*, 5 Nov. 1878; *New York Herald*, 22 Feb. 1879; *Socialist* (New York), 24 Oct. 1875, vol. 1, SGP; Howard Gitelman, "Adolph Strasser and the Origins of Pure and Simple Unionism," *Labor History*, 6 (Winter 1965), p. 80; Fred Fairchild, *Factory Legislation of the State of New York* (New York, 1905), p. 11; Howard Lawrence Hurwitz, *Theodore Roosevelt and Labor in New York State, 1880–1900* (New York, 1943), pp. 16–17, 79–88, 59, 174; Troxell, "Labor in the Tobacco Industry," pp. 136–38. See also Gompers, *Seventy Years of Life and Labor*, pp. 184–86, 190–92. Regarding the anti–tenement house campaign, see articles and letters in *CMOJ*, Mar. 1879, July 1879, Mar.–Aug. 1880, Dec. 1881, Mar.–Apr., July 1882 (D.S.).

30. Schneider, "Trade Unions and Community," chap. 4; Gitelman, "Adolph Strasser and the Origins of Pure and Simple Unionism," p. 80; *CMOJ*, Apr. 1882, p. 3; Sept. 1883, supp., p. 5; Oct. 1883, p. 4; Dec. 1883, p. 1; Sept. 1884, p. 4; Mar. 1893, p. 4; Ware, *Labor Movement in the United States*, pp. 184, 265, 313; Mandel, *Samuel Gompers*, pp. 35–36; *U.S. Tobacco Journal*, 31 July 1886, p. 2; 26 Aug. 1882, p. 2; *New York Times*, 24 July 1882.

31. *U.S. Tobacco Journal*, 31 July 1886, p. 2; 26 Aug. 1882, p. 2; *New York Times*, 24 July 1882; Ware, *Labor Movement in the United States*, pp. 184, 313; *CMOJ*, Apr. 1882, p. 3; May 1882, p. 1; June 1882, p. 4; Aug. 1882, p. 1; Aug. 1883, pp. 6–7; Jan. 1884, pp. 4–5; Sept. 1884, p. 5; July 1886, p. 2; *Progress*, Aug. 1882, p. 1; 20 Sept. 1882, p. 1; 20 Oct. 1882, p. 1; 20 June 1883, p. 2; 24 Oct. 1884, p. 3; *Progress* had English, German, and Czech sections. Tamiment Institute in New York has a full run of the journal, from 1882 to 1885 when it ceased publication.

32. Schneider, "Trade Unions and Community," chap. 4; Richard Oestreicher, "Solidarity and Fragmentation: Working People and Class Consciousness in Detroit, 1877–1895," (Ph.D. dissertation, Michigan State University, 1979), pp. 193, 199–207, 217, 230, 373, 380–89, 456. (Now published by the University of Illinois Press as *Solidarity and Fragmentation: Working People and Class Consciousness in Detroit, 1875–1900.*)

33. Schneider, "Trade Unions and Community," chap. 4; *CMOJ*, Oct. 1882 (D.S.); Sept. 1883, supp., p. 4; Mandel, *Samuel Gompers*, pp. 30–33, 70; Ware, *Labor Movement in the United States*, p. 258. See also *CMOJ*, Sept. and Oct. 1882 issues.

34. Schneider, "Trade Unions and Community," chap. 4; Oestreicher, "Solidarity and Fragmentation," pp. 205–6, 218, 227, 230, 338, 380, 384, 389, 390–91; *Detroit Free Press*, 24 May 1886, vol. 1, SGP; Gregory S. Kealey and Bryan D. Palmer, *Dreaming of What Might Be: The Knights of Labor in Ontario, 1880–1900* (Cambridge, 1982), pp. 140, 153–66; *CMOJ*, July 1886, p. 4; Apr. 1889, p. 4; June 1891, p. 7; Ware, *Labor Movement in the United States*, pp. 265–66, 270; Troxell, "Labor in the Tobacco Industry," p. 137.

35. Mandel, *Samuel Gompers*, p. 70; Ware, *Labor Movement in the United States*, pp. 258, 270–71; *CMOJ*, Sept. 1883, supp., pp. 6, 9–11; Sept. 1884, p. 4.

36. Schneider, "Trade Unions and Community," chap. 4; Mandel, *Samuel*

Gompers, pp. 73–74; *U.S. Tobacco Journal*, 12 Apr. 1884; Oestreicher, "Solidarity and Fragmentation," p. 398; *CMOJ*, Aug. 1883, pp. 6–7; Philip Taft, *The A.F.L. in the Time of Gompers* (New York, 1957), pp. 26, 38, 85. See also Kealey and Palmer, *Dreaming of What Might Be*, pp. 103, 135–69, 371. See also on the Knights, *CMOJ*, Oct. 1884, p. 6; Jan. 1886, p. 5; May 1886, pp. 6, 8–9; July 1886, p. 6; Aug. 1886, p. 6; Sept. 1886, p. 4.

37. *CMOJ*, Feb. 1887, p. 4; Smill, "Stogy Industry," pp. 6, 11, 21, 24; Butler, *Women and the Trades*, pp. 75–94; U.S. Commissioner of Labor, "Regulation and Restriction of Output," p. 558; *CMOJ*, Oct. 1887, p. 6; Dec. 1897, p. 4; Jan. 1898, p. 4.

38. *CMOJ*, Feb. 1884, p. 6; June 1886, p. 4; June 1894, p. 3; July 1894, p. 4; Aug. 1897, p. 9.

39. Alexander Saxton, *The Indispensible Enemy: Labor and the Anti-Chinese Movement in California* (Berkeley, 1971), pp. 73–77, 119, 167, 214–18; *CMOJ*, May 1876, p. 3; Aug. 1876, p. 3; Nov. 1877, p. 4; Jan. 1878, p. 2; June 1878, p. 4; Nov. 1881, p. 1; Feb. 1886, p. 4; Mar. 1886, p. 4; June 1886, p. 4; Aug. 1886, p. 4.

40. Long, "La Resistencia," pp. 193–213; Pozzetta, "Italians and the Tampa General Strike of 1910," pp. 32–35; Mormino, "Tampa and the New Urban South," pp. 340–42, 344–47, 350–55; Pérez, "Cubans in Tampa," pp. 136–39; *CMOJ*, Feb. 1887, p. 6; July 1895, p. 10. The *CMOJ* reported a union of Spanish and Cuban cigar makers in Philadelphia in 1877 (see *CMOJ*, Dec. 1877, p. 1), and there were, according to the *New York Times*, two Spanish-speaking locals in New York City in 1883 (see *NYT*, Apr. 23, 1883, p. 8, vol. 1, SGP).

41. Schneider, "New York Strike," p. 352; *CMOJ*, Nov. 1879, p. 1; Oct. 1882, p. 4.

42. U.S. Commissioner of Labor, "Regulation and Restriction of Output," pp. 568–69; Yellowitz, *Industrialization and the American Labor Movement*, pp. 65–66, 69, 71; Slichter, *Union Policies and Industrial Management*, pp. 218–19; *CMOJ*, June 1878, p. 1; Sept. 1879, p. 2; Sept. 1883, supp., p. 4.

43. Union cigar makers always liked to think of themselves as more literate than many other workers. One member expressed this attitude in a letter in the *CMOJ* which referred to "the often boasted assertion that cigar makers are the most intellectual body of workmen in the country." See *CMOJ*, Feb. 1892, p. 4.

44. William Dick, *Labor and Socialism in America: The Gompers Era* (Port Washington, N.Y., 1972), p. 76; Henry Gruber Stetler, *The Socialist Movement in Reading, Pennsylvania, 1896–1936: A Study in Social Change* (Storrs, Conn., 1943); William C. Pratt, "The Reading Socialist Experience: A Study of Working Class Politics" (Ph.D. dissertation, Emory University, 1969); Henry Bedford, *Socialism and the Workers in Massachusetts, 1886–1912* (Amherst, Mass., 1966); David J. Saposs, *Left Wing Unionism: A Study of Radical Policies and Tactics* (New York, 1926), pp. 33–34; *CMOJ*, Jan. 1881, p. 4; Jan. 1884, pp. 4, 5; Sept. 1884, p. 4; Sept. 1895, p. 6. The Jacksonville, Illinois, local could always be counted on to provide an extreme view in the *CMOJ* on almost any issue. On Local 90, for example, see *CMOJ*, Aug. 1888, p. 1; July 1889, p. 4; Dec. 1890, p. 8; June 1891, p. 2; Aug. 1891, p. 4; Dec. 1891, p. 11; May 1896, pp. 4–5.

45. J. F. Finn, "AF of L Leaders and the Question of Politics in the Early

1890s," *American Studies*, 7 (Fall 1973), 243–65; Ira Kipnis, *The American Socialist Movement, 1897–1912* (New York, 1942), pp. 27, 237, 239; Howard Quint, *The Forging of American Socialism: Origins of the Modern Movement* (Columbia, S.C., 1953), p. 161; Solon DeLeon, ed., *The American Labor Who's Who* (New York, 1925), p. 10; *CMOJ*, Mar. 1894, p. 4; Jan. 1894, p. 8; Jan. 1895, pp. 9–11; Feb. 1895, p. 4; Dec. 1895, p. 3; Feb. 1896, p. 9; Mar. 1896, p. 3; June 1896, p. 9; Jan. 1897, p. 3.

46. Perrier, "Socialists and the Working Class in New York," pp. 499–500. On Local 90, see *CMOJ*, Dec. 1896, pp. 6–7; Jan. 1897, p. 3.

47. *CMOJ*, June 1886, p. 9; Sept. 1901, p. 9; U.S. Industrial Commission, *Report*, vol. 7, p. 193; vol. 15, p. 385; Schneider, "Trade Unions and Community," chap. 4; U.S. Commissioner of Labor, "Regulation and Restriction of Output," p. 585. Local 90 lamented in 1895 that team work had nearly replaced out and out handwork in New York City and that suction tables and women workers were increasingly common in the city's factories. New York City declined as a center of the U.S. cigar industry during the 1890s. See Troxell, "Labor in the Tobacco Industry," p. 52.

48. Philip Foner, *History of the Labor Movement in the United States*, vol. 2, *From the Founding of the American Federation of Labor to the Emergence of American Imperialism* (New York, 1975 [1955]), pp. 133–36, 160; Gary M. Fink, *Labor's Search for Political Order: The Political Behavior of the Missouri Labor Movement, 1890–1940* (Columbia, Mo., 1973), p. 28. For example, Philip Wagaman of Local 316, McSherrystown, Pa., served as seventh vice-president of the Pennsylvania Federation of Labor in 1919. George Thompson of Local 14 in Chicago served as financial secretary for the Chicago Federation of Labor (see *Chicago Federationist*, 15 Dec. 1897, p. 5), and Adam Menche served as president of the Illinois Federation of Labor in 1901 (see *Chicago Federationist*, 2 Nov. 1901, p. 4). Daniel Harris of the New York cigar makers served as president of the New York State Federation of Labor between 1906 and 1915 (see vol. 1, SGP). Note, for example, that in 1896 the CMIU had four delegates to the AFL, each with 270 votes. No other union had as many total votes as the CMIU. In 1900 the CMIU had three delegates with 107 votes each. Only the International Typographical Union had more total votes. See American Federation of Labor, *Report of Proceedings of the 16th Annual Convention*, 1896, pp. i–vi, and *Report of Proceedings of the 20th Annual Convention*, 1900, pp. i–viii.

49. U.S. Industrial Commission, *Report*, vol. 7, p. 197; vol. 15, p. 387; U.S. Bureau of Labor, Bulletin 67, *Conditions of Entrance to the Principal Trades*, by A. M. Sakolski (Washington, D.C., 1906), p. 722; Jacobstein, *Tobacco Industry*, p. 111; U.S. Commissioner of Labor, "Regulation and Restriction of Output," p. 585.

50. Baer, *Economic Development of the Cigar Industry*, pp. 13–50, 74–75, 81, 89, 107, 119, 257; Troxell, "Labor in the Tobacco Industry," pp. 11–42, 86–89; U.S. Bureau of Corporations, *Report*, part I, pp. 149–64, 266, 423–47; U.S. Congress, Senate, *Report on Condition of Woman and Child Wage-Earners*, vol. 18, pp. 95–102; Bureau of the Census, *Census of Manufactures: 1900*, vol. 9, pp. 669–71; Alfred D. Chandler, *The Visible Hand: The Managerial Revolution in*

American Business (Cambridge, Mass., 1977), pp. 249–51; Jacobstein, *Tobacco Industry*, p. 99.

51. Robert, *Story of Tobacco*, pp. 138–53; Chandler, *Visible Hand*, p. 290; Troxell, "Labor in the Tobacco Industry," p. 4; Richard Tennant, *The American Cigarette Industry* (New Haven, 1950), pp. 17–20.

52. Robert, *Story of Tobacco*, pp. 141–42; Chandler, *Visible Hand*, pp. 249–50, 291–92, 382–84; Tennant, *American Cigarette Industry*, p. 19.

53. Troxell, "Labor in the Tobacco Industry," p. 4; Tennant, *American Cigarette Industry*, pp. 26–31; Chandler, *Visible Hand*, pp. 382–84; Robert, *Story of Tobacco*, pp. 142–43.

54. Tennant, *American Cigarette Industry*, pp. 32–33; Robert, *Story of Tobacco*, p. 149; Chandler, *Visible Hand*, p. 388; U.S. Bureau of Corporations, *Report*, part I, pp. 50, 278.

55. Chandler, *Visible Hand*, pp. 388–90; U.S. Bureau of Corporations, *Report*, part I, pp. 149–64, 312, 317, 423–24.

56. Santana, interviews, 1976–80.

2

The Workday of a Union Man

No union factory bothered to keep a record of the hours cigar makers worked; it would have been a bookkeeper's nightmare. Although a union cigar maker's day typically began between seven and eight in the morning, he* did not have to be at the factory doors when they opened. A cigar maker was free to keep his own hours and come and go during the day, unless, of course, his attendance became unusually erratic. Attempts to alter this custom and fix the hours of labor would be met with firm resistance. In 1900 when a Philadelphia union manufacturer attempted to require all cigar makers to be at work by 8:30 A.M. "instead of drifting in at any time," cigar makers walked out and refused to work until the rule was abolished. Frank Shea, the foreman at R. G. Sullivan in Manchester, New Hampshire, one of the CMIU's premier label factories, remembered that "the door used to be open and people used to walk in and out" all day long. "Their hours?" mused Shea. "Bankers' hours."[1]

This freedom depended on a fundamental characteristic of their craft: it was piecework. Like coal miners, hatters, stove mounters, potters, and many other skilled workers in the early twentieth century, cigar makers were paid not according to the hours they spent on the job but the number of items they produced—so many dollars per thousand cigars. Working alone, each man was responsible only for his individual production. So while piecework often signified exploitative working conditions, as it did in the garment and other "sweated" trades, to union cigar makers it meant the boss did not own their time. "When you're working piecework," observed John Ograin, a cigar maker in Salt Lake City and later Chicago,

---

*There were women in the union, but I have chosen to use the masculine pronoun to emphasize the organization's masculine nature.

"your time is your own." In Denver, cigar maker William Theisen recalled that it did not matter how busy the factory might be. If a man wanted to "knock off early," he just wrapped up his things and left. "You didn't have to say anything because it wasn't costing them anything."[2]

Cigar makers controlled their time not only by insisting on flexible hours, but by designating the specific hours of operation for all union factories. In 1904 in Cincinnati, for example, union factories were open from 7:30 A.M. until noon, and from 1:30 until 4:30 P.M. In Manchester, the cigar makers set hours from 7:45 to 11:45 A.M. and from 1 to 5 P.M. All factories in Buffalo opened at 8 A.M. and closed between noon and 1 P.M., closing again at 5 P.M. On Saturdays, hours varied. During the first decade of the century, many locals shortened Saturday hours to four or five, and these Saturday "half-holidays" were especially popular in the summer. The other limitation which union cigar makers imposed with regard to hours involved the eight-hour day, won in 1886. Through it, cigar makers expected to make more work available to fellow craftsmen, a form of restriction of output.[3]

As the cigar maker arrived at the factory each morning, he made his way to the cigar-making floor. Except for the smallest shops in which all operations could be squeezed into one or two rooms, most factory buildings usually had more than one story. In Denver, William Theisen began working in a very small factory with only five men, and finished learning the trade in another small shop. Soon, however, he went to work for Solis Cigar, the largest factory in the city, employing about 125 cigar makers. The Solis factory had two floors, with the cigar makers occupying most of the upper story. Stemmers and packers worked at the back of the same floor, and downstairs were company offices. Tobacco and cigars were stored in the basement, where the casing and preparation of the tobacco also took place.[4]

The R. G. Sullivan factory in Manchester, like other New England cigar factories, grew dramatically during the first decade and a half of the twentieth century. In 1908, Sullivan opened a new factory which had five stories above ground and a basement below, and measured ninety-two feet by eighty-three feet in ground space. Coal was stored in the basement, along with cigars. Company offices and additional storage rooms occupied the ground floor. The second floor included a stamping room for placing the U.S. Internal Revenue tax stamps and blue union labels on the cigar boxes. The second floor also had a large workroom (measuring eighty by sixty-four feet) for about 128 cigar makers. The last room was used for drying tobacco. The third story of the factory was completely taken over by some two to three hundred cigar makers. By 1914 the number had risen to nine hundred cigar makers (the company had only fourteen in 1882) and Sullivan had to expand to a nearby building, having outgrown the new one in only six years. The casing of tobacco took place on the fourth floor, where there was room for still more cigar makers. On the fifth floor the packers carefully spread out their cigars under the windows covered by green shades to make sure the light was not too harsh. There were no cafeterias or first aid rooms, and while Sullivan officials proudly pointed out the hot and cold running water in the washrooms off the shop floors, William Theisen in Denver noted that in many western factories "you were lucky if you had a bathroom to go to."[5]

In small shops the work was usually carried on in a few rooms either in a small detached building or part of some larger structure or even a private home. In a one-man shop, a cigar maker had to handle all aspects of production himself. In factories with only a few cigar makers, the union usually required some packers in the jurisdiction to make weekly visits to do the packing, since a small force could not give steady work to a packer. These shops often employed several women or even a few young boys to strip the tobacco. It was not uncommon for a young cigar maker to learn his trade in a small shop, as Theisen had, and then move on to a larger factory once he had mastered the trade.[6]

While each cigar maker had a preference for either a large or a small shop, most worked in both over the course of their careers. Herman Baust learned cigar making in a small factory in New Haven, Connecticut, and thereafter began working for F. D. Grave, one of the larger companies in the city. He preferred the large shops because he did not like to perform as many tasks as were required in the smallest enterprises. He also believed that large shops offered more security and were less likely to be affected by local economic downturns. In larger shops, Baust found there were more people to talk with and much more activity. Foremen and manufacturers had fewer opportunities to scrutinize an individual's work habits in a large factory, and many preferred that more anonymous setting. Yet the small shop had its own advantages, notably its more personal, informal atmosphere.[7]

The cigar maker did not necessarily begin working right away in the morning. John Ograin remembered that in winter it took some time before the coal stoves could warm up the cavernous work areas in the large factories. "You'd come in there and it was cold," he recalled. "You sit

around and wait till it gets warm." It was not uncommon for a cigar maker
to wear his finest suit to work and then change clothes at the factory into
something more appropriate for handling the gritty tobacco. (Whether
women unionists observed the same custom is, unfortunately, unknown.)
In Salt Lake City, Chicago, and St. Louis, where Ograin had worked, men
often changed their trousers when they reached the factory. Cigar makers
also liked "Prince Alberts," long coats that came down to their knees, especially in New England. No self-respecting cigar maker could go to work
in a union shop with shabby clothing. It was the cigar makers' "pride to be
well-dressed" and clothing reflected their sense of respectability and the
dignity of their trade. José Santana added that good clothes, such as those
he had bought when he first got a steady job, visually placed workers on
an equal footing with employers.[8]

James Durso's experience in New Haven was that cigar makers always
wore hats to work, "derbies and straw hats," and that most of them wore
neckties while on the job. A union cigar maker who wore no coat or vest
and tie stood out from the rest. Charles Peet, a foreman at a Bridgeport,
Connecticut, factory in the early years of the century, observed that "the
cigar makers are very particular about their clothes and will blow all their
pay for a snappy wardrobe. I remember one maker . . . everyone called
him January. He stayed on a long time one season and saved up a substantial sum. Then he went out and blew himself to a new suit and shoes and
socks and a hat in the latest fashion. . . . He went to the best tailor in
town and ordered it."[9] The clothing of the cigar makers became almost
mythical, and in later years was quite exaggerated in some accounts. One
manufacturer, speaking in the early 1960s, claimed that the cigar maker in
Manchester, New Hampshire, had been an exceptional worker in that
city: "On Sunday he'd wear a high hat and carry a cane because he com-
manded a salary that made him a man of affluence."[10]

After a cigar maker changed clothes in the morning, he completed his
costume by donning his apron. (In Boston, cigar makers paid an outside
concern to provide clean aprons and towels at least once a week.) Next the
cigar maker proceeded onto the work floor and to his "bench," his cigar-
making work space. For those who had daily walked through the doors of
the cigar factory, the odor no longer gave them pause, but sometimes
older cigar makers, in describing their first days at work, recalled the nausea and the intoxication of the thick, penetrating smell which, according
to one observer, rendered "it difficult for them to walk in a straight line"
and made it "necessary to get to the fresh air." Before long the feeling

died away. The air in the factory held other smells besides tobacco, since coal stoves and gas lights used in some factories could fill the rooms with smoke.[11]

The cigar-making floor was a large gallery which sometimes took up the entire factory floor, depending on the number of cigar makers employed. Since cigar makers needed all the natural light they could get, the room usually had tall windows on all four sides. The men sat at benches, basically wooden tables with raised edges on three sides. The back of the bench rose higher than the two sides and formed a shelf, just below eye level from the seated cigar maker. A canvas sack was tacked to the open front of the table for catching excess leaf and cuttings. Despite this precaution, tobacco scraps still fell to the floor and by the end of the day the room was littered with them.[12]

The benches were attached to each other in double rows, so that the cigar maker sat with people on either side and across from him. These rows extended across the floor, occasionally broken by aisles. In some factories the benches were clustered close to the windows, but in most they were evenly spaced across the floor. The benches were only a few feet in width, so the workers sat, as Ograin noted, so close together that "you only got a little elbow room here." The seating arrangement conserved space, which manufacturers appreciated, but health inspectors criticized it for facilitating the spread of germs, particularly in view of cigar workers' high mortality rate from tuberculosis (second only to stonecutters'). Cigar makers liked to sit that way because it made conversation easier. Each cigar maker sat at the same bench every day and exercised a proprietary right over his place.[13]

In a small shop the arrangement was similar. Nine workers in one New York City factory in 1917 sat in one room, with four facing one wall and five facing another. In Manhattan a small shop such as this might be attached to a retail counter, since the street trade there was so active. The work space and retail shop would be separated only by a wire netting, as required by law. (Elsewhere such a combination of retailing and manufacturing was rare. Most small shops distributed their cigars to other outlets and did not engage directly in retail sales.) In 1913, the John O. Lund factory in Warren, Pennsylvania, employed seven cigar makers who worked in one room, but sat facing each other just as in the larger factories. In Kalamazoo, Michigan, in 1906 the McGlannon shop employed fourteen cigar makers who were seated the same way, in one long room.[14]

Winter and summer were the least pleasant seasons for the cigar mak-

John O. Lund's cigar factory, Warren, Pa., circa 1900. (Lund is at the extreme left of the picture.) Photo courtesy of the Warren County Historical Society, Warren, Pa.

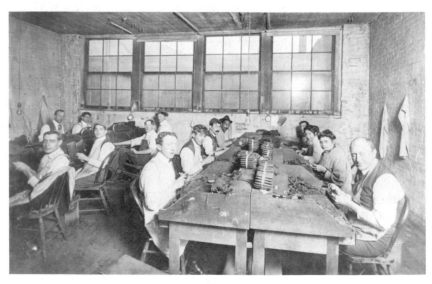

The Cuban Cigar Company, Denver, 1913. Photo courtesy of William Theisen, Denver, Colo.

ers, who could be plagued either by fumes from the coal stoves or by intense heat and humidity. Except for the work tables, where the cigar makers' busy motions kept the surface clean, a fine brown dust settled everywhere; it mounted on the window sills, since the windows were rarely opened, and the glass became so coated that it was no longer transparent. The cigar makers insisted that the floor be swept regularly, although preferably not during working hours, and that it be done with a wet mop to hold down the dust.

Scraps swept up from the floor were sold and used for making cheaper cigars. Factory inspectors sometimes complained of this practice since other—less desirable—matter also found its way to the floor. Because smoking in the factories was often prohibited by state law, many cigar makers chewed tobacco, and cuspidors were kept scattered throughout the shop. As one investigator reported, there existed some carelessness about the use of cuspidors, "many of the workers seeming to think that if they spat in that general direction it was sufficient." Still, unionists demanded that the cuspidors be cleaned weekly and in some cases hired someone themselves to do the job.

Boston factories at the turn of the century did not have water fountains, so the cigar makers brought in glasses or bottles of water with them. Despite a Massachusetts state law requiring factories with over one hundred employees to maintain first aid facilities, none of the cigar companies bothered to comply during the early decades of the century. Other amenities varied depending upon the particular shop. In some factories the men simply hung their coats and hats on nails and hooks around the workroom, while in others there were separate coat rooms.[15]

Some of the cigar maker's chief concerns during the workday related to his degree of control over his working conditions, which affected his output and earnings, but also reflected his self-image as a skilled and dignified craftsman. There were times in the summer when the combination of dust, smell, and heat became so unbearable that cigar makers simply refused to come to work. In most union factories the subject of ventilation was extremely controversial. Usually the windows remained closed, and in some shops they were nailed shut. As one Massachusetts Board of Health inspector observed: "Any suggestion to open the windows even a small distance for a limited period of time was politely but firmly disregarded as I was told again and again of the absolute refusal of the men to work in rooms with the windows open unless it happened to be the right kind of day." Open windows created a draft for the men who sat in virtually the same position all day, but more important the fresh air dried out the tobacco and made it harder to work with, resulting in slower production. If a cigar maker wanted to make his maximum, he would brook no interference with his efforts. It was more than simply a matter of earnings. No cigar maker wanted to make cigars with tobacco that was dry and unpliable, and the job was simply not worth performing if he had to use inferior grade stock. Sometimes cigar makers went home instead of working under conditions they considered unacceptable, even though the net result—lower wages—was the same in either case.[16]

The process of making cigars involved a considerable degree of skill and experience. The union required three years' apprenticeship, but cigar makers agreed they could learn the rudiments in half that time. What took longer was acquiring a combination of speed and skill. A 1907 government study of the work remarked that "union cigar makers are usually well trained in their trade and give satisfaction as regards both the quantity and quality of their product." Theoretically the apprenticeship system also helped to limit entry to the trade so that they could protect the basis of their power—their limited numbers and their skill. Each local set the number of apprenticeships it would allow and in New England it was particularly difficult to get one. In other areas, such as Denver and Chicago, the regulations were more lenient. Yet frequently, especially in cities where the union was weak, such as New York City or Philadelphia, the union did not have the power to enforce these apprenticeship laws. Few union manufacturers, however, wanted to train their own cigar makers, particularly in view of the amount of tobacco that could be wasted in the learning process. So although manfacturers opposed the apprenticeship system because it limited the number of skilled cigar makers, they did not systematically move to circumvent it, and there were periodic shortages of union labor in some areas.[17]

A foreman taught James Durso how to roll a cigar by first demonstrating the process and then returning later to comment on his work. "He'd show you once or twice where your mistakes were and after a while you've got it by yourself," Durso recalled. In Boston and in many union factories different cigar makers would stop to show the apprentice how to make a cigar, wrote Henry Abrahams, longtime secretary of Local 97 there. "After being shown by probably half a dozen different men . . . [he] became a skilled mechanic and would become very fast."[18] The apprentices learned to make cigars but also were required to sweep out the shop, run errands, and perform odd jobs, all for very low wages. The manufacturers justified the low wage scale on the grounds that they lost so much tobacco from the mistakes of these beginners.

Usually apprentices started to work between the ages of thirteen and sixteen. Herman Baust, who began in 1914 at fourteen years old, remembered that "we had to serve three years and we only got five dollars a week." Durso added that "your last year they move you in with the cigar makers so that you can get speed with them—you can make them fast." John Ograin explained that in Chicago the apprentices usually made the cheapest five-cent cigars while they were learning, and they were often expected to smoke their own cigars to test how good a product they were making. A union apprentice was supposed to learn all phases of cigar making, from stripping to packing. As Ograin put it, "We learned the trade from top to bottom."[19] Once a cigar maker finished his apprenticeship, he took his place among the other full-fledged workers. He began on the cheaper grades of cigars and worked his way up to the best grades, which paid the highest wages.

Once he sat down at his bench, the cigar maker began to work. Union members made cigars by hand and used only a few tools. With some exceptions, they made the entire cigar from beginning to end. José Santana explained that a division of labor violated the integrity of the cigar. Since each one was virtually an artistic creation, he could not imagine finishing the work that another cigar maker had begun. John Ograin felt that "if you are making it individually, you're responsible for it."[20]

A cigar maker's basic tool was a heavy wooden board measuring nine by fifteen inches and about two and a half inches thick, made of seven or eight sections of extremely hard wood which were bolted together. The board rested on the surface of the work bench, called the table. Although factories routinely provided cigar boards, some cigar makers preferred to purchase their own. Regardless of ownership, it was an unspoken rule that no one touched the work board or other items on the cigar maker's table without permission. A board in use for several years became seasoned with tobacco juice and gently worn in places where the cigar maker's rapid motions were concentrated. His other major tool was his cutter. Preferences for styles varied, with some cigar makers using a knife with a wooden handle, while others used the traditional Cuban blade, a thin, flat piece of metal two inches wide and four or five inches long, which was curved on the cutting side and was used in a rocking motion to slice the tobacco leaves to proper size.[21]

The work process itself and the wages the cigar maker received for his work depended on the particular cigar he made, since cigars came in so many styles and sizes. "They'd be making different shapes," said William Theisen. "It all depends on which we're selling best." In the larger shops, the orders that manufacturers received determined which cigars were made, while in the smallest, choices of cigars related both to orders and local tastes since many small producers sold their products in neighborhood stores and taverns.[22]

Every cigar style and size had its own wage rate. All wages were stated in terms of one thousand cigars made and were customarily noted as dollars "per M." The cigar makers' formal wage agreement, the bill of prices, was an elaborate listing of every cigar made in the shop and sometimes grew quite large and complicated. In Philadelphia in 1903 on a 4¾-inch handmade cigar using seed filler (Havana tobacco, grown in the U.S.), cigar makers charged $10.50 for straight work, $11.50 for shaped, and $14.00 for the perfectos, which were the hardest to make. If real Havana tobacco were used, the prices jumped by $1.50 on filler, and $1 each on binder and wrapper. On "Spanish Hand Work," where all tobacco was Clear Havana, the prices for the same cigars were $17, $18, and $21. In Boston, the bill was higher. Handwork on a seed filler cigar for a perfecto cost $17.[23]

The bills of prices varied from city to city, but were uniform in each local's jurisdiction. A committee in each local drew up a bill and submitted it to a meeting of the members of the local. If they approved, the committee presented it to all union manufacturers in the area. The stronger the local, the more demanding its members could be. In Boston, changes in the bill were usually accepted with little resistance. In Philadelphia or New Orleans where there were many skilled nonunion cigar makers or where competition from nonunion companies exerted downward pressure on wages, cigar makers might use more caution in formulating the bill. The CMIU constitution set a national minimum of $6 and later $7 for a thousand cigars made in a union shop.[24]

The process of making the cigars was known in the trade as "working up" the tobacco. If enough tobacco had been left over from the day before, the cigar maker could begin to work as soon as he sat down. In most union factories there were cans or bins at the benches for storing the tobacco overnight and keeping it from drying out. To begin, the cigar maker arrayed the various tobaccos on his table. Wrapper leaves needed to be kept moist and pliable, and the cigar maker could keep some of them on top of the bench during the day if they were covered with a dampened

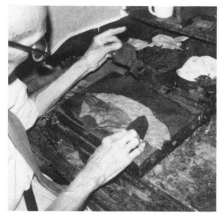
1. Selecting the binder leaf.

2. Starting the bunch.

3. Making the bunch.

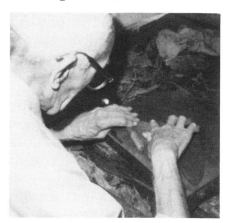
4. Adding the wrapper.

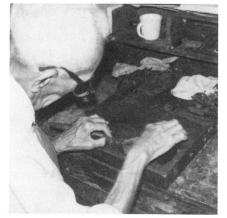
5. Cutting the wrapper.

6. Finishing the head.

José Santana at work in his shop, 1977. Photographs taken by author.

cloth. The coarse binder leaves and the fairly dry filler leaves did not usually require special attention, as long as the factory itself was humid.[25]

A cigar maker first selected a binder leaf, or two leaves in factories using a "double binder." The F. R. Rice factory in St. Louis always used single binder, while the R. G. Sullivan factory in Manchester preferred double binders. The difference, Ograin explained, was only in what a manufacturer thought made a better smoke. Cigar makers always charged more for the single binder, in part because it was difficult to make but, most important, because the manufacturer stood to make more of a profit on the cigar because he used less tobacco. Conscious of themselves as wage workers and as creators of their employer's wealth, they sought to claim their share of profits.[26]

For a double binder the cigar maker selected two pieces, tore them to the right size, and placed them slightly overlapping each other on the board. Next he took the long filler leaves into the palm of his left hand, sometimes blending different types of filler tobaccos to reach the flavor combination that the manufacturer wanted. "You had two different bins and you knew what percentage of each you had to put in each cigar," William Theisen recalled. "Maybe it would be two-thirds of one and one-third of the other." Boston cigar makers charged a dollar extra if they had to blend more than three of these fillers, which ranged from sweet to bitter and from mild to harsh. The extra charges for blending sometimes became so prohibitive that manufacturers mixed the tobaccos themselves in large bins. In Chicago, the cigar makers rarely blended on the table. "The bosses knew they wouldn't do it," Santana explained, because such effort consumed too much time and therefore reduced wages.[27]

After building up pieces of filler leaf in the palm of his hand, the cigar maker would break off the filler to the length of the cigar. He kept adding tobacco to this bunch until he got a "feeling" for how much he needed. He held them gently, feeling the thickness of the bunch he was forming and also the tightness or looseness of the leaves as they pressed against each other, making sure he used neither too much nor too little pressure as he squeezed and formed the leaves. In "open head" work the tips of the filler leaves all had to be at the tuck or lighting end of the cigar. In some factories "you made open head work or you didn't work," so that union cigar makers had to learn to do it. (Styles, color, method, and materials varied with each manufacturer's personal taste. Many manufacturers came from families in the cigar-making business and carried on family traditions as to what made a truly fine cigar.) The tips of the filler leaves were considered to be more tender and sweet, so that the smoker's first puff held the very best flavor if the tips were at the lighting end. It took more time, however, to make cigars this way and cigar makers usually charged an extra 50¢ to $1 for open head work.[28]

Once the filler had been shaped in the cigar maker's hand, he placed the bunch on the corner of the binder leaf and curled the edge around the filler leaves, rolling them up inside. This action could not be careless or haphazard, because the shape and form of the cigar had to be introduced and maintained at this point. The combination of the shape already given the filler and the pressure applied while rolling the binder leaf around the filler helped to clarify the precise contours of the cigar.[29]

The bunch-making stage required great skill and sensitivity because the actual smoking value of the cigar depended upon it. A wrong twist in the leaf or too many leaves crossed at one place created blockades for smoke and flavor which the experienced smoker could detect. All the taste had to reach the smoker and the "draw" had to be smooth and complete. A cigar packed too loosely allowed too much hot air to pass through too quickly, "like a chimney with too much draft." The smoke had to travel at just the right pace so that the smoker had only to puff and not pull on the cigar, but not too quickly so as to be harsh or burning. These were the subtleties that the cigar makers learned by experience over the years, and many, especially Clear Havana workers like José Santana, considered themselves to be artists.[30]

After the cigar maker completed the bunch he laid it to the side, cleared the board, and reached for a wrapper leaf. This was the most delicate leaf on the cigar and had to be handled carefully. A hole or tear in it would ruin the cigar's appearance. The wrapper had to be moist and pliable for working, but not soggy. The cigar maker stretched the wrapper onto the board with the glossy outside facing down, smoothing it with his fingertips. Next he cut the wrapper to proper shape, long and thin and slightly curved. He could expect several "cuts" from a good piece of leaf (which was actually half of a whole leaf that had been stripped). If the leaf was a "right," then the veins moved out from the stem to the right and the cigar maker began on the left and rolled toward the right. If the leaf was a "left," he moved in the opposite direction. Beginners usually learned only one direction at a time, but an experienced hand could instantly distinguish between the two leaves and could move easily from one to the other.[31]

Instead of simply folding the wrapper around the bunch, the cigar maker began at the tuck and rolled the bunch up inside the narrow wrapper in a spiral motion, coiling it around toward the other end, gradually covering the entire bunch. At each turn he carefully overlapped the leaf slightly. His goal was to have the outside of the cigar appear smooth and uniform. A new problem arose when the cigar maker had rolled the wrapper to the head; it had to be perfectly rounded so that the wrapper covered it completely. Fashion and custom dictated this, although the smoker cut off the tip before lighting the cigar. The cigar maker therefore made a sort of flag on the end of the leaf. As he neared the end he dipped his finger into a paste cup containing gum tragacanth, a clear, tasteless glue, and took the remaining piece of leaf between his thumb and forefinger, sliding on the paste as he turned the cigar and wound the flag smoothly about the head. The juncture in the wrapper leaf would almost disappear from sight. Some shapes required that the tuck end also be closed, a step which added effort and time. In some cases the pinpoint tuck needed was achieved by making a cut into the cigar once it had been rolled, removing some tobacco and reshaping and then sealing the cigar back up again—a delicate operation. A cigar maker had to judge everything by appearance and feel. Every cigar he made had to be exactly the same in every respect.[32]

Cigar makers placed great emphasis on the importance of a "keen sense of touch." In the opinion of Herman Baust, "not everybody could be a cigar maker. You had to have a certain feeling in your hands." Cigar makers regarded their hands as their most precious possession—"our skill lies in our fingers." As Ramy Rogers of Manchester described it, a "human being has eyes to look and hands to feel [the] tobacco to know [how] to make good [cigars]. . . . It takes a man ten years to learn to make cigars right and know the feel of the tobacco." If the cigar maker smoked cigars himself, he knew well the delight and pleasure that came from smoking an expertly made product.[33]

While "out and out" handwork prevailed in New England, mold work could be found in many other union shops and often hand and mold cigar makers worked together in the same factories. In 1912, the CMIU estimated that half of its members were "out and out" cigar makers while the rest used the wooden mold, a block which held from ten to twenty spaces the size of a cigar and molded the bunches into the correct size and shape. Many manufacturers preferred mold work because it simplified the process and economized on leaf. Wrappers did not have to be as large as for hand-rolled cigars, and wages for mold workers were slightly lower in comparison to overall output. Yet the manufacturers, many of whom had been cigar makers themselves, knew the qualities of a good cigar and some readily admitted that "even a short time in the mold serves to change the character of a cigar" so far as its burning qualities were concerned. One of the Ibold brothers, who ran a large union factory in Cincinnati, Ohio, once proudly proclaimed to a union official: "There's never been a mold in my shop."[34]

In mold work, used on many ten-cent cigars and most five-cent smokes, the cigar maker placed the tobacco bunches in the deep cigar-shaped grooves on one half of the mold. Then he locked on the top and placed the mold in an iron screw press, which usually stood to the side of the room or sometimes between two cigar makers. The press created enough pressure to shape the bunches, and the longer the bunches remained under pressure the more shaping took place. Naturally, any tie-up in the use of the presses slowed down work for the cigar makers and meant a disruption in their schedules and a potential drop in wages. Thus the cigar makers universally insisted that "there must be press facilities for all molds in use." The cigar makers established other rules concerning the use of the molds which involved the same principles, although they varied slightly among locals. Five twenty-block molds were called a set, and the cigar maker placed two molds in the press together, leaving them in for about twenty minutes while he filled the other three. For anything less than one hundred bunches in a set, the cigar makers charged more, since their work would take more time. The less time a mold had been in the press, the closer rolling the bunches was to handwork because they remained soft and therefore required more skill and care. Less than forty bunches, two twenty-block molds, was considered the same as handwork and the same prices were charged.[35]

Mold work was easier and quicker, and while a mold worker's production was greater, his overall pay might be less than or only equal to that of a handworker because of the lower price for mold work. Using the mold reduced the amount of skill needed in shaping the bunch, but it did not completely relieve the cigar maker of responsibility for shaping. "You know the mold didn't just shape it," William Theisen noted. "You kind of had to figure it out. If you had too much in one place, why it would press it down too hard and naturally the cigar wouldn't smoke."[36]

Although union cigar makers tended to work primarily in Seed and Havana cigars, some members worked on Clear Havanas. During strikes at the turn of the century and in 1910, the CMIU tried to organize workers in Tampa and thousands there joined at one time or another, but membership in the CMIU in Tampa was unsteady at best and only a small percentage of the city's ten thousand workers kept regular membership in the union. Hostility was fueled by persistent ethnic tensions since Cubans and Spaniards regarded the CMIU as German and too conservative. Ograin remembered that opponents of the union had spread the rumor that George W. Perkins, president of the CMIU, was the same person as George Perkins, the wealthy industrialist. However, the CMIU did have members working on Clear Havana cigars in New York City, San Francisco, London and Hamilton in Ontario, Denver, and especially Chicago. In most cases members doing this work represented many different groups, including Germans, Poles, and Russian Jews, but in Denver many of the Clear Havana workers were Spanish-speaking, as were many in New York City. Cigar makers charged the very highest prices on the bill for the Clear Havanas, which also were the most expensive on the retail market.[37]

Clear Havana work had a mystique all its own. For these cigars, made by either the "Spanish method" or the "German method," the key element was workmanship and precision, given the scores of distinctive shapes and sizes. Unlike the Seed and Havana cigar, which was measured for length but not for width except by the cigar maker's eye, the Clear Havana cigar had to fit through a "cepo" or "ring gauge." The ring gauge was a piece of wood with a metal ring in the middle, engraved with a gauge number graduated in sixty-fourths of an inch. The widest point on a Clear Havana cigar had to fit the ring gauge exactly.[38] In any given Clear Havana factory the particular requirements for the cigars might vary. Many shops had their own distinctive styles. One large Clear Havana shop in San Francisco was nicknamed the "tamale shop," John Ograin recalled. "You know how big a Mexican tamale is. Well, that's why they called it the tamale shop. It was a big, heavy cigar."[39]

Every bill of prices, no matter for what locale, carried the same rule, usually printed in boldface type: "All stock must be in good condition to work." Nothing could be worse in a cigar maker's day than inferior tobacco. First it increased his time and effort and decreased earnings and production. But it was not simply a matter of earnings. The cigar maker's freedom in the cigar factory was tied to his piecework and his ability to work quickly and efficiently. The cigar maker who came late or left early or spent his day talking might not make many cigars, but at least the choice was his. Cigar makers carefully distinguished between their own time and the boss's. Time should not be spent working cheap, poor quality

The Solis Cigar factory, Denver, circa 1914. Photo courtesy of William Theisen, Denver, Colo.

tobacco which served the boss's best interest but not the cigar maker's. The usually even-tempered cigar makers at the Kafka factory in New Haven changed their disposition when furnished with flawed tobacco. The "only time you'd see them get mad," said James Durso, "was when they got tobacco that wasn't good—hard to work." William Theisen explained that his daily production depended on the condition of the tobacco. "Sometimes the stock would be terrible. It would either be too wet or too dry and the wrapper would be a mess. A lot of things like that could slow you down." Inferior grade stock was regarded by many as an insult and was sufficient justification for a spontaneous walkout.[40]

As the cigar maker continued his work, he would use up all of the tobacco at his bench. Then he needed to get fresh supplies of leaf from stock boys who either brought him the tobacco or dispensed it from a central area just off the cigar-making floor. Where the union was strong, makers insisted that tobacco be brought to them so they did not waste their own time getting it. While in some factories cigar makers received all tobacco in preweighed packages, in others only wrappers were so measured.[41]

Once a cigar maker finished making a cigar he quickly inspected it. If well-made, it had no holes or tears in the wrapper. All of the cigars had to be uniform in appearance—the right weight, shape, and size. The cigar should be firm, but slightly springy when squeezed between the fingers. On the raised shelf before the cigar maker was a "bundler," a U-shaped holder made of wire or wood, which when filled would hold fifty cigars. When he had reached fifty, the cigar maker tied up the bundle with a string or buckled strap and placed a slip underneath with either his name or seat number on it. From there, exact procedures differed, but the bundles were gathered in a central location in the shop each day and were inspected. The cigar maker's production for the day was added to his totals for the week in order to calculate his weekly earnings.[42]

Saturday was payday and cigar makers preferred this day because they wanted spending money for the weekend. Wages were paid weekly in cash and were calculated according to the number of cigars one had produced during the week times the price for the size and style he had made. Thus he had a fairly good idea at the week's end just how much money he would be getting in his pay envelope. Sometimes factory bookkeeping required that the last tally be made on Friday, so the foreman circulated through the shop floor on Friday morning asking each man how many cigars he expected to make before he left work on Saturday. "You'd go around to a man," explained foreman Shea, "and he'd tell you how many

he was going to make that day and how many he'd make the next day."
Some of the cigar makers who had missed a day or who wanted more
money would "give in two big day's work to get the money." If the cigar
maker did not make as many cigars as he had estimated, then he would
have a "dead horse," work that would have to be made up the following
week. The term also meant, more broadly, anything the cigar maker
thought he had in his possession but actually did not. The expression had
originated in a nineteenth-century tale, often told and passed on to each
new generation, about a cigar maker who worked all winter long and
allowed his boss to keep part of his earnings for him until spring. When
the time came, the cigar maker wanted to get his money and travel, but
the boss no longer had the cash. He persuaded the cigar maker to accept a
horse instead. When the cigar maker led the horse out of the stable, it
promptly dropped dead and he had to pay seven dollars (the amount varied) to have the carcass carted away.[43]

Cigar makers' wages rose during the period between 1900 and 1919,
but in spurts. They rose steadily until 1908 or so and then leveled out
until about 1916, when they began rising sharply. Between 1904 and 1919
the wages of male hand cigar makers rose 64 percent in Boston, 73 percent in Chicago, 46 percent in Detroit, and 38 percent in New York City.
However, the Department of Labor estimated that between 1913 and
1920 the national cost of living rose 75 percent. Too, the wages of American workers generally rose during the century's second decade, while
those of cigar makers climbed only slightly. The divergence related to the
deteriorating fortunes of union men after 1910, as competition from the
expanding five-cent-cigar industry began to dampen union wages. The
lingering effects of a recession from 1907 to 1909 slowed the rate of increase as well.[44]

Because of regional differences in the power and strength of the CMIU,
wage rates of union cigar makers varied from place to place. The union's
formal wage agreement, the bill of prices, was uniform in each local's jurisdiction, but cigar makers had never been able to impose a national
scale of wages for members. Wages were highest in the union's stronghold
in New England, particularly Massachusetts, New Hampshire, Connecticut, and Rhode Island, where practically all cigar factories were unionized throughout the period.[45] In 1907 cigar makers in Boston earned
about 49¢ an hour or from $20 to $24 per week, average. In 1907 in New
Hampshire, male cigar makers averaged about $22 a week. By the end of
World War I, Boston wages had risen to an estimated 68¢ an hour or from

60

Table 1. Average Weekly Wage of Union Cigar Makers
in Selected Cities, 1913

City	Factory	Average Weekly Number of Cigar Makers	Weekly Wage
Colorado			
Denver	Solis Cigar Co.	86	$16.38
	Cuban Cigar Co.	44	17.44
Connecticut			
Hartford	Charles Soby	83	17.53
New Haven	F. D. Graves	161	18.85
	A. Kafka and Co.	89	18.98
California			
San Francisco	Frankel, Gerds and Co.	170	19.85
	Red Seal Cigar Co.	21	20.00
Illinois			
Chicago	Wengler and Mandell-Clear Havana	152	20.37
	J. Fernbach and Co.	72	19.93
	Duus and Gellert	14	20.41
Indiana			
Indianapolis	Crump Bros.	325	19.50
	A. E. Rauch	35	17.00
	Coony Bayer Cigar Co.	50	16.83
	C. L. Goetz and Mike Hazinski	60	16.00
Kentucky			
Louisville	A. Bickel and Co.	46	9.09
	J. T. Siler and Sons	28	13.08
Maine			
Bangor	W. S. Allen	12	26.72
Massachusetts			
Boston	Waitt and Bond, Inc.	648	22.16
	H. Traiser and Co.	486	19.94
Missouri			
St. Louis	F. R. Rice Mercantile Cigar Co.	100	16.05
New Hampshire			
Manchester	R. G. Sullivan	479	21.20
New Jersey			
Newark	Frank Mueller	29	19.03
	Stumm and Co.	22	16.15

Table 1 (cont'd.)

City	Factory	Average Weekly Number of Cigar Makers	Weekly Wage
	Harry Stone	20	18.15
	F. L. Luz and Co.	15	17.22
New York			
Troy	Quinn Bros.	41	14.20
	Fitzpatrick and Draper	43	17.80
Oneida	Powell and Goldstein	132	14.95
	J. M. Bennett and Son	19	14.62
New York City	B. Feifer and Sons	244	11.94
	Wm. Glaccum and Sons	71	12.62
	T. J. Plunket	50	15.32
	Central Cigar Manufac- turing Co.	133	17.60
Ohio			
Cincinnati	Peter Ibold	103	14.61
	M. Ibold	110	16.54
Pennsylvania			
Reading	Clarence E. Kutz	75	14.70
	Charles N. Yetter and Co.	65	12.22
McSherrystown	C. E. Miller	55	13.40
Erie	G. B. Wingerter	25	15.75
	A. M. Hess	8	14.50
Wisconsin			
Milwaukee	B. Fernandez	111	16.89
	Herman Busch	16	13.50

Source: *Congressional Record*, 5 Sept. 1913, 63d Cong., 1st sess., vol. 50, part 5, 1913.

$27 to $30 a week. Other areas of relatively high wages were Chicago, St. Louis, upstate New York, parts of Ohio and Wisconsin, and Denver. Elsewhere wages averaged from $10 to $18 a week. Union cigar makers in New York State in 1907, for example, averaged about $12 a week. Table 1 suggests comparisons among several areas for 1913.[46]

Cigar makers frequently called for higher wages, basing their demands on what manufacturers could afford to pay and what they believed they deserved. Frank Shea remembered that "they were always crabbing" that they "ought to be getting a dollar a thousand more." When they discussed the matter with other skilled workers or outsiders, however, cigar makers usually claimed that their wages were quite high, in keeping with their position as respectable craftsmen. Ograin asserted that the cigar makers "were usually getting the top salaries." Herman Baust of Connecticut declared that "when I first went in you were almost considered a millionaire because you were a cigar maker. Yeah, we made thirty dollars a week when they [other skilled workers] were only making ten and nine." In New Haven, James Durso thought cigar makers "were considered high class. They made more than the bricklayer, they made more than the carpenter." Santana felt rich when he first began working in Canada and later in Chicago. He easily made enough money to support himself and to send money home every week to his parents in Puerto Rico. [47]

Although cigar makers liked to believe they made more than other workers, evidence suggests that this was not strictly the case. In New England, where wages were highest, they did earn on a par with other skilled workers. In Manchester, cigar makers averaged about $20 a week in 1904 and easily outearned all but the most skilled workers in the city's textile factories. In Chicago during the first decade of the century, cigar makers earned the same as union coopers and machinists, and the latter worked a longer day. But other skilled workers, including pressmen, railroad engineers, bricklayers, and carpenters, made more when differing hours were taken into account. In New York State, cigar makers consistently earned less than workers in these occupations by about $1 a day, and less than bricklayers by as much as $3 a day. Union cigar makers did earn more than nonunion cigar makers, however. Estimates placed their wages anywhere from 10 to 50 percent higher than nonunion wages. [48]

Exact wages depended on production. A cigar maker could expect to make between two hundred and four hundred cigars a day, and on a "big day" he might make as many as five hundred. "Out and out" work was slower than mold work (although the piece rates were higher) and output also depended on the tobacco and the style of the cigar being made. On the most difficult styles, a cigar maker might average only 150 a day. A 5¼-inch perfecto with a small tuck took longer to make than a 4¼-inch londre in a mold.

Informal shop rules never limited output. The only restriction on it was the eight-hour day. In fact cigar makers tended to judge their skill and ability based on their individual speed and informally competed with each other. Even older workers used daily production figures to demonstrate their continued proficiency. One member wrote in the *CMOJ*, "I'm

76 now and I make 900 a week." Exceptional speed was a gift someone had naturally—it could not be acquired—and cigar makers revered and respected very fast workers. Frank Shea could recall years later the Belgian who could make eight hundred cigars in a day. Ograin explained that people's talents simply differed. He compared two cigar makers he had known. "Vic Carlson. He was the fastest man I ever worked with and he was up to two thousand a week. Two thousand cigars at $18 a thousand— $36 a week. . . . And the fellow working next to me was making $12 a week." Union rules and practice did not permit shoddy workmanship, so the less adroit maker would simply work more slowly and make less money. A truly fine cigar maker was expected to be both fast and accurate, qualities which coincided with manufacturers' needs.[49]

Around noon the cigar makers stopped work for forty-five minutes to an hour. Union factories generally did not have dining rooms. In the winter, men often brought their lunches and ate in the workroom. Throughout the year, many went out to eat. In New Haven, many cigar makers, recalled Durso and Baust, ate lunch in nearby taverns, while some walked home. When they returned to work in the afternoon, someone might bring in a pitcher or more of "near beer," although neither remembered anyone getting intoxicated while at work. The noon meal was not the only time the cigar makers visited a tavern. R. W. Steber, a manufacturer in Warren, Pennsylvania, complained that "in the morning sometimes, some fellow would say, 'Well, who wants to get drunk?' And the whole crowd of them would get up and walk out and go to the saloon, and we were shut down for the day." Customarily, however, cigar makers returned from lunch and began working again, trying to reach whatever quota they had set for themselves for the day.[50]

As the cigar maker sat working, he might pause and look across the shop. Surrounding him as he worked was a fairly diverse group of people. Most of them were men, although in larger factories, especially in New York City or Chicago, there might be a few "lady cigar makers." In Boston during the second decade of the century, there were as many as two hundred women working among the city's three thousand cigar makers, but almost all had learned the trade in Belgium or Holland, had belonged to the union there, and then had emigrated to the U.S. A majority of the CMIU's women members were in New York City. Nationally, female membership averaged about 10 percent of the union's total during these years, temporarily ballooning during World War I. For the most part these women seem to have had a fairly short union tenure, and their membership figures actually represented a coming and going of women with few long-term ties to the union. Unfortunately, little is known about them and the *CMOJ* is disappointingly silent. The number of blacks in the CMIU was apparently small, although the CMIU had one of the largest black memberships of any international union in the country. This was true, though, because so many other unions barred blacks from membership. New Orleans and Mobile each had black locals. In Chicago, both Ograin and Santana recalled working with black cigar makers who had come from Mobile.[51]

Another group visible in a cigar factory were physically handicapped men who were attracted to the trade because of its sedentary nature. James Durso was the son of a bricklayer, but when he broke his arm at the age of fourteen he damaged it so severely that he could not follow his father's trade and became a cigar maker instead. The F. R. Rice factory in St. Louis actually catered to "cripples," because Frank Rice, who owned the company, had lost a leg in the Battle of Fredericksburg in the Civil War. John Ograin recalled that able-bodied cigar makers had to walk up to the third-floor cigar-making room in the factory; only those with a disability could ride the elevators. There were always older workers in union cigar factories as well, since the union supported the right of older members to work as long as they could. It was not uncommon for such old-timers to have worked for the same manufacturer for twenty years or more.[52]

Cigar making attracted people from a variety of ethnic groups. Although Germans were the largest single nationality in the CMIU, John Swinton was only slightly exaggerating when he wrote that he could not name "another trade in which the workers are of so many races as there are in the cigar makers' trade." Although exact figures are unavailable, the 1910 census listed 58,725 male cigar makers (union membership that year was 43,837), of whom 18,032 were native-born of native parents, 15,004 had foreign or mixed parentage, and 23,569 were foreign-born. New York City had separate locals for Bohemian, Jewish, and Spanish-speaking cigar makers. In Chicago, Local 15 had originally been chartered as the German local, but in the early twentieth century it was known as a socialist union and attracted many different nationalities. Its meetings were all conducted in English. Some shops were known to be German or Belgian, but lines were not rigid and nationalities were mixed in most cases. Tensions between Cuban cigar makers and others in the union were more pronounced, particularly since Cubans often made it no secret that they considered themselves to be inherently better cigar makers. This tension, however, was most evident in the rocky association that Clear Havana workers in Tampa and Key West had with the union. Most meetings of CMIU locals in the early twentieth century were conducted in English, but the *CMOJ* carried additional brief sections in German, French, Czech, and Spanish.[53]

Despite cramped and stiff arm and neck muscles and the readiness of every union cigar maker to point out injustices regarding his work, cigar makers spoke in warm and positive terms about their jobs, largely because of the pleasant shop atmosphere they themselves had created. Cigar makers had a saying, "Once a cigar maker, always a cigar maker." That meant, explained Santana, that no matter what happened to a cigar maker, what he did or where he went, "you always have on your mind the cigar makers . . . and you will go back to the cigar shop." When away once himself, Santana had thought frequently of the "cigar shop and the liberty I had." Herman Baust agreed. If a cigar maker left the trade and went away for a while, something "draws them back . . . I think I liked it because it was so free—you never had them standing over your head. You were a pieceworker. . . . I liked it because you were free."[54]

Most important were the social aspects of their work culture and the sense of community and belonging cigar makers shared at work. Santana had prized the "companionship" of the factory most. The cigar makers were "so congenial one with the other that you enjoy." "I really enjoyed it," noted Herman Baust. "They were all friends." There was a great camaraderie among the cigar makers, noted Charles Peet, a foreman in Bridgeport, Connecticut. "They had their own names for each other too, names which never appeared on the company books, but names by which they were known to each other," such as "Fine and Dandy Smith," "Kentucky Pete," and "Old Standby." Travelers from other locals enlivened their factory conversations. Although newcomers to the shop in other trades might find animosity, Santana pointed out, in the cigar factory they were always welcomed. Shop discussions were also a means of passing along union stories such as that about the dead horse. Older members never tired of describing the terrible conditions before the union was organized when members had to pay for the oil to light the factories or accept "truck" in lieu of cash for wages. Young members learned the trade terms and language which helped draw them into the community as full-fledged members.[55]

Conversations and pranks helped relieve the monotony of the day. Cigar makers enjoyed jokes, but they usually acted together as a group rather than trying to fool each other. Foremen and stock boys were perennial targets. A new stock boy would be sent all through the factory in search of a binder "stretcher," or a "left-handed" something, and would be sent from person to person, all playing along with the joke until everyone would break out in laughter. Charles Peet recalled the cigar makers in his shop playing pranks on the boss's brother, and once hiding a garter snake in his cigars. Belgian cigar makers in Manchester spent much of their time racing pigeons and sometimes brought them to work in large baskets, which provided the opportunity for stock boys to retaliate by letting a bird loose in the shop.[56]

The sociability of the shop floor did not mean a lack of arguments or serious discussions. In fact heated discussions formed an important part of shop-floor work culture. Topics varied, but the strong socialist presence within the CMIU often meant that the conversation centered around "economics," albeit on a somewhat less literate plane than the debates in New York City in the 1870s. Socialist editor Algie Simons remarked that the cigar makers perceived themselves as a "race of philosophers," and loved to debate politics, the labor movement, current events, and life generally. "We were the best politicians in the country," claimed Herman Baust. "They would talk on every subject of the country—what the Congress was doing, everything. . . . They were very well read people." In Manchester, the Belgian cigar makers sometimes got into fights over issues. "Once in a while two of them would go outside and have it out," Frank Shea remembered. "Out in the street." While political and economic discussions could heat up the atmosphere, there were times when the shop would become so quiet "you could hear a pin drop."[57]

The custom of employing a reader—which became commonly associated with the cigar makers in the public mind—originated in Cuba and never became widespread in the United States outside of the Clear Havana shops employing Spanish-speaking workers. The custom may have extended to some other nationalities, especially in Jewish shops in New York City in the late nineteenth century, and as a young man Samuel Gompers served as a reader there in a Clear Havana shop. José Santana had listened to a reader in the factory where he had worked as a young boy in Puerto Rico, and also heard one in a Spanish-speaking shop in New York City and later in London, Ontario, but never saw the practice elsewhere. In those shops where the custom prevailed, the cigar makers themselves paid someone with a strong, clear voice to read to them from newspapers and books (which they voted on) while they worked.[58]

Normally most cigar makers remained until the official workday ended to make more cigars and earn more money. The day drew to a close when someone announced the time or, as in Manchester, the union shop collector blew a whistle to signal that there were only fifteen minutes left to work. Since the cigar makers did not like to hand in cigars in odd numbers, this notification gave them time to make enough to complete their work in "units of five or ten." Then a final whistle indicated that the workday was over. The men brought up their cigars or someone came round to collect them, and the foreman placed them in the humidor overnight, to be inspected the next day before being sent to the packing room. If anyone remained after the official end of the working day, the shop collector was supposed to report him to the union for a fine. After covering his tobacco, sweeping the scraps into the pouch in front of his bench, and changing his clothes again, he gathered up his three "smokers," the free cigars he received as a fringe benefit, put on his hat, and walked out.[59]

After work the congenial atmosphere of the cigar shop often migrated elsewhere. "When they got through at night they'd all gang up and go to the saloon," Herman Baust recalled of cigar makers in New Haven. "They were great drinkers," he continued. "They sometimes would have a bad weekend and sometimes there were thirty or forty out of Graves for a day, if they got too drunk." In Denver, Chicago, Manchester, New Haven, or wherever the cigar makers worked, the saloon was a favorite gathering place, and union secretaries often set up their offices there after work to conduct union business. Depending on the locale, cigar makers may or may not have shared the ride or walk home afterwards together. For example, in Manchester, most Belgians lived in one of two general areas, while in Roxbury, Massachusetts, in 1913, cigar makers came from all over Boston to work in a new, modern Waitt and Bond Company factory there. In some cities, a few cigar makers met again at meetings of the central labor body, or perhaps in community or neighborhood organizations. In Boston, the Belgian Federation, formed in 1907, worked to help countrymen still in Belgium achieve better working conditions while the Union Belge, organized in 1914, aided those suffering the ravages of the war back home. Certainly these and other organizations elsewhere provided cigar makers with opportunities for meeting and talking beyond the workplace and the saloon.[60]

During the course of the workday, cigar makers' activities reflected several aspects of their work culture, expressing concerns which were not simply economic and material. They placed great emphasis on controlling their time and differentiating it from the boss's, and they used the freedom their craft work and flexible hours provided them to shape the day according to their own needs. They took great pride in skills that had taken years to learn and in the products they made, refusing, for example, to work with inferior materials. Their sense of dignity and respectability extended even to the clothes they wore. Beyond these, however, were the close bonds and ties which developed in the factory, not separate from the context of local community, but cutting across ethnic and other differences among them. In the factory they built a work community in which they all took part, albeit one with differences and conflict. The "old craftsman spirit"[61] was still very much a part of the lives of union cigar makers in the early twentieth century.

Notes

1. U.S. Bureau of Labor Statistics, Bulletin 161, *Wages and Hours of Labor in the Clothing and Cigar Industries, 1911 to 1913* (Washington, D.C., 1914), p. 66; *Tobacco,* 1 June 1900, p. 4; T. Frank Shea interview, 26 June 1979, Manchester, N.H. Shea began working as a stock boy in 1909 in Roger Sullivan's large factory in Manchester. Later he became a foreman, a position he kept until the company closed in 1961.

2. Elizabeth M. Hennessey, "Report on Cigar and Cigarette Making Industry in Boston," typescript, report for the Massachusetts Bureau of Labor and Industries, ca. 1918, U.S. Women's Bureau, Box 23, Unpublished Surveys, General Correspondence, Record Group (R.G.) 86, National Archives (NA), Washington, D.C.; Lloyd Ulman, *The Rise of the National Trade Union: The Development and Significance of Its Structure, Governing Institutions and Economic Policies* (Cambridge, Mass., 1955), p. 549; U.S. Commissioner of Labor, *Eleventh Special Report,* "Regulation and Restriction of Output" (Washington, D.C., 1904), p. 570; John R. Ograin interview, 17 May 1980, Chicago; William Theisen interview, 17 Aug. 1979, Denver, Colo. John Ograin learned the trade in Chicago in 1903. William Theisen began learning the trade in Denver in 1912. His father was a laborer born in Germany, and his mother a U.S.-born homemaker. He belonged to the CMIU until 1924, when he left the trade.

3. "Bill of Prices," Local 4, Cincinnati, Ohio, 1907, U.S. Department of Labor Library (USDL), Washington, D.C.; "By-Laws of the Cigar Makers' Union No. 192," Manchester, N.H., 1915, p. 17, Manchester City Library (MCL), Manchester, N.H.; New York Bureau of Labor Statistics, *Annual Report* (Albany, 1901, 1908, 1912); Massachusetts Bureau of Labor Statistics, *Fifth Annual Report on Labor Organizations for the Year 1912* (Boston, 1912), p. 170.; U.S. Commissioner of Labor, "Regulation and Restriction of Output," p. 564; "By-Laws and Rules of Order of the Cigar Makers' Union No. 25," Milwaukee, Wis., 1903, p. 9,

State Historical Society of Wisconsin (SHSW), Madison; A. M. Simons, "A Label and Lives—The Story of the Cigar Makers," *Pearson's Magazine*, Jan. 1917, p. 69.

4. Theisen interview.

5. Shea interview; *Tobacco Leaf*, 25 Mar. 1903, p. 11; *CMOJ*, July 1882, p. 3; *Manchester Union*, 25 Aug. 1908; *Manchester Mirror*, 17 June 1914, clipping files, Tobacco Merchants Association Library (TMA), New York City; Theisen interview.

6. José Santana interviews, 1976–80, Chicago; U.S. Bureau of Labor, Bulletin 67, *Conditions of Entrance to the Principal Trades*, by A. M. Sakolski (Washington, D.C., 1906), pp. 711, 719. Santana was born in 1890 in Mayagüez, Puerto Rico, and moved to New York City in 1909. After 1911, he lived primarily in Chicago. I interviewed him extensively between 1976 and his death in 1980.

7. Herman Baust interview, 24 Mar. 1977, North Haven, Conn. Baust was born in 1897 and learned to make cigars in New Haven, at the factory of Barnett Plotkin. In 1927 he opened his own shop.

8. Ograin interview, 19 May 1979 and 11 Aug. 1976; Santana interview, 27 Feb. 1977 and 18 Nov. 1979 by telephone.

9. James Durso interview, 24 Mar. 1977, New Haven, Conn.; Santana interview, 18 Nov. 1979 by telephone; *Bridgeport* (Conn.) *Sunday Post*, 13 Feb. 1938; Frederick Bates interview, 27 June 1979, Manchester, N.H. Durso's Italian parents moved from New York City to New Haven when he was six. Bates was the son of a cigar maker and worked in the trade in the 1920s in Manchester.

10. *Manchester Union Leader*, 26 Apr. 1961, TMA.

11. Hennessey, "Report on Cigar Making in Boston," p. 12; New York State Commissioner of Labor, *Report of the Commissioner of Labor 1908* (Albany, 1909), p. 171.

12. See, for example, *Tobacco Leaf*, 25 Mar. 1903, p. 11; 7 Nov. 1906, p. 31.

13. Ograin interview, 19 May 1979; Hennessey, "Report on Cigar Making in Boston," p. 10; U.S. Bureau of Labor, Bulletin 82, *Mortality from Consumption in Certain Occupations* (Washington, D.C., 1909), pp. 545–67.

14. Lucy Winsor Killough, *The Tobacco Products Industry in New York and Its Environs: Present Trends and Probable Future Developments*, Regional Plan of New York and Its Environs, Monograph no. 5 (New York, 1924), p. 29; U.S. Industrial Commission, *Report of the Industrial Commission on the Relations and Conditions of Capital and Labor*, vol. 7 (Washington, D.C., 1901), p. 198. Photograph, John O. Lund factory, Warren, Pa., 1913, Warren County Historical Society, Warren, Pa. (see Fig. 1).

15. Working conditions of cigar makers are described in Massachusetts State Board of Health, *Thirty-Sixth Annual Report of the State Board of Health* (Boston, 1905), p. xxvi; U.S. Congress, Senate, *Report on Condition of Woman and Child Wage-Earners in the United States*, vol. 18, *Employment of Women and Children in Selected Industries*, S. Doc. 645, 61st Cong., 2d sess., 1913, p. 94; Hennessey, "Report on Cigar Making in Boston," p. 12.

16. Hennessey, "Report on Cigar Making in Boston," p. 11; Massachusetts State Board of Health, *Report of the State Board of Health upon the Sanitary*

70 *Once a Cigar Maker*

Condition of Factories, Workshops, and Other Establishments Where Persons Are Employed (Boston, 1907), p. 50; *CMOJ*, Sept. 1906, p. 9.

17. U.S. Commissioner of Labor, "Regulation and Restriction of Output," p. 571; Hennessey, "Report on Cigar Making in Boston," p. 5; U.S. Bureau of Labor, *Conditions of Entrance to Principal Trades*, p. 719; F. E. Wolfe, *Admission to American Trade Unions* (Baltimore, 1912), p. 37; Shea interview; U.S. Industrial Commission, *Report*, vol. 7, p. 264; "By-Laws of Union No. 208," Kalamazoo, Mich., 1905, p. 11, WMUL. On labor shortages see, for example, *Tobacco Leaf*, 17 June 1903, p. 11; 6 Feb. 1907, p. 26; 29 Nov. 1905, pp. 10, 48; 26 Nov. 1902, p. 6; 24 Jan. 1906, p. 4; 7 Feb. 1906, p. 6.

18. Durso interview; U.S. Congress, House, Committee on Ways and Means, *Cigars Supplied Employees by Manufacturers: Hearings before the House Committee on Ways and Means on H.R. 17253, H.R. 21357, and H.R. 21958*, 62d Cong., 2d sess., 1912, p. 29.

19. Baust interview; Durso interview; Ograin interview, 11 Aug. 1976.

20. Sumner H. Slichter, *Union Policies and Industrial Management* (New York, 1968 [1941]), pp. 218–19; Santana interviews, 1976–80; Ograin interview, 19 May 1979.

21. Willis N. Baer, *The Economic Development of the Cigar Industry in the United States* (Lancaster, Pa., 1933), p. 80; Baust interview; Santana interviews, 1976–80; *Cigar Makers' International Union Diamond Jubilee, July 26–28, 1939* (Washington, D.C., 1939), p. 11. Artifacts of cigar makers' tools can be seen at the Smithsonian Institution, Division of Extractive Industries, Washington, D.C., and at the Milwaukee Public Museum, Milwaukee, Wis.

22. Theisen interview; *CMOJ*, July 1907, p. 6; July 1909, p. 4; Oct. 1909, p. 10.

23. "List of Shops and Bill of Prices," Local 97, Boston, Mass., 1904, p. 6, U.S. Bureau of Corporations, Tobacco Investigation, file 3073, Record Group (R.G.) 122, National Archives (NA), Washington, D.C.; "Bill of Prices," Local 165, Philadelphia, Pa., 1903, USDL. The Manchester bill was, by custom, always $1 behind Boston.

24. *CMOJ*, May 1906, p. 20; July 1906, p. 3; *Constitution of the Cigar Makers' International Union of America*, 1896, 1912, 1916, Section 154, Series V, Box 2, Cigar Makers' International Union of America Collection (CMIU Collection), McKeldin Library, University of Maryland (UM), College Park.

25. Ograin interview, 19 May 1979; Shea interview; Theisen interview.

26. Ograin, letter to author, 15 Jan. 1979; Ograin interview, 19 May 1979; Santana interview, 16, 17, 20 May 1979. Examination of various bills of prices reveals this differential. See, for example, "Bill of Prices," Local 14, Chicago, p. 33, USDL.

27. Theisen interview; "Bill of Prices," Local 97, Boston, p. 12; Santana interview, 17 June 1979 by telephone.

28. Santana interview, 17 July 1979 by telephone; Baust interview; Ograin interview, 19 May 1979; Ograin, letter to author, 15 Jan. 1979; *CMOJ*, Feb. 1907, p. 8; "Bill of Prices," Local 4, Cincinnati, Ohio.

29. U.S. Commissioner of Labor, "Regulation and Restriction of Output," p. 565.

30. Shea interview; Santana interview, 17 June 1979 by telephone; Ograin, letter to author, 15 Jan. 1979.

31. Hennessey, "Report on Cigar Making in Boston," pp. 4, 15; Shea interview, 26 June 1979; Norman Eliason, "The Language of the 'Buckeye,'" *American Speech,* 12 (1937), 270–74; *Tobacco,* 7 Mar. 1902, p. 7; Ograin interview, 19 May 1979.

32. See n. 31 and Santana interview, 6 July 1976.

33. Charles Dickerman, "Cigar Makers' Neurosis," *National Eclectic Medical Association Quarterly,* 10 (Sept. 1918), 63; Baust interview, 24 Mar. 1977; Massachusetts Board of Arbitration and Conciliation, "Hearings and Evidence of the Unemployment Commission," typescript, 11896, Massachusetts State Archives, Boston; "Gold Star Buckeye," typescript, 1937, Papers of the Works Progress Administration, New Hampshire Federal Writers' Project, MCL.

34. *Tobacco,* 7 Mar. 1902, p. 7; Ograin interview, 19 May 1979.

35. Ograin to author, 15 Jan. 1979; "Bill of Prices," Local 97, Boston, p. 11; "Bill of Prices," Local 4, Cincinnati; "By-Laws," Local 192, Manchester, pp. 23, 25; "By-Laws," Local 25, Milwaukee, pp. 21–22; "By-Laws of Cigar Makers' Union No. 14," Chicago, p. 33, USDL.

36. Theisen interview.

37. *Tobacco Leaf,* 4 Dec. 1907, p. 18; 7 Oct. 1909, p. 11; U.S. Bureau of Labor, *Conditions of Entrance to the Principal Trades,* p. 722; Ograin interview, 11 Aug. 1976.

38. Ograin interview, 19 May 1979; Russell Mack, *The Cigar Manufacturing Industry* (Philadelphia, 1933), p. 50.

39. Ograin interview, 19 May 1979.

40. Durso interview; Theisen interview.

41. Theisen interview; Shea interview; Ograin interview, 19 May 1979; U.S. Congress, House, *Cigars Supplied Employees,* p. 44.

42. Carl A. Werner, *A Textbook on Tobacco* (New York, 1914), pp. 114–15; Theisen interview; Raymond W. Steber interview, 24 July 1978, Warren, Pa.; Shea interview. Raymond Steber and his father ran a union factory in Warren until 1914, when they temporarily moved to Reading.

43. Shea interview; Ograin interview, 8 July 1977 and 19 May 1979; *CMOJ,* Nov. 1910, p. 2.

44. U.S. Bureau of Labor Statistics, "Wages and Hours of Labor in the Cigar and the Men's Clothing Industries," *Monthly Labor Review,* 10 (Mar. 1920), 81; Paul H. Douglas, *Real Wages in the United States, 1890–1926* (New York, 1966 [1930]), pp. 53–60; U.S. Bureau of Labor Statistics, Bulletin 65, *Wages and Hours of Labor in Manufacturing Industries, 1890 to 1905* (Washington, D.C., 1906), p. 157; U.S. Bureau of Labor Statistics, Bulletin 161, *Wages and Hours of Labor in the Clothing and Cigar Industries, 1911 to 1913* (Washington, D.C., 1914), p. 75.

45. *CMOJ,* Nov. 1902, p. 4; David A. McCabe, *The Standard Rate in American Trade Unions* (New York, 1971 [1912]), pp. 125–27, 229; Ulman, *Rise of the*

National Trade Union, pp. 37–42, 79, 517; U.S. Industrial Commission, *Report,* vol. 15, p. 386. Meyer Jacobstein, *The Tobacco Industry in the United States* (New York, 1907), p. 150. Copies of wage agreements of the cigar makers in several different cities illustrate the various scales in effect in different union jurisdictions. See, for example, "Bill of Prices," Local 192, Manchester, N.H., 1915, MCL; "List of Shops and Bill of Prices under the Jurisdiction of Union 97, C.M.I.U.," Boston, Mass., 1904, U.S. Bureau of Corporations, Tobacco Investigation, file 3073, R.G. 122, NA; "Bill of Prices," Local 25, Milwaukee, Wis., 1903, SHSW; Indiana Labor Commission, *Fourth Biennial Report of the Indiana Labor Commission for 1903–1904* (Indianapolis, 1904), pp. 67–68; "Bill of Prices," Local 165, Philadelphia, Pa., 1903, U.S. Department of Labor Library (USDL), Washington, D.C.; "Bill of Prices," Local 1, Baltimore, Md., ca. 1901, USDL; "Bill of Prices," Joint Unions of New York City, ca. 1900, USDL; "Bill of Prices," Local 4, Cincinnati, Ohio, 1907, USDL; "Bill of Prices," Joint Unions of Chicago, Ill., 1904, USDL.

46. U.S. Bureau of Corporations, Tobacco Investigation, file 3073, R.G. 122, NA. State wage statistics are not directly comparable and unfortunately states did not prepare them regularly. However, the following demonstrate the differentials in several different states and cities: New Hampshire Bureau of Labor, *Biennial Report, 1904* (Concord, 1904), p. 14; *1907,* p. 32; *1911,* p. 17; Massachusetts Bureau of Labor Statistics, *Annual Report on the Statistics of Manufactures, 1908* (Boston, 1909), p. 10; *1916,* pp. 9, 16; *1919,* p. 9; Illinois Bureau of Labor Statistics, *Biennial Report, 1902* (Springfield, 1904), pp. 332–46; Ohio Bureau of Labor Statistics, *Report, 1901* (Springfield, 1901), p. 69; *1912,* p. 122; Minnesota Department of Labor, Industries and Commerce, *Biennial Report, 1908* (Minneapolis, 1908), pp. 144–46; *1911,* p. 330; New York Bureau of Labor Statistics, *Annual Report, 1908* (Albany, 1908), p. 358; *1912,* p. 423; California Bureau of Labor Statistics, *Biennial Report, 1909* (Sacramento, 1909), p. 138. See also U.S. Bureau of Labor, Bulletin 77, *Wages and Hours of Labor in Manufacturing Industries, 1890 to 1907* (Washington, D.C., 1908), p. 162; U.S. Bureau of Labor Statistics, Bulletin 161, *Wages and Hours of Labor in the Clothing and Cigar Industries, 1911 to 1913* (Washington, D.C., 1914), pp. 69, 71, 75; U.S. Bureau of Labor Statistics, "Wages and Hours of Labor in the Cigar and the Men's Clothing Industries," *Monthly Labor Review,* 10 (Mar. 1920), 81; *Tobacco Leaf,* 17 Sept. 1908, p. 36; *CMOJ,* Feb. 1913, p. 23; Mar. 1913, p. 21.

47. Shea interview; Santana interview, 11 Jan. 1976 by telephone; Baust interview; Durso interview.

48. New Hampshire Bureau of Labor, *Biennial Report, 1911* (Concord, 1911), pp. 15, 17; Douglas, *Real Wages,* p. 96; *CMOJ,* July 1902, p. 8; Hugh S. Hanna and W. Jett Lauck, *Wages and the War: A Summary of Recent Wage Movements* (New York, 1918), pp. 60, 281, 296, 303, 317; Illinois Bureau of Labor Statistics, *Biennial Report, 1902* (Springfield, 1904), pp. 346, 330, 332, 328; New York State Bureau of Labor Statistics, *Annual Report,* 1900–1912; U.S. Industrial Commission, *Report,* vol. 7, p. 307; vol. 15, pp. 385–87. Each year the Massachusetts *Statistics of Manufactures* listed average yearly earnings for workers in the state. Unfortunately these earnings include all tobacco workers, not just cigar makers. In 1905, tobacco workers in Massachusetts averaged $677 a year. That same year,

according to Meyer Jacobstein, union cigar makers in New York State averaged $592 a year. Annual incomes of the most skilled railroad workers for 1905 were $899. See Andrew Dawson, "The Paradox of Dynamic Technological Change and the Labor Aristocracy in the United States 1880–1914," *Labor History,* 20 (Summer 1979), 336; Jacobstein, *Tobacco Industry,* pp. 149–50; Massachusetts Bureau of Labor Statistics, *Annual Report on the Statistics of Manufactures, 1905* (Boston, 1906), p. 337.

49. U.S. Commissioner of Labor, "Regulation and Restriction of Output," pp. 566–67, 569; Shea interview; Santana interviews, 1976–80; *CMOJ,* Sept. 1906, p. 5; Ograin interview, 8 July 1977.

50. Baust interview; Durso interview; Steber interview; Theisen interview. Packers could also leave during the day, particularly if light conditions were not exactly right. In Manchester, even the tobacco stemmers left work during the day. Jennie Kramasz related that "if a sale appeared in Wednesday morning's paper, we left work around 10:30, and sometimes we weren't back until one." But they could not stay away so long that the cigar makers would run out of tobacco. Jennie Kramasz interview, 27 June 1979, Manchester, N.H.

51. Killough, *Tobacco Products Industry,* p. 25; Hennessey, "Report on Cigar Making in Boston," p. 30; *CMOJ,* Sept. 1912, p. 15; Sept. 1901, p. 8; Apr. 1920, p. 3; Wolfe, *Admission to American Trade Unions,* pp. 93, 123; Slichter, *Union Policies and Industrial Management,* pp. 218–19; Ograin interview, 19 May 1979; Santana interview, 17 May 1979. See also Chap. 10. Ira DeAugustine Reid, *Negro Membership in American Labor Unions* (New York, 1930), passim; Herbert R. Northrup, *Organized Labor and the Negro* (New York, 1944), passim; George E. Haynes, *The Negro at Work in New York City* (New York, 1912), p. 182.

52. Ograin interview, 19 May 1979; 8 July 1977; *Tobacco Leaf,* 28 June 1917, p. 44; Dickerman, "Cigar Makers' Neurosis," pp. 58–66.

53. *Tobacco,* 27 Apr. 1900, p. 7; *CMOJ,* Sept. 1912, p. 18. The precise ethnic composition of the CMIU is unknown because extant union records do not contain membership lists which could be linked to the 1900 census. For information on cigar makers' ethnicity see Killough, *Tobacco Products Industry,* p. 26; U.S. Industrial Commission, *Report,* vol. 7, p. 385; U.S. Congress, Senate, *Reports of the Immigration Commission; Immigrants in Industries,* part 14, *Cigar and Tobacco Manufacturing,* S. Doc. 633, 61st Cong., 2d sess., 1911, pp. 104–5; U.S. Department of Commerce, Bureau of the Census, *Census of Population: 1910,* vol. 4, *Occupation Statistics* (Washington, D.C., 1914), p. 396. The *CMOJ* offers clues on ethnicity such as names of members printed belonging to particular locals, but the subject did not appear in letters, organizers' reports for the most part, or editorials. Local 15, of course, had once been the number of a local in New York City.

54. Santana interview, 18 Jan. 1976 by telephone; *CMOJ,* Feb. 1903, p. 4; May 1915, p. 9; Baust interview; Santana interview, 6 July 1977.

55. Baust interview; *Bridgeport* (Conn.) *Sunday Post,* 13 Feb. 1938; Theisen interview; *CMOJ,* Mar. 1907, p. 10; Apr. 1910, p. 9; Mar. 1912, p. 14; *Tobacco Leaf,* 24 Dec. 1902, p. 22; Margaret Kehm interview, 25 July 1978, Warren, Pa.; Santana interview, 18 Jan. 1976; Eliason, "Language of the 'Buckeye,'" p. 272.

Eliason remarked that cigar makers, unlike workers in many other trades, had no derogatory terms for themselves. Kehm learned to strip tobacco in a factory in Warren. In 1916 she married a union cigar maker from York.

56. Shea interview.

57. A. M. Simons, "Label and Lives," p. 69; Baust interview; Shea interview. See also Chap. 5.

58. Santana interview, 11 and 18 Jan. 1976 by telephone; Louis Pérez, "Reminiscences of a *Lector:* Cuban Cigar Workers in Tampa," *Florida Historical Quarterly*, 53 (Apr. 1975), 443–49. Richard Oestreicher, "Solidarity and Fragmentation: Working People and Class Consciousness in Detroit, 1875–1900" (Ph.D. dissertation, Michigan State University, 1979), p. 126. Oestreicher cites the Labadie Collection's Charles Erb file to show that there were readers in Detroit. I find it doubtful that readers were anything but rare outside of Clear Havana shops. Gompers may well have been a reader as he claims, but this was not common in the nineteenth or twentieth century.

59. Theisen interview; Shea interview; U.S. Congress, House, *Cigars Supplied Employees*, p. 5.

60. Steber interview; Theisen interview; Kehm interview; Eliason, "Language of the 'Buckeye,'" p. 272; Robert Woods, *Zone of Emergence* (Cambridge, Mass., 1973), p. 123; *Tobacco Leaf*, 30 Jan. 1913, p. 40; "Report," 1 Aug. 1918, General Staff, Military Intelligence, file 10101–910, R.G. 165, War Dept., NA.

61. Simons, "Label and Lives," p. 69.

CHAPTER

3

The "Traveling Fraternity"

"The cigar maker," wrote one lifelong observer of the CMIU, "is a wanderer."[1] The description was simple but accurate. John Ograin, who learned cigar making in Salt Lake City in 1904, speculated that "99 percent, more or less" of the union's members, traveled at some time during their working years.[2] In any given year in the early twentieth century, one-third or more of the members of the various locals left their home base to travel and work elsewhere.[3] Herman Baust recalled that there were "cigar factories all over the country, and [cigar makers] would travel. They were great travelers. They'd work so long in a factory, then off they'd be." Travel was so much a part of the work lives of members that they sometimes referred to their union as the "traveling fraternity."[4]

Travel was an indispensable element of cigar makers' work culture. Rather than permitting mobility to undermine the union, cigar makers used it to advantage: to adjust work patterns and assert more control in the workplace. At the same time, however, it helped to make that work culture national, one which cut across ethnic and geographic lines to unite a fairly diverse set of workers. While community and neighborhood were vital aspects of cigar makers' lives, the traveling tradition linked them to a larger community of fellow unionists and fostered a recognition of their interdependence. Over the years, they had created a coherent, well-organized, and disciplined system to support and maintain this valued tradition.

Cigar makers were certainly not the only skilled workers to be so mobile—carpenters, hatters, and printers also had strong "tramping" traditions, particularly in the nineteenth century.[5] Such customs were likely rooted in the long association of craft work and travel in Europe. On the continent, seventeenth- and eighteenth-century French craft workers' convention of a *tour de France,* the German *Wanderjahre,* and customs of journeyman travel in Poland, Bohemia, Hungary, and elsewhere all required travel for completion of craft training. Expanding preliminary research by Eric Hobsbawm, R. A. Leeson has recently traced craft travel in England over six centuries, firmly linking thirteenth-century guilds with eighteenth- and nineteenth-century trade unions. Skilled craftsmen's mobility acted not only as a means of securing employment, but as a final stage of learning, a tradition passed from generation to generation.[6]

Yet cigar making was a relatively new craft in Europe, one which had no guild traditions. This was especially true among Germans, who made up such a large proportion of the CMIU's membership. The custom of cigar makers' travel may very well have started in the United States, though too little evidence exists to say for sure. In any case, cigar makers were certainly traveling by the 1860s, since one of the first orders of business of the newly formed National Cigar Makers' Union in 1864 was reciprocity among locals regarding members' mobility. Nonunion male workers also traveled throughout the nineteenth and early twentieth centuries, although these patterns are much less thoroughly documented.[7]

Unions had an inherent problem with geographic movement in the nineteenth century. Newcomers could undercut fellow workers and glut the local labor market, depressing wages and making organization difficult. The answer, most unions agreed, was to try to insist that newcomers belong to the union and abide by its rules. All tradesmen, including cigar makers, encountered particular problems during the depression of the 1870s, when the unemployed desperately drifted from place to place searching for work. Throughout the decade and into the early 1880s, letters in the *CMOJ,* established in 1875, criticized the great numbers of tramps and their tendency to scab on fellow unionists. An initial plan for handling travel broke down early in the decade, but as the depression drew to an end, the idea of reinstituting some kind of program to regulate it gained support. Members adopted a permanent system of loans to traveling members in 1880 and supplemented it with a host of rules to insure its economic viability.[8]

The debates over the traveling system suggested that already travel was much more than an individual strategy of the unemployed. Responding to the criticism of travel during the depression, the Warren, Pennsylvania, local made their case for a travel benefit by arguing that it "would reestablish the fraternal feeling of years ago, when a traveling craftsman was treated like a brother." A member in 1879 noted that during bad times travelers "willingly place themselves in the rank of tramps" so that those left behind would have more work. Perhaps more telling, however, was Strasser's adamant opposition to giving loans to the man "who travels for the fun of it." Early rules permitted travel loans only if no jobs were open. One defeated proposal would have prohibited loans during the summer for the same reason.[9] But by the early twentieth century, members ignored such restrictions. A member did not need to justify his desire to leave and travel elsewhere.

Certainly cigar makers' mobility in the early twentieth century was often spurred by economic necessity. Loss of a job due to local business downturns or strikes prompted many members to search for work elsewhere. The union's benefit package provided members who lost their jobs with $3 a week, and strikers with $5 a week. But such payments fell far short of regular wages, which could range as high as $20 to $30 a week. Many members therefore took to the road. By contrast, during periods of national economic distress, such as the depression of the 1890s, and the recessions of 1907–9 and 1914–15, cigar makers stayed home. Rather than borrowing money to travel, cigar makers accepted the union's out-of-work benefit, since they recognized the futility of traveling when economic conditions were poor everywhere.[10]

A small number of the union's yearly travelers were broken men, society's misfits. A few fled the law, including the occasional one or two who absconded with local union funds. The trade included rare examples of criminals, but cigar makers' most common transgression was little more than failure to repay loans. It is likely that some were alcoholics. Drinking and socializing after work in saloons were very much a part of the everyday patterns of union cigar makers and at times members complained about drunken travelers. Alcoholics and others whose workmanship was so poor they were unable to keep a job were possibly included in the ranks of travelers each year, but some of the most constant travelers were reputed to be also some of the finest workmen in the trade. Frank Shea defended the skills of the travelers, noting that "to knock around the country you had to be a pretty good cigar maker." Raymond Steber, a manufacturer in Warren, Pennsylvania, in business with his father, observed that "a lot of those fellows, those tourists, they'd worked in a million different factories and they were really experts."[11]

Travel worked as a group strategy to help cigar makers negotiate the limits of their position within the production process which made them so acutely vulnerable to shifts in the economy and the demands and power of employers. If orders were slack, unions required manufacturers to spread available work rather than lay anyone off. A young single member would "do as the large percentage of single men do under the system 'go on the road,' which at certain times of the year is not taken as a 'pleasure trip,' and will willingly go rather than break his obligation to the union."[12] The formal travel system helped reduce the drain on union finances, prevent mass suspensions or scabbing in hard times by circulating the unemployed, and relieve pressure in any one locale.

An understanding of the reasons and impact of the traveling system, however, does not end with strictly economic interpretations. Consider, for example, William Theisen. In 1915, temporarily laid off from his job in Denver, he left and took another in Livingston, Montana, where he had heard about plenty of openings. After he had worked there a few months, two fellow workers who were planning to hobo to Seattle, Washington, by jumping aboard freight trains west, coaxed him to join them. The trip to Seattle and back took about two weeks as they worked making cigars occasionally along the way. When he returned, he paid his fare back to Denver and assumed his former job. His unemployment had initially forced him to leave Denver, but he had continued to travel for unrelated reasons.[13]

Travel also acted as a sort of rite of passage, a cultural obligation of newcomers. This was especially true of hoboing. Most traveling was not hoboing, but everyone was expected to try it at least once. "I don't know why we did," remarked Ograin, "but you had to take a hobo trip. If you didn't hobo—why they used to say, 'All right. You're through with your apprenticeship. Now go out and learn the trade.'" For many, hoboing did not prove to be a permanently workable mode of travel. Ograin tried to hobo since it was the "fashion," but when his experiment left him "ditched" north of Salt Lake City and minus his belongings, he resolved that his first hobo trip would be his last. Thereafter he traveled and worked in Denver, St. Louis, and Chicago, but he always paid his fare. José Santana met many hoboes in the shop where he worked in London, Ontario. At first he wanted to join them, but he hesitated because of his slight frame. "I was anxious to do it, but I didn't trust myself physically," he recounted. "After I got myself on my feet . . . , money in my pocket and well-dressed, then I said to myself, not going to travel second class, going to travel Pullman. . . . I want to know how the rich people live. I know how the poor live."[14]

Shop conversation doubtless affected cigar makers' eagerness to travel.

Since cigar making was a noiseless, sedentary trade, the hours spent at work were open to wide-ranging discussion. Travelers described the places they had been and regaled each other with stories about their various exploits while on the road. James Durso, a cigar maker at the Kafka factory in New Haven, explained that "you heard all kinds of stories. . . . They used to talk about their experiences—everybody could hear it."[15] The urge to travel was fostered by peer pressure and braggadocio, products of the masculine nature of the work culture. William Theisen had been reluctant to hobo, for example, but the two cigar makers he met in Livingston "mash[ed] it in so much they'd make you think that you're chicken or something," so he had finally given in. Travelers bragged about how many times they had crossed the country, how their cigar-making talents had enabled them to get jobs anywhere, or how far they had hoboed in one stretch. These workplace conversations encouraged others to try their skills somewhere else in order to test their proficiency and to gain admission to the cultural world of shop-floor talk.[16]

Cigar makers traveled for a variety of reasons: a "pleasure trip," "adventure," "to escape the winter cold," and "itchings to be on the move."[17] Travel made work life more satisfying, because it provided the opportunity to change the work environment, experience new surroundings, and take a break from the monotony and routine of work. Many traveled out of curiosity. Santana remembered listening to a traveler "talk all day about 'Frisco'" and he decided to go there one day to see for himself what the city was like. Like the flexible hours they kept during the day, travel signified their freedom to control their own time. Travel asserted their independence from employers and their right to leave a job for any reason. The knowledge that one could leave and work elsewhere also permitted cigar makers, if they wished, to be very particular about working conditions. Herman Baust remembered that "if they came in the shop, and something didn't suit them, the tobacco wasn't right, they'd go right out."[18]

Most travelers were young and single, so the custom must be understood in terms of the cigar maker's life cycle. José Santana noted that he had been so mobile because "a man before he gets to the stage of raising a family, he needs to know about life."[19] Once cigar makers married and took on family obligations, they tended to be less mobile. A contingent of them, however, became almost addicted to constant movement and gave in to it throughout their lives—many of the hoboes apparently fell into this category. William Theisen called it "travel fever." At the R. G. Sullivan factory, Shea observed that "some of them, a couple of months or so—the call of the wild. For no reason they'd go out and put a few drinks in and say, 'I'm getting through, Frank.' That was it. Then the other fellows that knew him, they'd say, 'Aw, he's getting restless. He's been sitting on a chair too long.'" Margaret Kehm married a union cigar maker and the two traveled together for about five years. Traveling couples were apparently not altogether rare, but available evidence is silent regarding women traveling alone or with other women. Kehm and her husband worked in various midwestern cities including Cleveland and Cincinnati, but after a few months they left each one "because he just wanted to roam around different places. And we could always get work." Kehm had been more fortunate than some other relatives and spouses who had found themselves abandoned. Each month *CMOJ* carried notices from wives and children seeking to track down neglectful husbands or fathers. Such requests as "Anyone knowing the whereabouts of Fred Doxey will please notify his wife, Josie Doxey, 30 Dartmouth Street, Boston, Massachusetts," and "the children of Frank Meyer (40438) desire to know the whereabouts of their father, as they are in need" appeared monthly.[20]

These cigar-making "nomads" had a vast territory they could cover. CMIU locals were spread into every state and territory so that a cigar maker could head in any direction and find locals on his way. Santana explained that he could cover long distances because "I could work, make money and keep on, save some money and keep on moving." The CMIU grew from 414 locals in 1901 to 466 in 1919. Eighty percent of these locals had fewer than one hundred members, some as few as eight. Yet half of the members belonged to locals containing between two hundred to one thousand cigar makers, located in such cities as Boston, New Haven, Hartford, New York City, Philadelphia, Baltimore, Buffalo, Rochester, Syracuse, Chicago, St. Louis, Detroit, Dayton, Milwaukee, Cincinnati, Cleveland, Indianapolis, Denver, Louisville, and Manchester (New Hampshire).[21] Some of the locals were associated with particular ethnic groups. In Boston, for example, many members were newly arrived Belgians. Bohemians, German and Russian Jews, and Spanish-speaking cigar makers had separate locals in New York City, although the lines were not rigid. Cigar makers of German descent predominated there and in most other locals, particularly in the Midwest, but scores of other nationalities were represented in the union's membership—Austrian, Irish, Hungarian, Russian Jewish, Polish Bohemian, Belgian, Dutch, and British. The various nationality groups were spread out enough and the ethnic mix was so broad that it is unlikely that ethnicity ever formed a barrier to anyone's travel.[22]

The union factories that cigar makers found on their travels varied as much in size as did the locals, from small shops of only one or two men to large factories with as many as one thousand. In some areas, such as Terre Haute, Indiana, or Dubuque, Iowa, where the industry was marginal, the largest factory might employ only ten cigar makers. In 1905, CMIU president George W. Perkins estimated that possibly as many as half of the union's members worked in factories with fewer than sixty cigar makers. In Boston, three hundred members at that same time worked in forty to fifty small shops, while fifteen hundred others worked in the city's three largest factories.[23] The smallest units of production were "buckeyes," which generally consisted of a lone cigar maker operating his own shop, although some included one or two journeymen. Establishing buckeyes was still quite popular among CMIU members in the early twentieth century. These rarely grew into larger enterprises and were notorious for their small financial rewards, yet their appeal lay in their clear assertion of independence. Ograin observed that there had been "darn few of us that didn't have a buckeye some time or other. . . . You'd do it for a while and then if you didn't make a go of it . . ." the factory stood waiting.[24] Union rules permitted buckeyes to remain members as long as they worked alone. If they hired anyone, they had to retire from the union, but they could retain the sickness and death benefits the union provided by paying a monthly fee. In Milwaukee in 1918, the union had a total of 533 members, 90 of whom were buckeyes.[25]

The formal operation of the traveling system offers more clues about its impact on the cigar makers, both individually and collectively, and on the industry as a whole. A cigar maker who wanted to travel requested a traveling card from his local secretary which proved his membership in good standing, and left for whatever destination he desired. He could also take out a travel loan of up to $8. The exact amount was based on the train fare to the nearest local in whatever direction he wished to proceed and averaged around $4. In Chicago, for example, the loans were never large because the Hammond, Blue Island, and Milwaukee locals were all so close. He could accumulate a total debt of $20, but then his card was considered "full," and he could not borrow on it again until the debt had been reduced. Once he began working, 10 percent of his weekly earnings were taken to repay the loan.[26]

There were no set paths or routes, such as in the old European guild systems. Any union factory was a possible stopping point, but routes tended to follow the railroad lines. Decisions on destination might be based on the general knowledge cigar makers accumulated about other factories through working and listening in a union shop. They knew which locals had the best wages and conditions and which had the worst. Thus travelers interested in maximizing earnings might steer away from Detroit, New Orleans, much of Pennsylvania and New Jersey, and head instead for New England, upstate New York, and parts of the Midwest. In many cases, out-lying towns and cities averaged lower bills of prices than did large cities. Such was the case in Massachusetts, where wages in Boston were consistently higher than elsewhere. In New York, however, the opposite was true. The cigar makers were well organized in Syracuse, Elmira, Rochester, Utica, and Buffalo, but less organized in New York City where the bill was lower.

Particular factories had outstanding reputations and were so widely spoken of that a cigar maker might travel there just to see one of them. The R. G. Sullivan Company in Manchester began the century with only two hundred cigar makers, but the force rapidly expanded in the following years to include over nine hundred. Sullivan, a stern, quiet man with a huge mustache, had started the company in 1874. It was known for its high wages and rather liberal conditions, second only to the cigar factories of Boston such as Waitt and Bond and H. Traiser. Foreman Shea recalled seeing men arrive there from the Dakotas and beyond. In one case a cigar maker at the Sullivan factory left to travel and landed in Wisconsin where he got a job. When he returned, he told Shea that when the cigar makers he had met in Wisconsin learned where he usually worked, "they wanted to shake hands with him. They had heard about the place. It was fabulous, the name, you know."[27]

Travelers also needed current information on trade conditions. The *CMOJ*, delivered to factories in the middle of each month, contained a "State of Trade" column grouping locals under headings of "Good," "Fair," and "Dull." Locals experiencing poor conditions or enforcing boycotts or strikes against particular companies often published additional warnings in the "Union Notes" and "Bureau of Information" columns advising travelers to "steer clear." Information also came informally: friends wrote back letters describing conditions elsewhere and newcomers related their previous experiences and suggested attractive possible destinations. Union rules forbade a cigar maker from writing to factories or secretaries to ask

for a job and in some locals such action resulted in a fine. One could inquire of friends whether jobs were likely to be open, but writing ahead for
a specific job put a cigar maker ahead of his traveling colleagues, a violation of union principle stressing the interests of the collective group over
individual advancement.[28]

The *CMOJ* also provided information on boycotted and strike shops,
which were off limits. Striking locals only had to accept travel cards if a
member were ill and needed the sick benefit. In large cities such as New
York, Chicago, and Philadelphia, the union permitted members to work in
open shops since there were not enough strictly union jobs. Elsewhere,
open shops were supposed to be off limits. The "cheap district" of Pennsylvania always had jobs and undoubtedly some union cigar makers worked
there and elsewhere in nonunion shops on occasion, but there is no way
to measure the extent of this extralegal work.[29]

In most cases, travel could be undertaken because cigar makers had
reasonable expectations of finding jobs. José Santana traveled extensively
throughout the U.S. and Canada between 1909 and 1916 and explained
that "there was so much abundance of jobs that you didn't have to be
afraid. You quit and come back in a couple of weeks." Yet at certain times
of the year, a cigar maker might consider the decision to travel more carefully. While the trade was not highly seasonal, it did not offer full employment all year. Factories closed for about two weeks at the end of December and beginning of January for inventory, and again in July for the
same reason. At other times, when not enough work was available, factories placed cigar makers on a "limit" as demanded by union rules, or if the
situation worsened, they laid off cigar makers. During the months from
January through March, following the peak Christmas sales, orders for
cigars were usually lower and the number of cigar makers exceeded the
number of jobs. By late spring and summer, when the vacation season began and cigar sales rose, the levels of employment grew. As one Massachusetts official noted in 1904: "With good weather conditions, so that the
beaches and other summer resorts may open early, and with open cars
running, the dealers look for an exceptionally good season. A hot summer
makes a wonderful improvement in the cigar trade." Most union cigar
makers averaged only about forty-five weeks of employment during the
year. While slack periods offered an excuse for travel, one might be less
sure of securing work during an excursion then.[30]

Armed with his travel card, and some idea of where he wanted to head,
the cigar maker began his journey. When he was hoboing, the trip itself

was part of the experience. When William Theisen decided to hobo to Seattle he first found that he needed hoboing clothes, "overalls and what you call a jumper, like a jacket." Before boarding, he and his two companions stopped in the liquor store and bought three pints of whiskey. The trio soon climbed up into an empty coal-hauling car. As they were lying in the gondola, a brakeman approached, demanding, "Where are you going?"—"We're goin' out to Seattle." He asked, "What are you riding on?" "Riding on a union card," they responded. They showed him their union cards and pulled out the bottle of whiskey "and gave him a drink and everything is all right . . . but some of them, they'll tell you 'I can't eat a union card.' They want money." Brakemen and train guards could throw hoboes off the train and once Theisen had had to ride the rods underneath the car to escape detection.[31]

Upon arriving at any union factory, a cigar maker could expect to find friendly assistance and familiar patterns of work. The traveler might first look for the union secretary by stopping in any union shop or by heading to union headquarters, if the local were big enough to support one. In Boston, explained union secretary Henry Abrahams, a traveler could find at Local 97's office "a place where he can sit down, read the paper, write a letter. . . . Should he desire a wash or to clean his shoes, clean towels, bleaching, soap, brush and combs are furnished." Secretaries who worked at the bench kept separate hours for dispensing travel loans, which were posted in the *CMOJ* in the "List of Secretaries" column each month. A few included directions to their temporary offices—in a nearby saloon or hotel, "Water street, opp R.R. station, from 12 to 12:30 noon and from 5 to 5:30 P.M." The fact that some travelers may have waited for the secretary's arrival at the saloon possibly prompted one secretary to add to his message in the *CMOJ*, "travelers must come sober or they will be refused."[32]

For immigrant cigar makers who did not speak English, travel was more difficult, but they could minimize their problems by visiting places where fellow countrymen lived. Leon Rogiers, a cigar maker who arrived from Belgium in 1910, traveled from Boston, where his brother lived, to Manchester, New Hampshire, where he knew no one. Unable to speak English and apprehensive about finding his way once he reached the city, he followed relatives' instructions and walked into every saloon he saw on the west side of town until he heard Flemish spoken. Since many Belgians in the city were associated with the large Sullivan factory there, he could be sure of a warm reception and information on job openings and boarding houses.[33]

If the traveler intended to move on, the secretary could help him with loans. If he wanted to work, union rules required him to deposit his travel card before taking a job. Secretaries offered information on local rooming houses and in some places the secretary issued a "meal ticket" for a free dinner. In a few locals, travelers also received a "boardinghouse order" once they had secured jobs. This guaranteed to the boarding- or rooming-house keeper that the cigar maker had work and would be able to meet his obligations. Enough cigar makers failed to pay board bills before leaving town to make this a matter of concern. These interlopers were known in the trade, remembered Julius Sodekson, a Boston cigar packer, as "beats." Often a local covered the debt in order to preserve good relations with the boarding house and then attempted to track down the guilty party for reimbursement.[34]

Hobo accommodations usually consisted of a boxcar, although Theisen became so sore after a night in these quarters that he persuaded his companions to sleep in a hotel one night. Occasionally hobo cigar makers had contacts with "regular" tramps and hoboes, on the trains, in city flophouses, or even in hobo "jungles," the tramp camping grounds "usually on the outskirts of town, along the railroad tracks out." When Theisen and his friends "had money, why we ate in restaurants. Maybe once or twice we ate in the jungle."[35]

Travelers who wanted to work obtained a list of job openings from the secretary or simply stopped in to see a foreman in any of the union shops. Frank Shea remembered that at the Manchester factory "they'd be standing outside the door waiting for them to be opening in the morning." Once a traveler was hired, the shop collector approached to make sure the cigar maker's membership was in order, and then he worked the rest of the day to prove his skill. The job was his as long as he wanted it. In many smaller factories and buckeyes, cigar makers could work even if no positions were open. Travelers were given an "accommodation job": they could work for a day or an afternoon and make enough to move on.[36]

The custom of travel included not only the act of mobility itself, but the tradition of hospitality and aid to travelers, which worked to further reinforce a feeling of members' interdependence. A cigar maker could head in any direction, find a job, and depend on fellow unionists for support and assistance. Union locals provided private loans to individuals in addition to travel loans, but cigar makers did not always have to go into debt. If his travel loan card were "full," the system still worked to aid and assist him. The traveler gave his card to the shop collector who circulated it among the cigar makers in the shop, saying "this fellow needs a hand," passing the hat. Other workers would give a nickel, dime, or whatever they had. When the traveler collected a couple of dollars, he moved on. To eliminate the necessity of repeated hat-passing, which "gets kind of monotonous," a number of locals set up separate funds to be used to aid travelers. For example, Local 192 in Manchester had a "Tourist Fund" maintained by assessing members twenty-five to thirty cents whenever the sum dipped below $50. Each needy cigar maker was given $1.50. The Portland, Oregon, organization had a "Tramp Stake" of the same amount for members with full cards.[37]

Cigar makers regarded themselves as very generous, and took pride in their code of help and loyalty to each other. John Ograin described this feeling: "I stopped off in Eugene, Oregon. That was early morning and the boss hadn't got there yet. So I went in and there were five fellows working there. And asked them about a job. One says, 'Have you had breakfast yet?'" When Ograin shook his head, "this gentleman threw me a quarter into my hand for breakfast. I really believe we had the most fraternal-minded group in the whole country."[38]

The cigar makers' strong sense of mutual aid and the open, trusting atmosphere of many locals made it possible, however, for a minority to misuse and defraud the traveling system. Using various rules and safeguards, members attempted to discipline each other and keep the system operating. In Chicago, Local 14 had a tramp stake, and members made sure travelers did not take advantage of them. Some cigar makers "made regular calls. But we'd say, 'You got it a couple of weeks ago. The heck with you.'"[39] Because some nonunion cigar makers joined the CMIU only when they wanted to travel, several locals refused to accept cards less than six months old except for former apprentices who had just "finished their time." Those with private loans were careful to avoid any misunderstanding with regard to repayment. John F. Fischer chose to keep in touch with the secretary of Local 162, Green Bay, Wisconsin, concerning the money he had borrowed from the local. Writing from Cairo, Illinois, he thanked the local for the loan and explained that "I have just gone to work here and will pay up as soon as I can. I worked a little in Memphis, Tenn. Had to move. I am feeling somewhat better as it is getting a little cooler. Thanking the boys of local 162, Green Bay Wisc. I am Yours Truly."[40]

The *CMOJ*, which provided information on trade conditions, also assisted in enforcing discipline. Each month it contained notices from locals asking members to pay up travel or private loans. If general calls for repayment did not achieve results, the wayward cigar maker could have his name printed in the *CMOJ*, an ignominious fate to be scrupulously avoided by those who valued their reputations as "union men." To prevent such dishonor, some asked patience in letters to the union journal and promised to pay as soon as possible. Still each issue included names of many who had hoped to escape specific notice for their misdeeds. For example, Fred Doxey was wanted not only by his wife. The May 1905 issue of the *CMOJ* contained the following: "Will Fred Doxey please send the three weeks' board to Mrs. Wigley that he owes her, and oblige Susan Wigley, New port, R.I.?" "Chas. Rudy is wanted by Union 35. He knows what for. He is to answer before July, 1904," one cryptic notice read.[41]

Cigar makers used the journal not only to collect loans due but to track down other traveling "tramps, scamps, and bums," as Ograin termed them. All too often, someone who did not belong, or who had huge loans against his name, could relate a sad story of a sick wife and a lost card and be accepted by members of the fraternity with no identification. Others resorted to "altering figures" on their loan books. The journal helped members protect each other from this kind of abuse. The secretary of the Akron, Ohio, local cautioned others about a man who traveled all over the country who "plays the sympathy racket and obtains work," and another reported damaging information on "an ungrateful traveler who don't deserve any help." One secretary wrote that he wished "to warn the members against one R. C. Lang (Card No. 95936). That gentleman is going around the country beating board bills and other incidentals. He left Westville, Ill., and forgot to pay his board and also stole my suit of underwear. He also done every one else he could. The place that should happen to be honored by his presence, the members will do well to keep an eye on him, as he has a pitiful tale of hardship and family troubles to relate." The *CMOJ*, besides warning of particular unsavory characters, also listed each month the names of members who had reported lost cards so that secretaries could check their own records to make sure the reported losses were bona fide.[42]

The *CMOJ* further facilitated a "much boasted" communication and location system, providing a way for members to keep in touch with each other and with relatives. Local unions accepted mail for members and letters not delivered were listed in the "Letter Box" column. Cigar makers could thus read the journal, learn where mail was being held for them, and send for it. Letters unclaimed after a month, and there were few, were returned to the post office and listed in the next issue of the *CMOJ*. The "Bureau of Information" column printed names of cigar makers who wanted to hear from cigar-making friends: "J. M. Gallagher, La Salle, Ill., would like to hear from F. H. Baker, 4788," or "Richard Bonelli . . . Los Angeles, Cal., would like to hear from Chas. Ehrieke, formerly of Meriden, Conn. For Old-time sake." Mothers, fathers, brothers, sisters, and wives used the *CMOJ* to locate a relative or transmit news. "Nellie Rule would like to hear from her brother John, and let him know that his brother Michael died July 10, 1906," or "Fred Stroud, send address home at once. May seriously ill and mother almost frantic." Many notices included such phrases as: "When last heard from he was in Montana."[43]

The traveling system gave cigar makers added leverage in the daily shop-floor struggle with manufacturers. They could use it in some measure to regulate the size and distribution of the labor force. Threats of strikes had to be taken seriously because cigar makers had the machinery to remove members physically and reduce the chance for undercutting or scabbing. Further, after the strike ended, weeks passed before word spread that it had been settled and enough workers reappeared to return production to normal, a serious risk for the relatively small, local-market union manufacturer. Employers had learned to accept the traveling tradition because they depended on it to provide them with enough workers to fill their cigar-making benches. Raymond Steber admitted that there was little he could have done about the travelers. "I suppose maybe we could have fired all the tourists and not hired any. Well, then we'd have been out of business for labor." The extent and frequency of mobility in the midst of generally high employment levels and relative prosperity in the trade intensified a condition of relative labor shortage. As long as union manufacturers wanted the delicate skills that the union monopolized, cigar makers could use their influence over the distribution of needed workers as a resource.[44]

Travel meant that cigar makers could compare directly the varying bills of prices and the different factory conditions and employer policies in various cities and use this information in formulating their own demands. Fresh arrivals would "tell you where they'd come from, what they—how things were over there and over here," James Durso recounted. If present conditions were less favorable than past ones, noted Frank Shea, the travelers called attention to the difference, so that their presence could spark shop strikes, spontaneous protest walkouts unsanctioned by the union. Raymond Steber mistakenly blamed all of his labor troubles on travelers, but he responded to their influential role when he complained that "we had many 'hobo' cigar makers, tourists, we called them. They liked nothing better than turmoil, would . . . make ridiculous demands and go on strike at the drop of a hat." It is perhaps not surprising that tramping cigar makers in the nineteenth century had been the original organizers of the CMIU before such jobs were systematized in the 1880s.[45] When the collective power of the cigar makers could not match that of manufacturers in trade matters, cigar makers could leave conditions which they interpreted personally as compromising dignity and self-respect.

The traveling system provided union cigar makers several distinct advantages during the early twentieth century. Through it they could combine work and leisure, alter work environment, and advance their interests vis-à-vis manufacturers. Travel offered cigar makers individual freedom and independence, but it also reinforced a sense of collective identity and mutuality. The arrival of newcomers provided a source of outside information and news, connecting scattered locals and militating against the isolation of a single factory. The daily mixing of people and experiences helped to hold together a heterogeneous group of workers who shared a national occupational culture.

Notes

1. A. M. Simons, "A Label and Lives—The Story of the Cigar Makers," *Pearson's Magazine*, Jan. 1917, p. 70.

2. John R. Ograin, letter to author, 29 Sept. 1979.

3. It is impossible to determine precisely the extent of travel each year in the union. The CMIU published only yearly total loan amounts, not numbers of individual loans. Gauging turnover for one city using the 1900 census and city directories is not fruitful because the intervals are too long to capture the mobility of these workers who spent only a few weeks in one place. Any estimate is thus somewhat impressionistic. By dividing yearly travel amounts by $8, the maximum amount of any loan, to reach a rough approximation of the number of loans granted, one reaches an estimate of 25–35 percent of the membership between 1900 and 1916. Most took less than that amount and many did not borrow at all. What lends further credence to the estimate is the attention given to traveling in the union's monthly journal and the magnitude suggested by those interviewed. Considering other studies' findings on levels of geographic mobility in the general population, this rate is not surprising or exceptional.

4. Herman Baust interview, 24 Mar. 1977, North Haven, Conn.; *CMOJ*,

15 Sept. 1902, p. 6; *Cigar Makers' International Union Diamond Jubilee, 26–28 July 1939* (Washington, D.C., 1939), p. 11.

5. David Bensman, *The Practice of Solidarity: American Hat Finishers in the Nineteenth Century* (Urbana, Ill., 1985), pp. 9–13, 71–73; William Pretzer, "'Love of Grog and Desperate Passion for Clean Shirts': The Tramp Printer in Nineteenth Century America," paper read at the Organization of American Historians convention, Detroit, Mich., Apr. 1981; Jules Tygiel, "Tramping Artisans: The Case of Carpenters in Industrial America," *Labor History* 22 (Summer 1981), 348–76. These tradesmen were all less mobile in the twentieth century than in the nineteenth century.

6. Peter Burke, *Popular Culture in Early Modern Europe* (New York, 1978), pp. 36–40; William James Ashley, *Surveys: Historic and Economic* (New York, 1966 [1900]), pp. 251–57; Georges Renard, *Guilds in the Middle Ages,* trans. Dorothy Terry (New York, 1968 [1918]), pp. 13, 70; George Clune, *The Medieval Guild System* (Dublin, 1943), p. 179; Sidney Webb and Beatrice Webb, *History of Trade Unionism* (New York, 1973 [1920]), pp. 25, 444–51; Helga Grebling, *The History of the German Labour Movement: A Survey* (London, 1969), pp. 26, 29; Joan Scott, *Glassworkers of Carmaux: French Craftsmen and Political Action in a Nineteenth-Century City* (Cambridge, Mass., 1974), pp. 46–52; Eric Hobsbawm, "The Tramping Artisan," in *Labouring Men: Studies in the History of Labour* (London, 1964), pp. 34–63; R. A. Leeson, *Traveling Brothers: The Six Centuries' Road from Craft Fellowship to Trade Unionism* (London, 1979).

7. Dorothee Schneider, "Trade Unions and Community: Three German Trade Unions in New York, 1870–1900" (Ph.D. dissertation, University of Munich, 1983), trans. Schneider and Harry Liebersohn; *CMOJ,* Oct. 1908, pp. 2–3; Marie H. Hourwich, "Cigar Makers' Union History, 1851–1879," typescript, Research Files, Box 22, David Saposs Papers, State Historical Society of Wisconsin (SHSW), Madison; James B. Kennedy , *Beneficiary Features of American Trade Unions* (Baltimore, 1908), pp. 594–95. On early and nonunion travel, see Nathan H. Cohen, "Con Brio," in Stanley F. Chyet, ed., *Lives and Voices* (Philadelphia, 1972), pp. 48–59; Walter E. Baum, *Two Hundred Years* (Sellersville, Pa., 1938), pp. 101–14; Grier Scheerz, "Tobacco and Its Cultivation in Bucks County," *A Collection of Papers Read Before the Bucks County Historical Society,* vol. 5 (Bucks County Historical Society, 1924), p. 615; Henry L. Freking, "Cigar Makers," *Bucks County Traveler,* June 1954, p. 35 and July 1954, p. 34. My thanks to Don Ritchie for bringing Chyet to my attention.

8. Lloyd Ulman, *The Rise of the National Trade Union: The Development and Significance of Its Structure, Governing Institutions and Economic Policies* (Cambridge, Mass., 1955), pp. 53–54; *CMOJ,* Jan. 1878, p. 2; Apr. 1878, p. 4; July 1878, p. 3; Aug. 1878, p. 1; Apr. 1880, p. 4; Feb. 1881, p. 4; May 1883, p. 5; Feb. 1884, p. 1; Oct. 1884, p. 4; Kennedy, *Beneficiary Features,* pp. 594–95. Criticism of travel shows up in the twentieth century during the recession in 1914. See *CMOJ,* Oct. 1914, p. 7. On tramping, see *CMOJ,* Mar. 1876, p. 2; Dec. 1876, pp. 1–2; Mar. 1877, pp. 1–2; June 1877, p. 1.

9. *CMOJ,* Oct. 1878, p. 2; July 1879, p. 3; Mar. 1881, p. 6; May 1884, p. 4.

10. *Constitution of the Cigar Makers' International Union of America, 1896,*

1912, 1916, 1917, 1919, section 79, Series V, Box 2, Cigar Makers' International Union of America Collection (CMIU Collection), McKeldin Library, University of Maryland (UM), College Park; "By-Laws of the Cigar Makers' Union No. 192," Manchester, N.H., 1915, Manchester City Library (MCL), Manchester, N.H.; José Santana interview, 11 Jan. 1976 by telephone; *CMOJ*, Apr. 1902, p. 4; Sept. 1902, p. 5; Mar. 1906, p. 5; June 1906, p. 11; June 1910, p. 4; Apr. 1920, p. 4. A chart listing CMIU expenditures for all benefits is in *CMOJ*, Apr. 1920, p. 4; I compared the figures for travel and out-of-work expenditures, which generally had an inverse relationship to each other.

11. *CMOJ*, June 1881, p. 8; Sept. 1902, p. 5; Apr. 1903, p. 3; Dec. 1915, p. 39; Baust interview; T. Frank Shea interview, 26 June 1979, Manchester, N.H.; Raymond W. Steber interview, 24 July 1978, Warren, Pa.

12. Santana interview, 11 Jan. 1976 by telephone; *CMOJ*, Mar. 1906, p. 6; June 1906, p. 11.

13. William Theisen interview, 17 Aug. 1979, Denver, Colo.

14. Theisen interview; John R. Ograin interview, 11 Aug. 1976, 8 July 1977; Ograin to author, 29 Sept. 1979; Santana interview, 13 Aug. 1976; 15 Sept. 1978. Ideally a candidate for membership would have served a three-year apprenticeship in a union factory, but such a rule was not enforceable in most areas. Locals did require all new members, however, to prove they had worked at least three years in the trade. New members could also be accepted with a union card from another country. In this way many Belgian immigrants joined CMIU locals in New England during the early twentieth century. See F. E. Wolfe, *Admission to American Trade Unions* (Baltimore, 1912), p. 37; Massachusetts Bureau of Labor, *The Apprenticeship System*, by Charles F. Pidgin (Boston, 1906), p. 50.

15. James Durso interview, 24 Mar. 1977, New Haven, Conn.

16. Theisen interview; Durso interview; Baust interview; Ograin interview, 8 July 1977.

17. *Cigar Makers' Union Diamond Jubilee*, p. 10; *CMOJ*, Oct. 1904, p. 7; Mar. 1906, p. 5; June 1906, p. 11; Santana interview, 20 May 1979; 22 July 1979 by telephone; "Gold Star Buckeye," typescript, 1937, Papers of the Works Progress Administration, New Hampshire Federal Writer's Project, MCL; Margaret Kehm interview, 25 July 1978, Warren, Pa.; Leon Rogiers interview, 27 June 1979, Manchester, N.H. Rogiers learned the trade in Belgium and emigrated to the U.S. in about 1909 or 1910 as a teenager.

18. Santana interview, 18 May 1979; 22 July 1979 by telephone; Baust interview; *Cigar Makers' Union Diamond Jubilee*, p. 10.

19. Santana interview, 18 Nov. 1979 by telephone. All interviewees believed that most travelers were young and single. Ograin, however, did recall meeting a few cigar-making couples who traveled together.

20. Theisen interview; Shea interview; Kehm interview. See *CMOJ*, Jan. 1900, p. 14; Apr. 1908, p. 6; Feb. 1909, p. 14; June 1910, p. 14; Apr. 1908, p. 6; Feb. 1909, p. 14; June 1910, p. 7; Mar. 1911, p. 10; Sept. 1913, p. 13; Feb. 1914, p. 26. The *CMOJ* contained little comment on these cases of desertion, although when comments were made they were negative.

21. *Tobacco Leaf*, 24 Dec. 1902, p. 11; *CMOJ*, Apr. 1920, p. 4; Santana inter-

view, 11 Jan. 1976 by telephone. Every April the *CMOJ* printed the annual financial report of the union by listing receipts and expenditures of each local for the previous year. These also list the membership in each local. I tabulated these figures for 1900, 1904, 1909, 1914, and 1919 and found roughly the same breakdown for the entire period with regard to size.

22. See Chap. 2.

23. *CMOJ*, Jan. 1905, p. 10; Feb. 1906, p. 3; May 1906, p. 10; Feb. 1908, p. 13; July 1909, p. 4; U.S. Bureau of Corporations, Tobacco Investigation, file 3073, Section 9, Record Group (R.G.) 122, National Archives (NA), Washington, D.C.; *Tobacco Leaf*, 16 July 1902, p. 30.

24. U.S. Industrial Commission, *Report of the Industrial Commission on the Relations and Conditions of Capital and Labor* (Washington, D.C., 1901), vol. 7, p. 198; Ograin interview, 8 July 1977; *CMOJ*, Aug. 1906, p. 17; Sept. 1906, p. 20; Aug. 1909, p. 9; Apr. 1920, p. 3; *Tobacco Leaf*, 22 June 1911, p. 28.

25. Meyer Jacobstein, *The Tobacco Industry in the United States* (New York, 1907), pp. 89–92, 99–111; U.S. Industrial Commission, *Report*, vol. 15, pp. 385–87; vol. 7, pp. 191–98; *Constitution of the Cigar Makers' Union*, 1896, 1912, 1916; *CMOJ*, July 1918, p. 5; Santana interview, 11 Jan. 1976 by telephone; Norman E. Eliason, "The Language of the 'Buckeye,'" *American Speech*, 12 (Dec. 1937), 270–74.

26. *Constitution of the Cigar Makers' Union*, section 16; Jacobstein, *Tobacco Industry*, pp. 90, 148–50; Ograin interview, 17 May 1980; *Cigar Makers' Union Diamond Jubilee*, p. 11.

27. Shea interview.

28. *CMOJ*, Feb. 1900, p. 12; July 1901, p. 7; Feb. 1902, p. 4; Oct. 1914, p. 3; Santana interview, 18 May 1979; *Constitution of the Cigar Makers' Union*, section 96. Prohibitions against writing ahead were included in local union bylaws as well. For example see "By-Laws of Cigar Makers' and Packers' Union 97," Boston, Mass., 1912, p. 18, Boston Public Library; "By-Laws of Cigar Makers' Union No. 22," Detroit, Mich., 1904, p. 22, SHSW.

29. *CMOJ*, Feb. 1902, p. 4; *Constitution of the Cigar Makers' Union*, section 96.

30. Santana interview, 13 Aug. 1976; Massachusetts Bureau of Labor Statistics, *Massachusetts Labor Bulletin*, 30 (Mar. 1904), 126; U.S. Congress, House, Committee on Ways and Means, *Cigars Supplied Employees by Manufacturers: Hearings before the Committee on Ways and Means on H.R. 17253, H.R. 21357, and H.R. 21958*, 62d Cong., 2d sess., 1912, p. 28.

31. Theisen interview.

32. *CMOJ*, May 1897, p. 4; Apr. 1903, p. 3; July 1903, p. 1; Oct. 1906, p. 9. Although atypical because of its location, McSherrystown Local 316 records show an average of one traveler arriving each month in 1916 and three a month in 1908. See Monthly Reports, Papers of Local 316, McSherrystown, Adams County Historical Society, Gettysburg, Pa.

33. Rogiers interview.

34. *Constitution of the Cigar Makers' Union*, section 113; Ulman, *Rise of the National Trade Union*, pp. 79–84; Santana interview, 6 July 1977; Theisen inter-

view; Julius Sodekson interview, 29 June 1979, Hebrew Rehabilitation Center, Roslindale, Mass.; *CMOJ*, June 1900, p. 3; Jan. 1908, p. 4; *Chicago Federationist*, 2 Jan. 1904. R. A. Leeson in *Traveling Brothers*, which documents craft travel in England from the fourteenth to the nineteenth centuries, found the same problem in guild travel between 1450 and 1550. See Leeson, *Traveling Brothers*, p. 58. See also *CMOJ*, Aug. 1881, p. 4; Nov. 1881, p. 6; Feb. 1891, p. 7.

35. Theisen interview.

36. Santana interview, 24 Feb. 1980 by telephone; Shea interview; Eliason, "Language of the 'Buckeye,'" pp. 270–74; Ograin interview, 17 May 1980; *CMOJ*, Sept. 1909, p. 3.

37. *Cigar Makers' Union Diamond Jubilee*, p. 11; Durso interview; Baust interview; "By-Laws of the Cigar Makers' Union No. 192," Manchester, N.H., 1915, p. 13, MCL; *CMOJ*, Aug. 1907, p. 6; Ograin interview, 19 May 1979.

38. Baust interview; Ograin interview, 19 May 1979.

39. Ograin interview, 19 May 1979.

40. *Cigar Makers' Union Diamond Jubilee*, p. 11; *CMOJ*, Sept. 1902, p. 3; Dec. 1915, p. 39; Fischer to Jules Babeau, 25 Sept. 1919, Cigar Makers International Union of America, Papers of Local 162, Green Bay, Wis., SHSW.

41. *CMOJ*, Apr. 1903, p. 5; Jan. 1904, p. 5; June 1904, p. 13; May 1905, pp. 16, 38; June 1910, p. 7; Feb. 1915, p. 30; Mar. 1917, p. 22; Ograin interview, 17 May 1980. The *CMOJ* began listing such notices in 1878.

42. *CMOJ*, Jan. 1904, p. 5; Jan. 1903, pp. 4–5; June 1912, p. 24; *Constitution of the Cigar Makers' Union*, sections 109 and 111.

43. *CMOJ*, Feb. 1900, p. 7; Apr. 1903, p. 5; Dec. 1906, p. 20; Dec. 1907, p. 13; June 1910, p. 7; Jan. 1916, p. 31. See also *CMOJ*, Dec. 1878, p. 4 (the first letterbox column) and July 1882, p. 12.

44. Steber interview; Santana interview, 16 Sept. 1978; *Tobacco*, 2 Feb. 1900, p. 7; 23 Nov. 1900, p. 7; *Tobacco Leaf*, 26 Nov. 1902, p. 6; 17 June 1903, p. 11; 29 Nov. 1905, pp. 10, 48; 7 Feb. 1906, p. 6; 24 Jan. 1906, p. 4; 6 Feb. 1907, p. 26; 14 Sept. 1911, p. 11. Cigar makers had their own ratio of cigar makers to population: "We used to figure that one cigar maker for every 1,000 population." (Ograin interview, 17 May 1980.)

45. Durso interview; Shea interview; Steber interview; Samuel Gompers, *Seventy Years of Life and Labor: An Autobiography*, vol. 1 (New York, 1967 [1925]), p. 177; *CMOJ*, July 1884, p. 4. See also Charles Stephenson, "A Gathering of Strangers? Mobility, Social Structure, and Political Participation in the Formation of Nineteenth-Century American Workingclass Culture," in Milton Cantor, ed., *American Workingclass Culture: Explorations in American Labor and Social History* (Westport, Conn., 1979), pp. 48–49.

CHAPTER
4

"Learning to Love the Union"

In 1901 when Clovis Gallaud reported in the *Cigar Makers' Official Journal* about his organizing work in New Orleans, a weak union city, he reassured members about the new recruits by noting that "the boys are learning to love the union."[1] The cigar makers' union organization played an important part in the national work culture of the cigar makers. Given their other identities and loyalties based on neighborhood, ethnicity, or religion, the union helped to institutionalize an identification with work and occupation which cut across ethnic and other lines. The union reinforced the close ties of the shop floor and extended cigar makers' sense of occupational community to a national setting, facilitated by their carefully organized traveling system. Members established their formal ties and responsibilities to each other and defended their work culture through union structure, particularly its disciplinary features. Still, work culture and union were not neatly equivalent, and cigar makers viewed the union as a vehicle, not an end in itself. They tolerated some transgressions so long as one's basic loyalty to the union remained unquestioned. The boys in New Orleans and elsewhere were doing more than just paying their dues; they were proving their commitment and becoming an accepted part of the fraternity. Yet the unity and strength that unionism built, coupled with their patriarchal work culture and the practical economic competition they faced in the marketplace, set up a dynamic tension between solidarity and exclusivity that they would find difficult, if not impossible, to resolve.

Cigar makers had their closest contact with the union on the local level. Reminders of the local inside the shops ranged from the bill of prices posted on the wall to the shop collector making his rounds. Cigar makers in every union shop, even if it had only one employee, elected a shop collector to handle benefits, keep track of union labels placed on the cigar boxes, check dues books monthly, and collect both weekly dues and periodic additional "assessments." The shop collector greeted each newcomer to the factory to verify the traveler's card and "due" book and to record any outstanding loans. He also represented the cigar makers before the boss. "Anything went wrong and they didn't want it, they'd speak to him and he was their go-between." In shops with more than five cigar makers, members sometimes elected a shop committee to call shop meetings or investigate grievances. These committees, however, had no formal powers.[2]

The monthly union meetings provided the cigar maker's link to the local organization. Since not all members shared an equal interest in union affairs, the locals established attendance requirements. Unless a cigar maker wanted to pay fines ranging from fifty cents to one dollar, he went to at least one meeting every three months. Size varied from as few as eight members in Muncie, Indiana, to nearly two thousand in Local 90 in New York City.[3]

Every local's governing body included a president and vice-president, but each parceled out the duties of treasurer and recording, corresponding, and financial secretaries to one or more people depending on membership size and particular needs. Other elected officers audited the union's books, deposited union funds in the bank, and monitored attendance at union meetings. Local 14 in Chicago even elected the janitor who cleaned the union offices and prepared them for meetings. The financial secretary-treasurer universally received some salary, while other officers were paid small amounts for their services. Large locals employed their secretaries full time; elsewhere secretaries worked at the bench much or all of the day. In some cities, such as New York, Chicago, and Tampa, there might be more than one local cigar makers' union—including a packers' local as well. Then the various locals sent representatives to a citywide governing body known as the Joint Advisory Board (JAB).[4]

George W. Perkins, from Albany, New York, held the position of president-secretary of the Cigar Makers' International Union from 1892 until his retirement in 1927. His duties as president ranged widely: he handled all the administrative functions of the union, including arranging the conventions (held in 1896, 1912, 1920), writing all official correspondence, sending out circulars, editing the *Cigar Makers' Official Journal*, and receiving and acting on appeals from members fined or otherwise disciplined by their locals. He had to supply and order all due books, travel cards, and membership records, and keep an account of all benefits paid out. Operating out of the International's headquarters in Chicago, established in 1895, Perkins had the help of only one or two paid assistants. Perkins, the rest of the executive board of seven vice-presidents from different locals around the country, and a treasurer were elected every five years through a referendum vote, rather than at a convention as had been the case before 1891. Each member voted in his local, and results were forwarded by mail and printed in the *CMOJ*. Samuel Gompers consistently won election as the first vice-president, representing Local 144 in New York City.[5]

The relationship between locals and the national organization had been contested since the reorganization in the late 1870s. The plan had augmented the control of national officers and had centralized authority, but cigar makers retained a considerable degree of influence within the CMIU. Members' greatest power came through the initiative and referendum system begun in 1879. This system replaced the yearly convention where everyone present voted, and permitted each local only one vote—no advance for democratic principles. However, cigar makers soon changed these rules so that each member had an equal vote. Cigar makers could amend any part of the union constitution, so long as they secured first an endorsement from twenty locals and then a two-thirds vote of the entire membership. Proposed amendments appeared in every issue of the *CMOJ*. Although most agreed that their union should be "democratic," differences of opinion emerged over just how this could be accomplished. The rank and file tended to be "jealous of our democratic principles," and favored more local control. Cigar makers in one local in 1912 even proposed that members elect union organizers. National officers and those in the locals who supported them argued for more centralized power and authority. Since the constitution left some room for interpretation, conflict over local versus national control continued to occupy members' attention.[6]

Locals held all money collected by them through assessment, fines, dues, interest, and initiation fees, but could only spend 20 percent of this amount for operating expenses. The rest, known as the general fund, officially belonged to the International and could be used only to pay benefits. Under the equalization system the International could transfer money from those locals which had spent less than their pro rata amounts to those that had legitimately spent over their allowed percentages. Equalization had been designed to prevent hostilities and inequities from dividing union members from each other, but it had also contributed to a sense of community among members.[7] It emphasized that the locals worked together for the common good, not independently as competing parts.

Because the union was so diverse and its members known for being so trusting, cigar makers had over the years agreed to measures to protect union funds. Perkins supported these rules because he thought they inspired "confidence and security," and members seem to have agreed for the most part. Locals made extensive monthly reports to the International president and also had to report all loans. The International's constitution required that each local keep certain minimum deposits in its bank account, and it stipulated a minimum for the general fund of ten dollars per capita. If the level dropped below the minimum, Perkins had the power to assess members to make up the difference. An elaborate system of controls within each local divided the financial duties and required monthly auditing of the books by a special finance committee. In addition, President Perkins randomly dispatched two auditors (known as "financiers") to go through locals' books. Despite these precautions, notices of missing funds appeared occasionally in the *CMOJ*. Members of the local were responsible for making up the deficiency, José Santana noted, because after all they had elected the officers and thus bore the responsibility for their actions. This was a matter of considerable importance because cigar makers elected officers for qualities they valued, particularly militancy and an antipathy toward employers, rather than qualities needed for office.[8]

Members paid an initiation fee of three dollars and weekly dues of thirty cents, although sometimes during organization drives both were temporarily lowered, as in a 1908 effort to enroll Tampa workers. For several months, cigar makers there could join for only one dollar. As we have seen, not everyone was eligible to join the CMIU. Only a few locals admitted team workers and stogie makers could not join until 1916. The union's constitution specifically excluded "Chinese coolies and tenement-house workers." Buckeyes could belong, but once they hired journeymen they had to take out a twenty-cent retiring card. This meant they could pay dues of twenty cents a week and still receive sickness and death benefits. Should their situations change, they could become regular members again without paying the initiation fee. Union rules also required locals to admit anyone with a foreign union card, but when hundreds of Belgians began pouring into New England after 1900, members voted to require proof that an applicant had actually served three years' apprenticeship.[9]

Being a union member meant having numerous advantages and privileges compared to nonunion workers. At the most basic level, CMIU membership provided a degree of security and a source of group pride. Not only was their union strong and respected, but one of its founders and leaders had become the most widely known labor leader in the country, Samuel Gompers. The union also created a vehicle for achieving substantial material gains: good wages and working conditions and a system of benefits reputed to be the best benefit package of any union in the country. Certainly it was one of the most costly. Despite the fact that there was fairly widespread support for the combined high dues and benefits, Perkins felt some need to keep up a steady stream of self-congratulatory editorials in the *CMOJ* extolling the virtues of the system.[10]

Cigar makers' benefits were designed to provide members with financial aid when they needed it the most, but they also, as one member noted, had a "tendency to create a fraternal and binding effect on us." In addition to travel loans, these included sickness, out-of-work, strike, and death benefits. The last graduated according to the length of membership at the time of death: $50 if more than two years, $200 if more than five, $350 if over ten, and for those who had belonged more than fifteen years, $550. In 1887 the union adopted a $40 burial payment for male members who lost a wife or dependent mother. This benefit was never extended to include female members. Once they had been members for a year, cigar makers who became ill or incapacitated and unable to work for any reason other than "intemperance, debauchery or other immoral conduct" could receive a payment of $5 a week after seven days and could continue to receive it for a total of thirteen weeks during any one year.[11]

Most AFL unions offered sickness, death, and travel benefits, but out-of-work benefits were not common. The CMIU adopted the plan in 1890, and as late as 1916 only three other unions offered it. If a cigar maker lost his job for anything other than poor workmanship or intoxication, he could, after seven days, receive $3 a week for up to six weeks. Seven additional weeks had to elapse and then payment could resume for up to twelve weeks, allowing a total of $54 in one year. In cases of more general trade depression in an area, a local might set up a special aid fund and assess working members or ask for contributions. For years cigar makers debated the feasibility of disability and old-age pensions, but these measures failed in referendum despite a sizable minority vote in their favor. In 1902 members decided to permit blind or incapacitated members to receive all but $50 of their death benefits in advance—the $50 to be held for funeral expenses. Cigar makers also never agreed on establishing a home for tubercular or aged members, although Local 129 in Denver led campaigns for it every few years. Strike benefits were $5 a week for sixteen weeks and $3 a week thereafter.[12]

To protect union benefits from fraud or misuse, cigar makers constructed a web of safeguards. Locals fined those who accepted benefits to which they were not entitled, but getting that far could be difficult. For example, a member reporting sick received a relief card from the local secretary. Each week members of an appointed committee individually visited the sick member and signed the card. In Detroit, sick members' names were read aloud at union meetings as a further check on the veracity of their claims. Although alcohol may have had its medicinal effects, Local 192 in Manchester warned members that visits to saloons "in pursuit of pleasure" by anyone on the sick list automatically meant forfeiture of a week's benefits.[13]

Strike benefits in particular had been laden with procedures and limitations. Part of the 1879 reorganization required locals to receive permission from the union in order to strike. Strike rules were tightened in the 1880s after several disastrous strikes during the decade.[14] Members in a local who wanted to strike first had to meet and vote in favor. Joint advisory boards, where they existed, had to concur in the vote. Members of a committee then drew up a petition including details of grievances, number of members involved, and the exact strike vote and sent it to the International office (i.e., Perkins) in Chicago. If fewer than twenty-five members were involved in the strike, the executive board alone could grant permission; however, if more members were affected, Perkins had to send circulars reprinting the petition to every local. Two-thirds of the entire membership had to vote in favor of the strike for it to be approved. Disapproval only meant that strikers did not receive benefits, while in several other internationals an illegal strike was grounds for revocation of a local's charter. The cigar makers may have agreed grudgingly to restrictions on strikes, but they would not permit severe punishments, given their well-deserved reputation for striking quickly and frequently. Another rule limited requests for wage-increase strikes to particular regions in certain times of the year. Thus, between November 1 and April 1, only southern states could apply and thereafter locals elsewhere could. Ograin explained that "the idea of limiting strikes to different sections was to prevent too heavy a burden to hit the International Union at any one time." Although the process of applying for permission was slow, members rarely turned down each other's requests.[15]

Perkins regarded strikes with a good deal of consternation. He believed that members' impatience led to permanent ill will with employers and drained the union's treasury. Most differences of opinion between cigar makers and employers could be adjusted, he thought, without stopping work, and he argued that the strongest locals actually had fewer strikes. As the union's national leader, Perkins was most concerned about the health and survival of the institution itself, and not incidentally his own job, since he had not worked at the bench as a cigar maker since the early 1890s. Technically, his executive powers to control strikes were limited. He had the right to send agents to any strike situation to help reach a solution, but they had no formal powers. However, the executive board could appoint arbitrators who could actually force a settlement of a strike and therefore theoretically usurp the authority of the local strike committee. Since Perkins's supporters held a majority on the board throughout this period, he could intervene through them.[16]

In four strikes between 1902 and 1909, involving a large number of socialist members in Oneida, Boston, Hartford, and New Haven, Perkins stiffly disapproved of the strike issues. When arbitrators were dispatched, strike leaders charged them with undermining the strikes. In Boston in 1906, for example, cigar makers struck for a wage increase which Perkins regarded as unjustified. Responding to an appeal from employers, Perkins sent in Willard Best and the less-than-diplomatic Adolph Strasser, who proceeded to meet secretly with manufacturers and suggest a compromise. Boston cigar makers, however, held their ground and won a complete victory. For months, the atmosphere in Boston remained "thick with suspicion," and Strasser's and Best's behavior so angered members, socialist and nonsocialist alike, that they voted to prohibit arbitrators from any meeting with manufacturers unless a member of the local strike committee were present.[17]

Despite these advantages, cigar makers' lives were still uncertain. Older workers naturally lost the ability to make many cigars, and their earnings began to drop. Worse, the older cigar maker might strain to keep his production at its customary level, and the pressure could damage muscles and nerves, actually hastening the deterioration of skills. Nor did one have to wait until youth had passed to be affected by the physical aspects of work. Although rates of tuberculosis dropped dramatically within the CMIU after the 1880s, it was still the leading cause of death among members. Another common affliction was "cigar makers' neurosis," a muscular dysfunction which reduced a worker's speed and sometimes resulted in a total inability to work. Probably caused by repetitive work and cigar makers' cramped and stationary position, it included shoulder, arm, and head pain and in the worst cases the cigar maker lost some muscle control in one of his hands.[18]

This vulnerability underscored the importance of their union and their ties to each other. Over and over the message of interdependence was replayed throughout the operation of the union, and cigar makers could frequently be found digging into their pockets to help a brother. Stranded travelers needed a tramp stake to bridge the gap until the next town and a job. Sickness, accidents, death, personal tragedies, and everyday misfortune prompted shop mates to offer each other what money they had. "They were very generous. I was always giving something," remarked Herman Baust. José Santana referred to the cigar makers' charitable nature as their "humanitarianism." The preamble to the bylaws of Local 14 in Chicago captured in a few words cigar makers' emphasis on mutual aid and assistance. Each local union had the duty of giving "all moral and pecuniary aid in its power to members of the union, encouraging and assisting each other in hour of trial, [and providing] a kind and sympathetic attendance upon the couch of suffering."[19] Local 165 in Philadelphia took all of the money it derived from local fines and contributions and created a local fund to be used for "donations to our own members in need through long spells of sickness or a long period of enforced idleness."[20]

The resources of one local, particularly a smaller one, at times fell short of demand. Then locals widened their appeals and approached fellow unions nearby or sent circulars asking for donations throughout the entire CMIU. "Fellow Craftsman—We respectfully appeal to you in behalf of Mr. Ben Coster, an old and esteemed member of the C.M.I.U., who has been a continuous member since 1880, and has been active in different locals in the interest of our craft. Mr. Coster was attacked by a sickness which culminated in the total loss of his sight and the complete collapse of his nervous system, rendering him incapable of supporting his family." In another case, J. Braunstein of Local 14 "had the misfortune to lose his left hand, forever disabling him from plying his vocation." Locals held raffles and raised money by selling tickets at ten to fifteen cents each to members elsewhere.[21]

A few locals chose or were forced by circumstance to play even more prominent roles. Members of Boston's Local 97, which was comparatively wealthy, pointed with pride bordering on hubris to their record of outgiving others. Local 97's legendary generosity to fellow unionists provided it with national recognition and respect, but the local constantly published how much money it had donated in each case, and did so, union secretary and spokesman Henry Abrahams claimed, "for the benefit of the future historian." Because of 97's high bill of prices and its great wealth and strength, Abrahams unabashedly referred to his local as "the brightest gem in the galaxy of stars in the International Union."[22] In 1910, Local 97 spent $17,000 for "charitable and fraternal purposes," a fact which even *Tobacco Leaf* noted. Local 129 in Denver shouldered a greater burden than most locals because consumptives often migrated there searching for a cure. Many came too late. These frequently arrived without sufficient funds to care for themselves and Denver members' financial resources were strained to pay for care in a TB sanitarium, since hospitals and boarding houses would not take anyone afflicted with "the great white plague." Yet fellow unionists' appreciation partly offset the debt. "Union 395, Waterbury Conn., extends a vote of thanks to Union 129, Denver Colo., for the way they treated our deceased brother, G. C. Gwinn; also his wife, when she was there to take back his remains."[23]

Members were not the only beneficiaries of the cigar makers' benevolence, for "many a lone widow" could thank the cigar makers for their chivalrous financial contributions and assistance. Several did. In 1909, for example, Mrs. Carrie Warner asked that the following be placed in the *CMOJ*. "To friends in the J. Seubert Cigar Factory. I wish to thank you all most sincerely for your sympathy and kindness in my hour of sorrow, and especially the liberal purse you gave." Gallantry could take other forms as well. William McKinistry, secretary of Local 208 in Kalamazoo, received from the sister of a cigar maker killed in an accident in 1905 a request for a picture of her brother. He appealed to the fraternity in the journal: "Now boys, make inquiries and keep making them till we get this girl what she desires."[24]

Calls for aid could also be made in behalf of an entire local, and often the response was quite generous. Members in San Francisco in the wake of the 1906 earthquake received such an outpouring of money so quickly that they soon requested that no more money or supplies be sent. Most often, however, these calls went out during strikes. Frequently members voted to assess themselves a fixed amount to support the strike to insure a sufficient collection. Some locals, such as 97, stood at the forefront of giving. The local donated an additional $14,000 beyond the required contribution during the great New York strike of 1900, and donated over $6,500 to the Tampa strike of 1910. Secretary Abrahams never kept these donations a secret and most found their way into the pages of the journal via his monthly message to the "Union Notes" column of the *CMOJ*—"97 donated one hundred and fifty dollars to the boys on strike in York, PA." Cigar makers gave to their own strikes, but they also took pride in sending money to aid other workers, including miners in 1902, stockyard and garment workers along with British cigar makers in 1904, teamsters in 1906, telegraphers in 1907, hatters in 1910, corset makers and boot and shoe workers in 1912. In 1914, Denver cigar makers assessed themselves three dollars each to aid striking miners after the deaths at Ludlow, Colorado.[25]

Yet this harmonious picture masked some underlying tensions. Members sometimes complained about too many assessments and an especially unpopular or drawn-out strike might not elicit such liberal giving. While such attitudes only occasionally made their way into the *CMOJ*, it is possible that the anti-Semitism expressed in Francis X. Colgan's letter to Perkins in 1913 might not have been altogether rare. Colgan served as secretary of Local 316 in McSherrystown, Pennsylvania, and he unenthusiastically sent in the money his local had been assessed to aid Local 90 in New York City but complained that "Those jews [sic] are in a great hurry to get the money when the same is ordered to be sent to them. . . . If Union No. 90 would exercise a little more care in looking after the funds of the International Union perhaps they would not have to call so often for assistance."[26]

Members' code of responsibility to each other extended even to death. Locals usually requested that their charters be draped in mourning upon the death of a member. Union rules stipulated that every member receive a proper burial, regardless of a person's eligibility for the union's death benefit. Locals always sent at least one floral arrangement to a funeral, and in every case a member of the local, if not the entire local, attended. "The Union attended the funeral in a body, and laid to rest one of the best union men 395 ever had." In Chicago, Local 14 had its own section of Forest Home Cemetery where members and their families could be buried.[27]

The cigar makers' union also functioned as a social organization, which deepened members' attachment to it and to each other. Each local varied, but union cigar makers did not necessarily live in the same neighborhoods or share the same ethnic, religious, or cultural backgrounds. Both the union and the workplace provided common experiences and meeting grounds upon which to form identities based on work and occupation. James Durso remembered that union meetings in New Haven had been social gatherings and that after adjournment "they all went to saloons, all to drink beer." Herman Baust described how many of his cigar-making companions at the F. D. Grave Company worked Saturday mornings during the summer, and afterwards went to the park for the afternoon once they received their pay envelopes. They spent the afternoon making speeches and telling stories and "they'd all be drunk when they went home." William Theisen spent much of his time after work with Cuban friends he had met in the factory in Denver.[28]

Union locals sponsored a variety of activities away from the workplace and such outings had been reported in the *CMOJ* since the 1870s. Baseball teams were popular from California to Minneapolis to Rochester and locals shared their triumphs in the pages of the *CMOJ*, as when the Bakersfield, California, team played the butchers in 1902 in a benefit game for the striking miners and announced that, despite a hard fight, they had been "slaughtered" by their opponents. Locals held picnics, dances, "annual excursions," smokers, and parades both for fun and for raising money. An anniversary of a local was a particularly good excuse for celebrating with songs, speeches, or dancing, and Local 14 was known for its "impressive masquerade ball" each year. Labor Day occasioned tireless efforts to construct an exceptional float or banner, sometimes in competition with other skilled trades.[29]

The friendships formed in the factory and the sense of solidarity reinforced by union structure and fraternal spirit drew members together and created a strong sense of belonging to a special group. "You have to have gone through it to know what it was all about," Santana reasoned as he tried to explain the spirit inside the union. "Developing from day to day, for years and years, it was a brotherhood. . . . Cigar makers' union was more like a brotherhood. Friendship and brotherhood." That closeness at times translated into a "tendency towards clannishness. They worked together, stuck together, played together." After work, "brick layers and railroad men might get together," one observer noted, "but cigar makers stayed by themselves." "We were," concluded Ograin, "a fraternity by ourselves."[30]

One of the union's important symbols was the union label. Hatters, bakers, garment makers, printers, and many other craft unions adopted labels in the nineteenth century to set their products apart from non-union goods, although the cigar makers claimed to have been the first union to do so, in 1880. The blue label went on every box of cigars produced in a union shop. To have the label, a manufacturer had to agree to the bill of prices and every cigar maker and packer in his factory had to belong to the union. The label read: "This certifies that the cigars contained in this box have been made by a FIRST CLASS WORKMAN, a member of the Cigar Makers' International Union of America, an Organization devoted to the advancement of the Moral, Material and Intellectual Welfare of the Craft. Therefore we recommend these cigars to all smokers throughout the world." Someone from the local had to dispense labels to each factory, where one member had responsibility for seeing that they were used properly. Shop collectors had to keep accurate records on the receipt and use of all labels, which were consecutively numbered. Counterfeiting was fairly common and both the locals and the CMIU nationally fought to win state legislation making label counterfeiting a crime. Manufacturers recognized that the CMIU was "one of the most aggressive labor bodies in this country when the rights of its blue label was infringed on," and cigar makers rarely missed an opportunity to take such cases to court.[31]

Each local had a label committee, appointed by the local president, which conducted "label agitation" activities to advertise and popularize the label both within the labor movement and to the public in general. These efforts included newspaper ads, posters in store and tavern windows, and public distribution of various items emblazoned with the label, including matches, playing cards, and calendars. The more creative the attempt to display the label the better. In 1903, the Oneida union hired a parachute jumper to advertise it, and in 1912, cigar makers attending the national convention in Baltimore voted to erect and maintain "a large electric sign at Niagara Falls to advertise our union label." Members also worked to get local tobacco dealers to support union products by displaying them prominently in their stores. In New Haven, recalled Herman Baust, the committee was continuously "threatening the storekeepers, if they brought any nonunion cigars in. We had a committee. We paid that committee so much a year to go from store to store and they'd boycott that store. . . . Oh, the cigar makers' union was strong, very strong." Cigar makers also attempted to win concessions in ballparks or with a city for various municipal events in the summer.[32]

Much of the activity promoting the label in the early part of the century was directed against the "trust," the American Tobacco Company. Boston's Local 97 in particular had considerable success in keeping trust

CMIU Blue Label, 1914. From author's collection.

products out of the city through advertising which "created sentiment" against the trust in the general population. The American Tobacco Company's retail outlets, United Cigar Stores, rarely carried union products, and occasionally local label committees attempted to cooperate with independent retailers in resisting the trust stores, but these alliances proved temporary at best.[33]

To pay for label activities, locals could use one dollar per member each year from the general fund. In 1903 the various locals spent a total of $44,339.82 and in 1916 $34,300.84 for label agitation. Local 97, as might be expected, outspent other locals; in 1903, when the union had only 1,832 members, it spent $10,000. Beginning in the 1890s, state Blue Label Leagues had been organized in Michigan, Pennsylvania, New York, New Jersey, Minnesota, Indiana, Ohio, Illinois, Wisconsin, and Rhode Island to coordinate efforts of locals in the state on behalf of the label, but

most had difficulty drawing enough interest. Only the New England Label League, led by Boston cigar makers, functioned well during the early
twentieth century.[34]

Much of the union's energy as an institution went into activities related
to the label. The "organizers" Perkins hired and sent to different areas of
the country occasionally worked to interest nonunion cigar makers in
joining as they had in the nineteenth century, but by the early twentieth
century they actually spent most of their time visiting unions in other
trades and urging them to buy only blue label cigars. Union regulations
required that cigar makers return the favor and buy only union products.
Perkins frequently printed reminders in the *CMOJ:* "Cigar makers can
and should show their appreciation by always insisting that the stamp of
the Boot and Shoe Workers is firmly imbedded in the shoes they purchase. The same advice applies to all other labels." How consistently rules
on buying label products were followed or enforced varied. Ograin noted
that in Chicago members were insistent on the question of cigars or cigarettes, but were less particular about other products. In New England,
cigar makers took the principle of patronizing union labor more seriously.
Two cigar makers in Manchester, related Frank Shea, had built a home
outside of town. Men in the local "found out they had hired nonunion
contractors because they were cheaper. Oh boy, they had a meeting up
there that night. . . ." The fine came to seventy-five dollars each. In another case, a cigar maker in the Sullivan factory had taken his shirts to a
nonunion, Chinese laundry in the city, but had dropped the ticket inside
the factory at work. Another cigar maker found it and tacked it up on the
wall. "They were waiting for the fellow to claim the ticket. He never
claimed it. They'd jump all over him. . . . That's the way the union was."
In New Haven, Herman Baust noted that union members obeyed the rules
on buying only union products. Their motto had been "all for one. You had
to be. If they caught you buying nonunion goods, you were fined."[35]

As the case of patronizing union goods suggests, cigar makers may have
agreed on broad principles but they did not always live according to these
stated ideals. Through union rules and discipline cigar makers protected
themselves and their union and called miscreant members to task. Locals
levied fines against members for a multitude of sins; some were enumer-
ated in local bylaws, while others were recognized by "common consent."[36] Sins included failure to fulfill the duties of elected union office or
to carry out a committee assignment, tampering with a union election,
passing bad checks anywhere, embezzling union funds or defrauding the

union, working more than eight hours a day, taking a new job without first quitting the old one, asking a friend to line up a job, being suspended for nonpayment of dues while holding a steady job, selling cigars for the boss, taking a job as a foreman in a nonunion shop (taking the position in a union shop was acceptable), or, for a shop collector, failing to report a job opening to the secretary. All members were required to march in the yearly Labor Day parade and those who did not faced a fine. One cigar maker in Burlington, Iowa, failed to appear for the parade there in 1906 and offered as the excuse for his absence that he had been "in the country squirrel hunting." The executive board of the local found the explanation unacceptable and fined him five dollars. Local 156, Suffield, Connecticut, announced in 1901 that the union would fine any cigar maker who took a room in a boardinghouse where men scabbing in a local machinists' strike also boarded. [37]

Cigar makers recognized the divergence of opinion among members on many issues, and set up guidelines for the conduct of local meetings which could contain and structure conflict. Regulations on meetings prohibited "boisterous," "unruly or obnoxious," "improper," and "indecorous" language or behavior. "To maliciously slander" another member meant a fine, and "disrespect to the chair" could bring expulsion from the meeting. Ideally, meetings were supposed to be the arena for handling all disagreements and rules required members to make all charges openly in meetings. "The Union meeting is the place for criticism and grievances." Internal divisions would be kept within the union family and not aired to outsiders. Members were forbidden to pass along union business to any nonmember. [38]

Collecting dues had been a problem since the 1870s. Union rules after reorganization stipulated that if a member fell more than eight weeks behind in paying dues, he could be suspended. A contingency clause postponed such drastic action if the member, within two weeks, paid enough dues to fall within the eight-week limit. He kept his membership, but was placed on the so-called ninety-day list and could not use any benefits for three months. Just as Gompers had argued decades earlier, benefits helped to tie members to the organization and helped to keep them paying their dues. For those who had earned the $550 death benefit, suspension could be a critical matter. "You thought twice before you dropped your card," noted John Ograin. Still, Ograin explained, not everyone regarded continuous membership in the same light. "I only joined the union once," he commented. "I know a lot of people that joined it a dozen times. . . . They didn't think nothing of dropping their cards." No other available evidence indicates that mass suspensions were a problem for the CMIU, yet Ograin's observation suggests that one's identity with the union fraternity did not always mean an acceptance of all of its rules.[39]

The most serious offenses involved scabbing and working for, or paying below, the wage scale in the bill of prices. "Conduct unbecoming a union man" was a catchall phrase for various serious offenses such as "working against the interests of the union" or leaving debts. "Union 290, Janesville, Wis., fined Al Yates (number not given) $10 for conduct unbecoming a union member—jumping a board bill and trying to induce others to do the same. His card is tied up at Nashville, Tenn., and was formerly from Canton, Ill."[40]

Fines ran from fifty cents and one dollar to one hundred dollars or more depending on the offense, and applied not only to members but nonmembers as well, particularly recalcitrant manufacturers. In the case of the latter, however, fines were imposed out of principle, but rarely became much of a source of revenue. "We didn't collect many fines," Ograin confessed. "We levied a lot, but we didn't collect many."[41] In all cases of charges against an individual, the local executive board acted as a "court of trial," calling witnesses and conducting an investigation. Members were bound to present any injury from another member to the local for redress before appealing to civil authorities. Anyone who objected to the decision of the local could appeal to President Perkins, including nonmembers. Still unsatisfied, an aggrieved member could appeal to the executive board (which nearly always sustained Perkins) or, as a last resort, he could ask for a referendum vote of the entire membership.[42]

Most punishments involved fines, although in some cases members were temporarily suspended or completely expelled. In 1904 Local 32 in Louisville, Kentucky, voted "to fine H. Gutman (41271) $25 for sailing under various names and quitting a union job and accepting employment in the notorious non-union factory of Hetherman Brothers. Also suspended him." Using the *CMOJ* to publicize the names of transgressors not only made the indignity of public disgrace a further punishment, but reflected a collective enforcement of community norms. Any member convicted of a crime involving union funds automatically had his name printed in the journal and any fine over five dollars had to have the approval of the International board and was then published in the *CMOJ*. Each month the journal included the names of "frauds," "chiselers," and "scoundrels."[43]

Discipline, however, went beyond mere formal penalties. Indeed ostracism from the work group served as a powerful informal means of enforcing acceptable behavior. Members wrote in asking patience for repaying loans or fines, and occasionally a local apologized for printing the name of the wrong person. Results of misinformation could be most unpleasant. In January 1907, James Knudston wrote the *CMOJ* to say that the J. Knudston whom the Peoria union had fined thirty dollars for scabbing was a different person. "The reason I ask that this explanation be made is that on account of the similarity of names I have been subject to considerable humiliation from my fellow unionists since the above mentioned item appeared in the *CMOJ*."[44]

Rules hardly worked uniformly or even completely fairly. Members were willing to tolerate certain behavior although it might technically violate union law, or to ease and adjust a previous decision. In September 1913, the members of Local 122 in Warren, Pennsylvania, voted to exempt their former secretary from further payments in regard to his conviction for misusing union funds. The secretary, they pointed out, was a slow worker and had already been humiliated by the affair. Demanding further payment on the fine seemed to be a case of "kicking a man when he is down." In addition the "boys" from around the country had, in a fraternal spirit, sent in donations to help cover the loss of funds.[45] However, sometimes members bent rules to suit their own self-interest, as when cigar makers in Pawtucket, Rhode Island, voted to fine a member who had refused to chip in to buy beer. Perkins supported the temperate member's appeal. On some issues, International officers proved more lenient and forgiving than a man's fellow members. A cigar maker in Flint, Michigan, took a job in 1906 in a scab shop but quit shortly thereafter. The local voted to fine him fifty dollars. The executive board urged that the fine be reduced to twenty-five dollars because "there is every reason to believe that the man did not intentionally 'scab.'" If treated with understanding, eventually this cigar maker would "become a good, staunch, true union member."[46]

The work culture's emphasis on loyalty to the union protected cigar makers' interests and reinforced their collectivity, but it drew a tighter circle around them. If unionism were valued and rewarded both formally and informally, outsiders appeared all that more suspicious. The concern with having members also be true union men meant that on a practical level cigar makers were circumspect about whom they admitted. They warned each other about unscrupulous characters in the *CMOJ* and they made efforts on the local level to screen out undesirables, those who might not share the same values and ideals. One cigar maker, writing from "on the Road," urged members to "work to the end that an applicant for membership . . . be of good moral character, sober (not a prohibitionist), honest and have no bad debts against him." Some locals refused to accept cards less than a year old from travelers to punish anyone who had joined just to make travel easier. In Denver, one cigar maker pointed a finger at those "worthies, some with gray whiskers, who never thought of paying a cent to the interest of the union, until they were ready to start west for their health, which some of them lost in scab shops, working against the interests of the union."[47]

The question of loyalty was illustated well in the case of Fred Nauman, who began his apprenticeship in Green Bay, Wisconsin, and served two years before the shop closed. Unable to secure a union position, he worked for a time in a nonunion shop. He left and took a job as a tobacco stemmer in a small union factory, hoping to get a place as a cigar maker when one opened. When he applied to Green Bay Local 162 in 1915 for membership and credit for his final year of apprenticeship under non-union conditions, the members of the local initially denied his application. One member, however, refuted previous arguments and reasoned that the man had left the union against his will in the first place and had taken a large cut in pay in order to return. These actions, he posited, were "enough proof that he is a Union-Man at heart." The argument worked and Nauman was admitted. Even when asking fellow cigar makers for donations for a sick member, it was good policy to establish his long and faithful association with the union.[48]

All this distrust created serious problems for the CMIU with regard to admitting nonunion cigar makers. Outsiders by definition did not obey union rules and were therefore suspect. Cigar makers routinely referred to all nonunion cigar makers as scabs whether or not they actually broke strikes. Members worried about "mushroom membership"—people who poured into the union at the height of a strike, only to drop out thereafter. Being a member entailed a genuine commitment. Whenever the label was proposed as an organizing tool, many members objected. The label served the union in many ways, but anyone who joined the union not out of some conviction, but simply because his employer wanted to use the union la-bel, would likely make a poor union member. Cigar makers needed to "educate" prospective members first. Clovis Gallaud had addressed cigar makers' fears about new members when he reassured them that new recruits in New Orleans were developing the proper understanding of unionism.[49]

Older members sometimes had their doubts about the commitment of the young, who had not witnessed the great changes the union had wrought and might not therefore be able to appreciate and understand the union's history and purpose. One Kansas City old-timer wrote: "It makes me stop and wonder sometimes if the cigar makers who have come into our trade in the last fifteen years who have been handed the eight-hour work day, the new scale of wages and the provision on each bill that wages must be paid in cash weekly on a silver platter . . . not to say anything about our sick and death benefit, our out-of-work benefit, loan benefit—if he realized what some of our old scraps have done, what sacrifices they have made to bring these new results about."[50]

Certainly the largest group outside the CMIU were team workers, a growing proportion of whom were women making five-cent cigars. The debate over organizing these workers had begun in the early 1870s and continued throughout the early twentieth century. The union's constitution ostensibly prohibited discrimination on the basis of sex or method of work, but the local option clause effectively kept team workers out of many jurisdictions. In 1902 the Syracuse local struck against the large Justin Seubert Company to force it to abandon team work, and in 1903 Chicago locals voted to ban team workers. Local 97 in Boston and Local 22 in Milwaukee also prohibited a division of labor in their jurisdictions. Members in these and other locals argued that allowing the introduction of the team system benefited only the manufacturers, because it permitted them to reduce their wages. Accepting the team system and organizing these workers gave employers permission to adopt it. True enough, others countered, but many employers were using the team system anyway, and the unions which prohibited it simply eliminated all possibility of organizing these workers. Not only did such a policy ultimately make team workers more attractive to manufacturers since it was unlikely that they would be organized, it also gave other organizations, including the Socialist Trades and Labor Alliance, the Industrial Workers of the World, and independent unions such as the Progressive Cigar Makers in Chicago, openings to organize these workers.[51]

Craft pride gave cigar makers a sense of dignity and accomplishment, but it contributed to an attitude of superiority and even condescension. Their own concern with the quality of the product as part of the content of their work meant that they did not regard other, less-skilled work used on an inferior product to be of equal merit or importance. John Ograin believed that members' view of themselves and their own work had kept them from seeing their common interest with other workers. "That was the first blunder we made when we wouldn't recognize the team work. . . . We were too narrow minded. We were so darned proud. 'We're something special. We're artists.'" The contradictions did not escape all members. When cigar makers in Chicago in 1903 voted to ban team work, one angry cigar maker there cried: "What will other unionists say when they learn that we refuse to accept cigar makers into our organization because they make but half a cigar?"[52] Even when they wanted to reach nonunion workers, their sense of difference with these outsiders created barriers neither side wanted to cross. José Santana believed in organizing all workers and had walked out in an unauthorized strike in 1916 in solidarity with women team workers, but these convictions did not diminish the vast difference he saw between his work and theirs. "They're not cigar makers," he and his male friends had joked. "They're carpenters!" Another cigar maker urged his fellow unionists to organize team workers, and went so far as to assert that the division of labor should make absolutely no difference, provided, he could not resist adding, that "the quality was good."[53]

Inside the factory cigar makers made distinctions between themselves (and here they included the elite cigar packers as well) and other factory operatives—to the point of not organizing the latter. In Boston Local 97 worked with and supported the strippers' union, but in a strike in 1926 women strippers stayed out after cigar makers returned to work and complained about "continual snubbing in the past." A federal conciliator remarked that "this friction between the two locals . . . has been going on for the last twenty years." Tampa cigar makers were some of the worst offenders. Their unions frequently included all tobacco-factory operatives, but this move toward industrial unionism did not signify a belief that all were equal. They observed a rigid status hierarchy in the factory: packers and selectors looked down on cigar makers, who sneered at strippers, and so on down the line.[54]

All of these factors made organizing in the country districts of southeastern Pennsylvania, north and west of Philadelphia, especially difficult. Cigars produced in the area, particularly in the Ninth Internal Revenue District of York and Lancaster counties, were, according to members, "no good whatever." When these workers organized and received the union label, members elsewhere complained that the poor quality of the smokes gave union cigars a bad name. Jobbers, pressed to supply union cigars, bought these goods because they were cheaper than union products made elsewhere. They undersold union cigars made locally and angered many union members. "We have been paying year after year for advertising of the union label by local assessments and along comes Pennsylvania union made cigars sold in the Chicago markets under our very eyes, taking advantage of our agitation, selling their cheap goods at our expense and putting the cigarmakers of Chicago on the streets." One went so far as to suggest that the union withhold the label from all Ninth District factories. Beginning in the late 1870s, the CMIU had repeatedly tried to organize in Pennsylvania. Time after time locals were formed in Lancaster and such towns as Quakertown, Pennsburg, Lititz, and Manheim with little success, although York and McSherrystown managed to keep unions going throughout the period. Organizers pointed out the poor working conditions and tried to understand why people there did not join—"these men and women sit and work in hopes of better stock tomorrow." Organizers also urged members not to "condemn but build up" the cigar makers of Pennsylvania. Frequently Pennsylvania workers who were members did not work in union shops. The union counted 452 members in Berks County, Pennsylvania, in 1907, but only half of them worked in union shops and of those half were buckeyes. McSherrystown Local 316 had 900 members in 1905, but membership had dropped to 596 in 1915 and only about half of the members worked in union shops, many of whom once again were buckeyes. Members vacillated between trying repeatedly to organize in the area or branding the place "hopeless" and ignoring it. Longtime Pennsylvania member and frequent CMIU organizer, I. W. Bisbing, asked of fellow members in 1897 what he and others repeated over and over in the coming years. Did members intend their union to be "an aristocratic or a democratic" institution? If the latter, he insisted, cigar makers would have to open the doors to their union, treat all fairly, and be willing to spend money and energy organizing in Pennsylvania.[55]

Enrolling team workers was complicated by the fact that they were not just another group of workers: they were women, a fact that was no accident. Manufacturers wanted women workers for specific reasons. But gender fundamentally shaped cigar makers' exclusivistic outlook. Union members shared a masculine culture, and while they drew strength from this kind of solidarity, their attitudes toward women were reflections of the male-dominated society in which they lived. For years, much of the material in the *CMOJ* had argued that women's rightful place was in the home and that men should make enough to support daughters and wives so they could stay there. A married woman who worked robbed a man, the rightful breadwinner, of a job. Women were also viewed as victims and appeals to organize them were often phrased in chivalrous tones imploring members to "protect womanhood" and defend "degraded womanhood." Even when they were members, women were viewed as somehow marginal. Local 25 in Milwaukee, for example, required all members to march in the Labor Day parade, except those "over fifty years of age, disabled, and female members and mutes."[56] Socialists had no better insight into the position of women cigar makers. In 1908, Boston's Local 97 proposed barring all married women from CMIU membership. The proposal was framed in the collectivist language of sharing work, but it was rooted in patriarchical attitudes about the family. Elizabeth Henry, a handworker and member in Reading, Pennsylvania, rebuked 97 and the male membership of the CMIU generally. She called attention to the problems that female cigar makers faced within particular locals despite their so-called equal treatment and pay. "There is a tacit understanding among the male members of the unions in such localities that women are not to be given employment. . . . Is this your idea of justice?" A referendum vote killed the measure.[57]

The tension between solidarity and exclusivity lay at the core of unionists' work culture and would make the issue of organizing the unorganized a central paradox throughout the life of the CMIU. In specific cases, the members chose one policy or another, but the underlying philosophical problem remained. Hand stogie makers were admitted to membership in 1916 and the union began organizing seriously in Puerto Rico (because of competition from Puerto Rican cigars) that same year. The CMIU rarely worked hard to organize other factory operatives, but even when it did support their organization, as in the case of women stemmers in Boston, these workers often complained of the cigar makers' "continual snubbing." Approaches to the question of team work varied. Some socialists had long called for complete organization in the trade, while at the other end of the spectrum, members tenaciously held on to the hope that the union would never have to change. Perkins vehemently opposed the concept of industrial unionism, but he grew increasingly worried about the increase in the numbers of team workers and the growing popularity of the five-cent cigar. A dual union movement of team workers developing in Chicago convinced him by 1912 to take some action. Delegates meeting that year in Baltimore, during the first convention since 1896, adopted Perkins's program for facilitating the organization of these workers. The

Class A plan provided that team workers could join the union by paying an initiation fee of one dollar and weekly dues of fifteen cents, half the regular dues, and receive in return half of each benefit. Although the convention adopted the proposal, bitter opposition to it among many members killed it narrowly in the subsequent referendum vote.[58] In October 1915, however, members finally adopted the Class A system, although they refused to drop the local option clause. The total vote on Class A, 5,985 to 2,207, represented only about 21 percent of the union's regular thirty cents dues-paying members, and hostility to the plan remained even after it was adopted. Class A locals did form in several cities, and in 1916 the CMIU counted a total of 3,976 Class A members. Yet two years later only 1,365 remained. John Ograin offered a telling clue when he commented that those who enrolled under the plan were only "half members."[59]

Thus craft union exclusivity among cigar makers was more than simply the attempt by privileged workers to preserve their economic position, although undeniably it was partly that. The "logic of craft unionism" was based on the need to limit access to skills and sell those skills at a premium. Cigar makers' need to protect themselves grew out of actual experience and recognition that only a fine line separated them from more degraded conditions. José Santana had worked in nonunion shops in New York City when he had first reached the mainland in 1909 and never wanted to return. He strongly supported the CMIU throughout his life to make sure that he did not. Open shops meant low wages, but worse, "the worker was considered a slave. No man was given decency. We were treated in open shops like dogs. Anytime anybody came around and because he doesn't like the way you comb your hair, he fire you."[60]

While much about their culture and their union fostered solidarity, it simultaneously nourished exclusivity. Their shop conversations and the congenial atmosphere on the shop floor, the social and fraternal customs, the helping hand every member gave a traveler, and union discipline all expressed the value they placed on their collective interests, rather than personal advancement, but they also acted as a boundary mechanism— keeping members in, yet at the same time keeping others out.[61] Pride in work provided them with a deeply human sense of worth and satisfaction, but it inevitably inhibited their ability to encompass all workers.

Union cigar makers' strength—a dynamic work culture which emphasized mutuality and solidarity—was at the same moment their key weakness. Exclusivity was not simply a matter of pure economics whereby a craft union attempted to limit the pool of skilled labor and bolster wages and job security for a select few through this shortage. It was more. It grew out of a whole cultural matrix which connected pride, loyalty, and unity with a fear of potential subversives. All of this was grafted onto a sex/gender system based on belief in male supremacy and the subordination of women. Male unionists viewed the expansion of female employment in the industry as a kind of economic threat, yes. Their policies and reactions to women cigar makers, however, signified their deep interest in preserving a degree of male privilege. Union cigar makers belonged to a community, but one with distinct bounds and limitations.

Notes

1. *CMOJ*, Oct. 1901, p. 4.

2. T. Frank Shea interview, 26 June 1979, Manchester, N.H.; "By-Laws of the Cigar Makers' International Union Local No. 165," Philadelphia, 1908, pp. 17–19, State Historical Society of Wisconsin (SHSW), Madison; "By-Laws of Cigar Makers' Union No. 14," Chicago, Ill., 1902, pp. 13–14, U.S. Department of Labor Library (USDL), Washington, D.C.; "By-Laws of the Cigar Makers' Progressive International Union No. 90," New York City, 1905, pp. 16–18, SHSW.

3. *CMOJ*, Jan. 1905, p. 3; "By-Laws of Cigar Makers' and Packers' Union 97," Boston, Mass., 1912, p. 17, Boston Public Library; "Constitution and By-Laws of Cigar Makers' and Packers' Union No. 2," Buffalo, N.Y., 1905, pp. 11–12, SHSW; John R. Ograin interview, 17 May 1980. Membership figures for each local were presented each year in the *CMOJ*'s April issue as part of the financial report of each local.

4. "By-Laws," Local 14, Chicago, p. 15; *CMOJ*, Dec. 1909, p. 10; "By-Laws of Cigar Makers' Union No. 22," Detroit, Mich., 1904, pp. 9–16, SHSW; "By-Laws of Cigar Makers' Union No. 192," Manchester, N.H., 1915, pp. 5–10, Manchester City Library (MCL), Manchester, N.H.

5. *Constitution of the Cigar Makers' International Union of America*, sections 12, 50–55, 1896, 1912, 1916, Series V, Box 2, Cigar Makers' International Union of America Collection (CMIU Collection), McKeldin Library, University of Maryland (UM), College Park; Meyer Jacobstein, *The Tobacco Industry in the United States* (New York, 1907), pp. 154–55; Marie H. Hourwich, "Cigar Makers' Union History, 1851–1879," typescript, Research Files, Box 22, David Saposs Papers, SHSW; John P. Troxell, "Labor in the Tobacco Industry" (Ph.D. dissertation, University of Wisconsin, 1931), p. 141.

6. Hourwich, "Cigar Makers' Union History," pp. 9, 14, 16; *CMOJ*, Jan. 1889, p. 23; Sept. 1904, p. 6; Jan. 1905, p. 9; Aug. 1906, p. 3; May 1912, p. 12; Lloyd Ulman, *The Rise of the National Trade Union: The Development and Significance of Its Structure, Governing Institutions and Economic Policies* (Cambridge, Mass.,

1955), p. 253; Theodore W. Glocker, "The Structure of the Cigar Makers' Union," in Jacob H. Hollander and George E. Barnett, eds., *Studies in American Trade Unionism* (New York, 1970 [1912]), p. 59; Theodore W. Glocker, *The Government of American Trade Unions* (New York, 1971 [1913]), pp. 196, 199, 228, 229; Troxell, "Labor in the Tobacco Industry," p. 141.

7. *Constitution of the Cigar Makers' Union*, 1912, sections 181–82; Troxell, "Labor in the Tobacco Industry," p. 136; Glocker, "Cigar Makers' Union," p. 62; *CMOJ*, Apr. 1903, p. 8; Hourwich, "Cigar Makers' Union History," p. 9.

8. *Constitution of the Cigar Makers' Union*, 1912, sections 175–80, 183–84; "Minutes of Local 208, Kalamazoo, Michigan," 13 Oct. 1913, Western Michigan University Library, Kalamazoo; U.S. Industrial Commission, *Report of the Industrial Commission on the Relations and Conditions of Capital and Labor*, vol. 7 (Washington, D.C., 1901), p. 193; Jacobstein, *Tobacco Industry*, pp. 156–57; Helen Sumner, "The Benefit System of the Cigar Makers' Union," in John R. Commons, ed., *Trade Unionism and Labor Problems* (New York, 1967 [1905]), p. 541. José Santana interview, 29 July 1979 by telephone; *CMOJ*, Apr. 1904, p. 8; May 1906, p. 4; Apr. 1908, p. 6; Jan. 1912, p. 9; Dec. 1915, p. 39; Glocker, *American Trade Unions*, p. 108.

9. Constitution of the Cigar Makers' Union, sections 61–65; *CMOJ*, May 1903, p. 4; May 1907, p. 5; July 1907, p. 9; Jan. 1912, p. 5; Feb. 1912, p. 3; May 1912, pp. 8, 30, 33; Oct. 1912, p. 70; Nov. 1912, p. 11; Jan. 1913, p. 2; W. H. Riley, president, National Stogie Makers' League, *Information Relative to Stogies*, n.d., SHSW; *Tobacco Leaf*, 6 Dec. 1905, p. 18; Perkins to Gompers and vice versa, Oct., Nov., 1909, Reel 6, *American Federation of Labor Records: The Samuel Gompers Era* (Sanford, N.C., 1979).

10. James B. Kennedy, *Beneficiary Features of American Trade Unions* (Baltimore, 1908), pp. 510–13, 568; *CMOJ*, July 1904, p. 5; July 1910, p. 8; July 1912, p. 3; Nov. 1912, p. 2.

11. Sumner, "Benefit System of the Cigar Makers' Union," pp. 528, 530; Kennedy, *Beneficiary Features*, pp. 548, 557, 568, 570; *CMOJ*, Oct. 1890, p. 5; June 1903, p. 6. See also *CMOJ*, Oct. 1877, p. 3.

12. Kennedy, *Beneficiary Features*, p. 583; *CMOJ*, Oct. 1877, p. 3; Jan. 1885, p. 6; July 1901, p. 1; Apr. 1905, p. 3; July 1906, pp. 9–10; Jan. 1910, p. 7; May 1911, p. 4; Sumner, "Benefit System of the Cigar Makers' Union," pp. 530, 532–33, 544; D. P. Smelser, *Unemployment and American Trade Unions* (Baltimore, 1919), p. 130; U.S. Industrial Commission, *Report*, vol. 7, p. 194; Murray W. Latimer, *Trade Union Pension Systems and Other Superannuation and Permanent and Total Disability Benefits in the United States and Canada* (New York, 1932), p. 16. In cases of more general trade depression, locals might set up a special fund to help the unemployed. See Francis Colgan to David Smelser, 21 Feb. 1913, Papers of Local 316, McSherrystown, Pa., Adams County Historical Society (ACHS), Gettysburg.

13. Sumner, "Benefit System of the Cigar Makers' Union," p. 531; "By-Laws," Local 22, Detroit, Mich., p. 16; "By-Laws," Local 192, Manchester, N.H., p. 10.

14. Sumner, "Benefit System of the Cigar Makers' Union," p. 530; *Constitution of the Cigar Makers' Union*, sections 79–93; *CMOJ*, Jan. 1910, p. 10;

Glocker, "Cigar Makers' Union," pp. 61–63; George M. Janes, *The Control of Strikes in American Trade Unions* (Baltimore, 1916), p. 17.

15. *Constitution of the Cigar Makers' Union*, sections 79–93; Ograin to author, 15 Jan. 1979; Janes, *Control of Strikes*, pp. 44, 48, 76–78, 122.

16. *CMOJ*, June 1903, p. 8; Sept. 1903, p. 8; Apr. 1906, p. 8; May 1906, p. 8; Dec. 1906, p. 12; Apr. 1907, p. 1; Mar. 1909, p. 8; Sept. 1912, p. 20; Apr. 1920, p. 6; Janes, *Control of Strikes*, p. 30.

17. *CMOJ*, Feb. 1902, p. 6; Apr. 1902, p. 5; July 1906, p. 4; Aug. 1906, p. 4; Oct. 1906, p. 1; Sept. 1907, p. 1; May 1908, p. 7; Feb. 1909, pp. 4–5; Massachusetts Bureau of Labor Statistics, *Labor and Industrial Chronology* (Boston, 1906), p. 404.

18. *CMOJ*, Apr. 1904, p. 4; Sept. 1910, p. 3; Charles Dickerman, "Cigar Makers' Neurosis," *National Eclectic Medical Association Quarterly*, 10 (Sept. 1918), pp. 62–63.

19. Herman Baust interview, 24 Mar. 1977, North Haven, Conn.; Santana interview 27 Feb. 1977 by telephone; "By-Laws," Local 14, Chicago, Ill., p. 1.

20. *CMOJ*, Mar. 1908, p. 7; *Tobacco Leaf*, 7 Aug. 1907, p. 38; "By-Laws," Local 165, Philadelphia, Pa., p. 22.

21. "Minutes of Local 208," Kalamazoo, Mich., 18 Oct. 1907; 11 May 1908; 13 Feb. 1911; 10 July 1916 (these are only examples since nearly every meeting involved a request for aid); *CMOJ*, Nov. 1901, p. 4; Jan. 1912, p. 5; circular from Local 14, Chicago, Ill., n.d., Cigar Makers International Union of America, Papers of Local 162, Green Bay, Wis., Box 1, folder 1, SHSW.

22. *CMOJ*, June 1885, p. 9; Sept. 1900, p. 7; Mar. 1904, p. 9; Sept. 1904, p. 6; *Tobacco Leaf*, 28 Apr. 1910, p. 28; 9 June 1910, p. 3. Henry Abrahams became secretary in 1885. See *CMOJ*, Jan. 1885, p. 12.

23. *CMOJ*, May 1903, p. 6; June 1903, p. 3; July 1904, p. 2; Feb. 1909, p. 10; Mar. 1909, p. 3.

24. *CMOJ*, Oct. 1885, p. 5; Apr. 1901, p. 6; Aug. 1904, p. 4; July 1905, p. 3; Feb. 1909, p. 10.

25. *CMOJ*, June 1904, p. 4; Aug. 1904, p. 12; June 1906, p. 3; Oct. 1906, p. 9; Feb. 1909, p. 5; July 1910, p. 9; *Tobacco Leaf*, 17 Nov. 1910, p. 14; 30 Apr. 1914, p. 8; Union Due Book, George W. Perkins, 1899–1911, National Museum of American History, Smithsonian Institution, Washington, D.C.; *Financial Statement of the JAB of Cigarmakers' Unions of New York and Vicinity, Relating to the Defense Fund of the Striking and Locked Out Cigarmakers of New York City, 1900–1901*, 1901, USDL; "Minutes of Local 208," Kalamazoo, Mich., 12 Feb. 1912; 22 Mar. 1912. CMIU members voted down a proposal to permit sympathy strikes, however, in 1903. See *Tobacco*, 23 Oct. 1903, p. 6.

26. *CMOJ*, Apr. 1876, p. 2; Francis X. Colgan to George Perkins, 17 Feb. 1913, Papers of Local 316, ACHS.

27. "By-Laws," Local 97, Boston, Mass., pp. 20–21; *CMOJ*, June 1903, p. 3; Oct. 1914, pp. 11–12. The first *CMOJ* mention of draping a charter is Mar. 1876, p. 3.

28. James Durso interview, 24 Mar. 1977, New Haven, Conn.; Baust interview; William Theisen, interview, 17 Aug. 1979.

29. *CMOJ*, Jan. 1879, p. 1; Nov. 1881, p. 4; Dec. 1902, p. 11; Mar. 1904, p. 6; Apr. 1904, p. 6; Nov. 1904, p. 3; Mar. 1905, p. 2; Aug. 1905, p. 10; Aug. 1906, pp. 9–10; Sept. 1906, p. 13; Oct. 1906, p. 3; Nov. 1906, p. 16; May 1911, p. 5; *Cigar Makers' International Union Diamond Jubilee, July 26–28, 1939* (Washington, D.C., 1939), p. 29; *Tobacco Leaf*, 11 June 1902, p. 7; 16 Sept. 1903, p. 34; "Minutes of Local 208," Kalamazoo, Mich., 8 July 1907.

30. Norman Eliason, "The Language of the 'Buckeye,'" *American Speech*, 12 (Dec. 1937), 272; Ograin, interview, 19 May 1979; Santana, interview, 13 Aug. 1976; 22 July 1979 by telephone.

31. A. M. Simons, "A Label and Lives—The Story of the Cigar Makers," *Pearson's Magazine*, Jan. 1917, p. 70; *Tobacco*, 30 Mar. 1900, p. 5; 1 Nov. 1906, p. 4; *U.S. Tobacco Journal*, 3 Feb. 1906, p. 5; *Tobacco Leaf*, 24 Sept. 1908, p. 38; *Cigar Makers' Union Diamond Jubilee*, p. 17; *CMOJ*, Mar. 1905, p. 4.

32. *CMOJ*, May 1903, p. 7; *Constitution of the Cigar Makers' Union*, 1912, section 221; *Tobacco Leaf*, 27 May 1903, p. 22; 30 Mar. 1911, p. 15; Baust interview; Theisen interview; "Minutes of Local 208," Kalamazoo, Mich., 13 Nov. 1909; 11 May 1914; 10 May 1915.

33. U.S. Bureau of Corporations, Tobacco Investigation, file 3073, Record Group (R.G.) 122, National Archives (NA), Washington, D.C.; *Tobacco*, 11 July 1902, p. 1; U.S. Bureau of Corporations, *Report of the Commissioner of Corporations in the Tobacco Industry*, part I, *Position of the Tobacco Combination in the Industry* (Washington, D.C., 1909), pp. 88, 313–15; David Goldstein, *The Tobacco Trust as Related to Cigar Stores: A Reply to Louis K. Liggett* (Boston, [1909?]), pp. 1–13.

34. *CMOJ*, Sept. 1892, 4; Mar. 1894, p. 11; Apr. 1894, p. 7; May 1894, p. 10; June 1894, p. 7; Nov. 1894, p. 9; Feb. 1903, p. 6; Mar. 1903, p. 2; Feb. 1904, p. 6; Mar. 1904, pp. 4, 9; Apr. 1904, pp. 18, 32; July 1906, pp. 9–10; Apr. 1917, p. 68; *Denver Times*, 30 Dec. 1900; *Tobacco Leaf*, 17 Jan. 1900, p. 14; 4 June 1902, p. 32; *Tobacco*, 14 Nov. 1906, p. 3; 16 Apr. 1914, p. 56; Blue Label League of Indiana, *Official Proceedings of the Meetings of the Provisional Organization and the First and Second Conventions, 1909, 1910*, 1910, USDL.

35. Ograin interview, 17 May 1980; Shea interview; Baust interview; *CMOJ*, Mar. 1912, p. 6.

36. U.S. Industrial Commission, *Report*, vol. 7, p. 168.

37. *Constitution of the Cigar Makers' Union*, 1912, pp. 59–60; "By-Laws," Local 22, Detroit, Mich., pp. 20–21; *CMOJ*, June 1901, p. 5; Nov. 1914, p. 22; Dec. 1906, p. 1. Fines over five dollars were printed in the *CMOJ* each month.

38. *CMOJ*, July 1900, p. 1; "By-Laws," Local 192, Manchester, N.H., p. 7; "By-Laws," Local 97, Boston, Mass., p. 17; "By-Laws and Rules of Order of Cigar Makers' Benevolent Union No. 17," Cleveland, Ohio, n.d., p. 6, SHSW; "By-Laws," Local 2, Buffalo, N.Y., p. 24.

39. *Constitution of the Cigar Makers' Union*, section 67; Ograin interview, 17 May 1980; *CMOJ*, Nov. 1883, p. 6; Oct. 1911, p. 15; Glocker, "Cigar Makers' Union," pp. 65–66.

40. *CMOJ*, Jan. 1900, p. 1; Feb. 1904, p. 2; July 1906, p. 17; Aug. 1911, p. 4; Dec. 1912, p. 32; June 1914, p. 22; "By-Laws," Local 165, Philadelphia, Pa., p. 26.

41. *CMOJ*, June 1905, p. 3; June 1911, p. 2; Ograin interview, 17 May 1980 and 19 May 1979.

42. "By-Laws," Local 192, Manchester, N.H., p. 7; *CMOJ*, Jan. 1900, p. 1; Nov. 1907, pp. 1–3; Nov. 1914, p. 22; July 1915, p. 23; Apr. 1916, p. 48.

43. *CMOJ*, June 1878, p. 4; July 1900, p. 7; May 1903, p. 7; Mar. 1904, p. 2; Nov. 1904, p. 2; Mar. 1907, p. 9.

44. *CMOJ*, Feb. 1902, p. 4; Jan. 1907, p. 6; June 1907, p. 17. See also Nov. 1909, p. 6.

45. *CMOJ*, Sept. 1913, p. 9.

46. *CMOJ*, Mar. 1906, p. 1; Aug. 1906, pp. 1, 2; Apr. 1910, p. 1; Sept. 1914, p. 20.

47. *CMOJ*, Sept. 1901, p. 3; Nov. 1901, p. 3; Jan. 1904, p. 5; May 1906, p. 4; Jan. 1908, pp. 4–5; May 1908, p. 6.

48. Papers of Local 162, Green Bay, Wis., Box 1, folder 1, SHSW; *CMOJ*, Nov. 1901, p. 4; Jan. 1912, p. 5.

49. *CMOJ*, June 1900, p. 6; Oct. 1901, p. 4; Dec. 1901, p. 8; Jan. 1903, p. 4; June 1903, p. 4; Feb. 1913, p. 23; Ograin interview, 19 May 1979. Gallaud had been trying to organize in New Orleans for years. See *CMOJ*, Sept. 1884, p. 4.

50. *CMOJ*, July 1910, pp. 2–3.

51. Ann Schofield, "The Rise of the Pig-Headed Girl: An Analysis of the American Labor Press for Their Attitudes towards Women, 1877–1920" (Ph.D. dissertation, State University of New York at Binghamton, 1980), pp. 54–60; *CMOJ*, Aug. 1907, p. 9; *Constitution of the Cigar Makers' Union*, 1912, section 61; *Tobacco Leaf*, 30 Apr. 1902, p. 26; *CMOJ*, Apr. 1903, p. 5; May 1906, p. 9; Nov. 1906, p. 9; Apr. 1911, p. 2; May 1911, p. 4; June 1911, p. 3; Mar. 1913, p. 2; "List of Shops and Bill of Prices under the Jurisdiction of Union 97, C.M.I.U.," Boston, Mass., 1904, p. 12, U.S. Bureau of Corporations, Tobacco Investigation, file 3073, R.G. 122, NA. In 1875 when the CMIU constitution was changed to prohibit discrimination against a cigar maker because of sex or system of working, the Baltimore and Cincinnati locals withdrew from the union for several years in protest.

52. Ograin interview, 11 Aug. 1976, 17 May 1980, and letter to author 29 Jan. 1976; *CMOJ*, Mar. 1903, p. 4; Apr. 1903, p. 5. Ograin believed that the cigar makers had been "victims of pride. . . . We were a proud group and our pride proved to be our weakness." (Ograin to author, 29 Jan. 1976.)

53. Santana, interview, 27 Feb. 1977 by telephone; 6–11 July 1977; 17 May 1979; *CMOJ*, Apr. 1903, p. 5.

54. R. A. Brown to Hugh Kerwin, 3 July 1926, file 170/3524, R.G. 280, Federal Mediation and Conciliation Service (FMCS), NA; George Pozzetta, "Italians and the Tampa General Strike of 1910," in George Pozzetta, ed., *Pane e Lavoro: The Italian American Working Class* (Toronto, 1980), pp. 32–33, 43 n. 15.

55. *CMOJ*, Oct. 1897, p. 6; Dec. 1897, p. 4; Sept. 1903, p. 2; June 1903, p. 4; Nov. 1903, p. 4; Apr. 1903, p. 5; May 1905, pp. 6–7; Sept. 1906, pp. 12–13; Oct. 1906, p. 3; May 1907, pp. 4–5; July 1907, p. 3; May 1908, p. 3; Jan. 1910, p. 6; Dec. 1912, p. 25; May 1911, p. 4; Feb. 1913, p. 23. On the nineteenth century see, for example: *CMOJ*, Dec. 1877, p. 2; Oct. 1880, p. 2; Feb. 1881, p. 1; Mar.

1881, p. 1; Mar. 1882, p. 4; Sept. 1882, p. 4; Jan. 1886, p. 8; Mar. 1894, p. 6.

56. *Tobacco*, 17 Apr. 1903, p. 6; Schofield, "Rise of the Pig-Headed Girl," pp. 55–60; *CMOJ*, Sept. 1910, p. 2; Oct. 1910, p. 8; "By-Laws and Rules of Order of the Cigar Makers' Union No. 25, Milwaukee, Wis., SHSW, p. 10. Three useful but conflicting interpretations of why male unionists have an interest in excluding women workers can be found in: Ruth Milkman, "Organizing the Sexual Division of Labor: Historical Perspectives on 'Women's Work' and the American Labor Movement," *Socialist Review*, 49 (1980), 95–150; Heidi Hartmann, "Capitalism, Patriarchy, and Job Segregation by Sex," *Signs,* 1 (Spring 1976 supplement), 137–40; Alice Kessler-Harris, "Where Are the Organized Women Workers?" *Feminist Studies*, 3 (Fall 1975), 92–109. See also Schofield, "Rise of the Pig-Headed Girl."

57. *CMOJ*, Jan. 1908, p. 3; Feb. 1908, pp. 3, 4. See also Nov. 1877, p. 2; Dec. 1877, p. 4; Jan. 1908, p. 3; Feb. 1908, pp. 3.

58. R. A. Brown to Hugh Herwin, file 170, 3524, R.G. 280, FMCS, NA. *CMOJ*, May 1912, p. 7; Oct. 1912, p. 12; Nov. 1912, p. 3; Dec. 1912, p. 14; Jan. 1913, p. 2; Feb. 1913, p. 2; May 1914, pp. 5–6. See for contrast Perkins's view in 1905 (*CMOJ*, Jan. 1905, p. 9).

59. *CMOJ*, Oct. 1915, p. 23; Apr. 1920, p. 14; Ograin interview, 8 July 1977 and 17 May 1980.

60. Milkman, "Organizing the Sexual Division of Labor," p. 95; Santana interview, 11 Jan. 1976 by telephone.

61. See John F. Runcie, "Occupational Communication as Boundary Mechanism," *Sociology of Work and Occupations*, 1 (Nov. 1974), 419–41.

5

The Battle in the Workplace

Cigar makers' work culture revealed their pride, their sense of mutuality, loyalty, and brotherhood, and their concern for control over their lives and work. It also expressed a clear recognition that their interests and those of employers' were inherently different and antagonistic. They resisted employer policies on the shop floor through unspoken practices and formal work rules backed up by a reputation for labor militancy. Both sides recognized the combative nature of this relationship. In 1903 a leading industry trade journal, *Tobacco Leaf,* angrily declared that union cigar makers regarded "employment as a battle, and the employer as the enemy." Yet this ideology did not necessarily lead cigar makers to a more revolutionary political consciousness. The daily struggle on the shop floor had provided the setting in which they created a powerful oppositional work culture, but it was a culture containing contradictions and limitations. The grafting of more deliberate and conscious political ideas onto this culture, hindered in part by the history of the ideas themselves, interpersonal wrangling over issues of power, craft defensiveness in the face of deteriorating conditions, and the consequences of the dominant gender ideology, would have to wait for another day. The strengths and weaknesses of cigar makers' work culture together with the power and objectives of manufacturers formed the fundamental outlines of the battle in the workplace in the cigar industry.[1]

Cigar makers enforced a set of ethical principles which required members to maintain an assertive distance from those who employed them. In relations with the "bosses," there could be no doubt on which side the cigar maker stood. Associations with employers had to be free of obligation and could suggest no hint of collaboration. In some locals, cigar makers prohibited a shop owner from working in his shop, and most locals forbade members from renting property or housing from employers. Manufacturers complained that cigar makers would not perform errands or undertake any activity other than making cigars. They also "refused to make concessions or sacrifices in order for a manufacturer to secure a larger contract." Union rules forbade borrowing money from anyone with a manufacturer's license, selling cigars for a manufacturer, or in any way acting as the agent of one. In early 1908, members of Local 208 in Kalamazoo, Michigan, filed charges against a member for "being on too intimate terms with the proprietor."[2] One cigar maker in Connecticut came under fire for appearing in public with his foreman. Any separate dealings or efforts to curry favor with bosses were known as "dark lantern methods" and were harshly censured by the work group.[3]

Members were expected to assert their pride, self-respect, and dignity by maintaining a "manly" demeanor before employers.[4] Cigar makers paid special attention to their clothes not only because they were proud of their position as craftsmen, but as a demonstration of their fundamental human equality with employers. John Ograin remembered that very often cigar makers dressed most fastidiously on payday.[5] At times, rank-and-file members took these ethical principles more seriously than did union leaders. In the 1906 strike in Boston for a wage increase, members of Local 97 angrily denounced the intervention of arbitrator Adolph Strasser, whom the CMIU executive board had dispatched to the scene. Not only had Strasser undermined cigar makers' authority in their own strike, he had, they charged, violated the code of manhood with regard to the bosses. He had taken the initiative and had requested a conference with manufacturers—a move cigar makers described as "humiliating."[6] The manly course required that manufacturers ask first.

Even George Perkins noted that each trade had its own moral code: "It defines violations of the trade rules and provides punishment for offenders. Carpenters call 'lumping' an offense; cigar makers denounce some men as 'suckers,' and so along the whole line." The term had originated in the nineteenth century for it appeared in the German *Social Demokrat* in New York in 1875 and soon after in the *CMOJ*. A sucker was someone who "sucked up" to the boss, who did "things for the boss that wasn't called for," noted John Ograin. "There were little things on the job you could do to please the boss, like cleaning up" at the end of the day. Instead, "we put on our coat and hat and got out." Cigar makers had a reputation for embracing newcomers who made a show of antipathy toward manufacturers, frequently electing them to local office without any knowledge of their backgrounds. This same spirit also influenced their view of team work. They opposed it in part because it served manufacturers' interests, not their own.[7]

Cigar makers also insisted on certain rules of decorum with regard to the evaluation of their work. In Chicago, José Santana remembered the foreman walking through the shop randomly examining the work of the men. If someone's cigars fell short of the standard, he could not go and speak directly to that cigar maker. Shop custom required him to present the matter to the shop collector, who in turn spoke to the cigar maker in question, and the latter had to have a fair chance to improve his work. Elsewhere, although a foreman might speak directly to the cigar maker, he did so carefully. Herman Baust, working in New Haven, exploded when a foreman yelled at him about his work after he had been in the shop only a few days. "I got up. I says, 'Frank, you don't yell at me. I can make my living. . . .' The shop was quiet. I says 'If I don't make it right, you show me, then if I don't prove it, then you can fire me. But you can't stand there and make a monkey out of me in front of the cigar makers.'" Baust had proved himself to his new shop mates: he was no sucker.[8]

Relations with a foreman could be pleasant and convivial, but cigar makers quickly reacted to any affront or insult. From Frank Shea's perspective in the Sullivan factory in Manchester, a foreman had to "walk a tightrope" in the factory to avoid offending the men. He had initially encountered resistance from the cigar makers when he became a foreman because he had not spent much time at the bench. "They thought I was too young to be going around telling them how to make cigars when I didn't know how to make them myself." In another case, a cigar maker explained that he had quit his job "because I would allow no boss or foreman to question my principle." In a strike in Philadelphia in 1900, cigar makers demanded not only the firing of the foreman, but also the right to hire a new one. The manufacturer consented to their wage demand but rejected the foreman issue. "Why, I might as well let them come in and run my business as to let them name my foreman," he retorted.[9]

Cigar makers strictly enforced their code of behavior vis-à-vis manufacturers but were sometimes less than vigilant among themselves. Frank Shea had been very careful to speak softly when he approached any of the men about their work, so much so that the other cigar makers jokingly complained that they had to strain to overhear what he said. While they resented abusive behavior, their pride in workmanship and speed made them naturally curious and even competitive regarding each other's performance and abilities. José Santana recalled that at times traveling members did write ahead about jobs in spite of union rules prohibiting the practice. In Chicago, John Ograin related, cigar makers informally agreed to work a little longer than eight hours in some shops, without fear of reprisal. Even in Boston, shop collectors at times looked the other way while a man made a few cigars during lunch. In 1900, a Connecticut manufacturer insisted that his union workers obey their own eight-hour rule; they struck and demanded a dollar more in wages for every thousand cigars. The manufacturer, unwilling to risk a long walkout, agreed. The lesson the cigar makers intended was that cigar makers, not manufacturers, set the rules.[10]

Motives of manufacturers were always suspect. After a Boston manufacturer installed metal lockers to replace the nails where the men had been hanging their coats, cigar makers walked out not because they disliked lockers but because they had not been consulted about the change. In debates during these years about the best way to organize nonunion workers, particularly in Pennsylvania, some members suggested that a massive "label agitation" campaign would encourage manufacturers to unionize their shops in order to get the label to help sell their products. Others stridently opposed using the label in this way. Explained one opponent, "I don't look with favor on a union that comes into being because of the boss."[11]

Despite the strength of oppositional values, there were many points of ambiguity and contradiction. An older cigar maker associated with a particular manufacturer over many years might feel a dual loyalty, for example. Because of their pride in speed and workmanship, they accorded fast, accurate workers prestige in their ranks. The best workers in some union factories won the right to make the highest-paying, most expensive cigars. Such values not only created hierarchy in their ranks, but also served the interests of employers. Another disjunction, one which they confronted more openly, was the position of buckeyes within the CMIU. In the mid-nineteenth century, most cigar makers had been independent proprietors or journeymen who expected to become such, and the CMIU had originally formed when this independence seemed under attack. By the 1880s, however, CMIU members had begun to see small producers as a problem in terms of competition. In the twentieth century, the debate related to buckeyes' anomalous position as both members and manufacturers. In some small towns, buckeyes comprised a sizable segment of the local. Although they could be members only if they were not employers, their class position was ambiguous. Reflecting this concern, CMIU members voted in 1906 to support an amendment offered by Boston's Local 97 to bar buckeye manufacturers from holding local union office.[12]

Makers refused to spend their own time walking up to get more tobacco when they ran out and insisted that it be brought to them instead. "And were they fussy," commented Shea, regarding his experience as a stock boy. They wanted the tobacco prepared and deposited well before they actually needed it. Indeed, the cigar makers disapproved of performing any work in the boss's service which went uncompensated. For every extra quarter inch on a cigar, any additional time required to make a special shape, any requirement about using all the scraps on the table, or the distraction of working in a show window, the manufacturer would have to pay incrementally more money. Union rules also forbade cigar makers from taking back any cigars they had made and rerolling them, unless the manufacturers paid for the extra work. A foreman could warn a cigar maker about his work, but could not require him to give up his time to perform the work over again.[13]

The bill of prices demonstrated that cigar makers also recognized the relationship of their wages to the selling price of the cigars and felt entitled to a fair share of profits. As part of their general concern with controlling the conditions of work, cigar makers insisted on a role in determining wages and a local committee meticulously constructed the bill "according to the price that the manufacturer was selling the cigar. . . . All was related to the selling price," Santana explained. By this cigar makers meant the price per thousand cigars to the wholesaler or dealer, since the prices for single cigars were fairly rigidly set at five cents, ten cents, and so on. They were also aware that their most expensive cigars would be purchased by those who had the money to pay more. In Chicago in 1904, cigar makers walked out of the W. D. Algeo factory in June demanding a wage increase. Their rallying cry illustrated the point: "Candidates for Governor can afford to pay well for their campaign cigars. Let us strike for higher wages." As the industry was expanding in the early twentieth century, manufacturers enjoyed discussing their success, but one observer warned them in *Tobacco Leaf* that bragging about profits had a bad effect and certainly would not contribute to making cigar makers any more satisfied with their position.[14]

Frank Shea recalled that the cigar makers "always talked about privileges." As a foreman he wondered whether a privilege was "something somebody gives you or is it something you take and then claim as a privilege? That's what the cigar makers did." Indeed, unionists felt a strong sense of entitlement with regard to shop practices and rules, which was illustrated well in the case of their smokers. The custom of taking home three cigars at the end of the day and six on Saturday was regarded as a "personal right" and constituted nothing less than "unwritten law" in all union shops, in Tampa factories, and even in scattered plants elsewhere. While the origins of the custom were unclear, workers and manufacturers alike claimed it had characterized the industry from the start in the U.S. and had possibly originated in Cuba. "We took our smokers and that's all there was to it," declared John Ograin. Each man made his own, sometimes using scraps and extra leaves from his table in the process. Most union factories allowed three, but in Boston cigar makers got four smokers a day. In some cases, cigar makers took more than the standard amount, but in keeping with their collectivist approach and perhaps in recognition that gross abuse might spell the end of the practice, they disapproved of any one person taking too many. Size, however, was another matter. At the R. G. Sullivan factory cigar makers rolled giant smokers, "a good, big, long smoke. Everybody used to want to get a cigar maker's smoke," explained Shea.[15] Cigar makers counted the "acknowledged right" to roll smokers for their own use as part of their "compensation." Thus technically cigar makers could only roll smokers in the course of the working day. However, Shea remembered that in Manchester some men tried to claim their smokers even when they had not been working. They came in "and if their stick was still lit [their tobacco was still workable], they'd sit down while they're in and make some smokes and take them and go back out again."[16]

Manufacturers offered little resistance to the free smoker custom, despite the losses of expensive tobacco that resulted. They stood to gain somewhat from the custom since a cigar maker who smoked his own cigars would thereby test the tobacco quality and also discover any flaws in his own work. More important, manufacturers were unwilling to risk the consequences of tampering with this tradition. If Roger Sullivan had tried to ban smokers, reasoned Shea, "well, then you'd have a strike. Oh boy, they'd have raised up hang." Herman Baust noted that in New Haven a strike might not have been necessary if smokers had been threatened. "It would be no good taking them away because the cigar makers would make them and stick it in their pocket."[17]

In 1908 when the editors of *Tobacco Leaf* launched a campaign to do away with smokers (they had also done so back in 1878), pronouncing the practice an "intolerable abuse," few manufacturers joined in the crusade. Soon the journal gave up the effort, but chided manufacturers: "The truth of the matter is that the manufacturers are afraid to do what they have a right to do, and what the principle of self-preservation urges them to do, namely to discontinue the practice of furnishing gratuitously the 'smokes' of their employees. They dread having trouble with the workers," and feared a "general revolt."[18]

There the matter rested until late 1911 when Commissioner of Internal Revenue Royal E. Cabell ruled that smokers would have to be taxed just as any cigar in the factory. Either the cigar makers or the manufacturers would have to pay. Recognizing the turmoil about to ensue, both groups joined in petitioning Congress for legislation to lift the tax on smokers. In the meantime, cigar makers in scores of locals angrily protested the ruling, striking in several cities. An observer complained that the ruling had "disturbed the relations of employers and employees in the entire industry." Many manufacturers simply ignored the ruling and hoped to avoid any trouble. In Manchester, R. G. Sullivan immediately began handing out three cigars to each cigar maker in the late afternoon and paid the tax himself. This procedure did not satisfy the cigar makers, however, because they each wanted to roll their own. "They'd look at their little bits of things," noted Shea, and shake their heads. Gradually they stopped taking the ones the company handed out and continued rolling their own as before. Sullivan then calculated and paid tax for three cigars for every cigar maker and sent Shea and several others circling the factory daily to count the number of cigar makers present.[19]

At congressional hearings, representatives of all parts of the industry explained the hopelessness of trying to regulate such a deeply held tradition. "The men look upon it as a right, established by long custom, and they will not be deprived of it," noted the bill's sponsor. A number of CMIU members testified, including Henry Abrahams of Boston, who asked Congress not to "take from us that which we have always possessed and which our Government does not need." He was affronted by the ruling's implication that cigar makers would steal tobacco or cigars from employers. Sol Suntheimer, a cigar maker from Connecticut, pointed out to the committee that cigar makers "cultivate the idea of honesty" among newcomers. Manufacturer Charles Soby counseled that "the question of free smokers to cigar makers is as old as the trade; and while manufacturers could wish the men would not smoke their good tobacco, I fear any attempt to stop the custom will not only make friction, but will not stop the practice." In Tampa, smokers were used as currency and a representative from the Tampa industry warned that cigar makers considered smokers a "gratuity." Any move to withhold them would only result in "discord and strikes." Cabell's ruling was dropped. No smokers would be taxed.[20]

Work culture on the shop floor stressed the importance of the group and their collective position vis-à-vis manufacturers. Rather than permit layoffs of individuals when orders fell off, cigar makers' rules stipulated that manufacturers place all members on a "limit" of weekly production and refrain from hiring any new workers until business picked up again and the limit was lifted. In these cases custom required younger, single members to travel elsewhere to create more work for those left behind. When not enough prepared tobacco was available, cigar makers stipulated that "none shall work until all can." To maintain their united position against manufacturers, cigar makers could not risk undercutting each other. Stiff punishments awaited anyone who attempted to have another member discharged, or who worked below the bill of prices. Boston cigar makers considered it inappropriate for an individual cigar maker to inquire privately of a manufacturer why he had been dismissed. All such matters would be handled by the group.[21]

While manufacturers did not care about the hours a cigar maker worked or even his daily production, they generally kept records on each cigar maker's output in relation to the amount of tobacco he used. Employers insisted on weighing tobacco not only to discourage pilfering, but to pressure cigar makers into "working economically" and conserving the tobacco. Specific practices varied. Some weighed all tobaccos, while others weighed only filler or wrapper. Stock boys kept track of each cigar maker's request for tobacco, usually by punching the amount on a card. In Manchester at the Sullivan factory, there was a room with a wooden rack covering one wall located just off the main cigar-making floor. In slots on the rack were cards for each cigar maker, containing a daily record of the tobacco given him. In smaller factories, the record-keeping procedure was simpler.[22]

Manufacturers particularly watched the use of wrapper tobacco because of its delicate nature and high cost. To hold down expenses, manufacturers' interests were best served when cigar makers struggled to get several wrappers or "cuts" out of each half of wrapper leaf. In Denver, the Solis factory went so far as to sort the wrapper leaves and prepare them into pads according to quality. Each was marked "'three cut,' 'two cut,'

[or] 'one cut.' If your bundle was a 'three cut,' you were supposed to get enough out of that one leaf to make three cigars and if you didn't you were short," explained William Theisen. Getting the desired number of cuts depended on the quality of the tobacco—whether it was torn or had holes in it. "The one cuts were terrible. They were really bad . . . every time somebody went up there, [they said] 'Boy, I sure hope I don't get a one cut.'" Usually, wrappers of varying quality were mixed together in the pads cigar makers received, and they were expected to average so many cigars per pad.[23]

For cigar makers caught short, no real punishment was forthcoming. Union rules prohibited manufacturers from fining cigar makers, and attempts to try it resulted in strikes, but cigar makers could not stop a manufacturer from firing someone who consistently used too much tobacco. They also did not have the power to stop the weighing altogether but they did strike if manufacturers tried to extend the practice to filler or binder leaves. In 1908, New Haven cigar makers lost a fight to stop such extension of weighing, but they succeeded in instituting the "average" plan. Cigar makers averaged together everyone's production and the total use of tobacco, but refused to permit an "individual account" of stock used. In 1913, New Haven's sixty-eight manufacturers locked out their five hundred cigar makers to end the average plan. The strike resulted in a compromise with individual weighing permitted but with liberal allowances of tobacco. In most cases the latter worked as the best formal resolution of the question. Where quotas on usage were liberal, as in St. Louis, most cigar makers encountered few difficulties. In Kalamazoo, cigar makers could exchange poor tobacco for good, but in 1908 asked for more generous allotments instead.[24]

Since overt attempts to resist and control weighing were not always fruitful, cigar makers devised covert approaches. In Manchester, for example, Roger Sullivan personally reviewed the cigar makers' cards each week. Every day he asked the foremen and stock boys to bring him a few of the cards to inspect. Cigar makers who were having trouble getting enough cuts from a leaf at times resorted to bribing a foreman to make sure their cards never reached Sullivan. Shea recalled that the cigar makers would pay such a foreman weekly to "pass them over." "If they weren't good, he didn't say anything and if they weren't good cutters he'd take care of them." Shea never felt tempted, especially since Sullivan fired anyone he suspected of the practice.[25]

Collectively, cigar makers could resist in several ways. If someone con-

sistently proved too eager to get the maximum number of cuts, his fellow
workers might call him down. Shea recalled that once a cigar maker from
Lancaster, Pennsylvania, where few of the factories were unionized, arrived in Manchester and went to work for Sullivan. He began working the
same way that he had in Pennsylvania, and was getting three cuts out of a
side of wrapper. After a while the other cigar makers stopped him: "Hey,
what are you trying to do, queer it, crab it for us?" The puzzled newcomer
asked what they meant, and his shop mates replied: "Look at all you're
getting out of your wrappers. They'll want to know why we can't, see?
Only two cuts instead of three." In Boston, cigar makers attempted to
protect each other by masking each person's use of tobacco, an informal
version of what New Haven cigar makers institutionalized. One manufacturer complained in 1905 that his wrappers were not "worked closely. . . .
When two or three poor ones failed to get the proper number of wrappers
out of material given, the entire force calls for more leaf thereby shielding
the deficient." In Denver in 1902, the Cuban Cigar Company announced
that it would allow only six ounces of binder for every one hundred cigars.
Cigar makers discussed the provision and demanded seven. The company
agreed but stipulated that on Saturday all unused stock would be returned. When the stock came back, the company recorded the exact
amount each man returned. The cigar makers did not appreciate the affront and "without notice" took control of the next Saturday's collection.
They pooled all unused tobacco in the hands of a shop committee which
turned it over to a foreman.[26]

Inside the workplace, cigar makers waged an ongoing fight and pressed
whatever openings they saw to advance their own position. However,
they recognized the boundaries of their power. Their work culture force-
fully challenged manufacturers' authority on the shop floor and preserved
craft traditions, but cigar makers operated within significant constraints.
"No matter what," maintained José Santana, "they are always bosses."
Working for someone else meant that one was subject to his direction, Santana continued. "I hate humiliation to the boss." There were few alter-
natives to this fundamental relationship, especially when one had other
responsibilities. "You have to think of your family first," he explained.[27]

The buckeye offered one avenue of escape, but opening one's own shop
was no road to social mobility. Often cigar makers went into business for
themselves when their fortunes were lowest. A leaf dealer in Syracuse,
New York, pointed out that every time a cigar maker there lost his job, he
"starts up a little shop of his own." Buckeyes worked long hours and risked

much to make only a little more than before. They needed cash for rent, tobacco boxes, and revenue stamps. Tobacco was expensive because of the small lots in which they had to buy it. If a buckeye used the saloon as a retail outlet, he had difficulty paying his bills because saloonkeepers notoriously pressured him into patronizing the bar in return for the privilege of selling there. His dependence on the saloon meant that he stood to lose the entire business if the town voted to go dry. Opening a buckeye offered independence from employers, but it usually did not release cigar makers from the worries of their precarious economic position. Most would have to resign themselves to wage work.[28]

Many forces were beyond their control. Illness, disability, or unemployment could throw cigar makers out of work, and union benefits and aid were not always enough to carry them through such emergencies. Competition from nonunion cigars, especially the steadily improving five-cent smoke, and from cheaper imports from the Philippines and Puerto Rico undermined the position of cigar makers in several areas. Wage differentials among locals even threw members into competition with each other. In addition, not all members enjoyed the same advantages and degree of power in the shop-floor battle with manufacturers. In areas where successful nonunion factories abounded, as in New York or Philadelphia, members were "forced to make many concessions" to union manufacturers. Although a vast majority of the union's members worked in label factories, some did not, particularly those in Pennsylvania.[29]

Cigar makers conceded manufacturers the right to fire anyone for genuinely poor workmanship, but they realized they could not insure that members would be fired solely for that reason. In some locals, secretaries could lose their jobs if travelers interrupted their work too frequently, so they asked those needing loans to wait until after closing. Since they could not control dismissals, cigar makers tried to establish some restrictions. They insisted that members be discharged with dignity and respect. In Racine, Wisconsin, cigar makers could not be fired on Monday, while elsewhere the day might be Saturday. If a member were fired for union activity or if a firm fired a large number of men at once, cigar makers might feel they had no choice but to strike. In 1907 when one Boston manufacturer hired and fired several cigar makers in rapid succession, the local declared the shop "off limits"—a virtual strike—and quickly resolved the problem.[30]

Each side calculated and weighed its strengths and weaknesses in a balance. For cigar makers, striking was without question their most important weapon, and union strike restrictions did not inhibit members from withholding their labor. As an expression of their manhood and a bold assertion of their rights, cigar makers reacted quickly against affronts or unjust policies by walking out in short spontaneous protests, called shop strikes, for which they were well known. These walkouts usually lasted only a day or an afternoon, but cigar makers used them to express their collective displeasure and demand the immediate attention of employers. "If anything was wrong, they'd get up," Herman Baust explained. "All out. We're out. Grievance." Socialist editor Algie Simons concurred. If the cigar makers got angry, "they went home." [31] The causes varied. Poor stock slowed production and insulted the craftsman, and a change in company policy could provoke a contest. Frequently shop strikes erupted when a foreman overstepped his bounds. Frank Shea noted that Roger Sullivan had once hired his brother as a foreman, but "he was so strict, the men struck him out. . . . Now mind you that's his own brother." [32]

Although shop strikes were by far the most common form of protest, cigar makers engaged in many official strikes as well. Between September 1, 1901, and August 1, 1912, CMIU members approved 1,010 strike applications and disapproved only 41. Thirty-six percent of these strikes were for an increase in wages, 17 percent against a wage cut, 12 percent against "victimization of members," which included unfair dismissal, 7 percent against violation of apprentice laws, and 25 percent for "other causes" such as "poor heating and ventilating" or against the team system. From 1912 through early 1920, cigar makers approved 938 strikes and disapproved 22. Fifty-seven percent included a demand for increased wages, another 12 percent related to wage reductions, and others pertained to apprentice laws, victimization, lockouts, union rules, and the organization of packers. Nine were sympathy strikes. With few exceptions, during these years cigar makers had a remarkable record of winning their strikes or at the very least achieving a favorable compromise. [33]

Cigar makers followed an unwritten procedure when striking. If they walked out and stayed out for several days, tobacco left at work benches would be ruined, an indirect form of sabotage. In strikes they expected to last longer than an afternoon, cigar makers traditionally "worked up" their remaining tobacco before walking out. Ograin explained that cigar makers felt that decreasing the animosity would "probably create a little good will." Such courtesy may have reflected a respect for employers' property, another possible internal contradiction. [34]

The threat to withhold labor had the most impact when cigar manufacturers stood to lose the most money. When inventory was low and companies had many orders on hand, for example, cigar makers found themselves in a strategically more favorable position, more so than after Christmas when orders were slack. In Cleveland in 1902, cigar makers demanded wage increases of from fifty cents to one dollar on the bill, and they struck when manufacturers refused to grant them. Employers offered a compromise because business was brisk and in such a competitive industry they could not endure a strike for long without losing customers. But the cigar makers rejected this offer and within three weeks had won a complete victory.[35]

Strikes involved costly delays for manufacturers, both during the strike and afterwards in the time needed to get a full force back at work once it had ended. Trade journals sometimes mentioned manufacturers who gave in to wage demands in order to avoid strikes and the attendant delays. *Tobacco* speculated that in a Pawtucket, Rhode Island, wage dispute the manufacturers would agree to the one-dollar increase "as the easiest way out of the difficulty." Manufacturers' fearfulness and the pressure to settle without a strike in one case aided rank-and-file members in their efforts to retain local autonomy. In 1903, cigar makers in St. Louis at the F. R. Rice and the Jacob Lampert companies demanded an increase in many of the bill's prices, which was granted. Then the cigar makers demanded one dollar more for single binder and both firms appealed to Perkins, who supported their position. Still the cigar makers reiterated their intention to strike and to avoid "trouble" Rice and Lampert conceded the dollar.[36]

Union cigar makers' reputation for striking was surpassed only by that of Tampa cigar makers. Tobacco journals reported frequent shop strikes and brief walkouts to protest some slight or another and manufacturers complained of the tyranny of workers who, they charged, wanted to control the factories and dictate terms to manufacturers. Tampa workers had forestalled the weighing of tobacco far longer than unionists, and because of the high-grade cigars they made, successfully kept molds out of Tampa until the early twentieth century, when several new five-cent firms moved there. Their militancy did not translate into either permanent or egalitarian labor organizations, however. Resistencia had admitted all factory operatives and subsequent Tampa organizations would continue to do so, but rigid hierarchies of workers were observed despite this gesture toward industrial unionism. After the demise of Resistencia in 1901, workers maintained no labor organization, although some continued to belong to the CMIU.[37]

An extensive and well-publicized organizing campaign in 1909, however, enrolled over six thousand Tampa workers in five unions. In June 1910, cigar makers began a general strike of about twelve thousand workers after a number of selectors had been fired and manufacturers had violated the unofficial wage agreement, the *cartabon*. They demanded wage increases and a closed shop. Manufacturers refused the latter because it would make conditions "so intolerable and unsatisfactory that we could not operate at a living profit." Marked by violence, vigilante action on the part of Tampa's Anglo elite, and the importation of strikebreakers from Havana, the strike was ultimately defeated in January 1911. The loss came as a blow to the International, which had hoped at long last to organize the trade there and which had spent an estimated $100,000 to support the effort. Relations between workers and the union cooled, although they were not as bitter as in the aftermath of the 1901 strike. Perkins clearly viewed Tampa union leaders as radicals and denounced a new union formed in March of 1911. CMIU membership in Tampa fell to 2,230 by 1913. While Tampa strikers never won their big strikes after 1899, they conducted some of the most turbulent and widely publicized of any in the industry.[38]

Union cigar makers had some advantages because of their skills and the relative shortage of such expert labor. Throughout most of the first two decades of the century, manufacturers outside of Tampa making goods priced from ten cents on up needed the workmanship that the CMIU provided. Consumers of these brands had a distinct prejudice in favor of handmade cigars and demanded quality. Fear of a shortage of workers kept many manufacturers from seriously considering dropping the label so long as they continued to make the same types of cigars. Whenever anyone did drop it, the trade journals quickly pointed out that sufficient labor had been acquired to operate under the open-shop system. The relative shortage of labor meant not only that hiring scabs might be difficult, but that manufacturers with the blue label felt a need to maintain good relations in order to insure an ample supply of cigar makers, especially when orders were plentiful. Frank Shea believed that the Sullivan factory was "easy," a "pushover." Sullivan had been partly responsible: he had been "too lenient." Yet in many respects, Sullivan "didn't have much choice." Cigar makers "supported each other" in strikes, and in day-to-day operations Sullivan needed a steady force of skilled cigar makers.

Using union cigar makers his factory had grown from fewer than one hundred workers to over nine hundred, making him a comfortable and successful Manchester businessman. He preferred good labor relations to costly strikes.[39]

Most observers agreed that the union label served cigar makers well in their efforts during the early twentieth century. Consumer preference for handmade cigars helped to sustain a market for union label products, but union cigar makers worked hard themselves to create demand. Cigar makers' extensive advertising of the label made it "a real advantage to the manufacturer," even "essential," in many areas and encouraged them to get and keep the label on their products. The Bureau of Labor noted in one study that "manufacturers who use the label do not advertise their cigars, largely because they consider the label itself a good advertisement; in fact worth several dollars per thousand." Algie Simons, writing in 1918, viewed the label as the "backbone" of the union. "Its advertising value is the reward held out to the boss to secure concessions. It is the most effective fighting weapon." Manufacturers such as H. Traiser in Boston also supported the label because the union had used it successfully to keep trust products out of New England and therefore out of competition. Using the label, cigar makers were able to set a national minimum price for making cigars, first six dollars and later seven dollars per thousand.[40]

Cigar makers could threaten to remove the label and declare a shop off limits if a manufacturer continued to break union rules after a conference. Such a threat had more or less power depending on the type of cigars being made and the availability of nonunion labor. In New England such a move was quite effective, since removal of the label was tantamount to a strike. Local 39 of New Haven, Connecticut, accused Barnett Plotkin of violating the bill of prices and the union took away the label in May 1916. Since the union did not allow "union men to work in my place," and nonunion labor was scarce, Plotkin's factory stood empty. Officers of Local 39 also visited local retailers who agreed not to handle Plotkin's goods. In a desperate letter Plotkin asked the U.S. commissioner of conciliation to intervene and help settle the matter "to prevent the utter ruination of my business." When Plotkin agreed to comply with the bill the union returned the label, but only after he furnished a bond of one hundred dollars "for the faithful carrying out of the provisions of the agreement."[41]

Cigar makers' strikes also benefited from the fierce competition in the industry which kept manufacturers from forming associations. One cigar maker in Philadelphia revealed that a manufacturer there offered him one thousand dollars to start a strike in a rival firm.[42] Small factories with local markets conceded quickly in strikes which could permanently damage their businesses, and such a rapid succession of agreements created an impression that the strikers were winning. Many union companies remained in the hands of individuals and families who had a long association with the industry and believed that only expert hand labor could make cigars good enough to merit the family name. One manufacturer expressed his concern with tradition when he answered a Bureau of Corporations question regarding why he had chosen not to sell out to the American Tobacco Company despite an extremely attractive offer. He replied that the trust, which used female labor and machinery, would have effectively "killed the brand." Although eventually such a stance would prove to be a luxury few could afford, for now these manufacturers preferred reaching a compromise with striking cigar makers rather than trying to locate an alternative labor supply.[43]

The CMIU as an institution did not represent a unified interpretation of workers' place in the battle or the best strategy for waging the war. One of the principal sources of internal conflict was the disagreement over national versus local prerogatives, which figured prominently in the matter of cigar makers' readiness to strike. While striking signified a manly bearing to most members, to Perkins it reflected irresponsibility and risked goodwill and existing wage agreements with manufacturers. "Some members admire and love a fight in any form, ready to move to new fields at a moment's notice," he charged. Perkins urged members to exhaust every remedy and to weight the decision to strike carefully. "Always be cautious and never overconfident." Members had best follow the advice of "cool conservatives," rather than "hot headed" leaders. Such sentiments were not new to cigar makers. Former president Hurst had admonished them not to strike so much in the *CMOJ*'s earliest issues and Strasser continued the litany throughout his presidency. Most members concurred with the notion that the reckless strikes of others served no purpose and drained union resources. Their own strikes, however, might be viewed quite differently. In any case, members regarded the strike as their "main weapon." A spokesman for Local 97 warned that if Perkins curbed members' authority in calling strikes, then the CMIU would "degenerate from a trade union to a sick and death benefit society."[44]

Cigar makers even disagreed on the union label. A few believed that the label's benefits had been overrated, and others complained about the "assessing mania" necessary to finance all the label work. Many argued that although the label had been a useful tool in the past, the union needed new approaches for the future. Some agreed with an Industrial Workers of the World charge that supporting the label basically meant drumming up business for capitalists. However, the label's greatest advocates, members of socialist Local 97, argued that the label made them strong and more evenly matched with manufacturers. As long as the label helped "to maintain the manhood of the cigar makers and the independence of the craft," one member wrote, it served an important purpose.[45]

Cigar makers' views on partisan politics differed as well. In Reading, Pennsylvania, socialists were active in city politics and cigar makers were well represented among their ranks. Many CMIU members eschewed all association with the regular parties and supported the Socialist Party or some other alternative. Frequently, however, locals rallied to defeat candidates unsympathetic to their interests. Cigar makers in Albany, New York, organized in 1903 to defeat a mayoral candidate who sold nonunion cigars in his store. In 1912, Albert Beveridge of Indiana appealed for labor's support in his campaign for governor. Cigar makers in the state, however, successfully fought against an endorsement by the state Federation of Labor because Beveridge had allowed his name to be used on a nonunion cigar. Other encounters with the state were largely defensive—dealing with misuse of the label, court injunctions, or sanitation issues.[46]

Cigar makers' work culture stressed collectivist, anticapitalist values on the shop floor, but it offered only a guide to one's activity outside the factory. Generally, members subscribed to the goals as stated in the constitution, "the amelioration and final emancipation" of labor, but they disagreed on the timing of final emancipation and the exact steps to achieve it. President Perkins and others who supported him, such as John Kirchner of Philadelphia, took up the pen in the *CMOJ*, arguing that sound, "conservative" trade union policies were the only path to emancipation. Unionists would do best to concentrate on steady work, fair wages, clean shops, and fair treatment. Others agreed simply because the membership was so diverse: other, broader issues would only divide them. "There are a variety of nationalities, characteristics, religious and other social instincts among us, but when it comes to enter the struggle for a livelihood, all working people in their respective trades and industries have one common purpose and one common object—to secure a better livelihood."[47]

Even in this regard, however, cigar makers might not share the same approach. Louis Alster, a member of Local 14, addressed the *CMOJ* in 1911, noting that cigar makers' lack of enthusiasm in organizing team workers meant that "they fight each other" rather than their "natural enemy," the manufacturers. For many unions, including the CMIU, the solution seemed to be admitting competing workers, often women, on a differential basis: in this case half dues and half benefits. Others called for broad industrial organization. The CMIU should organize all factory workers, regardless of occupation. As in some unions which followed a policy of "obstruction," some members preferred to fight the system of work rather than organize it.[48]

The idea of establishing cooperative cigar factories won considerable popularity among cigar makers, some of whom identified themselves as socialists. This strategy had captured cigar makers' imaginations since the nineteenth century as the promise to "become our own employers" seemed to hold out the answer. Some, like William Shakespeare of New York, argued in favor of cooperatives, but called for more immediate improvements as well. Supporters argued that co-ops would take cigar makers "out of the conditions of a wage slave into that freedom of working for your own interest." Another explained that "the profit system is a curse on humanity; it robs you of your full earning; it perpetuates a class of drones . . . living in luxury on your labor," and added that cooperatives could eliminate the system. Some proposed a policy of setting up cooperatives whenever members struck, and argued that the threat alone would make manufacturers "very careful not to give you any cause to strike." Perkins opposed cooperatives because they would compete with union manufacturers. Many socialists who fought these schemes argued that cooperatives simply meant workers becoming capitalists: they would not bring an end to the profit system. None of the proposed plans received the two-thirds majority needed to get off the ground.[49]

Socialists still formed a sizable and influential component of the union's membership—although they never gained a majority during these years—and contributed to the considerable socialist presence within the AFL. Their most prominent spokesman was J. Mahlon Barnes, a member of Local 165 in Philadelphia who served as secretary of the Socialist Party from 1904 through 1911, when he was ousted by the "Left Wing," a more radical segment of the party. Throughout the period, he also was elected yearly as a CMIU delegate to the AFL convention.[50]

Socialist members, representing many different strains of thought, by and large advocated a more far-reaching solution for ending class oppression. Final emancipation could not come while property remained in private hands. Some urged a wider participation in politics and many called for the formation of a labor party to unite all workers in political opposition to capitalism. Others reflected a more syndicalist view that workers needed to seize direct control of the means of production and the state, apart from the operation of political parties. The Jacksonville, Illinois, local proposed in 1906 that the CMIU leave the AFL and affiliate with the IWW, but only one local endorsed the measure and it quickly died. On a more immediate level, socialists in the union called attention to figures they compiled on industry wages and profits. They argued that cigar makers did not receive a fair share and that manufacturers were doing better financially than they were willing to admit. Charles Claus of Boston called for production "for use, not for profit." [51]

Socialist arguments, however, could never be considered on their own merits because socialism was inextricably intertwined with both power and personalities in the CMIU and in the AFL. The politicization of ideology complicated the efforts of self-conscious radicals to appeal to the sensibilities of fellow unionists. Most discussions of so-called economic issues in the *CMOJ* took the form of vituperative exchanges between bitter enemies, rather than careful presentations of positions and philosophy. From 1907 to about 1909, David Goldstein, the eccentric former SLP member from Boston who had recently converted to rabid antisocialism, dueled with Morris Brown of Local 144 in New York in the pages of the *CMOJ*. Even their initial supporters eventually found the letters "tiresome," and one member begged for the elimination of the "nauseating matter" disgracing the journal's pages. Cigar makers could not escape the history their various political ideas contained and their debates were hardly reflections of the implications of their work culture. [52]

The seeming contradiction that the cigar makers expressed in sending as delegates to the AFL convention every year both Samuel Gompers and J. Mahlon Barnes actually reflected an encompassing and yet tempestuous quality of their work culture. Cigar makers not only permitted conflict within their community, they embraced it, and had done so since the nineteenth century. Accepted patterns of shop-floor life included verbal sparring and exchanges between socialists and nonsocialists or anyone else on economic matters. Algie Simons once noted that often when visiting a new town on the "soap-box trail," he would not have the name of a local socialist. "I always asked for a cigar factory. Never did I fail to find a socialist or an anti-socialist who would gladly direct me to his beloved opponent." At times conflict fueled and energized them. [53]

Conflict could, of course, be divisive. Cigar makers may have made room for a range of opinion in their ranks, but they elected conservative George W. Perkins as their president every year. Being a leader in the same union where socialists such as Barnes were influential placed Perkins in a most unhappy position. Ograin noted that Barnes had been "a thorn in the side of Gompers and Perkins all the time." Perkins used whatever opportunity he could to discredit socialist members and their programs. He argued that the Knights of Labor had tried industrial unionism and the order's demise proved that the policy had failed miserably. He pointed out that in countries where the government owned the cigar factories, the industry was weak and ill-paid. Cooperatives, he said, created ill will with union manufacturers, who deserved special treatment because of their loyalty to the union, and placed the union in competition with them. The CMIU's major goal was to eliminate unfair competition and the current trade union path and its "conservative" approach had the best chance for success. Perkins granted that final emancipation seemed to come slowly, but argued that only conservative trade unions could bring the awaited day. Politics only divided members: they should leave politics and religion alone and concentrate on improving conditions in cigar factories. Socialists were little more than "idle dreamers." "Let wise councils prevail!"[54]

Worst of all, socialists advocated "hasty and impulsive strikes." In 1909, New York members protested a Perkins ruling that they believed needlessly drew out the process by which they could call a strike. A shop could vote to strike and then submit the matter to the New York Joint Advisory Board (JAB) for approval. However, Perkins ruled that once the JAB approved, members of all locals represented by the JAB also had to vote their assent. The New York JAB argued that by giving a manufacturer a full month before a strike could begin, they provided him with "plenty of opportunity to manufacture a large stock of cigars" and further placed "him in a position where he can do battle with more determination and longer duration because of supply." It was no coincidence that many members of the New York JAB were both socialists and frequent critics of Perkins and Gompers. Perkins denounced New York's amendment to change the ruling as a "radical departure" in the last issue of the *CMOJ* before the vote and charged that it was simply an attempt to encourage more impulsive strikes. The amendment was defeated, although Morris Brown, a member of the New York JAB, pointed out that Local 144 had not had the opportunity to rebut Perkins's charges before the final vote had been cast.[55]

As the first decade of the century closed, the division between socialists and CMIU leadership was becoming increasingly complicated by a growing restiveness among rank-and-file members in general. Tension between local and central authority had traditionally made the relationship ambiguous, but matters now worsened. The principle that no member should advance his interests before another's, and the growing mistrust of national leaders generally, contributed to a strain between local and national levels which was even reflected in Perkins's salary. In 1907 he made thirty dollars a week, one of the lowest salaries of any union president in the country. Members argued that because Perkins was no better than any other man in the union, as president he should only make what he could have expected to earn at the bench as a cigar maker. They consistently voted down salary increases every time the matter was raised. By 1912, his salary had risen only to forty dollars a week.[56]

The escalation of discontent and contention within the CMIU during these years was spurred by a number of disturbing trends and setbacks. In 1907, the general fund decreased for the first time since 1897. It continued to dwindle each year thereafter, as death benefit payments consumed a larger and larger proportion of union expenditures. While locals in Boston, Manchester, and elsewhere in New England added many new members during these years, other locals were losing ground. Between 1905 and 1912, membership levels in St. Louis dropped from 924 to 746, in Albany from 286 to 171, in New York's Local 90 from 2,010 to 1,411, and in Philadelphia from 1,501 to 1,107. Overall, the number of thirty-cent regular members declined after a high of 44,000 in 1909 to about 40,000 four years later, while the number of retired members increased from about 6,000 to 7,344. Members also worried about the spread of local-option prohibition, since it cut off an important union retail outlet. Sunday closings also hurt sales of union cigars. Cigar makers' well-known inclination toward drink and the heavy German influence in the union also contributed to their consistent stand against prohibition.[57]

Growing concentration in the leaf business, exacerbated by the aggressive buying tactics of the American Tobacco Company, drove tobacco prices upward after 1910 and pressured manufacturers to cut other costs, namely labor. The recession of 1907–9 affected unionists as consumers cut back on luxury items. Even Local 97 felt the effects. "For the first time in our history," Henry Abrahams noted in the *CMOJ* in 1909, "we are compelled to warn travelers in quest of work to keep away. . . . We have at this writing three hundred men out of work and no jobs in sight. There has been such distress this winter that assessments aggregating thirteen dollars and fifty cents were levied upon every man at work and another is pending." Although the industry recovered, conditions slumped again between 1911 and 1913. Cigars imported from Puerto Rico and the Philippines competed with union smokes and the CMIU fought in Congress for higher import duties on them.[58]

The expansion of team work and the growing popularity of the five-cent cigar made the issue of organizing the unorganized particularly salient. Perkins began warning members as early as 1907 that, contrary to popular belief, five-cent and ten-cent cigars now came into direct competition with each other primarily because cheap labor on nickel smokes enabled manufacturers to use better tobacco and markedly improved the quality of the five-cent cigar. Where once these cheaper smokes had been made using only domestic tobaccos, by the end of the first decade they increasingly were made using some imported leaves. Sumatra, once reserved for better brands, now could be found as wrappers on some five-cent cigars. As the two grades of cigars began to compete, union manufacturers found themselves at a disadvantage because of the cost of labor. Whole centers emerged based on the five-cent cigar: the Detroit industry grew from almost nothing in 1900 to a major thriving business ten years later. Responding to the expanding popularity of cheap cigars, the H. Traiser Company in Boston in 1909 placed 350 union men to work on "nickel goods," and in 1912, the bulwark of union manufacturers, Waitt and Bond in Boston, introduced a five-cent cigar.[59]

Although the *U.S. Tobacco Journal* certainly exaggerated when it claimed in a 1913 editorial that "our cigar industry is fast running into the grip of monopolization,"[60] a clear trend toward concentration in the industry was becoming evident. Despite antitrust action which presumably broke up the American Tobacco Company in 1911, the American Cigar Company continued to play an influential role in the industry. It had been joined, however, by other corporate enterprises which were expanding rapidly by the end of the first decade, including United Cigar Manufacturers (UCM), Otto Eisenlohr and Company, Deisel-Wemmer, I. Lewis, and others, with numerous branch factories. UCM absorbed several large companies after 1910 and by 1912 became the second largest producer in the country, accounting for 3.9 percent of production, behind American Cigar Company (combined with its affiliate, Federal Cigar), which produced 8.3 percent of all U.S. cigars. The nation's twenty largest companies in 1906 had controlled 28.5 percent of production. In 1912, the ten largest companies accounted for 22.6 percent. The number of factories continued to dwindle as the scale of production increased: in 1896 the industry had produced 4 billion cigars in 31,000 factories, but in 1914 it produced 7.5 billion in 13,515 factories. Between 1912 and 1913 alone, 1,272 factories disappeared. Cigar makers and smaller manufacturers alike began calling for a return to more competitive conditions.[61]

Other trends raised more questions about the industry's overall health. Cigar output faltered slightly in 1910 and observers noted that cigarette production had outpaced cigar production for the first time. The number of cigars manufactured increased only 1.5 percent in 1912, while the number of cigarettes produced that year over the previous year jumped 25 percent. By 1913, cigarette production doubled that of cigars. In view of such statistics, manufacturers adamantly opposed any increase in the tobacco tax. *Tobacco Leaf* editorialized that manufacturers did too little to promote cigar smoking, unlike cigarette manufacturers who used extensive advertising. To reverse the industry's stagnation, the journal urged cooperation with the CMIU in a campaign to boost cigars. *Tobacco Leaf* noted that the Clear Havana industry in Tampa had experienced a slowdown, but blamed the owners for giving away their profits through too much specialty work for their customers. In another break from the past, several manufacturers of cheaper grades of cigars were beginning to locate in Tampa by 1910.[62] Some industry leaders tried to calm spirits, however. Jacob Wertheim, president of United Cigar Manufacturers, predicted optimistically in early 1913 that cigar output would continue to rise. In his view the slow growth of cigar production stemmed from a shortage of labor. Once this could be relieved, cigar production would rise rapidly. The same problem did not affect cigarette manufacture, he continued, because it was so completely mechanized. When asked whether cigars could ever be made by machine, he replied: "Not until they grow every leaf just exactly like every other leaf."[63]

The socialist voice within the CMIU grew louder and more appealing amid this deteriorating situation. Perkins claimed that the union was doing all it could to meet these challenges and blamed dissatisfaction on socialist agitation, and in his autobiography Gompers later charged that the initiative and referendum system had given socialists too much power in the union. "Socialist publications, Socialist organizers and propagandists spread the poison of hatred and discontent," Gompers wrote, "thus weakening confidence in the integrity of the officers of the International Union."[64] For Gompers such a ground swell of opposition not only threatened his position within the CMIU, it embarrassed him as president of

the American Federation of Labor. In his opposition to the socialist presence in the CMIU, he was ably assisted by Perkins. In a letter to AFL
secretary Frank Morrison, Perkins acknowledged the increase in the socialist vote among the "indoor trades," including cigar making, and speculated that the younger generation of cigar makers did not understand
unionism because they had not witnessed the struggles of the past. His
fears about the growing influence of socialists in the union caused him to
equate dissent with treason, and his tone in the *CMOJ* grew more trucu-
lent. He railed against "knockers" who criticized union policies, and
lumped them all together as socialists. The "greatest enemy" to the
union, he wrote, was the "politician in our own ranks." [65]

Perkins, counseled by Gompers, sometimes censored critical letters to
the *CMOJ* and on those he did print he attached long notes attacking the
writers and their ideas. Antisocialists such as David Goldstein encountered no problem publishing letters in the journal, but opponents were
not so fortunate. Some members accused Perkins of wielding the "Big
Stick" in the *CMOJ* and restricting freedom of expression. They scoffed at
the union's appeals process and labeled it a "Czar of Russia" approach
since the executive board had upheld nearly every decision Perkins had
made since 1892. He ruled some amendments out of order when he
simply did not like them, and when he sent out circulars on others, he
included statements explaining why they should be defeated. He printed
his opinions on crucial issues in the journal but voting frequently took
place before responses to his opinions could be received and printed in
return. He defended himself against these charges but bowed to them
somewhat in 1911, when he began attaching the heading "Editorial Notes"
to many of his comments and confining them to the editorial page. [66]

Tensions mounted. In 1912 Perkins ran for reelection against Harry C.
Parker, a socialist from Philadelphia's local 165 and a friend of Barnes. In
his campaign statement in the *CMOJ*, Parker called for a hard fight in the
"great war between laborers and capitalists throughout the world—a war
that must go on until capitalism and wage-slavery shall be overthrown."
Perkins promised to continue "the past successful, conservative fruitful
methods." Perkins won, but his margin was a slim 16,138 to 14,221. In a
runoff election for executive board members, three of the seven elected
were Perkins's opponents. It was in this acrimonious atmosphere that the
cigar makers held their first convention in sixteen years. [67]

In September 1912, delegates came together in Baltimore, Maryland,
to decide the union's future course. The convention lasted three weeks

and delegates debated scores of issues. Two in particular addressed the deterioration of the union's position. One proposal increased the number of years a cigar maker was required to be a member in order to receive each successive level of death benefit. The other related to the increasing numbers of nonunion workers in the industry. Here delegates agreed on the need to take some action, but disagreed on what to do. Socialist Andrew P. Bower of Reading proposed lowering the dues and entirely changing the benefit structure, making membership more accessible to nonunion workers.[68]

In contrast to this complete overhaul, Perkins had his own plan which he hoped could enroll new members without seriously altering the structure of the CMIU. The issue was not just the potential threat of nonunion workers; Perkins was also alarmed about the dual-union movement that had recently begun in Chicago. Former members, many of whom identified themselves as socialists, led by Jake Billow, founded the Cigar Makers' Progressive Union to organize the city's team workers, particularly women. Perkins wanted to prevent Billow from charging—accurately—that the CMIU would not admit these workers. At the convention, Perkins was ultimately successful in his efforts. The delegates dropped Andrew Bower's plan and adopted Perkins's proposal for Class A membership for team workers. But all actions of the convention were subject to a referendum vote and the membership at large later defeated the death benefit change and Class A membership. Local 97 opposed the Class A plan and sent a circular to all locals urging them to vote against it.[69]

Both Perkins and Gompers believed that the convention had helped to clear the air, but while it had cooled tempers, dissatisfaction remained. Trade conditions picked up in 1914, which brightened the spirits of some, but letters to the journal continued to express concern about the union and the trade. In 1916 Perkins narrowly beat Parker once again, by a vote of 16,179 to 13,526. The executive board remained the same. Members finally passed the Class A plan in late 1915.[70]

The overriding issues of the 1912 convention—what the CMIU should do about the fast-growing nonunion sector of the industry and what its relationship with female team workers should be—remained critical and illustrated some of the limitations of cigar makers' work culture. Without doubt, that vibrant work culture had tremendous strengths. It operated subversively, challenging competitive capitalism and celebrating alternative values of egalitarianism and collective resistance to employers. This work culture had grown out of work experience, the contributions of a multi-ethnic work force, and a half century of history as an occupation and as a union. Yet its vision was limited. Its militancy and bold assertion of class rights did not extend beyond the bounds of the union fraternity, despite some good intentions and exceptions. Union cigar makers shared a world of insiders, where women workers were alien. While the concept of manhood gave them strength, it was grounded in reactionary values of male supremacy. The tension between solidarity and exclusivity meant self-destruction. Their policies of keeping out female team workers simply made hiring women at lower wages look more attractive to manufacturers and undercut their own position. As five-cent cigars increasingly competed with their own, they could not continue to preserve a niche in the industry sufficiently large to employ all members at customary wages. Nor did work culture translate directly into an immediate revolutionary movement. While José Santana spoke the language of class warfare, regarded anarchist Emma Goldman and Socialist Party chief Eugene Debs as heroes, and regularly attended socialist-sponsored meetings and addresses, he also drew pride from his union's association with Gompers. While cigar makers' work culture thus wove together different and conflicting elements, it contained the seeds of a more deliberate ideology, one which applied workplace values to the larger society.

Manufacturers, particularly nonunion ones, regarded the cigar makers' union and culture with hostility. Their perception, as reflected in trade journals, centered on several characteristics deemed most objectionable about these workers. First the CMIU overstepped its rightful bounds. Cigar makers should "confine their activity to their own sphere of labor" rather than attempting to interfere in matters outside their jursidiction. If manufacturers could function without the union, the organization would revert to its more appropriate activity. "It is only a question of a few years when all manufacturers will be independent of labor unions, as far as coercion is concerned, when they will then relapse into beneficial orders, which is their proper sphere." The union instituted "numerous arbitrary and tyrannical rules and practices" in the factories. Cigar makers went so far as to "set prices." One manufacturer affirmed that he would resist any attempt to unionize his factory because the union would "bring in any amount of friction. . . . For instance, should I wish to bring out a new cigar of a little different shape or size, I would have to submit it to the union for an estimate as to what I must pay for having it made. They could virtually prohibit me from making it at all if they wished to do so."[71]

Cigar makers were also unduly confrontational, from management's perspective. They needed instead to "cultivate friendly terms with employers." One angry *Tobacco* editorial declared that "few organizations have gone farther and faster toward anarchy than some of the local branches of Cigarmakers' International Union. Many of them seem to think that employers and employees have nothing in common, but must be always at war with each other." Cigar makers struck too often and at times when they should have been satisfied with what they had. "But the genus cigarmaker is so constituted that when he is best off he kicks the hardest."[72] Cigar makers seemed unlike any other group of workers when it came to striking. "Of all labor unions those of the cigar makers are the most shortsighted and crassly stupid of any in existence," posited one trade journal. "For forty years or more the ruling members of this craft have proved themselves incapable of understanding or appreciating fair and liberal treatment; striking has become to them a pastime." In addition, their demands were not only unjustified but capricious. "If ever written the history of cigarmakers' strikes in this country will make mighty interesting reading. . . . They have kicked against cuspidors, . . . the style of stools on which they sat, the color of wrappers and the feel of fillers." Another commentator stated that many manufacturers believed "that you can make no comparison between cigarmakers as a class, and say, mechanics or any other division of skilled labor; that the latter are often unreasonable, but the former impossible at all times." A *Tobacco* editorial in 1900 commented that the Boston manufacturers had "gone a step further in the direction of surrender" by signing, under pressure from the cigar makers, an agreement with the Stripper's Union. "Although nothing is mentioned as to supplying them with lemonade and strawberry short-cake," the report continued, "it is doubtless expected."[73]

Worse, manufacturers felt sure that cigar makers aimed for nothing less than taking control of the factories themselves. Union policies, according to employers, sought "diminished authority on the part of the employer," thus propelling many manufacturers to expel the union and run their factories "to suit themselves." Cigar makers would do better to place "just as few handicaps as possible" on manufacturers. In the strike of cigar makers in New York City during 1900, one trade journal asked, "Can the factory owners afford to place themselves in the hands of the union and surrender for good all their legal and natural rights to control their own factories?" Cigar manufacturers were not acting unfairly; they "only refuse to be dictated to in regard to the management of their business." Reporting on another strike *Tobacco* remarked, "It is not a strike for wages, but the old story of the employees wanting to run the business." Union cigar manufacturers occasionally received favorable attention in the trade press, but often they were portrayed as weak and manipulated. It was generally recognized, one article pointed out, that the CMIU had a "half-Nelson lock on" Boston.[74]

The "absurd and unreasonable" demands of the cigar makers stemmed partly from the radical element in the rank and file, various articles contended. An indignant description of a Labor Day parade in Philadelphia illustrated the nature of the problem and manufacturers' notion that cigar makers were different from other workers. Each group of marchers carried a banner; the bricklayers' sign reportedly said, "We prosper by arbitration," and a sheet metal workers' banner read, "Protection to our employer is protection to ourselves." The cigar makers', by contrast, announced, "Profit is robbery."[75]

Manufacturers rarely criticized the union's top leadership, and in some cases praised it. One *Tobacco Leaf* editorial described Perkins as "one of the brainiest and correctly conservative labor leaders" in the country. Lower-level union organizers, however, were not treated so kindly. James Wood, an especially effective CMIU organizer, aroused *Tobacco*'s ire while organizing in Binghamton, New York, in 1903. Wood was a "natural-born agitator" who had the "knack of making impassioned speeches," and was "extremely rabid in his utterances." He had recently told women workers in one nonunion shop meeting that the wives of manufacturers wore diamonds while they worked for starvation wages. "And strange as it may seem, he could lash his hearers into hysterics with such stuff."[76]

Manufacturers' weaknesses were cigar makers' strengths. The popularity of the label, the labor shortage on higher-priced goods, and the competition among cigar manufacturers meant that neither union nor nonunion manufacturers could simply dismiss the CMIU. Manufacturers had been notoriously unwilling to organize into permanent associations to cooperate against labor, because the trade was so competitive. There were other blocks to organization. For example, with the exception of the Henry Offterdinger factory, Washington, D.C. was considered a "buckeye town." In 1906, in the midst of a strike of his union workers, Offterdinger warned that he might look into forming a manufacturers' association in the city. Cigar makers were not worried about this threat because they knew that the majority of the city's buckeye manufacturers were themselves members of the union.[77]

However, manufacturers recognized their own advantages and used every means they could to avoid, undercut, or even break the union. Individual manufacturers and trade journal editorials tried to create the impression that union cigar makers did shoddy work and that their cigars were substandard. Manufacturers could use the courts against strikes through injunctions. In the pages of the trade journals, employers shared methods of avoiding the union and breaking strikes and warned each other about possible efforts to organize. Most important, they opened branch factories in nonunion areas, and new companies opened in places where the union was traditionally weak, as in Detroit and areas in New Jersey, Pennsylvania, and Ohio. The U.S. Industrial Commission noted that the "strength of the union has had a peculiar effect" by spreading the industry into new areas where it had not traditionally existed.[78] Although many union firms remained convinced of their need for the union, several decided to risk loss of the union label. Henry Offterdinger ended relations with the union, declared his factory an open shop, and cut wages on June 1, 1908, less than two years after he had lost a strike to union cigar makers. Anyone, he contended, could "earn his former wages if he would work nine hours and a half instead of eight hours." He kept a few handworkers and introduced a new brand. Before long his force was almost entirely composed of women working under a division of labor. Other factories made the transition as well, such as G. Pflaum and Sons in Minneapolis, which dropped the label in 1914 after forty years. In 1915, Syracuse manufacturer Justin Seubert, long a supporter of the CMIU, closed his factory and then reopened it without the blue label, convinced he could now sell nonunion cigars.[79]

In the end it was cigar makers' exclusivity that proved to be manufacturers' key strength in the battle. The structure of the cigar industry was shifting, especially by the second decade of the century. Large firms using some machinery, a division of labor, branch factories, and a labor force composed of women had begun to change the balance of power within the industry. Seeking an alternative to the challenges of union men, the manufacturers of five-cent cigars consciously chose another group of workers. They recognized that they could expand their operations by adopting the team system and employing women, without fears that their employees would join the union. Cigar makers' patriarchal exclusivity ensured the success of this policy. The work culture that gave them strength also blinded them to the new realities they confronted and prevented them from acting to save themselves from sure defeat. Manufacturers could easily exploit the factionalism: they could just divide and conquer. Fortunately, one *Leaf* editorial commented confidently, "there are so many diametrically opposed elements in the cigar making section of labor that the possibility of one great union being formed is outside the pale of practical effort."[80]

Notes

1. *Tobacco Leaf*, 24 June 1903, p. 6. The following were especially useful to me in formulating my ideas for this chapter: Andrew Dawson, "The Paradox of Dynamic Technological Change and the Labor Aristocracy in the United States, 1880–1914," *Labor History*, 20 (Summer 1979), 345–48; Andrew Dawson, "History and Ideology: Fifty Years of 'Job Consciousness,'" *Literature and History*, 8 (Autumn 1978), 223–41; Jim Green, "Culture, Politics and Workers' Reponse to Industrialization in the U.S.," *Radical America*, 16 (Jan.–Mar. 1982), 101–28; Michael Hanagan and Charles Stephenson, "The Skilled Worker and Working-Class Protest," *Social Science History*, 4 (Winter 1980), 3–13; Jean Monds, "Workers' Control and the Historians: A New Economism," *New Left Review*, 97 (May–June 1976), 81–104; Michael Burawoy, *Manufacturing Consent: Changes in the Labor Process under Monopoly Capitalism* (Chicago, 1979); James Hinton, *The First Shop Stewards' Movement* (London, 1973); David Montgomery, *Workers' Control in America: Studies in the History of Work, Technology and Labor Struggles* (Cambridge, 1979); George Rudé, *Ideology and Popular Protest* (New York, 1980). While I disagree with his reading of Montgomery's work, see also Lawrence T. McDonnell, "'You Are Too Sentimental': Problems and Suggestions for a New Labor History," *Journal of Social History*, 17 (Summer 1984), 629–54.

2. *Tobacco Leaf*, 12 Dec. 1902, p. 6; "Minutes of Local 208, Kalmazoo, Michigan," 21 Jan. 1908, Western Michigan University Library, Kalamazoo; "By-Laws of Union No. 208," Kalamazoo, Mich., 1905, pp. 13, 14, Western Michigan University Library, Kalamazoo; "By-Laws of Cigar Makers' and Packers' Union 97," Boston, Mass., p. 19, Boston Public Library, Boston; "By-Laws of Cigar Makers' Union No. 22," Detroit, Mich., 1904, p. 22, State Historical Society of Wisconsin (SHSW), Madison; "By-Laws of the Cigar Makers' Union No. 192," Manchester, N.H., pp. 12, 17, Manchester City Library (MCL), Manchester, N.H.

3. *CMOJ*, June 1902, p. 7; Dec. 1902, p. 7; Apr. 1904, p. 8; Sept. 1904, p. 8; Oct. 1906, p. 3.

4. David Montgomery, *Workers' Control in America: Studies in the History of Work, Technology and Labor Struggles* (Cambridge, Mass., 1979), pp. 14–15.

5. John R. Ograin interview, 11 Aug. 1976; 19 May 1979, Chicago; José Santana interview, 27 Feb. 1977 by telephone.

6. *CMOJ*, Sept. 1906, p. 3; Dec. 1906, pp. 8–10. See also *CMOJ*, Nov. 1880, p. 9.

7. *CMOJ*, Sept. 1904, p. 8; May 1906, p. 4; Ograin interview, 17 May 1980;

"By-Laws," Local 22, Detroit, Mich., p. 7; *Social-Demokrat*, 24 Jan. 1875; *CMOJ*, Nov. 1879, p. 3; Feb. 1880, p. 3; May 1880, p. 4; Theodore W. Glocker, "The Structure of the Cigar Makers' Union," in Jacob Hollander and George Barnett, eds., *Studies in American Trade Unionism* (New York, 1970 [1912]). My thanks to the Samuel Gompers Papers and to Dorothee Schneider for the *Social-Demokrat* reference.

8. Herman Baust interview, 24 Mar. 1977, North Haven, Conn.; Santana interview, 25 Feb. 1980 by telephone; Margaret Kehm interview, 25 July 1978, Warren, Pa.

9. T. Frank Shea interview, 26 June 1979, Manchester, N.H.; *CMOJ*, June 1902, p. 7; *Tobacco Leaf*, 7 Mar. 1900, p. 11.

10. Shea interview, 26 June 1979; *CMOJ*, July 1906, p. 4; *Tobacco*, 1 June 1900, p. 4.

11. *U.S. Tobacco Journal*, 2 Aug. 1919, p. 3; *CMOJ*, Jan. 1903, p. 4; June 1903, p. 4.

12. *CMOJ*, Apr. 1903, p. 6; June 1906, p. 4; July 1906, p. 10; Aug. 1906, p. 16; Santana interviews, 1976–80; *Boston Herald*, 19 May 1912. There are some hints that special relationships developed. See *Tobacco Leaf*, 24 Sept. 1902, p. 11; *Tobacco Leaf*, 4 May 1904, p. 10. On the nineteenth century see, for example: *CMOJ*, Oct. 1886, p. 4; Jan. 1887, p. 4; May 1888, p. 17; Aug. 1888, p. 8. Regarding the problem of elevating the importance of work, see Jim Green's reference to Daniel Rodgers's *Work Ethic in Industrial America*, in Green, "Culture, Politics and Workers' Response," p. 123.

13. Santana interview, 18 Nov. 1979 by telephone; "By-Laws," Local 192, Manchester, N.H.; Shea interview; "Bill of Prices," Local 192, Manchester, N.H., 1915, MCL; "List of Shops and Bill of Prices, Local 97, Boston, Mass. 1904, U.S. Bureau of Corporations, Tobacco Investigation, file 3073, Record Group (R.G.) 122, National Archives (NA), Washington, D.C.; "Bill of Prices," Local 25, Milwaukee, Wis., 1903, SHSW; Indiana Labor Commission, *Fourth Biennial Report of the Indiana Labor Commission for 1903–1904* (Indianapolis, 1904), pp. 67–68; "Bill of Prices," Local 97, Boston, Mass., in Carl A. Werner, *A Textbook on Tobacco* (New York, 1914), pp. 305–9; "Bill of Prices," Joint Unions of New York City, ca. 1900, U.S. Department of Labor Library (USDL), Washington, D.C.; "Bill of Prices," Local 1, Baltimore, Md., ca. 1901, USDL; "Bill of Prices," Local 4, Cincinnati, Ohio, 1907, USDL; "Bill of Prices," Local 316, McSherrystown, Pa., 1919, Adams County Historical Society, Gettysburg, Pa. All locals fined anyone for doing "reroll work."

14. Santana interview, 17 May 1979; *Tobacco Leaf*, 9 May 1900, p. 3; 1 June 1904, p. 28. If more Havana tobacco were used, then the price would be higher. For any extra work which would mean a higher selling price for the manufacturer, then the cigar makers charged more.

15. Shea interview; U.S. Congress, House, Committee on Ways and Means, *Cigars Supplied Employees by Manufacturers, Hearings before the Committee on Ways and Means on H.R. 17253, H.R. 21357, and H.R. 21958*, 62d Cong., 2d sess., 1912, pp. 5, 40; Ograin interview, 17 May 1980; Elizabeth M. Hennessey, "Report on Cigar and Cigarette Making Industry in Boston," p. 5, typescript, re-

port for the Massachusetts Bureau of Labor and Industries, ca. 1918, U.S. Women's Bureau, Box 23, Unpublished Surveys, General Correspondence, R.G. 86, NA; Shea interview.

16. U.S. Congress, House, *Cigars Supplied Employees*, pp. 38, 39; William B. Wilson to treasury secretary, May 1913, file 16/76, Office of the Chief Clerk, U.S. Department of Labor, R.G. 174, NA; Shea interview.

17. William Theisen interview, 17 Aug. 1979, Denver, Colo.; Shea interview; Baust interview.

18. *Tobacco Leaf*, 3 June 1908, p. 3; 9 July 1908, p. 6; *CMOJ*, July 1878, p. 1.

19. U.S. Congress, House, *Cigars Supplied Employees*, p. 7; *Tobacco Leaf*, 14 Sept. 1911, pp. 1, 6; 21 Sept. 1911, p. 5; 28 Sept. 1911, pp. 3, 4, 7; Shea interview.

20. U.S. Congress, House, *Cigars Supplied Employees*, pp. 5–6, 27–29, 36, 38, 40, 43, 47, 50; *U.S. Tobacco Journal*, 9 Mar. 1912, p. 5; 4 May 1912, p. 24.

21. "By-Laws," Local 192, Manchester, N.H., pp. 12, 13; *CMOJ*, Jan. 1900, p. 1; Mar. 1907, p. 12.

22. Shea interview; *CMOJ*, Mar. 1909, p. 2.

23. Theisen interview; Ograin interview, 17 May 1980; *Tobacco Leaf*, 4 Mar. 1908, p. 7.

24. Kehm interview; *Tobacco Leaf*, 3 Dec. 1902, p. 12; 1 May 1907, p. 44; 4 Mar. 1908, p. 7; 1 Apr. 1908, p. 38; 22 Apr. 1908, p. 7; *CMOJ*, Mar. 1909, p. 2. See also *Tobacco Leaf*, 24 Sept. 1902, p. 38; 1 May 1907, p. 44; *U.S. Tobacco Journal*, 26 Apr. 1913, p. 5; 17 May 1913, p. 7; *New Haven Evening Register*, 5 May 1913.

25. Shea interview.

26. Ibid., U.S. Bureau of Corporations, Tobacco Investigation, file 3073 R.G. 122, NA; *Tobacco Leaf*, 24 Sept. 1902, p. 38.

27. Santana interview, 18 Nov. 1979 by telephone; *CMOJ*, May 1906, pp. 5, 6.

28. *CMOJ*, May 1895, p. 7; July 1909, p. 4; Aug. 1909, p. 9; *Tobacco Leaf*, 30 July 1902, p. 12.

29. U.S. Congress, House, *Cigars Supplied Employees*, p. 37; *CMOJ*, Sept. 1906, p. 5; Oct. 1906, p. 3; Feb. 1907, p. 10; May 1907, pp. 4–5; May 1908, p. 3; June 1910, p. 4; Dec. 1911, p. 3; U.S. Bureau of Corporations, Tobacco Investigation, file 3073, Section 10, R.G. 122, NA; *Tobacco Leaf*, 23 Apr. 1903, pp. 34, 45; 5 Feb. 1905, p. 6; 15 Jan. 1908, p. 7.

30. *CMOJ*, July 1904, p. 1; Mar. 1907, p. 12; Ograin interview, 8 July 1977; "Bill of Prices," Local 329, Racine, Wis., 1918, Box 1, folder 3, Cigar Makers' International Union of America, Papers of Cigar Makers' Local 162, Green Bay, Wis., SHSW. It is not clear to me what the significance of being fired on a particular day had. See also *CMOJ*, Aug. 1884, p. 4.

31. *CMOJ*, Apr. 1904, p. 9; Samuel Gompers, *Seventy Years of Life and Labor: An Autobiography*, vol. 1 (New York, 1967 [1925]), p. 124; Baust interview; A. M. Simons, "A Label and Lives—The Story of the Cigar Makers," *Pearson's Magazine*, Jan. 1917, p. 73.

32. *CMOJ*, Apr. 1904, p. 4; *Tobacco*, 27 July 1900, p. 5; *Tobacco Leaf*, 14 Jan.

1903, p. 42; 24 June 1903, p. 6; 28 Feb. 1906, p. 36; 29 Aug. 1906, p. 28; James Durso interview, 24 Mar. 1977, New Haven, Conn.; Theisen interview; Shea interview.

33. *CMOJ*, Sept. 1912, pp. 20–21; Apr. 1920, pp. 6–7; Ograin interview, 19 May 1979 and 17 May 1980; New York State Department of Labor, "Cigar Makers of Syracuse," *New York Labor Bulletin*, no. 28 (Mar. 1906), 22.

34. Ograin interview, 19 May 1979 and 17 May 1980.

35. *Tobacco Leaf*, 7 Mar. 1900, p. 6; 18 June 1902, p. 14; 2 July 1902, p. 38; 7 Nov. 1906, p. 1.

36. *Tobacco Leaf*, 28 Mar. 1900, p. 5; 4 Apr. 1900, p. 12; 14 Nov. 1906, p. 24; *Tobacco*, 4 Sept. 1903, p. 7; 26 June 1907, p. 20.

37. *Tobacco*, 12 Sept. 1907, p. 8; *U.S. Tobacco Journal*, 11 Mar. 1911, p. 9; 22 Apr. 1911, p. 20.

38. George Pozzetta, "Italians and the Tampa General Strike of 1910," in George Pozzetta, ed., *Pane e Lavoro: The Italian American Working Class* (Toronto, 1980), pp. 34–36, 41; *CMOJ*, Apr. 1910, pp. 32–37; Dec. 1909, p. 8; Oct. 1910, p. 8; Feb. 1910, p. 9; Dec. 1910, p. 9; Feb. 1911, pp. 3, 8; July 1911, p. 4; Nov. 1911, p. 4; Apr. 1914, pp. 50–61; *Tobacco Leaf*, 11 Aug. 1910, p. 5; *U.S. Tobacco Journal*, 22 Apr. 1911, p. 20; 11 Mar. 1911, p. 9; 13 May 1911, pp. 3, 7; 2 Mar. 1912, p. 6. The CMIU charged that manufacturers tried to use racism to divide workers. In the end manufacturers did at least agree to conform to the cartabon.

39. *Tobacco*, 18 July 1900, p. 5; 14 Nov. 1906, p. 6; *Tobacco Leaf*, 3 June 1906, p. 3; 17 June 1908, p. 24; Shea interview; Willis N. Baer, *The Economic Development of the Cigar Industry in the United States* (Lancaster, Pa., 1933), p. 196.

40. U.S. Congress, Senate, *Report on Condition of Woman and Child Wage-Earners in the United States*, vol. 18, *Employment of Women and Children in Selected Industries*, S. Doc. 645, 61st Cong., 2d sess., 1913, p. 111; *Tobacco Leaf*, 7 Nov. 1906, p. 1; 3 Nov. 1908, p. 28; Meyer Jacobstein, *The Tobacco Industry in the United States* (New York, 1907), p. 110; U.S. Commissioner of Labor, *Eleventh Special Report*, "Regulation and Restriction of Output" (Washington, D.C, 1904), pp. 581–85; Simons, "Label and Lives," p. 70; U.S. Bureau of Corporations, Tobacco Investigation, file 3073, sections 1, 10, R.G. 122, NA; *Constitution of the Cigar Makers' International Union of America*, 1912, section 154, Series V, Box 2, Cigar Makers' International Union of America Collection (CMIU Collection), McKeldin Library, University of Maryland (UM), College Park.

41. *CMOJ*, Mar. 1905, p. 4; Barnett Plotkin to Board of Mediation and Arbitration, 19 May 1916, and John H. Moffitt to William B. Wilson, 12 June 1916, file 33/216, U.S. Federal Mediation and Conciliaton Service (FMCS), R.G. 280, NA; *Tobacco Leaf*, 12 Oct. 1904, p. 34; 24 Sept. 1908, p. 38.

42. *Tobacco Leaf*, 17 Dec. 1902, p. 30; 22 July 1903, p. 11; 18 May 1911, p. 11; *Tobacco*, 11 May 1900, p. 8; 6 Mar. 1903, p. 2.

43. *Tobacco Leaf*, 7 Nov. 1906, p. 1; U.S. Bureau of Corporations, Tobacco Investigation, file 3073, R.G. 122, NA.

44. *CMOJ*, Apr. 1881, p. 1; Oct. 1881, p. 3; Feb. 1882, p. 1; Dec. 1882, p. 8; June 1903, p. 8; Sept. 1903, p. 8; July 1906, p. 4; Aug. 1907, p. 10; May 1912, p. 4.

45. *CMOJ*, Dec. 1902, pp. 5–7; May 1903, p. 1; Nov. 1904, p. 4; July 1909, p. 4; Sept. 1909, p. 4; Feb. 1910, pp. 2, 10; Apr. 1910, p. 2. See also *CMOJ*, Apr. 1876, p. 4.

46. William C. Pratt, "The Reading Socialist Experience: A Study of Working Class Politics" (Ph.D. dissertation, Emory University, 1969); *Tobacco Leaf*, 11 June 1902, p. 34; 22 Oct. 1902, p. 22; 15 Apr. 1903, p. 20; 28 Oct. 1903, p. 18; 11 Nov. 1903, p. 14; John Braeman, *Albert J. Beveridge, American Nationalist* (Chicago, 1971), pp. 225–26. Thanks to Don Ritchie for the latter reference.

47. *Constitution of the Cigar Makers' Union*, 1912, p. 2; *CMOJ*, Aug. 1903, p. 2; Dec. 1905, p. 17; Jan. 1906, pp. 3, 10; Aug. 1906, p. 16; Oct. 1906, p. 8; Jan. 1907, pp. 4–5; May 1907, p. 2; June 1909, p. 4; Mar. 1911, p. 3; Apr. 1911, p. 3; May 1912, p. 12; Mar. 1913, p. 7.

48. *CMOJ*, Apr. 1911, p. 3; Sumner H. Slichter, *Union Policies and Industrial Management* (New York, 1968 [1941]), pp. 201–82. Concerning various trade union approaches and strategies, see also Irwin Yellowitz, *Industrialization and the American Labor Movement, 1850–1900* (New York, 1977).

49. *CMOJ*, Jan. 1885, p. 4; Feb. 1885, p. 4; Apr. 1885, p. 4; May 1885, p. 4; Jan. 1887, p. 4; Aug. 1894, p. 4; Feb. 1902, pp. 7, 9–11; Sept. 1906, pp. 5–6; Nov. 1906, p. 9; Feb. 1913, p. 14. Local 97 generally opposed plans for cooperatives.

50. Ira Kipnis, *The American Socialist Movement, 1897–1912* (New York, 1942), pp. 27, 237, 239; Howard Quint, *The Forging of American Socialism: Origins of the Modern Movement* (Columbia, S.C., 1953), p. 161; Solon DeLeon, ed., *The American Labor Who's Who* (New York, 1925), p. 10; Henry Gruber Stetler, *The Socialist Movement in Reading, Pennsylvania, 1896–1936; A Study in Social Change* (Storrs, Conn., 1943); William Dick, *Labor and Socialism in America: The Gompers Era* (Port Washington, N.Y., 1972), p. 76; *Boston Sunday Herald*, 4 Jan. 1903; Henry Bedford, *Socialism and the Workers in Massachusetts, 1886–1912* (Amherst, Mass., 1966); David J. Saposs, *Left Wing Unionism: A Study of Radical Policies and Tactics* (New York, 1926), pp. 33–34. The political spectrum of cigar makers was wider outside the CMIU than inside. See, for example, Paul Avrich, *An American Anarchist: The Life of Voltairine de Cleyre* (Princeton, N.J., 1978), pp. 74, 76, 80, 171.

51. *CMOJ*, Aug. 1976, p. 3; Mar. 1897, p. 4; Aug. 1903, p. 2; Dec. 1905, p. 17; Jan. 1906, pp. 3, 10; Aug. 1906, p. 16; Oct. 1906, p. 8; Jan. 1907, pp. 4–5; May 1907, p. 2; Mar. 1911, p. 3; May 1912, p. 12; Mar. 1913, p. 7; *Tobacco*, 23 Oct. 1903, p. 6.

52. *CMOJ*, Dec. 1906, p. 11; Feb. 1907, p. 12; May 1907, p. 5; Mar. 1909, pp. 6–7, 11; Apr. 1909, p. 10; June 1911, p. 4. In 1907 one local proposed banning the word socialism in the journal. See *CMOJ*, Feb. 1907, p. 12. Perkins's relationship to socialists in his union was complicated by their political opposition to Gompers in the AFL. There were frequent skirmishes. See, for example, Perkins to Frank Morrison, 23 Mar. 1902; Gompers to Morris Brown, 1 Mar. 1906; Perkins to Gibson Weber, Oct. 1903, Papers of the American Federation of Labor, "Cigar Makers, 1901–1937," Reel 36, *American Federation of Labor Records: The Samuel Gompers Era* (Sanford, N.C., 1979). Bedford discusses the colorful David

Goldstein of Boston, who broke with Daniel DeLeon at the turn of the century and became a rabid, and rather daffy, antisocialist.

53. Simons, "Label and Lives," p. 69.

54. *CMOJ*, Nov. 1904, p. 8; Jan. 1905, p. 4; Feb. 1905, p. 8; Mar. 1905, p. 8; Aug. 1906, p. 16; Oct. 1906, p. 16; July 1907, p. 8; Feb. 1910, p. 8; Dec. 1910, p. 10; Apr. 1912, p. 4; July 1912, p. 3; Sept. 1912, p. 5; Mar. 1913, pp. 2, 5; Dec. 1915, p. 9; Ograin interview, 17 May 1980.

55. *CMOJ*, Oct. 1909, p. 4; Jan. 1910, pp. 9, 12; Feb. 1912, pp. 4–5; May 1912, p. 9. In 1920, Gompers was defeated as delegate to the AFL by an old antagonist, Morris Brown. See Bernard Mandel, *Samuel Gompers: A Biography* (Yellow Springs, Ohio, 1963), p. 505.

56. *CMOJ*, Apr. 1904, p. 5; Aug. 1907, p. 6; Oct. 1907, pp. 2–3; July 1909, p. 2. See also Blue Label Club, Chicago, Circular, 17 July 1919, Box 1, folder 4, Papers of Cigar Makers' Local 162, Green Bay, Wis., SHSW. In 1881, Strasser was paid $800 for the year. See *CMOJ*, Oct. 1881, pp. 7–10.

57. *CMOJ*, Apr. 1906, pp. 19–27; May 1906, p. 4; Aug. 1906, p. 2; Aug. 1907, p. 9; July 1909, p. 4; Oct. 1909, p. 10; June 1910, p. 2; Sept. 1910, p. 8; Apr. 1912, pp. 3, 5; Feb. 1912, p. 11; Sept. 1912, p. 25; Apr. 1913, pp. 36–75; Apr. 1920, p. 14; *Tobacco Leaf*, 25 Dec. 1907, p. 3; 27 Aug. 1908, p. 36; 31 Mar. 1910, p. 32; 22 Jan. 1914, p. 18; *U.S. Tobacco Journal*, 29 Apr. 1911, p. 7; 13 May 1911, p. 15.

58. *CMOJ*, July 1907, p. 6; Apr. 1909, p. 2; Jan. 1910, p. 9; June 1910, p. 2; Apr. 1911, pp. 1, 2; *Tobacco Leaf*, 4 Feb. 1909, p. 42; *U.S. Tobacco Journal*, 27 May 1911, p. 4; 3 May 1913, p. 5; George W. Perkins to William B. Wilson, secretary of labor, file 16/45A, R.G. 174, Records of the Office of the Chief Clerk of the Department of Labor, NA.

59. *CMOJ*, Sept. 1902, p. 5; Aug. 1907, p. 9; Aug. 1910, p. 8; Sept. 1912, p. 38; Apr. 1916, p. 2; *U.S. Tobacco Journal*, 23 Mar. 1912, p. 20; 27 Apr. 1912, p. 4; 11 Jan. 1913, p. 4; *Tobacco Leaf*, 4 Feb. 1909, p. 42; 3 Dec. 1914, p. 50.

60. See n. 59 and U.S. Bureau of Corporations, *Report of the Commissioner of Corporations on the Tobacco Industry*, part I, *Position of the Tobacco Combination in the Industry* (Washington, D.C., 1906), p. 426; *U.S. Tobacco Journal*, 3 Feb. 1912, p. 20; 30 Mar. 1912, p. 4; 27 Apr. 1912, p. 4; 4 Jan. 1913, p. 4; 5 Apr. 1913, p. 3; 9 Aug. 1913, p. 3; Jack J. Gottsegen, *Tobacco: A Study of Its Consumption in the United States* (New York, 1940), p. 14; *U.S. Tobacco Journal*, 29 Mar. 1913, p. 4. American Cigar Company profits in 1913 were $1,817,979. See *Tobacco Leaf*, 5 Mar. 1914, p. 5.

61. Gottsegen, *Tobacco*, pp. 18, 26; *Tobacco Leaf*, 30 July 1908, p. 3; 24 Dec. 1914, p. 5; *U.S. Tobacco Journal*, 1 Feb. 1913, p. 4; 16 Aug. 1913, p. 4; 29 Aug. 1914, pp. 4, 7; 2 Jan. 1913, p. 6; Baer, *Economic Development of the Cigar Industry*, p. 257; *U.S. Tobacco Journal*, 13 Jan. 1912, p. 5; 15 Feb. 1913, p. 3; *Tobacco Leaf*, 20 Feb. 1913, p. 3.

62. *Tobacco Leaf*, 2 Jan. 1913, p. 6; 30 Apr. 1914, p. 6; 13 Aug. 1914, p. 6; 20 Aug. 1914, p. 5; 12 Nov. 1914, p. 5; 24 Dec. 1914, p. 5; *U.S. Tobacco Journal*, 27 Apr. 1912, p. 4; Gary Mormino, "Tampa and the New Urban South: The Weight Strike of 1899," *Florida Historical Quarterly*, 60 (Jan. 1982), 354–55.

63. *Tobacco Leaf*, 6 Feb. 1913, p. 4.

64. *CMOJ*, July 1907, p. 6; June 1910, p. 2; Apr. 1911, p. 2; Gompers, *Seventy Years of Life and Labor*, vol. 1., pp. 179–81.

65. Perkins to Morrison, 29 Mar. 1911, and 26 Feb. 1913, "Cigar Makers, 1901–1937," Reel 36, American Federation of Labor Records; *CMOJ*, Jan. 1905, p. 8; Oct. 1908, p. 8; Sept. 1909, p. 9; Oct. 1910, pp. 8–9; Nov. 1911, p. 8; Nov. 1916, p. 25.

66. Perkins to Samuel Gompers, 22 July 1905, Samuel Gompers Papers, Library of Congress, Washington, D.C.; *CMOJ*, Jan. 1906, p. 11; Mar. 1906, p. 4; May 1906, p. 4; Nov. 1906, p. 15; Apr. 1907, p. 2; Dec. 1908, p. 8; Dec. 1910, p. 10; Nov. 1911, p. 9; Apr. 1912, p. 9; Circular, 5 Feb. 1912, "Cigar Makers, 1901–1937," Reel 36, *American Federation of Labor Records*. Socialists charged that Perkins printed every letter Goldstein ever wrote. Periodically critics urged that someone else edit the *CMOJ*, but no specific steps toward this end were ever taken.

67. *CMOJ*, Dec. 1910, p. 12; Apr. 1911, p. 17; Aug. 1911, p. 17; Aug. 1911, pp. 14–16.

68. *CMOJ*, "Proceedings," Oct. 1912, pp. 2, 47–133.

69. *CMOJ*, Oct. 1912, p. 2; Nov. 1912, pp. 3, 4; Dec. 1912, p. 14. Perkins had previously argued against changing union rules and had defended the union against charges from the IWW that the CMIU did not admit all cigar makers. Perkins pointed out that union membership was technically open to any cigar maker, but that many team workers had been strike breakers. See *CMOJ*, Jan. 1905, p. 9.

70. *CMOJ*, Dec. 1912, pp. 3, 14; July 1914, p. 13; Oct. 1915, p. 25; Apr. 1916, pp. 2, 42. Perkins angrily denounced those who voted against Class A in 1912. See *CMOJ*, Feb. 1913, p. 2.

71. *Tobacco Leaf*, 24 Mar. 1900, p. 6; 24 June 1903, p. 6; 4 May 1904, p. 4; 3 July 1908, p. 18; *Tobacco*, 23 Mar. 1900, p. 3.

72. *Tobacco Leaf*, 29 Oct. 1902, p. 44; *Tobacco*, 4 May 1900, p. 3; 19 Dec. 1902, p. 4.

73. *Tobacco Leaf*, 14 Mar. 1900, p. 5; 21 Mar. 1900, p. 6; 27 June 1900, p. 6; 6 July 1900, p. 1.

74. *Tobacco Leaf*, 7 Mar. 1900, p. 6; 22 June 1904, p. 6; 31 May 1905, p. 6; *Tobacco*, 14 Mar. 1900, p. 5; 17 Apr. 1903, p. 4; 13 Aug. 1903, p. 8.

75. *Tobacco*, 20 Apr. 1900, p. 1; 27 Apr. 1900, p. 7; May 1900, p. 3; *Tobacco Leaf*, 24 Sept. 1902, p. 38; 10 Jan. 1906, p. 22.

76. *Tobacco*, 17 Apr. 1903, p. 7.

77. *Tobacco Leaf*, 28 Oct. 1903, p. 18; 4 Mar. 1906, p. 4; 27 Jan. 1910, p. 6; *U.S. Tobacco Journal*, 3 Nov. 1906, p. 9; *CMOJ*, July 1909, p. 4; Nov. 1909, p. 5.

78. *Tobacco Leaf*, 4 June 1902, p. 16; 17 May 1905, p. 7; 6 Feb. 1907, p. 11; 24 Nov. 1910, p. 4; 5 Jan. 1911, p. 11; *Tobacco*, 19 Jan. 1900, p. 7; 24 July 1903, p. 6; U.S. Industrial Commission, *Report of the Industrial Commission on the Relations and Conditions of Capital and Labor*, vol. 15 (Washington, D.C. 1901), p. 387.

79. *Tobacco Leaf*, 3 June 1908, p. 3; 17 June 1908, p. 24; 18 Mar. 1909, p. 5; 8 Jan. 1914, p. 5; 11 Oct. 1915, pp. 274, 282.

80. *Tobacco Leaf*, 28 Mar. 1900, p. 6.

6

"Taking the Factory to the Workers"

The men on strike against Lilies Cigar Company in Kalamazoo, Michigan, filed into the meeting hall of CMIU Local 208 to discuss the strike situation. It was a cold Saturday night, the last day of February in 1908, and the men were uneasy. Lilies, which employed 116 of the local's 200 members, had unexpectedly changed management when the factory reopened after New Year's Day. The new shop rules of the factory not only offended the union cigar makers' sensibilities, but they also violated the union's bill of prices and rendered "working with any degree of comfort impossible." The men resented the poor tobacco stock, the "obnoxious signs" posted throughout the factory which instructed them to make smokers using only scraps, and the degrading new rules on inspection of their work and the pickup of completed cigars. Within two weeks the union men had voted to strike and had received authorization from the International. They stopped work on January 29, when the company refused to give an immediate reply to their demands. As the days and weeks passed, company officials showed no signs of distress, and by the February 28 meeting, Lilies's management had only offered to take the strikers back under existing conditions. A gloomy mood prevailed in their assembly that night, but members voted to "stand pat" and continue the fight rather than return to the shop. The company's resolve was unsettling, but the cigar makers were not accustomed to losing.[1]

Within a week, Lilies Cigar Company announced that it would close its Kalamazoo factory and move to Detroit. The firm relocated at 222-58 Forest Avenue, in the center of one of the largest Polish neighborhoods in Detroit. Here Polish men worked in heavy industry, while about five thousand Polish women, mostly under the age of twenty-five, worked in the cigar factories located near their homes. Union cigar makers, who numbered about 430, were concentrated in small factories located in the city center, a number of which had no more than ten employees. They had little contact with the larger-sized companies which moved into the Polish district to tap its vast female labor pool, and which employed as many as one hundred or more women in each factory. A company spokesman for Lilies explained that the "labor trouble in Kalamazoo" would be "eliminated in Detroit."[2]

The Kalamazoo firm's actions were not isolated. Thousands of cigar manufacturers during the late nineteenth and early twentieth centuries adopted policies to maximize profit levels and control production. Their labor policies defined the organization of work and the context of social relations on the shop floor. They divided the labor process, instituted tighter regimentation of work, sometimes adopted modest welfare programs, and, most important, aimed at securing a cheap, pliant labor force. Young women, particularly recent immigrants, were thought to be the ideal employees. It was this conviction, together with women's own choices regarding occupation, which helped foster women's growing participation in the industry and which shaped the character and organization of the workplaces they encountered.

Although women had been a decisive influence in the cigar industry since the 1870s, it was not until the early twentieth century that they came to outnumber men in the trade. Regrettably, figures on women's participation in cigar making alone are unobtainable because census data combined several groups of tobacco workers and because cigar factories included women other than cigar makers. However, using census data and CMIU statistics, it is possible to estimate female participation in the industry, as Tables 2–4 illustrate.

In 1910 and 1919, other census figures reached a closer approximation of cigar makers' numbers. The 1910 Census of Occupations broke down tobacco industry data into specific jobs. Adding together figures for bunch makers, cigar makers "unspecified," and rollers, 1910 figures show 65,835 men and 41,056 women (38.4 percent of the total). These figures roughly correspond to the union's estimates for 1912. In 1919, the Census of Manufactures listed workers in cigar factories separately and found 78,253 women and 53,153 men. Women were almost 60 percent of the total cigar factory labor force.[3]

More women worked in the cigar industry each year, but they worked primarily in the large-scale firms with regional and national markets, specializing in cigars which retailed for five cents or less. For instance, the

Table 2. Male and Female Employment in Cigar and Cigarette Factories
Workers Age 16 and Over[a]

	Census of Manufactures			
	1900	1905	1909[b]	1919
Men	62,168	72,790	90,417	65,099
Women	37,762	57,174	84,193	93,341
Total	99,930	129,964	174,610	158,440
Percent women	37.8	43.9	48.2	58.9

Source: U.S. Department of Commerce, Bureau of the Census, *Census of Manufactures:*
1900, vol. 9, *Special Reports on Selected Industries* (Washington, D.C., 1902), p. 653;
Bureau of the Census, *Census of Manufactures: 1905*, Bulletin 87, *Tobacco* (Washington,
D.C., 1907), p. 8; Bureau of the Census, *Census of Manufactures: 1909*, vol. 8, *General
Report and Analysis* (Washington, D.C., 1913), p. 254; Bureau of the Census, *Census of
Manufactures: 1919*, vol. 8, *General Report and Analytical Tables* (Washington, D.C.,
1923), p. 490.

[a]excludes those under age 16
[b]includes all tobacco factory operatives

Table 3. Male and Female Employment
All Cigar and Tobacco Factory Operatives
Age 10 and Over

	Census of Population		
	1900[a]	1910[b]	1920[b]
Men	87,996	79,966	61,226
Women	43,498	71,845	83,960
Total	131,494	151,811	145,186
Percent women	33.1	47.3	57.8

Source: U.S. Department of Commerce, Bureau of the Census, *Census of Occupations:*
1900, "Special Reports" (Washington, D.C., 1904), p. 12; Bureau of the Census, *Census of
Population: 1920*, vol. 4, *Occupations* (Washington, D.C., 1923), p. 38.

[a]semiskilled and laborers combined
[b]semiskilled operatives only

Table 4. Male and Female Employment
Cigar Making and Packing

	1901	1912	1920
Men	38,902	61,031	50,375
Women	22,250	38,561	61,003
Total	61,152	99,592	111,378
Percent women	36.4	38.7	54.8

Source: *CMOJ*, Sept. 1901, p. 8; Sept. 1912, pp. 14–15; Apr. 1920, p. 3. President of the
CMIU, George W. Perkins, noted that 1901 figures significantly undercounted all cigar
makers. It is likely that all union figures undercounted women.

American Cigar Company, the cigar branch of the giant American Tobacco Company, adopted a women-only hiring policy. American Cigar plants were located in several cities in New Jersey, New York City, Philadelphia, Lancaster, Baltimore, Charleston (South Carolina), Louisville, New Orleans, Cincinnati, Chicago, and Detroit. A Bureau of Labor survey of the largest cigar factories in 1903 found that women made up 80 percent of their employees. Another survey in 1912 showed that most of the largest companies hired women as a majority of their production workers. With some exceptions, women cigar makers worked primarily in sex-segregated workplaces, creating all-female environments on the shop floor. Even when men and women worked together, most women worked in factories where they outnumbered men.[4]

Female employment increased because of the conscious hiring policies of these manufacturers. Firms just entering the industry, joined by older nonunion companies and others such as the Henry Offterdinger Company or Lilies Cigar who had dropped association with the union, looked to women workers to meet their labor requirements. Even when manufacturers had a choice between nonunion men and women, increasingly they preferred women. The trade journals commented on this tendency in several areas, such as New York City, where "a person must wear skirts and petticoats to get a job in any large factory uptown."[5]

Since the nineteenth century, manufacturers' interest in women had been based both on a rejection of the union and its strong culture, and on certain assumptions about the characteristics of women workers, particularly immigrant women. Manufacturers hoped to reduce the costs of labor and maximize their control over the production process. They could pay women lower wages on less-skilled work. As the trade journal *Tobacco Leaf* noted in 1902, "what manufacturers require is female labor—cheap hire, which responds so favorably to the cost of production in modern competition." A constellation of gender-based reasons influenced their decisions. The CMIU charged that employers believed "that women are more tractable and docile than men." Manufacturers explained that they wanted women because they "don't drink," were "better adapted and cheaper," were "more reliable," were "cheaper and more careful," and were "more easily controlled." A New York City study at the end of the period concluded that the "employers' preference for women . . . seems to arise partly from the fact that women will take lower wages and are less subject to labor agitation."[6] One manufacturer thought that women possessed "an innate skill and nimbleness." Another liked women because they were "always here on Monday morning." Also, women did not smoke cigars, so "they do not use any of the raw material they are handling." Manufacturers universally applauded women for not taking smokers and therefore not wasting tobacco. While union factories had been locked in the controversy over free smokers, Detroit manufacturers had been publicly congratulating themselves because they had no "free-smoker nuisance" to contend with among their female employees.[7]

By the century's second decade, the majority of women cigar makers in the country worked in Pennsylvania, New York, and New Jersey, followed by Michigan and Ohio. The heaviest concentration of female employment clustered along the so-called cigar belt, which ran southwest from New York City through New Jersey to Philadelphia, ending one hundred miles to the west. Traditionally New York City had been the center of women's employment in the industry. During the early years of the twentieth century, cigar manufacturers—particularly larger firms employing women— began leaving New York for New Jersey and Pennsylvania. Female employment in Manhattan declined, from 8,600 in 1900 to 4,500 in 1922. In New Jersey, large firms employing women opened in several cities during the early twentieth century, including New Brunswick, Trenton, Newark, Jersey City, and Camden. The number of women in cigars and tobacco in the state climbed from 736 in 1900 to 3,977 in 1905 to 8,243 in 1920.[8]

In Pennsylvania cigar production and employment were concentrated in three areas: Philadelphia, the Lehigh Valley, and the so-called country districts stretching from Bucks County in the east midway across the state to York County, just below Harrisburg. In addition, Pittsburgh, on the western border, served as one of the national centers of the stogie industry and employed 2,600 women and 961 men in 1905.[9]

Women cigar makers in Philadelphia could be found in the large factory buildings owned by Otto Eisenlohr Brothers, Bobrow Brothers, Bayuk Brothers, Theobald and Oppenheimer, Jeitles and Blumenthal, and the American Cigar Company. In 1915, 1,522 men and 4,300 women worked in the city's cigar factories. Over 1,000 worked for Bayuk alone. The Lehigh Valley spanned the region beginning fifty miles north of Philadelphia and eighty miles west of New York, which included the cities of Allentown and Bethlehem and the "almost continuous line" of small towns along the Lehigh River northward to Palmerton. The cigar industry in the region grew dramatically after 1905, when Jeitles and Blumenthal first erected a factory below Allentown. Other large firms quickly established branches in the neighborhoods where foreign-born women, whose husbands and fathers worked in the steel and cement industries, lived. In 1900 only about 186 women in the valley worked in the trade, but in 1910, 1,715 did. The country districts, the subject of Chapter 7, began growing at about the same time. Over 18,000 women worked in Pennsylvania cigar factories in 1916.[10]

In the South, Tampa and New Orleans were centers of women's employment. Twelve hundred women worked in the tobacco industry in Florida in 1900; 2,741 did in 1920. In New Orleans, the number jumped from a couple of hundred in 1900 to twelve hundred in 1920. Several cities in the Midwest in addition to Detroit had many female-employing factories, including Cincinnati, Dayton, Cleveland, and Chicago. Large firms were also located in several smaller midwestern cities, notably Evansville, Indiana, and Lima, Ohio. Few of the large firms were located in the West, so female employment there was low.[11]

Who were the women they hired? Just over half were either foreign-born or children of foreign-born parents in 1910 and less than 1 percent were black. Although by 1920 their numbers had increased, most black women were still segregated from white women in cigar factories and were assigned to tobacco stemming preparation jobs rather than cigar making itself. This was also true in the rest of the tobacco industry, where black women had traditionally been employed in large numbers. Throughout this period women cigar makers came from the ethnic groups which had immigrated most recently, including Poles, Hungarians, Italians, Slovaks, and Russian Jews. Three "older" groups also remained important in the trade: Germans, Irish, and Bohemians.[12]

Ethnicity varied geographically. In 1910 the U.S. Industrial Commission found that in cigar and tobacco factories in New Jersey, Pennsylvania, Delaware, and New York, about 28 percent of women workers were native-born of native parents; while in Ohio, Illinois, Missouri, and Wisconsin, 37 percent were.[13] In Detroit, a majority of the women were Polish; in Chicago, Polish and Russian Jewish women prevailed. In New Orleans, factories had traditionally employed Cuban and Spanish men. Once the American Cigar Company took over the largest factory and hired white women only, more manufacturers began hiring women, primarily Cubans and Spaniards, whom they viewed as white. Beginning in the late 1910s, however, some factories began hiring black women. In 1900, only 44 percent of women working in city tobacco factories were native white of native parents and less than 1 percent were black. In 1920, just over 64 percent were native white of native parents and about 16 percent were black. Note that the census assumes that blacks are native-born.

In the counties north of Philadelphia but below Allentown, the country districts, women were native-born "Pennsylvania Dutch" (more accurately Pennsylvania German). From Allentown and Bethlehem north, however, women were overwhelmingly foreign-born—86.4 percent in 1920. They were primarily German, Austrian, Hungarian, Slovenian, and to a lesser extent Polish and Italian.[14] Women stogie makers in Pittsburgh were primarily Jewish in the early twentieth century, but by the second decade Polish and Italian women were most often hired. In New York City, Bohemian women traditionally dominated cigar making, but by the 1910s fewer and fewer daughters of cigar makers entered the trade because of the social stigma they attached to the work. Other women, particularly Italians and Russian Jews, moved into the city's factories. By 1915, only 15 percent of the Czech women in the city were engaged in cigar making. In New Jersey cities, Hungarian women formed the largest group of cigar makers, but they shared the trade with native-born women, Italians, Poles, and Germans. In 1920, 52.6 percent of women tobacco workers in the state were foreign-born.[15]

Women cigar makers tended to be young and single, throughout this period. The 1912 Bureau of Labor report on *Woman and Child Wage-Earners in the United States* found that while half of the male cigar workers in their national sample were over age twenty-five, 70 percent of the women were younger. The same study found that almost 80 percent of the women questioned were single.[16] Figures for cigar makers from the 1910 census indicated that only 13 percent of males but 46 percent of females were under the age of twenty-five. One-quarter of the men were over age forty-five, while only one-twentieth of the women were. Census figures for 1900 showed that 16.1 percent of women in tobacco factories were married; in 1920 35.8 percent were. Thus, while a majority remained single, more married women could be found among the female cigar-making labor force at the end of the period. In Philadelphia in 1900, 8 percent of the women in tobacco factories were married, but in 1920 over 25 percent were. In Allentown, the proportion of married women likewise grew from 1.5 percent in 1900 to 33.2 percent in 1920. Just over 48 percent of women tobacco workers in New Jersey were married by 1920.[17] Age and marital status of women workers were related to ethnicity. Polish women tended to be young and single while Bohemian women were older and more likely to be married. Recently arrived Hungarian women were generally older and more likely to be married than other women in the trade.[18]

To acquire the most desirable employees, manufacturers followed a policy of "taking the factory to the workers," placing operations in areas readily accessible to targeted groups. Detroit manufacturers, as we have seen, moved into Polish neighborhoods to tap available female labor pools there. Even Pittsburgh stogie manufacturers moved out of Jewish areas in the wake of a strike and into Polish neighborhoods in the hopes of hiring more docile workers. A report on the industry in the New York/New Jersey region noted that "some manufacturers have even made a special attempt to get married women and have located their factories and arranged their hours so that the women can be at home to get the family meals and start the children to school and still work in the factory."[19] So while cigar companies used traditional methods of hiring through a foreman rather than a personnel office, they screened workers to the extent that they hired women and carefully decided where to locate plants.

Larger firms tended to open numerous branch factories in several different places, rather than concentrating production in one plant. Selection of sites related to local competition for labor, the strength of the CMIU, and the availability of large numbers of women. A cigar company desiring a pool of women workers would not locate in Paterson, New Jersey, for example, since competition for women from textile firms might reduce the labor supply and force wages up. An unpublished 1912 Commission on Industrial Relations study concluded that female-employing industries, such as cigar making, tended to locate in heavy-industry, male-employing areas where there were few other jobs for women. United Cigar Manufacturers (UCM), American Cigar, Bayuk, and Otto Eisenlohr Brothers opened branch factories throughout the East, particularly in Pennsylvania and New Jersey. UCM apparently divided Philadelphia territory with the American Cigar Company "in such a manner as not to compete for labor." The former opened plants north and west of the city, the latter primarily in Philadelphia, Camden, and Trenton. The branch factory system had also worked well as a strikebreaking measure in the nineteenth century and again more recently in the 1900 New York City strike when several firms opened branches in Pennsylvania, New Jersey, and Kingston, New York. The branch factory pattern permitted manufacturers to minimize disruption during strikes, for if operations were halted in one factory, production could shift to another.[20]

Manufacturers who located branches in fairly small, isolated areas, such as southeastern Pennsylvania or western Ohio, gained the additional advantage of securing a nearly captive labor force. Women who wanted to work had few choices available, unlike their sisters in a mixed-industry city like Philadelphia. The Deisel-Wemmer Company, founded in 1891, took the strategy to its furthest limit by locating branch factories in a score of small towns within a seventy-five-mile radius of its main office in Lima, Ohio. Between 1906 and 1916, the company established seventeen branches and employed four thousand women. The company found a ready supply of workers. "It was the only place to work in Lima," noted cigar roller Pearl Hume. Since there was no competition for labor from other factories in these towns, company owners could set whatever rules or wages they desired. As a conciliation commissioner of the U.S. Department of Labor noted: "The company can successfully impose any reduction in wages or changes in working conditions as it sees fit, as the workers . . . cannot secure similar work except by leaving their homes to seek employment in other places." Anyone who quit ran the risk of "being denied work in the future."[21]

Cigar manufacturers generally preferred to hire the most newly arrived immigrant women who had little facility with English. As the U.S. Immigration Commission noted in 1912, the increase in employment of southern and eastern European women in cigar factories was partly the result of "a conscious policy of the manufacturers in establishing new factories in communities where immigrant labor of this class—especially that of women and girls—is available." In the Lehigh Valley, manufacturers' policy of locating near and hiring foreign-born women actually precipitated increased immigration, according to a Women's Bureau study. Having heard from friends and relatives in the area, single women immigrated confidently expecting to get jobs in the cigar factories. Manufacturers wanted young women, immigrant or native, with little previous work experience. When the American Cigar Company, one of the most systematic in hiring women, opened a new factory in Altoona, Pennsylvania, in 1902, the company made a special effort to "select green hands, so as to train them into a disciplined force."[22]

That manufacturers consciously sought out women and tried to attract them did not mean, of course, that women themselves were passive in the process. They made choices about work, even if those choices were quite limited. Retail sales work offered the only alternative to cigar making in

The Deisel-Wemmer cigar factory, Lima, Ohio, from a 1906 pamphlet, *The Model Cigar Factory of America*, published by the Deisel-Wemmer Company. Photo courtesy of Allen County Historical Society, Lima, Ohio.

Lima, Ohio, but these jobs were few in number and many women felt the wages were too low. Pearl Hume followed the pattern of many cigar makers when she started working for Deisel-Wemmer in Lima in 1912. She took the job because her four sisters already worked there. Working itself was taken as given because "we were all poor, let's face it." Anna Bartasius worked in Philadelphia and based her work decision on the fact that the cigar factory was close enough to walk to and she did not need to know English to work there. Rita Johnson, a black cigar maker in New Orleans, had chosen the trade in 1918 as a welcome alternative. "I didn't like domestic work," she explained, "because it was too confining." In Chicago, Dora Rosenzweig chose cigar making, her brother's trade, over sewing "which I hated." Still cigar manufacturers placed themselves in a position to take advantage of women's need for convenient, paid work.[23]

Most manufacturers employing women organized the work into the team system, which by 1910 had become the dominant form of labor in the entire cigar industry. Normally two rollers worked with one buncher, although occasionally the ratio was one to one. Machinery gained ground during the second decade, but evidence suggests that more than half of the women cigar makers worked by hand with only the aid of molds throughout the period. While manufacturers purchased the molds, they saved money by requiring cigar makers to buy their own workboards and cutters. They liked using the team system because a team could easily change from one shape to another, but more so because it encouraged good work from all members. A roller would not be likely to risk rolling an imperfect bunch since it could waste her time and diminish her earnings if the cigars were rejected. Rollers could produce more rapidly if they worked on bunches made by one person rather than having to adjust to several different styles. Too, many manufacturers trained rollers to work only on right or left hand leaves, not both. This cut training time, and manufacturers hoped it would also reduce turnover by making it slightly more difficult to move to another job. Stogie manufacturers followed the same procedure.[24]

The advantage of the team system did not lie in its increased efficiency, a 1903 Bureau of Labor study confirmed. Its primary advantage could be found "not in the increased speed of the operatives but in the cheaper labor which can thereby be employed." The report continued that "undoubtedly the main reason why manufacturers favor team work is that thereby they can cheapen production." It required less time to teach only

part of the process and thus lessened the financial investment in each individual cigar maker.[25]

Manufacturers also looked to machinery to help achieve their labor
goals. Throughout this period, however, most machinery was hand- rather
than power-operated and did not bring substantial economy or efficiency.
"While certain machines are used in many of the factories furnishing
data," the Bureau of Labor Statistics reported in 1912, "they require so
much handwork in addition that they are more properly helpful appli-
ances than machines; they aid but they do not supersede handwork." At
first the only bunching machinery available was a device introduced in
the 1880s by Miller, DuBrul and Peters Manufacturing Company. It was
simply a sheet of canvas attached to a metal frame. The filler leaf was
placed either in the canvas trough at the base of the machine or in a metal
shaping cup. The cigar maker arranged the binder leaf on the canvas
apron above and when she pulled a lever attached to rollers toward her,
she wrapped the filler inside the binder. A closed mold, half mold, or special clips were then used to shape the bunches. Molds were customarily
used unless the cigars were a higher grade and expected to compete with
handmade cigars. (Molds drew out the moisture from the tobacco and created hard spots in the cigars, especially when used for periods over
twenty minutes.) A power-driven bunching machine was used for cheap
short-filler cigars, such as those made in York County, Pennsylvania, and
Pittsburgh stogies, although many of these same smokes were bunched
by hand as well. Working these machines was especially onerous because
most models required the operator to stand.[26]

In the 1890s the Lieberman Company of Philadelphia introduced a suction table for rolling cigars which came into wider use after 1900. The suction table consisted of a metal die which rested on the table top, through
which suction was applied from air ducts underneath. It was much easier
for a cigar maker to lay out the wrapper leaf on the table and stretch it
using suction. The roller operated a pedal with her foot which raised the
die slightly. Then she pushed a knife along a preset track around the die,
cutting the wrapper out uniformly. Since cutting the wrapper was one of
the most skilled operations involved in rolling a cigar, the suction table
thus eliminated the need for specialized training. While hand cutting and
rolling might take two years to learn, cutting with a suction table only
took a few months. In a few cases companies divided the work further so
that one person cut out the leaf and another rolled the bunch into it.[27]

Suction tables were used almost exclusively by women and their chief advantage to manufacturers lay in reduced labor costs.

The use of machinery depended on what manufacturers could afford and whether they felt the savings and reduced training time would justify the investment. Suction tables were not widely used during this period, but manufacturers in Philadelphia and New York City did install them, especially in the largest plants, because they speeded up the training process. Pittsburgh stogies, except for the handmade brands, were rolled using suction machines. Almost all American Cigar Company plants used one or both kinds of machinery for the same reason. These factories installed machinery and then advertised their use of it as proof of their modern methods and "scientific processes." The trust had hoped that more sophisticated machinery would be developed by the American Machine and Foundry Company, but AMF had been unable to fulfill its directive. AMF entered the cigar machinery business, however, and bought out several smaller producers of bunching and rolling equipment. During these years, countless rumors spread concerning the invention of automatic machinery (including a bunching device invented by impresario Oscar Hammerstein). However, none of these machines proved practicable on a wide scale.[28]

Advertising for the devices revealed the link between gender, reduced expenses, and control over production. Miller, DuBrul and Peters tempted potential buyers by pointing out that while the suction table increased speed and output, it also simplified the labor process: "Then, too, the operator rolls only right-hand or left-hand, and learns to roll only one-handed, thus reducing the time to become an expert cigar maker, and enabling the operator to learn in a few weeks what otherwise takes months to pick up." The suction table also set a uniform shape for the wrapper and took away from the rollers the opportunity for making these decisions. "Having one thoroughly-experienced person's judgment to rule the whole factory, in the matter of wrapper stock, is a great savings." Overall the suction table provided a "great saving in labor, which is natural from the fact that hands are quickly taught to make cigars, and by reason of increased output which is due to the suction table, a lower price can be fixed, for the same grade of work."[29] Another suction table advertisement noted that the foreman's job was hard because it took so long to train hand-workers. "For any shop employing girl labor, the economy of suction work . . . could make it worthwhile to equip with the suction system." Manu-

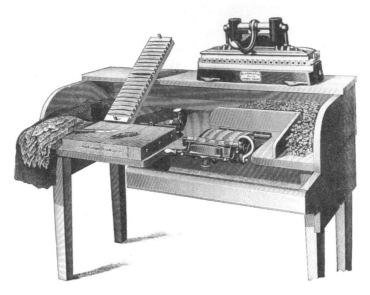

An advertising version of a bunch maker's work table complete with board, knife, mold, buncher, and small press. It is unlikely that many bunch makers ever got to work at such a clean and modern work space. Miller DuBrul and Peters Manufacturing Company, *Catalogue*, 1895, Tobacco Collection, Extractive Industries, Museum of American History, Smithsonian Institution, Washington, D.C.

Suction table, Miller DuBrul and Peters Manufacturing Company, *Catalogue*, 1895, Tobacco Collection, Extractive Industries, Museum of American History, Smithsonian Institution, Washington, D.C.

facturers liked suction tables because they forced workers to stretch the tobacco to get more cuts out of one wrapper. Finally, machinery offered "the opportunity of employing girls at low wages." By itself, the increased efficiency might not be sufficient to justify its use, but when combined with the lower wages of women, it did provide considerable savings.[30]

Wages and hours of women cigar makers were set with a view toward maximum profitability through low labor cost and high levels of production. Women worked by the piece as male unionists did, but piecework had less of a liberating effect, since low piece rates encouraged them to work long hours at maximum speed, in order to make incomes sufficient for their needs. Generally, women might make as little as $4 to $6 a week at the turn of the century. Meyer Jacobstein, writing on the tobacco industry using 1905 data, estimated that weekly wage rates for nonunion cigar makers ranged from $5 to $7 a week. By 1910 wage levels had risen to about $8 to $10 a week. From 1915 to 1920, they shot up to $15 to $20 a week.[31]

Not surprisingly, precise data on women's wages and hours in cigar factories are uneven and fragmentary at best. Factories did not keep records of hours and women's varying work patterns distorted wage statistics. Nevertheless, a look at various surveys of wage data permits some generalizations about women's wages in the early twentieth century.

Unfortunately, the U.S. Bureau of Labor (later Department of Labor) presented cigar makers' wages in the form of hourly earnings. (See Table 5.) Because of irregular hours, these are somewhat difficult to translate into weekly estimates. A possible average for use in conversion can be found in a 1913 Bureau of Labor study of fifty-eight cigar factories employing 15,782 workers. In the ten factories in union states, it shows hours averaging 9.42 Monday through Friday and 6.6 on Saturday.[32] For a woman earning 11¢ an hour, the weekly wage would be $6.44. At 44¢ an hour, it came to $23.63. Obviously these figures should be used with caution. The hourly totals do suggest, however, differentials among different cigar-making jobs and among various cities and towns. They also suggest a rise in wages during the second decade—with a particularly sharp jump between 1913 and 1919, a result of numerous strikes during the war period.

Slightly more helpful are the bureau's own comparative figures for 1913, which calculated that the following percentages of women workers in the cigar industry received more than eight dollars a week in wages: New York, 56.6 percent; New Jersey, 27.2 percent; Pennsylvania, 22.4 percent; Maryland, 23.1 percent; Louisiana, 24.1 percent; Ohio, 21.2

Table 5. Hourly Earnings for Women and Men[a] Cigar Makers
(Cents per Hour)

Occupation	Region	1900 W	1900 M	1901 W	1901 M	1902 W	1902 M	1903 W	1903 M	1906 W	1906 M	1907 W	1907 M
Hand Bunchers	North Atlantic	15.6	16.7	17.2	17.9	16.6	17.0	19.1	19.6	18.5	25.6	18.9	26.5
	North Central	12.4	—	13.2	—	12.3	—	16.7	—	22.2	23.1	21.3	23.5
	South Atlantic	—	—	—	—	—	—	—	—	15.1	19.6	17.3	20.1
	South Central	—	—	—	—	—	—	—	—	13.9	20.0	15.5	17.9
Machine Bunchers	North Atlantic	11.8	—	11.5	—	12.4	—	12.4	—	16.4	—	15.0	—
	North Central	—	—	—	—	—	—	—	—	17.1	—	17.9	—
Hand Rollers	North Atlantic	16.1	16.3	18.8	19.6	20.2	21.4	19.3	20.0	18.3	27.0	18.5	30.0
	North Central	12.3	21.2	14.1	23.6	12.2	23.9	18.8	23.6	19.3	24.8	18.9	25.4
	South Atlantic	—	—	—	—	—	—	—	—	13.2	21.0	13.4	22.9
	South Central	—	—	—	—	—	—	—	—	12.8	17.6	13.6	16.4
Suction Rollers[b]	North Atlantic	12.7	—	15.3	—	14.5	—	15.3	—	15.9	—	16.3	—
	North Central	—	—	—	—	—	—	—	—	15.2	—	14.3	—
	South Atlantic	—	—	—	—	—	—	—	—	16.2	—	18.5	—
	South Central	—	—	—	—	—	—	—	—	10.1	—	11.2	—
Cigar Makers[c]	North Atlantic	—	25.2	—	25.8	—	25.7	—	25.4	—	34.8	—	30.0
	North Central	—	28.1	—	28.6	—	29.1	—	32.0	—	31.9	—	33.3
	South Atlantic	—	25.7	—	27.5	—	27.6	—	27.5	—	30.1	—	29.6
	South Central	—	—	—	—	—	—	—	—	—	27.7	—	30.4

Source: *Nineteenth Annual Report of the Commissioner of Labor, Wages and Hours of Labor*, 1904, pp. 430–31; U.S. Bureau of Labor, Bulletin #77, *Wages and Hours of Labor, 1906 and 1907*, p. 59.

[a]These are all male workers surveyed, including union and nonunion workers.

[b]There were no male suction rollers.

[c]No division of labor.

percent; Indiana, 30.5 percent; and Michigan, 33.5 percent. One-half of all women surveyed earned less than six dollars a week, while only one-twelfth of the men surveyed did. Ten percent of the women studied made more than ten dollars a week, while 75 percent of the men exceeded that amount.[33]

New Jersey wage statistics for women working in cigar and tobacco factories showed little change between 1900 and 1910, when about 88 percent of them made less than $9 a week. In 1916, however, only about 53 percent made less than that amount. In Pennsylvania, women in cigar factories averaged $6.58 a week while men averaged $9.57 a week in 1916. In Ohio in 1913, 67 percent of women cigar workers made less than $7 a week while only 10 percent of the men in the trade earned that little. In factories where men and women worked together as team workers, both normally made the same piece rate. The Deisel-Wemmer Company in Lima, however, paid male cigar makers more than women for the same grade of work.[34]

Long hours and low wages were frequently combined. By 1908 Deisel-Wemmer had mandated a ten-hour day with no half holiday on Saturday. Pearl Hume had to rise "with the larks" at 5:30 each morning to get to work on time. In announcing the change a *Tobacco Leaf* reporter added that "before the holiday season sets in, they believe they will have to work overtime." Stella Sutton recalled this pre-Christmas rush: "They didn't ask. They just told you you worked and you worked or you didn't work at all."[35] In New Orleans, the Hernsheim factory, owned by the American Cigar Company, kept ten- to twelve-hour days. In 1914, 52 percent of the women working in cigar factories in the state, who were primarily concentrated in New Orleans, earned less than $6 a week. By 1919, the number earning less than $6 had fallen to 11 percent.[36] New York City wages were higher than in most areas, ranging from $8 to $12 a week throughout the first decade and upward thereafter. Hours were also shorter and the combination, plus the expensive real estate costs, stimulated migration of large companies out of the city during the second decade of the century.

Manufacturers did not necessarily need to make long hours compulsory, since piece rates were so low, as the case of Pennsylvania illustrated. In York County, factories stayed open late and women could work as long as they wished. "There was no pressure on you," noted Pauline Stauffer of Hanover in York County. "That we did ourselves," to get more pay. In the Lehigh Valley, janitors unlocked some factories as early as 5 A.M.; women could "go in as early as they please" and often did so, a Women's Bureau

Table 6. Hourly Earnings for Women and Men[a] Cigar Makers by City
(Cents per Hour)

	1912		1913		1919	
Occupation	W	M	W	M	W	M
Hand Bunch Makers						
Baltimore	19.31	23.10	21.15	22.90	39.30	47.50
Chicago	26.73	31.90	29.01	34.10	63.50	61.90
Cincinnati	20.46	24.90	21.56	22.60	—	—
Detroit	22.64	32.20	22.58	34.10	41.80	56.40
New York	24.07	28.70	24.64	29.60	45.20	46.90
Philadelphia	20.57	25.90	23.57	29.20	44.90	—
Lancaster	15.77	17.50	20.85	19.70	—	—
Reading	—	—	—	—	38.80	—
Machine Bunch Makers[b]						
Allentown	—	—	—	—	43.00	—
Baltimore	16.25	—	19.26	—	—	—
Dayton	18.48	—	20.45	—	32.10	—
Lancaster	16.07	—	18.53	—	—	—
New York	21.24	—	21.60	—	42.00	—
Philadelphia	20.21	—	21.33	—	36.10	—
Reading	—	—	—	—	41.30	—
Detroit	—	—	—	—	39.90	—
Hand Rollers						
Baltimore	22.72	26.10	23.62	25.90	45.80	50.60
Chicago	26.44	29.40	27.92	31.60	53.90	55.50
Cincinnati	22.01	22.50	23.49	21.50	—	—
Detroit	21.12	18.80	21.12	24.60	40.00	62.30
Lancaster	16.21	17.90	20.45	22.80	30.90	—
New York	24.15	29.90	24.57	31.10	29.90	47.10
Philadelphia	21.68	27.10	25.34	30.00	42.20	31.20
Suction Rollers[b]						
Baltimore	15.37	—	18.95	—	35.70	—
Chicago	20.40	—	21.33	—	—	—
Lancaster	13.07	—	15.17	—	34.90	—
New York	19.17	—	19.57	—	38.1	—
Philadelphia	17.26	—	18.39	—	38.80	—
Cigar Makers						
Baltimore	—	24.50	—	27.00	—	43.70
Boston	—	—	—	—	56.10	68.50
Chicago	43.70	40.30	40.10	41.80	—	58.40

Table 6 (cont'd)

Occupation	1912		1913		1919	
	W	M	W	M	W	M
Cigar Makers						
Cincinnati	—	30.20	—	35.20	—	38.90
Detroit	—	33.20	—	33.10	44.20	47.40
Lancaster	—	—	—	—	34.60	36.90
New York	28.60	33.60	27.70	33.90	—	43.50
Philadelphia	24.70	28.10	23.30	29.40	37.60	39.80
Reading	—	—	—	—	33.70	38.30

Source: *U.S. Bureau of Labor Statistics. Wages and Hours of Labor in the Clothing and Cigar Industries, 1911 to 1913*, No. 61, Oct. 24, 1914, pp. 72–75; U.S. Department of Labor, Bureau of Labor Statistics, *Monthly Labor Review*, 10 (Mar. 1920), 674–77.

[a]These include all male workers surveyed, both union and nonunion workers.

[b]There were no men in these occupations.

study reported, to earn more money. The hours women reported working did not conform to "scheduled hours of the plants, since many women . . . prolonged the firm's scheduled day by beginning earlier than the customary hour in the morning or by reducing the lunch period." In this way manufacturers not only got more labor for the money, they neatly circumvented the state maximum-hour law.[37]

While women learned the trade, wages were nonexistent or very low. In 1912, Anna Bartasius began working for Bayuk Cigar in Philadelphia and three weeks passed before she received any money. Then she earned 95¢ a week until she could build her piece rate. Pearl Hume, who learned the trade in Lima, Ohio, made $3.50 a week for two months until she was ready for the piece rate of 27½¢ a hundred—"not much money" but an improvement over the learner's wage. Anyone who could not make the former wage under the piece system was fired. One Lehigh Valley woman started learning to bunch in 1912 and made only $2.50 a week. Rather than a weekly learner's wage, some manufacturers tried to place women on the piece rate as quickly as possible as an incentive for greater output and efficiency. While the work itself could be learned in only a few months, gaining enough speed to raise average earnings took considerably longer. In 1915 the Havana-American Company in New Orleans paid apprentices weekly sums, but withheld $1 of the earnings each week over the period of a year as incentive to the learner to stay with the company.[38]

A few of the largest manufacturers, such as the American Cigar Company and various Detroit companies, adopted elements of what might be termed "modern" managerial practices. That is, to attract women, reduce turnover, and keep workers away from unions, several firms between 1900 and 1915 adopted modest employee welfare programs. In doing so, manufacturers further revealed their conceptions of gender. Paternalism was rarely practiced in cigar factories hiring primarily men. American Cigar's Hernsheim Company gave free hot lunches to women for several years, and in Charleston, South Carolina, the company provided employees with an assembly room, a piano, and a kitchen. The factory was exhibited to the public as a "model" concern. In its advertising, American Cigar drew attention to these modern facilities as part of its campaign to reduce the "social stigma" attached to cigar factory work. Trust factories in the North and South customarily provided dining rooms, dressing rooms, and sometimes even shower facilities.[39]

Other companies adopted these incentives both to compete for available labor and to avoid any efforts at unionization. They also liked to project the image of having "happy and contented" workers. Industry trade journals occasionally mentioned factories with "a professional pianist" hired to play for several hours daily, and one editorial urged manufacturers to think about adding these amenities because they could make their female workers "more productive." A Grand Rapids, Michigan, manufacturer in 1906 added a piano, formed a chorus, and once a week he invited a lecturer from the YWCA to speak on the value of "physical culture and sanitation," which—he insisted—his workers enjoyed. Several Philadelphia factories held dances for workers, although some floor managers privately denounced the "uselessness" of "special consideration for 'workers of this class.'" Theobald and Oppenheimer, one of the largest cigar companies in Philadelphia, provided shower baths on each floor for their seven hundred cigar makers, most of whom were women. Deisel-Wemmer in Lima had a "model factory," with "a commodious dining room . . . a result of the humanitarian ideas" of the company's owners. By 1917 the H. Fendrich Company in Evansville, Indiana, employed one thousand workers in its factory, which was described by the trade press as an "ideal environment." Not only were the "light, ventilation and sanitary conditions of the plant . . . modern in every respect," the factory was equipped with drinking fountains. The city library and the municipal market were only a short walk away. The company also maintained a dress code for employees. Some of the larger firms set up benefit or relief associations. Fendrich had such a plan, as did Otto Eisenlohr in Pennsylvania and the E. M. Schwartz Company in New York City. *Tobacco Leaf* encouraged manufacturers to "Make the Cigarmakers Independent of the Union" by setting up these benefit systems. By 1915 three Philadelphia firms had instituted profit-sharing. United Cigar Manufacturers also offered a "cooperative" plan whereby employees who earned over $1,000 a year got bonuses of company stock.[40]

Still, efforts at "welfare work" for women were limited. Even trust factories were not as clean, healthful, or as modern as public relations promotions suggested. Tuberculosis rates for cigar workers were still very high, and inspections of factories in many states drew attention to the dust, dirt, poor ventilation, poor heating, and lack of sanitary toilet facilities. Many factories provided no cafeterias or places for workers to eat. A medical study of Philadelphia in 1917 found several factories with cloakrooms, but only three with first aid rooms. The owner of the A. Falk Company in New Orleans argued that his women workers did not want welfare programs, which he felt interrupted their work.[41]

Large companies' primary goal in formulating these and other policies was to keep workers contented and out of the union. Not surprisingly they were particularly nervous during union organizing drives. The Harrisburg Cigar Company in Harrisburg, Pennsylvania, gave its employees a picnic, paid their transportation to the city park, and provided a band and refreshments when the CMIU was trying to organize during the summer of 1900. Mixing paternalism with a more traditional approach, the company also threatened to fire anyone who attended a union meeting. Some of the largest companies in Lancaster began relief associations in 1911, in the midst of a union organizing drive there. Workers paid ten cents a week dues and received five dollars sick benefits and one hundred dollars death benefits. Companies provided the initial funds to get the societies started. During the summer of 1907 the CMIU held several meetings in Lancaster and tried to get men and women cigar makers to attend. *Tobacco Leaf* reported that the Otto Eisenlohr management in Lancaster feared that at the very least its workers might ask for a wage increase. So the company suddenly sponsored a picnic for its employees and paid all expenses except for the trolley fare.[42]

More positive management gestures in no way overshadowed factory discipline, and most companies apparently relied more on the stick than the carrot. Women's fear of dismissal was the primary weapon of manufacturers. In factories throughout the country, women were pressured to use tobacco efficiently and in some cases had their pay docked for not doing so. In Lima, the offense might bring a thirty-day layoff. In Norristown, Pennsylvania, bunchers received ten-cent fines every time they failed to get one hundred cigars from the amount of binder leaf given, and rollers who failed to get one hundred cigars from their supply of wrappers received fines of forty cents. At the Deisel-Wemmer factory in Dayton, women who had shortages of tobacco at the end of the week were paid according to a lower schedule of piece rates. They remained on the lower schedule until the company judged their tobacco use to be more economical. When workers in the Lima factory showed an interest in the CMIU in 1916, management announced to a gathering of workers that the company would let "tobacco rot in the warehouse" before it would raise wages.[43] Larger factories, including American Cigar Company, often tried initially to establish reputations for good wages and working conditions as a way to win women from other companies, rather than having to train them themselves. The Otto Eisenlohr Company in Pennsylvania developed a reputation for liberal conditions for workers. The company held picnics and gave away gold pieces at Christmas and company anniversaries. Gradually, however, the policy "died out," and the company tightened control and became more rigid in its employment policies. In 1909 management announced that any worker quitting a job in an Eisenlohr factory in the state without a permit could not work again in any one of the firm's factories.[44]

American Cigar Company factories delved most heavily into systematic disciplinary measures. Lunch breaks in most of their factories were rigidly set, along with working hours. When the American Cigar Company bought the Hernsheim factory in New Orleans in 1901, its first action was to fire all the male handworkers. Then it hired women, installed machines, cut wages, and lengthened hours from eight to ten and twelve a day. Many of the new workers were under the age of eighteen. New rules there and in some trust factories in other cities prohibited women from talking to each other while at work. In Passaic, New Jersey, an independent manufacturer complained that the American Cigar Company there had imposed strict rules to keep its employees from going to work elsewhere. If a woman quit her job, she could not get her remaining pay unless she returned to work in the same factory. Rules and regulations were much more casual in the country districts of southeastern Pennsylvania, though even there it was possible to get fired. Still, unlike union men, women cigar makers had no procedures to protect them from arbitrary dismissal.[45]

One problem facing manufacturers during these years was the shortage of women workers trained to do the work. While there were nonunion men looking for jobs, manufacturers increasingly demanded women. Even Henry Offterdinger was having trouble getting enough women cigar makers for his Washington, D.C., factory by 1911. Companies sometimes increased wages as a way of attracting more workers. Trust factories in particular often entered local labor markets and tried to lure trained workers away from other manufacturers, both as a means of lessening the expense of training and also as a way of weakening the competition. The American Cigar Company was willing to sustain temporary losses in order to drive rivals out of business. Their wage rates were often higher and they "voluntarily" increased wages when they needed more workers. Other companies sometimes followed this pattern.[46]

For nearly a decade the American Cigar Company and H. Fendrich of Evansville, Indiana, waged an on-again, off-again war for labor in Evansville. American Cigar periodically opened and closed its factory there between 1902 and 1911. H. Fendrich had been making cigars in Evansville since 1855. The trust moved in and offered higher wages, winning away many of Fendrich's workers. Eventually the competition between the two companies forced Fendrich to recruit women workers from outlying areas, using advertising and flyers. They offered "pure drinking water," "perfect sanitary conditions," and "no machinery, hence, no danger." Headlines read: "500 More Girls Wanted at Once." The company even arranged for room and board for girls at the rate of $2.50 to $3.00 a week, "with respectable families." It also urged whole families to move to the city, claiming that "Evansville is in a prosperous condition. . . . Industrious men and boys, as well as girls, can find steady employment in Evansville."[47]

In Lima, employers also hoped to recruit workers from nearby areas as well as the town and used paternalist policies to win over doubtful parents. Superintendent Robert Plate often spoke of company policies in public speeches before local groups. He explained that the company felt it was "our duty" to develop "high standards of morality" among workers so that "parents will urge young people to seek employment there." The Lima Progressive Association, a local promotional organization, praised the company's facilities in its publications. "The officers of the Company have always shown that they have an interest in the welfare of their employees and believe in guarding the welfare of their work-people." Deisel-Wemmer's own publication, entitled *The Model Cigar Factory of America*, referred to its broad-mindedness, and noted "between employers and employes there is, therefore, a closer relation existing than is sometimes found in metropolitan centers. There follows, naturally, a special care for the welfare of the employes, shown in the conveniences furnished for them throughout the plant." When the American Cigar Company moved in after the turn of the century, some were alarmed, but Deisel-Wemmer raised wages, "cornering the help to a great extent," and the trust factory had closed by 1906.[48]

American Cigar had employed similar recruiting tactics in Charleston, South Carolina, trying to find young girls outside the city to work in its factory. Cincinnati manufacturers also recruited girls from rural areas, and complained about the limitations imposed by the lack of boarding facilities in the city. In Lancaster, the American Cigar Company had agents "scouring the country seeking families with young girls," and offered both employment for daughters and rental housing nearby.[49]

In the early twentieth century, those who did not feel the tug of tradition, who were not wedded to the notion of producing high-grade cigars, and whose markets were wide enough that they saw no major risk in foregoing the union label, found ways to deal with the issues of labor cost and control of the work force on their own terms. They wanted not only to avoid the CMIU, or even break it, but to have a cheap, pliant labor force instead. Their policies aimed at increasing employer control in the workplace and constricting workers' authority on the job. They assumed hiring women would fundamentally solve their labor problems. As one manufacturer in Detroit explained, he hired only Polish women because they were "easy to handle" and "orderly."[50] A closer look at two important centers of female employment, Detroit and the country districts of Pennsylvania, offers an opportunity to view employer policies at close range and to understand the context in which women's work culture emerged.

Notes

1. "Minutes of Local 208, Kalamazoo Michigan," Jan.–Feb. 1908, Western Michigan University Library, Kalamazoo.

2. *Tobacco Leaf*, 20 Sept. 1905, p. 44; 11 Mar. 1909, p. 7; *Detroit City Directory*, 1908 and 1909; *CMOJ*, Apr. 1908, p. 5.

3. U.S. Department of Commerce, Bureau of the Census, *Census of Population: 1910*, vol. 4, *Occupation Statistics* (Washington, D.C., 1914), p. 396; Bureau of the Census, *Census of Manufactures: 1919*, vol. 8, *General Report and Analytical Tables* (Washington, D.C., 1923), p. 490. CMIU membership for 1910 was 43,837, 41 percent of the census total. CMIU membership in 1920, 40,737, was only 31 percent of the census total.

4. U.S. Bureau of Corporations, *Report of the Commissioner of Corporations on the Tobacco Industry*, part I, *Position of the Tobacco Combination in the Industry* (Washington, D.C., 1909), pp. 141, 451; U.S. Congress, Senate, *Report on Condition of Woman and Child Wage-Earners in the United States*, vol. 18, *Employment of Women and Children in Selected Industries*, S. Doc. 645, 61st Congress, 2d sess., 1913, pp. 88–91; U.S. Bureau of Corporations, Tobacco Investigation, file 3073, sections 9, 10, "Location and Concentration of Cigar Industry," Record Group (R.G.) 122, National Archives (NA); Willis N. Baer, *The Economic Development of the Cigar Industry in the United States* (Lancaster, Pa., 1933), p. 257; U.S. Commissioner of Labor, *Eleventh Special Report*, "Regulation and Restriction of Output" (Washington, D.C., 1904), p. 575; *Tobacco Leaf*, 13 Jan. 1904, p. 36; Henry F. Smyth and T. Grier Miller, "A Hygienic Survey of Cigar Manufacturing in Philadelphia," *Medicine and Surgery*, 1 (Sept. 1917), 703; Mary Barbara Klaczynska, "Working Women in Philadelphia, 1900–1930" (Ph.D. dissertation, Temple University, 1975), p. 120.

5. *Tobacco Leaf*, 2 Apr. 1902, p. 11; 1 Oct. 1902, p. 24; *Tobacco*, 7 Feb. 1902, p. 7; Lucy Winsor Killough, *The Tobacco Products Industry in New York and Its Environs: Present Trends and Probable Future Developments*, Regional Plan of New York and Its Environs, Monograph no. 5 (New York, 1924), p. 26.

6. *Tobacco Leaf*, 1 Oct. 1902, p. 24; *CMOJ*, Jan. 1908, p. 3; Edith Abbott, *Women in Industry: A Study in American Economic History* (New York, 1913), p. 196; Killough, *Tobacco Products Industry*, p. 26; U.S. Bureau of Corporations, Tobacco Investigation, file 3073, "Labor Conditions in the Cigar Industry," R.G. 122, NA.

7. *Tobacco*, 8 Nov. 1906, p. 22; *Tobacco Leaf*, 23 July 1908, p. 18; Abbott, *Women in Industry*, p. 212; U.S. Bureau of Corporations, Tobacco Investigation, file 3073, "Labor Conditions in the Cigar Industry," R.G. 122, NA.

8. Killough, *Tobacco Products Industry*, p. 25; Bureau of the Census, *Census of Population: 1920*, vol. 4, *Occupations* (Washington, D.C., 1923), p. 1156; Bureau of the Census, *Census of Population: 1900*, "Special Reports," *Occupations* (Washington, D.C., 1904), p. 634; New York State Department of Labor, Special Bulletin no. 110, *Women Who Work* (Albany, 1922), p. 14; U.S. Department of Labor, Women's Bureau, Bulletin 37, *Women in New Jersey Industries* (Washington, D.C., 1924), p. 2; Bureau of the Census, *Census of Manufactures: 1900*, vol. 9, *Special Reports on Selected Industries* (Washington, D.C., 1900), p. 653.

9. Pennsylvania Department of Labor and Industry, Special Bulletin no. 10, *Conference on Women in Industry* (Harrisburg, 1926), pp. 16–19; Women's Bureau, Bulletin no. 74, *The Immigrant Woman and Her Job*, by Caroline Manning (Washington, D.C., 1930), pp. 2–14; Elizabeth Butler, *Women and the Trades, Pittsburgh 1907–1908* (New York, 1909), pp. 75–97.

10. U.S. Bureau of Corporations, Tobacco Investigation, file 3073, section 10, R.G. 122, NA; Bureau of the Census, *Census of Manufactures: 1919*, vol. 8, p. 490; Pennsylvania Department of Internal Affairs, *Report on the Productive Industries of the Commonwealth of Pennsylvania for 1916–1917–1918–1919* (Harrisburg, Pa., 1920), pp. 63, 79, 183, 710; *Tobacco Leaf*, 27 Aug. 1902, p. 28; Klaczynska, "Working Women in Philadelphia," pp. 85, 119–21; Pennsylvania De-

partment of Labor and Industry, *Second Industrial Directory of Pennsylvania, 1916* (Harrisburg, Pa., 1916), p. 1191; Carol Ann Golab, "The Polish Communities of Philadelphia, 1870–1920: Immigrant Distribution and Adaptation in Urban America" (Ph.D. dissertation, University of Pennsylvania, 1971), p. 121; Women's Bureau, *Immigrant Woman and Her Job*, pp. 2–10; Centennial Committee, *Centennial of Coplay, Pennsylvania* (Coplay, Pa., 1969), unpaginated; Alfred Mathews and Austin N. Hungerford, *History of the Counties of Lehigh and Carbon, in the Commonwealth of Pennsylvania* (Philadelphia, 1884), p. 164; Charles Rhoads Roberts et al., *History of Lehigh County, Pennsylvania*, vol. 1 (Allentown, Pa., 1924), pp. 1076–78; William J. Heller, *History of Northampton County, Pennsylvania* (New York, 1920), p. 314; Pennsylvania Department of Internal Affairs, *Report on the Productive Industries of the Commonwealth of Pennsylvania for 1916–1917–1918–1919*, pp. 63, 710.

11. Killough, *Tobacco Products Industry*, p. 25; Bureau of the Census, *Census of Population: 1920*, vol. 4, p. 1156; Bureau of the Census, *Census of Population: 1900*, "Special Reports," p. 634; Nancy Hewitt, "Women Cigar Makers in Tampa," paper delivered at Oral History Association, Pensacola, Fla., Nov. 1985.

12. Bureau of the Census, *Census of Population: 1910*, vol. 4, p. 396; Bureau of the Census, *Women in Gainful Occupations 1870 to 1920*, by Joseph A. Hill (Washington, D.C., 1929), p. 172; Bureau of the Census, *Census of Population: 1900*, vol. 4, pp. cxiv, cxv; U.S. Congress, Senate, *Reports of the Immigration Commission: Immigrants in Industries*, part 14, *Cigar and Tobacco Manufacturing*, S. Doc. 633, 61st Cong., 2d sess., 1911, pp. 17, 28; E. P. Hutchinson, *Immigrants and Their Children, 1850–1950* (New York, 1956), p. 182; New York State Assembly, *Report and Testimony Taken before the Special Committee of the Assembly Appointed to Investigate the Condition of Female Labor in the City of New York* (New York, 1896), pp. 150–56, 749–846, 901–27; Glenda Morrison, "Cigar Making as a Woman's Work," unpublished paper for Indiana Labor History Project, Indiana State University, Bloomington, p. 5. Regarding black women in the tobacco industry see Dolores Janiewski, *Sisterhood Denied: Race, Gender and Class in a New South Community* (Philadelphia, 1985), and Consumer's League of Eastern Pennsylvania, *Colored Women as Industrial Workers in Philadelphia, 1919–1920* (Consumers League of Eastern Pennsylvania, 1920), pp. 7, 17.

13. U.S. Congress, Senate, *Report of the Immigration Commission*, p. 19; Hutchinson, *Immigrants and Their Children*, pp. 172–75, 177–86.

14. Bureau of the Census, *Census of Population: 1900*, "Special Reports," pp. 523, 526, 635, 679; T. Grier Miller, "A Sociologic and Medical Study of Four Hundred Cigar Workers in Philadelphia," *American Journal of the Medical Sciences*, 155 (Feb. 1918), 164; Bureau of the Census, *Census of Population: 1920*, vol. 4, p. 1156; "Investigation of the Tobacco Industry in Lancaster, Pennsylvania," 1 Feb. 1919, file 46/2-C, Office of the Chief Clerk, U.S. Department of Labor, R.G. 174, NA; U.S. Congress, Senate, *Reports of the Immigration Commission*, p. 84; Caroline Golab, *Immigrant Destinations* (Philadelphia, 1977), p. 177; Women's Bureau, *Immigrant Woman and Her Job*, p. 9.

15. Alice Gannett, "Bohemian Women in New York: Investigation of Working

Mothers," *Life and Labor,* Feb. 1913, pp. 49–52; Emily Green Balch, *Our Slavic Fellow Citizens* (New York, 1910), pp. 70–76; 79, 211, 357; Thomas Capek, *The Čechs (Bohemians) in America: A Study of Their National, Cultural, Political, Social, Economic and Religious Life* (Boston, 1920), pp. 71, 72; Thomas Capek, *The Čech (Bohemian) Community of New York* (New York, 1921), pp. 20–26; Killough, *Tobacco Products Industry,* pp. 41–43; Jane Robbins, "The Bohemian Women of New York," *Charities,* Dec. 1904, pp. 194–96; *Tobacco Leaf,* 21 Jan. 1903, p. 42; New Jersey Bureau of Statistics of Labor and Industries, *Annual Report, 1910,* (Camden, 1910), p. 259; Eva Smill, "The Stogy Industry on the Hill in Pittsburgh, Pa." (M.A. thesis, Carnegie Institute, Pittsburgh, June 1920), pp. 9, 11, 27; Women's Bureau, *Women in New Jersey Industries,* p. 63; Patrick Lynch, "Pittsburgh, the I.W.W., and the Stogie Workers," in Joseph Conlin, ed., *At the Point of Production: The Local History of the I.W.W.* (Westport, Conn., 1981), p. 90; Ida Cohen Selavan, "Jewish Wage Earners in Pittsburgh, 1830–1930," *American Jewish Historical Quarterly,* 65 (Mar. 1976), p. 274.

16. U.S. Congress, Senate, *Report on Condition of Woman and Child Wage-Earners,* vol. 18, pp. 103, 345–46, 396.

17. Bureau of the Census, *Census of Population: 1910,* vol. 4, p. 396; Bureau of the Census, *Census of Population: 1900, Statistics of Women at Work* (Washington, D.C., 1907), pp. 34, 38, 282; Bureau of the Census, *Census of Population, 1920,* vol. 4, p. 702; Bureau of the Census, *Census of Population: 1900,* "Special Reports," p. 53; Miller, "Sociologic Study of Cigar Workers," pp. 164–65; Women's Bureau, *Immigrant Woman and Her Job,* p. 7; Women's Bureau, *Women in New Jersey Industries,* p. 65.

18. U.S. Congress, Senate, *Report on Condition of Woman and Child Wage-Earners,* vol. 18, p. 106; Balch, *Our Slavic Fellow Citizens,* p. 357; Abbott, *Women in Industry,* p. 211; New York Factory Investigating Commission, *Second Report,* vol. 2 (Albany, 1913), p. 492; U.S. Congress, Senate, *Reports of the Immigration Commission,* p. 57.

19. Smill, "Stogy Industry," pp. 8–9; Killough, *Tobacco Products Industry,* pp. 26, 29–30; Harvey Whipple, "Cigar Manufacture in Detroit," *The Detroiter,* June 1911, pp. 10–13.

20. *Tobacco,* 8 June 1900, p. 4; 20 July 1900, p. 8; U.S. Industrial Commission, *Report of the Industrial Commission on the Relations and Conditions of Capital and Labor,* vol. 15 (Washington, D.C., 1901), p. 388; *Tobacco Leaf,* 24 Nov. 1910, p. 4; 15 June 1911, p. 4; "Tendency of Industries Employing Largely Women and Child Labor to Locate in the Vicinity of Industries Employing Exclusively Male Labor," Commission on Industrial Relations, typescript, U.S. Department of Labor, R.G. 174, NA; *CMOJ,* Mar. 1901, p. 12; Sept. 1902, p. 5; Killough, *Tobacco Products Industry,* pp. 20–30, 34, 71; U.S. Bureau of Corporations, Tobacco Investigation, file 3073, section 10, R.G. 122, NA.

21. Report of Conciliator, 3 May 1922, file 170/1677, Federal Mediation and Conciliation Service (FMCS), R.G. 280, NA; *Tobacco,* 8 June 1900, p. 4; 20 July 1900, p. 8; *Tobacco Leaf,* 24 Nov. 1910, p. 4; *CMOJ,* Mar. 1901, p. 12; Deisel-Wemmer achieved this situation during the second decade of the century.

22. U.S. Congress, Senate, *Reports of the Immigration Commission*, p. 24; *Tobacco Leaf*, 12 Nov. 1902, p. 34; Women's Bureau, *Immigrant Woman and Her Job*, pp. 5–6.

23. Studs Terkel, *American Dreams: Lost and Found* (New York, 1980), p. 118; Pearl Hume interview, 23 Aug. 1982, Lima, Ohio; Lucille Speaker interview, 22 Aug. 1982, Lima; Stella Sutton interview, 19 Aug. 1982, Lima; Anna Bartasius interview, 31 Mar. 1982, Philadelphia, Pa.; Rita Johnson Amadee, interview 20 June 1979, New Orleans, La.

24. U.S. Commissioner of Labor, "Regulation and Restriction of Output," P. 568; Baer, *Economic Development of The Cigar Industry*, p. 85; Smill, "Stogy Industry," pp. 3–4, 11; *Lima News*, 9 Feb. 1922; Fred Brinkman interview, 24 Aug. 1982, Lima, Ohio; Hume interview. Over and over I found that women got their first jobs where a sister, other relative, or friend worked.

25. U.S. Commissioner of Labor, "Regulation and Restriction of Output," pp. 568–69; U.S. Commissioner of Labor, *Thirteenth Annual Report, 1898, Hand and Machine Labor* (Washington, D.C., 1899), pp. 392–95.

26. U.S. Bureau of Labor Statistics, Bulletin 135, *Rates of Wages in the Cigar and Clothing Industries, 1911 and 1912*, (Washington, D.C., 1913), p. 7; *U.S. Tobacco Journal*, 24 Mar. 1917, p. 8; Baer, *Economic Development of the Cigar Industry*, p. 84; U.S. Congress, Senate, *Report on Condition of Woman and Child Wage-Earners*, vol. 18, pp. 85–88; U.S. Commissioner of Labor, "Regulation and Restriction of Output," p. 572; Reavis Cox, *Competition in the Tobacco Industry, 1911–1932: A Study of the Effects of the Partition of the American Tobacco Company by the United States Supreme Court* (New York, 1933), p. 58; Butler, *Women and the Trades*, p. 78. See also Chap. 8; Smill, "Stogy Industry," p. 5; Clarence Jacobs interview, 17 Dec. 1982, Red Lion, Pa.

27. U.S. Bureau of Corporations, Tobacco Investigation, file 3073, "Machinery in Cigar Manufacture," R.G. 122, NA; *Tobacco Leaf*, 19 Sept. 1906, p. 36; 18 Feb. 1909, p. 11; 21 Oct. 1909, p. 20; U.S. Congress, Senate, *Report on Condition of Woman and Child Wage-Earners*, vol. 18, pp. 97–100; Bartasius interview.

28. Cox, *Competition in the Tobacco Industry*, pp. 48–51; Abbott, *Women in Industry*, pp. 203–4; *Tobacco Leaf*, 8 July 1903, p. 11; 14 Nov. 1906, p. 45; 19 June 1907, p. 22; 22 Oct. 1908, pp. 3, 5; U.S. Congress, Senate, *Report on Condition of Woman and Child Wage-Earners*, vol. 18, p. 84; U.S. Commissioner of Labor, "Regulation and Restriction of Output," p. 57; *Tobacco*, 21 Feb. 1907, p. 21; "From the Tobacco Leaf to the Cigar," *Scientific American*, 7 July 1906, pp. 10–13. Existing evidence does not provide a complete picture of the use and distribution of machinery in cigar factories during this period. As of 1912, suction tables were apparently not in use in Chicago and they were rare in Detroit and Cincinnati. See U.S. Bureau of Labor Statistics, *Wages and Hours of Labor, 1911–1912*, Bulletin 135, pp. 16–20; *Tobacco Leaf*, 21 Jan. 1903, p. 42; 24 Dec. 1908, p. 7; Gannett, "Bohemian Women in New York," p. 52; Butler, *Women and the Trades*, p. 78. The suction table was frequently used in conjunction with the team system, but in some New York City and York County factories, teams were abandoned and suction table operators worked separately from bunchers.

29. *Tobacco Leaf*, 14 Nov. 1906, p. 45; 25 Oct. 1905, p. 25; 21 Oct. 1909, p. 20;

Miller, DuBrul and Peters Manufacturing Co., *Catalogue*, Tobacco Collection, Extractive Industries, Museum of American History, Smithsonian Institution, Washington, D.C.

30. *Tobacco Leaf*, 15 Jan. 1902, p. 23; 26 Nov. 1902, p. 20; U.S. Commissioner of Labor, "Regulation and Restriction of Output," pp. 572, 575.

31. Meyer Jacobstein, *The Tobacco Industry in the United States* (New York, 1907), p. 140; U.S. Commissioner of Labor, *Nineteenth Annual Report, 1904, Wages and Hours of Labor* (Washington, D.C., 1904), p. 59; U.S. Bureau of Labor Statistics, *Wages and Hours of Labor, 1911 and 1912*, Bulletin 135, pp. 14–24; U.S. Bureau of Labor Statistics, "Wages and Hours of Labor in the Cigar and the Men's Clothing Industries," *Monthly Labor Review*, 10 (Mar. 1920), pp. 81–87; Congress, Senate, *Reports of the Immigration Commission*, pp. 44–45. The later jump was partly a result of wartime strikes. See Chap. 10.

32. U.S. Congress, Senate, *Report on Condition of Woman and Child Wage-Earners*, vol. 18, pp. 106–7.

33. U.S. Congress, Senate, *Report on Condition of Woman and Child Wage-Earners*, vol. 18, pp. 109–10, 464–71. See also Kansas Board of Public Welfare, Bureau of Labor Statistics, *Report on the Wage-Earning Women of Kansas City* (Kansas City, 1913), p. 22.

34. New Jersey Bureau of Statistics of Labor and Industries, *Annual Report, 1901*, p. 78; *1911*, p. 83; *1917*, p. 74; Pennsylvania Department of Internal Affairs, *Report*, p. 78.

35. U.S. Congress, Senate, *Report on Condition of Woman and Child Wage-Earners*, vol. 18, p. 470; *CMOJ*, Sept. 1910, p. 4; *Tobacco Leaf*, 7 Feb. 1906, p. 43; 8 Oct. 1908, p. 3. Wages for bunchers in Cincinnati in 1900 averaged about $1.20 daily and for women rollers $1.29 daily, so that weekly pay averaged about $6 to $8. See Ohio Bureau of Labor Statistics, *Report, 1901* (Springfield, 1901), p. 77; *Western Tobacco Journal*, 19 Sept. 1910, p. 4; *CMOJ*, June 1907, p. 9; Sutton interview; Hume interview.

36. *CMOJ*, June 1906, p. 11; U.S. Congress, Senate, *Report on Condition of Woman and Child Wage-Earners*, vol. 18, p. 464; National Consumers' League, New Orleans Chapter, *Wage Investigation: Report of the Louisiana State Commission to Study the Condition of Working Women and Children* (New Orleans, 1914), p. 8; U.S. Council on National Defense, Committee on Women's Defense Work, Louisiana Division, Women in Industry Committee, *Conditions of Women's Labor in Louisiana* (New Orleans, 1919), pp. 48–53.

37. Robbins, "Bohemian Women of New York," pp. 195–96; Gannett, "Bohemian Women in New York," p. 49; U.S. Commissioner of Labor, "Regulation and Restriction of Output," pp. 538; 570–76; Killough, *Tobacco Products Industry*, pp. 30–39; Women's Bureau, *Immigrant Woman and Her Job*, p. 95; Pauline Stauffer interview, 21 June 1977, Hanover, Pa.

38. *CMOJ*, Aug. 1901, p. 2; May 1915, p. 6; *Tobacco Leaf*, 4 June 1907, p. 22; Women's Bureau, *Immigrant Woman and Her Job*, p. 14; Hume interview; Speaker interview.

39. *U.S. Tobacco Journal*, 28 Oct. 1899, p. 4; *Tobacco*, 25 May 1900, p. 4; *Tobacco Leaf*, 24 Jan. 1906, p. 9.

40. *Tobacco Leaf,* 24 Jan. 1906, p. 9; 18 May 1911, p. 6; 8 Nov. 1910, p. 6; 7 Jan. 1915, p. 4; 14 Jan. 1915, pp. 6–7; 31 Jan. 1918, p. 3; *U.S. Tobacco Journal,* 21 Apr. 1906, p. 7; *CMOJ,* July 1910, p. 8; Morrison, "Cigar Making as Woman's Work," p. 5; Charles C. Miller, *A History of Allen County, Ohio and Representative Citizens* (Chicago, 1906), p. 196.

41. New York State Factory Investigating Commission, *Second Report,* vol. 2, pp. 487–513; Ohio Bureau of Labor Statistics, *Report, 1901,* p. 677; *Tobacco Leaf,* 20 July 1900, p. 7; "Investigation of the Tobacco Industry in Lancaster," file 46/2-C, Department of Labor, R.G. 174, NA; U.S. Bureau of Labor, Bulletin 82, *Mortality from Consumption in Certain Occupations* (Washington, D.C., 1909), pp. 562–63; Smyth and Miller, "Hygienic Survey of Cigar Manufacturing," p. 703; Fanny Seifirth, "Social and Recreational Work in New Orleans Industries" (M.A. thesis, Tulane University, 1925), pp. 239–40; Women's Bureau, *Immigrant Woman and Her Job,* pp. 126–27.

42. *Tobacco,* 6 July 1900, p. 8; 21 Nov. 1902, p. 2; *CMOJ,* May 1900, p. 9; May 1911, p. 4; Dec. 1912, p. 25; *Tobacco Leaf,* 7 Aug. 1907, p. 38; New York Factory Investigating Commission, *Second Report,* vol. 2, p. 504; *Detroit Labor News,* 18 Aug. 1916.

43. *CMOJ,* June 1907, p. 9; July 1912, p. 19; Aug. 1912, p. 28; Aug. 1916, p. 7; *Detroit Labor News,* 22 Sept. 1916; 17 Nov. 1916; New Orleans Factory Inspection Department, *Report* (New Orleans, 1908), p. 4; Hume interview.

44. *CMOJ,* Oct. 1909, p. 10; Norman Wieand interview, 21 June 1984, Quakertown, Pa.

45. *CMOJ,* June 1906, p. 11; June 1907, p. 6; U.S. Commissioner of Labor, "Regulation and Restriction of Output," p. 572; U.S. Bureau of Corporations, Tobacco Investigation, file 3073, section 9, R.G. 122, NA; *Tobacco Leaf,* 26 June 1907, p. 4.

46. *Tobacco Leaf,* 2 Nov. 1902, pp. 2, 21; 3 Dec. 1902, p. 28; 1 Nov. 1905, p. 58; 31 Jan. 1906, p. 11; 7 Feb. 1906, p. 32; 26 Sept. 1906, p. 34; 7 Dec. 1911, p. 3; *Tobacco,* 7 Feb. 1902, p. 7; *Western Tobacco Journal,* 2 Sept. 1910, p. 4. Periodically a few manufacturers set up schools to train cigar makers, but these never lasted long.

47. *Tobacco Leaf,* 16 Mar. 1900, p. 30; 26 Nov. 1902, p. 6; 3 Dec. 1902, p. 28; 23 Feb. 1911, p. 7; U.S. Bureau of Corporations, Tobacco Investigation, file 3073, section 6, R.G. 122, NA; H. Fendrich, Inc., *One Hundred Years of Cigar Making* (Evansville, Ind., 1950), p. 6, Southern Tier Library, Corning, N.Y.; *CMOJ,* Oct. 1916, p. 18. My thanks to Tony Hyman for bringing the Fendrich pamphlet to my attention.

48. Robert Plate, typed speech, no date, Lima Historical Society (LHS), Lima, Ohio; *The Lima Progressive Association* (1913), LHS; Deisel-Wemmer Corporation, *The Model Cigar Factory of America: The Deisel-Wemmer Co., Lima, O. USA.* (Lima, Ohio, 1906); *Republican Gazette* (Lima), 12 Aug. 1906.

49. *Tobacco Leaf,* 12 Nov. 1902, p. 22; 21 June 1905, p. 54; *CMOJ,* June 1907, p. 6.

50. *Tobacco,* 8 Nov. 1906, p. 22.

Five Cents or Less: Cigar Manufacturing in Detroit, Michigan, and Southeastern Pennsylvania

Both Detroit, Michigan, and the so-called country districts of southeastern Pennsylvania had emerged by the early twentieth century as important centers for women's employment in the cigar industry. On the surface, the two had little in common. The atmosphere in Detroit was unmistakably urban and overwhelmingly Polish. Women's lives were very much rooted in ethnic neighborhoods centered around the parish church. While women made cigars, Polish men worked in heavy industry in auto plants and foundries. Workers in eastern Pennsylvania were primarily native-born, of Pennsylvania Dutch heritage, and lived in or near small towns oriented toward farming. Despite differences, each formed cohesive communities where similarities in the cigar industry's operation meant that workers shared more than one might suspect. The contrast between the two areas not only suggests the diversity of working women's lives and experiences in the early twentieth century, but illuminates the relationship between work and community which helped to shape and define the character of women's work culture.

Detroit's Five-Cent Cigar Industry

When the Lilies Cigar Company moved to the heart of Detroit's largest Polish neighborhood in 1908, it became simply another statistic, part of a trend which had been underway in the city for about a decade. Until the 1890s, most of the cigar makers in the city had been German men who had brought their handcraft skills with them. Factories, two-thirds of which were buckeyes in 1890, were located in the city's center, separate from German residential neighborhoods. The largest factory in the city that year employed only 150 workers. In the 1880s, many Detroit cigar makers had belonged to a Knights of Labor Assembly, but by the 1890s, in the wake of the Order's decimation in the city, most had affiliated with CMIU Local 22. Women found work in some nonunion shops before the turn of the century, particularly as tobacco strippers, but unionists opposed female employment and struck in 1896 to prevent their employers from hiring women in cigar-making jobs. The struggle lasted two years and ended in defeat and a wage cut for Local 22 members. Soon female employment in the city ballooned.[1]

Drawing primarily on the labor of Polish women, Detroit became one of the most important cigar-making centers in the country. Between 1899 and 1905, cigar output in the First Internal Revenue District of Michigan, containing Detroit, rose by 73 percent. Polish immigration to the city also reached its peak during the fifteen years before World War I, providing the labor source. By 1915, the city's three largest factories (San Telmo, Wayne Cigar, and Lilies Cigar), employed nearly three thousand women, and the ten largest factories employed nearly seven thousand women.[2]

Women were migrating to Detroit from Poland because of changes in landholding patterns there. Serfdom had ended by the mid-1860s, but most peasants remained tied to and dependent on the land throughout the century. Indeed the entire rural social structure placed an extremely high value on owning land. Yet population growth, evictions, and shifts in market relations meant that increasingly over the nineteenth century peasants could only hope to acquire shrunken plots of land, if any land at all. Many "rural proletarians" thus began migrating to find work with the hope of saving enough money to purchase land. They searched for employment in nearby towns and cities within Poland, then in neighboring Prussia, Russia, and Denmark, and finally in more distant destinations such as Germany, France, the United States, Canada, or Argentina. Although Poles began moving to Detroit in considerable numbers during the late nineteenth century, the peak period of immigration took place between 1900 and 1920. Most had originally come from Galicia and Russian Poland, but many had lived and worked elsewhere in the United States before settling in Detroit. By 1920, Poles were the largest single ethnic group in the city, 19.6 percent of the population.[3]

Poles settled first on the east side, the area east of Woodward Avenue, initially among the Germans. They established the first Polish Catholic church in the city, St. Albertus, in 1871 and settlement expanded outward from there, along Canfield and Garfield avenues, south of Forest between Orleans and St. Aubin Street. During the early twentieth century the community expanded north of Forest Avenue. A second, smaller settlement began on the west side near Twentieth Street and expanded north and south of Michigan Avenue and west of Thirtieth Street after the turn of the century. From 1870 to 1900, six parishes were organized, five of them on the east side. Five more were added during the next fourteen years. Poles tended to form the most concentrated residential settlements of any ethnic group in the city. Eighty percent of Poles in 1920 lived on blocks where Poles were in a majority. They were also the most working-class of any of the city's ethnic groups, including the Germans. In 1900, only 5 percent held white-collar jobs; 31 percent were skilled; and 65 percent worked in unskilled occupations. The trend only intensified over the next twenty years. Most factory workers in the city were German or Polish.[4]

Once the first Polish women began to work in the city's cigar factories, they brought in friends and relatives to work with them, thus starting a recruiting pattern which supplied a steady flow of workers. The burst of growth in women's employment in the trade was facilitated when the downtown factories after 1899 adopted the policy of "taking the factory to the workers." They left their traditional center-city locations and moved into the midst of the Polish neighborhoods. As early as May 1900, *Tobacco Leaf* reported that "several manufacturers are contemplating moving into Polack districts, with a view to economy and convenience in securing help."[5]

What began as a trickle turned into a flood as companies already in Detroit placed branches in the Polish community or moved there altogether. A few union factories such as Lilies of Kalamazoo and Hemmeter of Saginaw moved to Detroit and dropped the union label in the process, but much of the growth came from the establishment of new firms. Most of the activity was first concentrated on the east side, although some also located on the west side. By 1908, the Independence, Mazer, Alexander Gordon, San Telmo, and William Tegge factories had all "located in the Polish district." American Cigar, by contrast, had bought out the largest factory in the downtown area, Brown Brothers, in 1902 and remained there.[6]

The cigar trade press reported a near frenzy of factory building as new companies formed and others relocated in Detroit. By 1906 the city had become a front-ranking center for five-cent cigars. By 1910 many regarded it as "the greatest five-cent cigar town in the country." That same year, cigar making was ranked as Detroit's fourth largest industry.[7] Stories periodically circulated throughout the city about new building construction and enlargements to factories already in place. When other cigar centers languished during the recession of 1907 to 1909, Detroit's factories boomed and continued to work full-time. As the larger companies prospered, however, the smaller ones, especially many of the buckeyes, disappeared and each year the city directory listed fewer and fewer shops named after only one individual.[8]

The San Telmo Company started operations in Detroit in 1897. Its owner, Oscar Rosenberger, moved the business to the east-side Polish neighborhood in 1901. He located on Chene Street and employed about fifty workers. Over the next few years he moved several times, but in 1906 he constructed his own large factory on Forest Avenue, near the "source of labor supply." A year later he built an addition to the plant, and by 1909 San Telmo accounted for nearly one-quarter of the production in the First Internal Revenue District. Observers marveled at the "phenomenal growth" of the company. In 1910 Rosenberger built a second plant "in the heart of the West Side Polish district." By 1915 he employed about fifteen hundred workers, most of them Polish women.[9]

Detroit cigars principally sold west of Chicago, and the made-in-Detroit stamp seemed to be "an open sesame in marketing the goods." They were made primarily using hand methods: only a few suction tables were in use before 1916. This enabled companies to advertise their products as handmade, which added to their appeal. Detroit manufacturers could make quality cigars which retailed for only five cents. They frankly acknowledged that this achievement rested on their "excellent labor conditions," which the trade journals described in glowing terms. Yet the thriving business there reached a kind of saturation point around 1910. The trade press then reported that the "labor market here is swept clean," and the rate of growth of the industry slowed somewhat thereafter.[10] As early as 1905 some manufacturers were complaining about labor shortages in the city. They agreed that they could expand production even further if only they had the labor. The slowed rate of growth in the city's cigar industry after 1910 was caused not by "lack of orders, but lack of labor." Labor turnover was high, and every year an estimated eight hundred women left the trade. Thus the manufacturers' plan for moving into the Polish neighborhoods had been too successful. The popularity of the Detroit cigar caused a near-constant labor shortage. In addition, because of "a certain feeling of caste regarding factory work," manufacturers realized that they would have difficulty recruiting young women from native stock families into the cigar factories. By 1910 some observers had concluded that the cigar industry could not grow much more in Detroit "because the labor market here is almost exhausted and manufacturers find it difficult to keep employees now on the payrolls."[11]

The competitive atmosphere for labor shaped the outlines of the industry and many company policies. *Tobacco Leaf* reported that "competition has been so keen among manufacturers for help that they are willing to provide almost any accommodation for maintenance." Many of the new three- and four-story factory buildings provided cafeterias and dressing rooms for employees, features manufacturers emphasized in the press when the buildings began operations. The 1906 William Tegge factory was among the first to provide such facilities and the company also gave employees a lunch and a ball to celebrate the factory's opening. Not all companies provided meals at the factory because they felt that women could walk home for lunch, but most of the largest ones did.[12] Manufacturers stressed the modern conveniences of their facilities and noted how well ventilated and lighted the buildings were. Trade journals referred to this or that structure as a "model factory." A 1909 trade article on the Lilies Company described its workrooms as "scrupulously clean and neat and it is automatically ventilated with a compressed-air device that at all times renders the atmosphere sweet and healthful." Lilies also installed shower baths. In 1911 at least one factory engaged a piano player to perform in the dining room during lunch break. The Mazer Company, which opened its doors in 1915, noted that the plant had drinking fountains, dining and cloakrooms, and steel lockers. As its grand opening celebration, the Mazer brothers gave a dance for employees.[13]

Women who worked in Detroit's cigar factories were for the most part the single daughters of fathers who worked in foundries, stove works, machine shops, and packinghouses, and of mothers who managed the household. Published census figures show that while more were native-born than foreign-born, 90 percent had foreign-born parents. In 1900 less than 1 percent of women cigar factory workers in the city were married, and many of these married women were concentrated in tobacco stemming rather than cigar making. By 1920, however, 22.4 percent of the women in the factories were married. Their average ages rose as well. In 1900, 92.8 percent were under age twenty-five. By 1920 the proportion had fallen to 64.2 percent. Increasingly during the early twentieth century, married women moved into cigar making, and single women stayed in the trade after they wed. In 1900 the average household had 5.33 members. Most women cigar makers lived at home with their parents, and 80 percent of them lived in families with two or more breadwinners.[14]

During the nineteenth century, Polish women in Detroit had found employment as domestic workers. Even after the cigar factories became the largest employer of Polish women in the city, some women in the community worked instead in dressmaking, overalls, domestic service, tailoring, and laundry work. The majority entered the cigar factories, however, and they did so for several reasons. The factories were close to their homes, and the work did not require them to be fluent in English. Openings were plentiful, and women could easily learn about them from sisters, cousins, and friends.[15]

Most important, Polish families needed the earnings of several family members because men's wages alone were not sufficient to fulfill basic expectations. Sons were sent to work in day labor and daughters to cigar factories in part to finance home ownership. So much did Poles prize this goal that their rates of home ownership were consistently high—44 percent in 1900. Olivier Zunz found that for sample blocks in 1920 between 30 and 75 percent of the families owned their own homes. Placing such a value on property might require sacrifice. For example, the father of one cigar maker, Frances Salantak, left Poland for Detroit in 1909, first bought a home, and only later saved the money to bring over the rest of the family. In many cases, owners rented out parts of the house in order to pay the mortgage and ease the housing shortage. The residential pattern then developed into one of owner-occupied homes shared with renters, rather than dilapidated houses filled with tenants. Income was also channeled into community building, particularly the establishment of the parish church, its organizations, and its schools. Families here adopted strategies they had used in Poland and expected contributions from all family members either through employment outside the home or work within it, including child rearing, cooking, and household duties.[16]

Daughters were expected to turn over their salaries for family expenses. Frances Salantak got a job with the American Cigar Company in January 1915, when she was thirteen years old. Although American Cigar was located outside her neighborhood, she took the job because a close relative also worked there. Rose Purzon took her first job at San Telmo, because her sister and many neighborhood friends also worked for the company. "All the women worked there," she explained. "That was the main thing for women to do." Helen Piwkowska chose cigar work because she knew that she did not need to be fluent in English to work in the cigar factories. The factories were close enough that she could go home for lunch, and jobs were easy to obtain. "I asked for a job and they gave me a job," said Salantak. "In that time, they take anybody that would come along. They teach them how to work." Rose Purzon remembered the employers saying: "You can apply today and start tomorrow."[17]

Although wages were low and therefore typical of women's wages in general in the city, Polish women were also attracted to cigar factories because they believed the wages there were higher than in other jobs open to them. Wage rates easily fell below the union's bill of prices. State factory inspections in 1900 found that women's wages in major nonunion cigar factories in Detroit ranged from seventy-seven to ninety cents a day. Five years later a state investigation of cigar factories found that 2,138 of the state's 2,716 women in cigar factories worked in Wayne County, which included Detroit. Only 410 of the state's 1,974 male cigar makers worked in the same county. Males there averaged $2.08 a day while women averaged $1.21 a day. Another 1905 study estimated that women in Detroit made $1.50 a day on both bunching and rolling. In 1911 and 1912, women hand bunchers earned just over ten cents an hour less than their male counterparts. In 1915 the Michigan legislature considered a minimum wage law for women which would have raised wages in the cigar factories. Cigar manufacturers threatened to leave the state if the measure passed, and it was defeated.[18]

The 1915 investigation of women's wages in the state found that 42 percent of the women in cigar factories earned less than $8 a week. The report concluded, however, that women's wages were relatively high. One family of sisters who were all cigar makers reported weekly earnings of $19, $14, $13, and $12. Piece rates for cigar makers ranged from $1 to $1.90 for machine bunching; $2 to $5.50 for hand bunching. A woman using hand-operated buncher could make between 1,000 and 1,400 bunches a day. Making an average of 1,200 a day, or 6,600 a week, at an average of $1.60 per thousand, she would earn $10.56 a week, the report stated. Hand bunchers on the most expensive brands could average 500 a day, making about $15 a week. Most hand bunchers earned about $10 to $12 a week, however, and average wages for rollers were similar.[19]

Most women learned the trade when they were very young. State law allowed girls aged fourteen and over to work, but the law was frequently broken. In 1914 a coalition of local reformers and clergy tried to raise the minimum age to sixteen, but the cigar companies joined forces to fend off the measure. Manufacturers never hired any woman in a starting or learning position who was over the age of eighteen because they felt there would not be enough of a return on the investment of training her. They assumed she would most likely quit work when she married. One union observer in 1915 guessed that 90 percent of the women he saw coming out of the factories were under twenty.[20]

Manufacturers regarded the teaching stage as crucial because of the supply problem and because of the expense of training. Since turnover was so high, it was "constantly up to the cigar manufacturer to break in new help," an expensive requirement. A good amount of tobacco was wasted in the process of teaching a woman to roll or bunch cigars, and some manufacturers complained that they lost $50 to $150 for each woman they taught, because of waste. Yet once she had completed the training, she could "hike over to another factory and get a new job," a source of endless irritation to Detroit manufacturers.[21] Considering the cost of the tobacco and the risks involved, manufacturers experimented with different methods of sustaining adequate levels of trained cigar makers.

One approach to the labor supply and training expense problem was to set up a joint cigar-making school. Late in 1908 a group of city manufacturers formed the Detroit Ideal Cigar Company and agreed to help support the enterprise. Located at the corner of Hale Street and St. Aubin Avenue, the factory trained beginners. Within two to three months the first class of thirty had completed their training. Then the new cigar makers were sent to member factories to work up their speed. *Tobacco Leaf* reported that representatives from cigar factories in Philadelphia visited the school with the thought of forming their own combined training center. The Detroit Ideal Cigar Company was supported mostly by large manufacturers. The school taught cigar work only on the basis of divided labor, the team system. Bunchers learned hand and machine work.[22]

In the school, rollers were taught to cut only the right or left side of the wrapper leaf, rather than both, a practice which specialized workers and made it slightly more difficult to move to another factory. The CMIU charged that such training was designed to make the workers "more submissive."[23] The primary function of specialization, however, was to save money since women could learn the task more quickly. Each girl paid a five-dollar fee to attend the school.

The school plan ultimately failed because of rivalry and competition among the cigar companies. According to an investigation by AFL organizer John Flynn, the school showed favoritism to larger companies by giving them more than their share of workers. This "caused dissatisfaction which grew to such proportions that the institution became weaker and a few years ago disbanded." Even while the school operated, some factories continued to teach the trade to "relieve the tension" on the labor supply, and in 1910 San Telmo had a school in each of its factories. Once the Detroit Ideal Cigar Company closed, individual companies again took responsibility for training. For a brief time in late 1910 and early 1911, manufacturers tried a plan whereby they would give each learner an apprentice card. They would then all ask to see it when hiring someone in order to prevent workers from going freely from factory to factory. Lack of cooperation killed this plan as well.[24]

Most factories followed similar systems of training. Usually women received a certain amount of money per week while learning the job. Instead of cash, however, they were given certificates for one dollar or more each week. At the end of six months the certificates could be cashed in, provided that the woman worked there steadily during the entire time. In 1915 the San Telmo Company extended the six-month period to one year before a woman could cash the certificates. If they left the factory before that period ended, they received no compensation at all for the work they had performed.[25]

A few factories required women to work two weeks for free. Thereafter the women were paid the regular piece rate and received money for however many acceptable cigars they made in a week. The management of one factory using this method indicated that they believed that the policy encouraged the women to be more careful and to work harder and faster. Their pay envelopes initially ranged from eight to thirty cents. "While this is not as profitable to employees as the rates of some of the other factories, it keeps the girls on the alert trying to beat one another, and expectant at the end of the week to learn just how many usable cigars they have made." Management felt that paying piece rates encouraged the cigar maker to try to gain speed as soon as possible so that her earnings would go up. Foremen and teachers remarked that the girls who were fourteen were more difficult to teach than the older girls because they seemed less interested. One scornfully commented that the youngest girls were generally "lazy."[26]

The work week ran Monday through Friday with a half-day on Saturday. A state fifty-four-hour law for women meant that employers could not report—officially—longer hours for the state factory inspection report. Thus all factories recorded fifty-four hours a week, appearing to comply with the law. It is likely that factories opened about 7 A.M. and closed between 5:30 and 6:30 P.M. The union argued that during rush periods women's hours were longer, until 8 P.M. at times. Hours per day must have averaged between nine and eleven. Officially women were allowed to leave any time, but because they needed the maximum earnings they usually worked steadily.[27]

Foremen in Detroit were always men. Only a foreman could assign team members, and his authority was basically arbitrary. He could reward favorites or he could place a slow worker on a fast team and hurt the entire team's production. The teams felt pressure to work quickly and accurately. Foremen and management inspectors could remove cigars from their bundles and mark them as rejects. Women had no recourse, and a cigar making team might lose five to ten cigars a day this way. The evaluation of management was final. The union, along with many workers, charged that in order to save money manufacturers routinely ordered foremen to remove several hundred cigars a day as rejects; the majority were sold anyway. Company officials in all of the large Detroit factories also fined rollers and bunchers from twenty-five cents to three dollars a week for inefficient use of tobacco. Cigar makers who failed to meet their quota for the use of stock had the money removed from their weekly pay envelopes. According to the union, women who questioned this practice were "docked double for asking."[28]

Southeastern Pennsylvania

Hundreds of miles away, another cigar center busily expanded operations in the early twentieth century. The so-called country districts stretched through the small towns and boroughs of Bucks, Berks, Montgomery, and lower Lehigh counties, Pennsylvania's First Internal Revenue District, and on to Lancaster and York counties, the Ninth. The entire region had remained primarily agricultural, although tobacco cultivation was now concentrated only in Lancaster County. Farmers there grew a mediocre filler leaf, used to make cheap cigars which supplied the entire region (and beyond) with the weed. Factories ranged in size from tiny buckeyes to sizable brick structures of several stories, though few could hold as many as one thousand workers. Perhaps most significant, however, was the fact that most of them were branches of large Philadelphia and New York firms and were spread throughout scores of towns and hamlets.[29]

Beginning as early as the 1870s, large Philadelphia firms began setting up branch factories in the small towns north of the city along the Philadelphia and Reading Railroad, and west along the Pennsylvania Railroad. By the early twentieth century, nearly every Philadelphia manufacturer of any consequence had a branch somewhere in the country, and most had several. These included Boltz, Clymer Company, Jeitles and Blumenthal, Theobald and Oppenheimer, United Cigar Manufacturers, and especially Otto Eisenlohr and Son. Offices remained in the city to give the public the impression that the cigars were made there.[30]

The country districts offered several attractions. There was an ample supply of labor and the CMIU had never enjoyed much success in the region. Also, wage rates were significantly lower. For a cigar that even nonunion cigar makers made at the rate of $7 per thousand in Philadelphia, manufacturers could pay as little as $5 to $5.50 outside the city. At that price, suction tables were simply not cost-effective and were seldom used, according to the U.S. Industrial Commission. Of course, only nickel smokes were made there because "much of the work is crude," but these manufacturers could have ten-cent brands made in the city. Keeping costs low on five-cent cigars was sensible business practice. A 1905 Bureau of Corporations study observed that "many manufacturers have gone there with a view to saving on this item of expense [wages]." The communities themselves offered manufacturers inducements to locate in their midst. They might donate ground, help pay for a building, or offer tax breaks. Trumbauersville, in Bucks County, for example, constructed several buildings out of town funds and offered them at low rents. Both Eisenlohr and Theobald and Oppenheimer had branches there by the turn of the century—this in a town with fewer than five hundred people. Manufacturers readily recognized the advantages of setting up factories in such isolated communities under conditions so conducive to profitability.[31]

Starting at the eastern side of the state, in southwestern Bucks County, cigar making concentrated in the North Penn Valley area, primarily in and near Quakertown, a small city of thirty-two hundred in 1900; Sellersville, a borough half that size, and Perkasie, home for two thousand in 1900.[32] All were stops along the train line between Allentown and Philadelphia.

Trumbauersville stood off to the side, a short distance from Quakertown. The largest incorporated community in the county, Doylestown, had no cigar factories, but did support several banks and served as the county seat. Area industries included creameries, sawmills, and textiles, but the North Penn area more or less depended on the cigar industry for its livelihood and owed what prosperity it enjoyed to the railroad and the "ascending popularity of the 5¢ cigar." Most residents found themselves "dependent in some way, upon the industry."[33]

Separated by only a few miles were the cigar-making towns of the Upper Perkiomen Valley just across the Montgomery County line. The train linked East Greenville, Pennsburg, Red Hill, and Green Lane, but these and other cigar-making communities were also joined by trolley lines which threaded the area. Just to the west of the valley lay Gilbertsville, Boyertown (home of a large casket factory), and Pottstown, a city of 15,600 in 1912 which included several industries in addition to cigar making. To the south, the largest city in the county, Norristown, offered employment in several industries, although cigar making continued to flourish there during the early twentieth century. Although more economically and ethnically diverse than Bucks County, half of Montgomery's population in 1920 lived in rural areas with fewer than two thousand people.[34]

Due west lay Reading and surrounding towns. This area depended less on cigar making than other sections of the belt, although in towns like Sinking Spring and Womelsdorf, cigar manufacture had "for years [been] the chief occupation of the borough." Reading's economy included a mix of industries with no single one dominating: food products, lumber, printing, bicycles, hosiery, paper, leather, rubber, clothing, clay, glass, and stone. It also served as a regional railroad center. Cigar making had begun there during the early nineteenth century with a male labor force, but women entered the factories in the 1870s. The CMIU had long had a strong local there, influential in the local labor movement and municpal politics, but the union organized less than 30 percent of the city's cigar workers in 1919.[35]

The Ninth Internal Revenue District included only York and Lancaster counties, but outpaced its neighbor in cigar production each year. Lancaster had the additional claim of producing most of the cigar filler tobacco used in the state. York County, where cigar factories were "as thick as flies," had more of them (factories, that is, not flies) than any other county in the state. In 1920, 20 percent of U.S. cigars were manufactured in York County. One local historian counted one thousand factories in 1906, most of which clustered in or near the borough of Red Lion, a town of fourteen hundred about ten miles southeast of York. Nearby towns of Yoe, Spry, Windsor, Dallastown, and East Prospect, as well as the small city of Hanover, were all devoted to cigar making, and there were several firms in the city of York as well. None, however, were so successful as the companies of Red Lion.[36]

Spread over such a large region, the country districts' separate communities each had distinctive characteristics and a unique past, but they shared many common elements. The smallest villages depended on neighboring boroughs for banks and newspapers, but most had their own local services such as blacksmiths, bakeries, schools, hotels, and even theaters. Churches, primarily Lutheran, Reformed, and Evangelical abounded, while Catholics clustered only in certain areas and Mennonite congregations, though numerous, were mostly found in the eastern counties. Churches organized much of the recreational and social life—the church picnic was a virtual institution in the summer months. The region's rather homogeneous population sprang largely from Pennsylvania Germans and the dialect was spoken throughout the belt. Few blacks lived in these rural areas, but Jews had slightly more of a presence. A revitalized Klan found many supporters in the region during the 1920s. Every town had its share of fraternal organizations such as Red Men, Eagles, Knights of Pythias, and Masons. Union organizers traditionally blamed these and other organizations, which offered sick and death payments and were popular among cigar makers' families, for making union organizing more difficult.[37]

Separated by about seventy miles, East Greenville and Red Lion were fairly typical. Only 331 people lived in East Greenville in 1880, but the population began to grow once the railroad from Philadelphia stopped there, and reached 1,235 in 1910 and 1,720 in 1920. Evangelical, Reformed, and Catholic congregations had all built churches there by the turn of the century. The first baseball team was organized in 1885, and in 1910 the town opened a baseball park complete with grandstand. That same year the first theater opened, providing a place to stage plays and show movies, and it was joined by a second in 1916. A Perkiomen Valley orchestra formed in 1909, and the town also had its own band. More industrially diverse than some communities in the valley, East Greenville boasted one each of a boot and shoe, furniture, and casket factory along with a few foundries, small silk mills, a hotel, and an ice business. Cigar making, however, was East Greenville's leading industry by the late nineteenth century and was responsible for much of the town's growth.[38]

Red Lion, south of York, "was a small town where everyone knew everyone else and knew where everyone lived."[39] Protestants chose from several denominations, but Catholics had to worship in nearby Dallastown. Town fathers set up the first bank in 1899, run by prominent local cigar manufacturers, including Thomas E. Brooks. The Red Lion Opera House was built in 1914 and that year the town also sported two banks, sixty-five cigar factories employing nine hundred, a pretzel factory, a furniture plant, three box factories, and a variety of small stores. The local baseball team was organized in 1889. Fairmount Park, located on a hill at one end of the town, featured a dance pavilion and refreshment stand until they burned in 1917. The Red Lion Grange sponsored a fair for three summers starting in 1915, but the war interrupted the annual celebration. A trolley network connected several towns, but residents walked from community to community without hesitation.[40]

Throughout the entire region, cigar making had begun as a cottage industry in the mid- to late nineteenth century. Initially tobacco farmers rolled cigars from unsold tobacco in the winter and marketed them locally or used them for barter. Local legend in Bucks County held that skilled cigar makers sometimes walked from house to house, making up cigars, much as itinerant shoemakers and tailors did. In any case, cigar factories began to appear throughout the region in the 1870s and 1880s. Home work did not disappear, however. Manufacturers subcontracted work to local families, delivering the tobacco and later picking up the finished cigars. While factory production was the norm by the early twentieth century, small shops abounded throughout the area, particularly in York County. Run perhaps by a married couple and staffed by children, they operated out of side rooms and basements. In Red Lion, families made cigars in "summerhouses," small structures in the yard where people ate and slept in the summer. Families sold cigars directly or to local factories and were no longer strictly part of a putting-out system, although their wares were still referred to as the "farmer cigar product." The subcontracting system survived, however, with regard to stripping binder and filler leaves. In many towns, it was common for widows and women with small children to strip tobacco at home for one of the local factories.[41]

The first factory opened in East Greenville in 1860, and the industry expanded thereafter. Local manufacturers included Daniel Dimmig, who also ran an undertaking business and acted as local postmaster in the 1890s, and John Hillegass, who operated a small factory in the town and was succeeded after his death by his wife, who ran the business until World War I. Thomas Gerhart moved his shop there from Pennsburg in 1872, but in 1890 sold out to Otto Eisenlohr, the large Philadelphia manufacturer, who extensively expanded the business. Gerhart then stayed on as manager for many years. This pattern typified much of what happened throughout the country districts. While local industry flourished initially, it was soon dwarfed by the location of large, outside firms such as Eisenlohr. By the early twentieth century, most country district towns had scores of cigar factories, but one or two large firms dominated the industry locally.[42]

Although it had begun in the same way, Red Lion's cigar industry developed somewhat differently. As elsewhere, many families maintained buckeye businesses and sold cigars to firms in town well into the twentieth century, although the practice was beginning to wane somewhat by World War I. Home work by women still accomplished much of the binder and filler stripping done in the area. Yet few branch firms located there during the period, perhaps because of the strength and size of local industry. American Cigar Company opened a factory early in the century but left after a short stay. United Cigar Manufacturers opened a factory just before the war but soon left, and Eisenlohr then finally set up operations in the town by 1919. Possibly the town's specialization in the cheapest smokes, scrap "twofers" (two for five cents) only steps removed from the lowly stogie, also affected location decisions. Large firms tended to concentrate on the more popular five-cent long-filler smoke.[43]

Most of the town's leading companies started as one-man operations founded by local men. T. E. Brooks had worked in the summers as a cigar maker when only a young boy. Later he became a school teacher in Windsor and Red Lion. In 1900 he went into business with two others to form the Porto Rico Cigar Company which manufactured cigars and sold leaf tobacco. Shortly thereafter he left and started his own firm. David A. Horn, C. N. Foreman, Alvin C. Frey, and Harry Haines all started successful businesses in the borough during these years. D. C. Kaltreider began manufacture in 1899 and built a new frame factory on Charles Street in 1901. Peter McGuigan moved to Red Lion from Bittersville and opened a factory in 1904, along with a branch in Felton, Pennsylvania. Foremen, owners, and men and women workers all knew each other through a web of acquaintances and kin in the town. Manufacturers claimed to understand, therefore, the character of the local labor force and "knew how to treat them and how to avoid all kinds of labor troubles." These local entrepreneurs formed part of the town's elite, and held some of its major political offices. Benjamin Zarfos, for example, began manufacturing cigars in 1882 and served as constable, member of the Town Council, and chief burgess in addition to helping to organize the Red Lion Water Company.[44]

The York County industry remained prosperous throughout the period despite the apparently dubious reputation of its cigars within the trade— which possibly explains why manufacturers from Texas to New York purchased York products but put their own labels on them. Manufacturers in the "Notorious Ninth," always concerned with improving their tarnished image and aware of the "bitter feeling" against them within industry circles, countered that others were simply jealous of York County's low prices and high profits.[45]

Since employment opportunities through the country districts were limited, cigar manufacturers enjoyed a plentiful, if dependent, labor supply. As Margaret McDowell, a Red Lion roller, observed, "I guess we had to like it . . . we had to do something and that was about all there was to do."[46] In contrast to Detroit and to trends in the industry nationally, companies in the country districts hired both men and women. Yet just how many male workers there were is not completely clear. York County interviewees unanimously agreed that women outnumbered men in general and in any given shop. Editha Mattingly in Hanover explained that she preferred the cigar factory to working in a local shoe factory for that reason: women predominated in the former.[47]

Further east, the picture was more ambiguous. A 1916 state Department of Labor and Industry report discussing employment conditions in the Upper Perkiomen Valley remarked that "farming is the only extensive class of occupation afforded the male inhabitants." Women, the report continued, could find jobs in silk, glove, shirt, and cigar factories which had sprung up in the area in recent years. Women, therefore, had more job choices than men, a "fact bitterly deplored by the latter." Norman Wieand, a cigar maker in Trumbauersville who worked throughout the North Penn and Upper Perkiomen valleys, considered himself somewhat of an exception. Men frequently worked in cigar factories in the winter, he noted, but "in summers, you saw very few." Three others interviewed from Bucks County remembered many men working in the factories, but

Table 7. Pennsylvania Cigar Factory Workers, by Sex, 1919
Selected Counties

Location	Men	Women	Percent Women
Pennsylvania Total	9,028	18,629	67.3
*Adams	284	245	46.3
Allegheny			
Cigar	73	392	84.3
Stogie	117	1,022	89.7
*Berks	907	1,012	52.7
*Bucks	852	871	50.5
Dauphin	103	1,065	91.1
*Lancaster	1,601	2,015	55.7
Lebanon	415	290	41.1
Lehigh	220	1,077	83.0
Luzerne	54	650	92.3
*Montgomery	860	1,002	53.8
Northampton	109	1,267	92.0
Northumberland	55	718	92.8
Philadelphia	1,252	4,276	77.3
*York	1,977	3,021	60.4

Source: Pennsylvania Department of Internal Affairs, *Report on Productive Industries of the Commonwealth of Pennsylvania for 1916-1917-1918-1919* (Harrisburg, Pa., 1920).

*Country district counties

could not recall the approximate sex ratio.[48] Table 7 gives state and selected county totals for 1919 by sex.

Unfortunately the state did not present county totals for the years before 1919, and figures for that year are suspect because of strikes which took place then throughout the region. These figures suggest a more evenly balanced sex ratio in the easternmost counties. Despite the authority of the state in publishing the figures, it is perhaps well to recall the difficulty that U.S. Bureau of Corporations investigators encountered in the country districts in 1905 as they gathered data on employment. They noticed an "evident reluctance" of manufacturers, particularly large ones, to divulge levels of female employment, since high levels of female employment might call into question the quality of the cigars. One manufacturer, for example, reported seventy-five women employees, but the investigator personally counted three hundred.[49]

Cigar companies drew on labor not only from the towns but from the outlying areas as well. In many cases these workers, the young sons and daughters of area farmers, walked considerable distances to reach their jobs. Jane Hollenbach's parents lived on a farm near Bloominglen, and after having worked there in a tailoring shop for three years to help out with family expenses, she began in 1904 to walk to work at Pent Brothers cigar factory in nearby Perkasie, where wages were higher. Norman Wieand's parents never owned a farm, but always worked as farm help. Wieand himself was "hired out" to a farm when he was only eleven. Soon, however, he got a job stripping tobacco in East Greenville and daily walked the four miles from his home in Geryville along a dirt road ("when it was muddy you had to carry your shoes"). Margaret McDowell lived on a farm in York County and got her first job when she was sixteen at the Eisenlohr factory in Dallastown. She and several friends began walking to work in the morning from scattered farms and met at designated corners to form a group. Some who lived farthest away rose at 4 or 4:30 A.M. to make the trip. Clarence Jacobs, who started making cigars in 1902 in Yorkana explained that the morning starting time at the cigar factories there depended "on where you lived and how far you had to travel. At that time . . . we had to walk." In 1911 he began working in Red Lion, boarded there, but walked home on the weekends. In an extreme case, Valeria Glatfelter, who left school when she was fourteen, lived so far from the factory in Souderton, south of Quakertown, that she left home each morning at 5:30 A.M. accompanied by nine friends from nearby farms and arrived home for work at 7. At 4:30, they started the long trek home. When she was sixteen and could work full time, she moved to Souderton and boarded with a family there, ending the arduous journey to work.[50]

Not surprisingly, cigar makers worked because families needed the money. Neva Fake started work in Windsor in 1915. Her mother was a widow with five children "and we had to get out and make a living for ourselves." Editha Mattingly worked because she "wanted the money" and got to keep her own earnings, as many of her friends did. Others turned wages over to their parents. "You didn't keep your own money," one Sellersville woman admonished, "if you did, well, you didn't have no respect for your family." Her wages went to meet the $16-a-month payment for the small home her parents owned. Pauline Stauffer started working as a bunch breaker when she was sixteen and used the money to buy clothes and other goods her parents could not afford. She also contributed part of her earnings to the family. Norman Wieand recalled that he and his friends had given their parents their earnings and then received an allowance in return. "What we got to spend didn't rattle too much," however.[51]

Since the cigar industry formed such an integral part of the economies of these towns, many future cigar makers learned to strip tobacco at home as young children, helping their mothers who did outwork for the nearby factories. Most of the women who performed this work were married or widows. Since small shops abounded some youngsters learned the trade from their parents. Raymond Markle's parents ran a factory of twelve employees in Pleasant Hill, near Hanover, and he learned to strip tobacco when he was four and to roll cigars a few years later. Mary Berkheiser and Pauline Stauffer both first learned the trade at home.[52]

Getting a position was a relatively simple matter, and stripping was often the first step toward a more remunerative job. At the Eisenlohr factory in East Greenville, most of the strippers were "little kids and old women." The former regarded the job as an entrance, the latter as an exit from factory life. Mary Diehl's father worked as a delivery man for a box factory in Sellersville, and heard from a foreman in one factory about the need for help in the stripping department. Diehl got the job and a year later, in 1908, her boss asked whether she wanted to learn how to make cigars. "Of course I jumped for this offer." Cigar making "was a good job and it was a steady job. When you were once a cigar maker, you could get into any place" to work. Valeria Glatfelter, who did not know the trade at all, had simply picked out a factory in Souderton and "just went to the door and asked." She and Jane Hollenbach both first learned stripping and later moved on to cigar making. Norman Wieand taught himself to make cigars by watching a farmer for whom his father worked. After only a few months he went to a Trumbauersville factory to find a job. "How long have you been making cigars?" the foreman inquired. "About a year and a half," he answered with a straight face. ("But it wasn't true," he said years later with a smile.) He got the job and immediately started making bunches.[53]

In most factories, neophytes had to pay to learn the trade—twenty-five dollars in Bucks County—and then worked for several months without pay. William Frutiger, who became a leading manufacturer in Red Lion, learned to make cigars in 1897, turning out the first ten thousand for free. Mervin Kaltreider, whose father ran a factory in Red Lion, explained that learners had to work "for free . . . because they'd ruin a lot of cigars." Jane Hollenbach learned bunching from a foreman and worked in a separate room in the factory in Perkasie. It took eight weeks before the "stuff would pass" inspection and she could "go down on the other floor." Neva Fake learned to make cigars from a couple with a buckeye in Windsor. Later she moved on to work in a bigger shop in town.[54]

Throughout the region, the standard workday ran about nine or ten hours from between 6:30 and 7 A.M. to about 5:30 or 6 P.M. In a few cases hours were rigidly enforced, especially in larger firms, while in others they were more casual, where "there was no time to stop and no time to start." Low piece rates, as we have seen, encouraged cigar makers to work long hours at maximum speed. As Margaret McDowell explained, "If you wanted to make a lot, you worked a lot." In Red Lion, the customary schedule for the cigar factories followed that of the local box factory. The latter's whistle blew at 6:30 A.M., at lunch, and again at 12:30 for the return, and finally at 5:30 P.M., marking the close of the day. Mervin Kaltreider recalled that the crowded streets soon emptied once the whistle blew each morning. At times, especially rush periods, cigar makers worked later, and in Red Lion a twelve- or even a fourteen-hour day was not unthinkable, prompting a CMIU organizer in 1900 to describe the town as "the worst proposition I have ever come across."[55]

Accurate wage data is sparse, but unquestionably piece rates throughout the region were low in comparison to urban areas. A 1919 Department of Labor investigation of cigar factories in Lancaster commented that the county was "spoken of by citizens, workers and employers as one of the cheapest labor markets in the country." The piece rate for one cigar in Lancaster was $11 a thousand, while the same cigar paid $21 in New Haven, Connecticut. While some cigar makers recalled making cigars for $1 to $1.40 per hundred, most pegged the rate at 14 to 25¢ a hundred. Few recalled the take-home pay, although Valeria Glatfelter made $8 a week, $4 of which went for room and board, and Margaret McDowell remembered averaging as much as $12 a week. On the state level, women cigar factory workers averaged $8 a week in 1916 and $12 a week in 1919. In any event, as Pauline Stauffer noted, "you didn't make big money."[56]

Manufacturers organized the work in the standard team system, although frequently only one roller worked with one buncher instead of two. No machinery was used: rollers and bunchers worked by hand and the latter used molds. Several firms, including some of the Eisenlohr plants, sometimes used a system where "instead of a mold," cigar makers wrapped the bunches in paper, "like a strong tissue paper," and then twisted the end. This method required more skill than mold work and was apparently much more common. York County, particularly Red Lion, departed from this pattern, however. With the exception of a few firms, most cigars were made from short filler rather than long. Red Lion also made a unique product—crooks, bent cigars which sold very well. Beginning about 1909, Red Lion manufacturers began installing power-operated bunching machines, which came into fairly common use there. While rollers wrapped cigars for specific bunchers, they did not sit together as a team, but instead worked in separate areas of the floor.[57]

As elsewhere, management paid close attention to the use of tobacco and the workmanship in the cigar. Fines were not given, but cigar makers were admonished to work efficiently and one could be fired for failing to do so. Foremen walked through the factory about twice a day, inspecting cigars and watching the cigar makers at work. Cigars were officially inspected when they were turned in as well. Clarence Jacobs recalled that while Yorkana manufacturers monitored tobacco usage to an extent, in "a place like Red Lion, they kept more watch on you." Most agreed that inspections by officials from the Philadelphia home office were especially rigorous.[58]

While city and country appeared to stand in marked contrast, many aspects of cigar manufacture in Detroit and southeastern Pennsylvania were similar. In both cases the industry consciously sought out the labor force and moved factories to be accessible to it. Detroit women may have found more commodious surroundings, but they encountered a work process and environment similar to that of their rural sisters. Manufacturers in both areas sought to reduce training expenses and labor costs while augmenting their control over the production process. They generally preferred women over men as employees. The women they hired seemed to reflect starkly different backgrounds and cultures, but in fact shared much. Their families had initially been rooted in rural settings and now, whether rural or urban, they came from relatively homogeneous communities where overlapping acquaintances and ties formed bonds inside and outside the factories. The daily patterns of Detroit women might have seemed strange to those from rural towns and hamlets in Pennsylvania's cigar belt, but the work cultures they created linked them together in ways they never had the luxury of recognizing.

Notes

1. *Tobacco Leaf*, 11 Mar. 1903, p. 22; George B. Catlin, *The Story of Detroit* (Detroit, 1926), p. 468; Richard Oestreicher, "Changing Patterns of Class Relations

in Detroit, 1880–1900," *Detroit in Perspective*, 3 (Spring 1979), 146; Richard Oestreicher, "Solidarity and Fragmentation: Working People and Class Consciousness in Detroit, 1877–1895" (Ph.D. dissertation, Michigan State University, 1979), p. 14.

2. U.S. Office of Internal Revenue, *Annual Report of the Commissioner of Internal Revenue*, 1901, 1906 (Washington, D.C., 1901, 1906); Sister Mary Napolska, *The Polish Immigrant in Detroit to 1914* (Chicago, 1946), pp. 19–23; *CMOJ*, July 1915, pp. 10–11; Michigan State Department of Labor, *Annual Report, 1916, Inspection of Factories and Workshops* (Lansing, 1916), pp. 296–344; *Report of the Michigan State Commission of Inquiry into Wages and the Conditions of Labor for Women and the Advisability of Establishing a Minimum Wage* (Lansing, 1915), p. 422; "Detroit's Interest in Tobacco Products," *The Detroiter*, June 1913, pp. 22–24.

3. Caroline Golab, *Immigrant Destinations* (Philadelphia, 1977), pp. 67–100; John Bukowczyk, "Polish Rural Culture and Immigrant Working Class Formation, 1880–1914," *Polish American Studies*, 41 (Autumn 1984), 23–44; Napolska, *Polish Immigrant in Detroit*, pp. 22, 23, 25, 30; Niles Carpenter, *Immigrants and Their Children* (New York, 1969 [1927]), pp. 373, 376, 385; Theodore Radzialowski, "View from a Polish Ghetto: Some Observations on the First One Hundred Years in Detroit," *Ethnic Studies*, 1 (July 1974), 128–31; Stanley Mackun, "The Changing Pattern of Polish Settlement in the Greater Detroit Area: A Geographic Study of the Assimilation of an Ethnic Group" (Ph.D. dissertation, University of Michigan, 1964), pp. 23–36, 52, 63. *Dziennik Polski*, a leading Polish-language newspaper, estimated in 1914 that between 110,000 and 120,000 Poles lived in Detroit that year. See Napolska, *Polish Immigrant in Detroit*, p. 30. See also Stefan Kieniewicz, *The Emancipation of the Polish Peasantry* (Chicago, 1969).

4. Radzialowski, "View from a Polish Ghetto," pp. 128–31; Napolska, *Polish Immigrant in Detroit*, pp. 24–25, 30–32; Mackun, "Changing Pattern of Polish Settlement," pp. 36–51; Olivier Zunz, *The Changing Face of Inequality: Urbanization, Industrial Development, and Immigrants in Detroit, 1880–1920* (Chicago, 1982), pp. 63, 136, 152, 188, 193–94, 222, 232, 236–37, 277, 349.

5. *Tobacco Leaf*, 2 May 1900, p. 5; *Tobacco*, 8 Nov. 1906, p. 22.

6. *Detroit Labor News*, 10 July 1914; *Tobacco Leaf*, 2 July 1902, p. 20; 20 Sept. 1905, pp. 44; 12 Nov. 1908, p. 22.

7. *Tobacco Leaf*, 8 Jan. 1908, p. 18; 14 Apr. 1910, p. 11; 11 Aug. 1910, p. 4; 12 Oct. 1911, pp. 24, 35; Napolska, *Polish Immigrant in Detroit*, pp. 33–36.

8. *Tobacco Leaf*, 11 Dec. 1907, p. 32; 16 July 1909, p. 11; 21 Jan. 1915, p. 20; *Detroit City Directory*, 1900–1916. See also Michigan State Department of Labor, *Annual Report*, 1900–1916, which lists each factory and the number of male and female employees.

9. *Tobacco Leaf*, 8 Jan. 1908, p. 18; 17 June 1909, p. 11; 6 Jan. 1910, p. 37; 14 Apr. 1910, p. 11; 15 June 1911, p. 24; 14 Jan. 1915, p. 18.

10. *Tobacco Leaf*, 25 Feb. 1909, p. 20; 23 Sept. 1909, p. 36; 5 May 1910, p. 20; 11 Aug. 1910, p. 4; *Tobacco*, 8 Nov. 1906, p. 22; *Detroit Free Press*, 8 Dec. 1908; *Report on the Michigan State Commission of Inquiry*, p. 426.

11. *Tobacco Leaf*, 27 Sept. 1905, p. 42; 2 Jan. 1906, p. 24; 14 Mar. 1907, p. 14;

9 July 1908, p. 14; 16 July 1908, p. 11; 11 Aug. 1910, p. 4; 3 Nov. 1910, p. 34; 10 Nov. 1910, p. 7.

12. *Tobacco Leaf*, 27 Sept. 1905, p. 42; *U.S. Tobacco Journal*, 3 Mar. 1906, p. 18; *CMOJ*, July 1915, pp. 10–11.

13. *Tobacco Leaf*, 11 Oct. 1905, p. 38; 2 Sept. 1909, pp. 36, 38; 23 Sept. 1909, p. 36; 21 Oct. 1909, p. 9; 5 May 1910, p. 7; *Detroit Free Press*, 8 Dec. 1908; U.S. Bureau of Corporations, Tobacco Investigation, file 3073, section 1, Record Group (R.G.) 122, National Archives (NA), Washington, D.C.; *Report of the Michigan State Commission of Inquiry*, p. 429; U.S. Congress, Senate, *Cost of Living in American Towns. Report of an Inquiry by the Board of Trade of London into Working Class Rents, Housing, and Retail Prices, Together with Rates of Wages in Certain Occupations in the Principal Industrial Towns of the United States of America*, S. Doc. 22, 62d Cong., 1st sess., 1911, p. 176.

14. U.S. Department of Commerce, Bureau of the Census, *Census of Population: 1900*, "Special Reports," *Occupations* (Washington, D.C., 1904), pp. 548–49; Bureau of the Census, *Census of Manufactures: 1909*, vol. 8, *General Report and Analysis* (Washington, D.C., 1913), pp. 695–96; Bureau of the Census, *Census of Population: 1900, Statistics of Women at Work* (Washington, D.C., 1907), pp. 328, 240, 241. The 1915 commission on women's wages found that of 807 women interviewed, 670 lived at home with their parents. See *Report of the Michigan State Commission of Inquiry*, p. 430; Napolska, *Polish Immigrant in Detroit*, pp. 67–68. See also National Industrial Conference Board, *The Cost of Living among Wage-Earners, Detroit, Michigan*, Special Report no. 21 (New York, 1921), pp. 4, 7; Zunz, *Changing Face*, pp. 229, 253.

15. Frances Salantak interview, 20 Sept. 1978, Detroit, Mich.; Napolska, *Poles in Detroit*, pp. 33–36, 38; U.S. Congress, Senate, *Cost of Living in American Towns*, pp. 173, 180; *Tobacco*, 8 Nov. 1906, p. 22; Golab, *Immigrant Destinations*, pp. 71–77; Zunz, *Changing Face*, pp. 235–37; Lawrence D. Orton, *Polish Detroit and the Kolasinski Affair* (Detroit, 1981), p. 171. Frances Salantak was born in Poland and came to the U.S. in 1913 when she was twelve. A friend of hers worked in a cigar factory and Salantak secured a job in the same place in 1915.

16. Salantak interview; Zunz, *Changing Face*, pp. 152–54, 157, 170–71, 173, 236–37, 240; Golab, *Immigrant Destinations*, pp. 71–77.

17. Napolska, *Polish Immigrant in Detroit*, pp. 35–41; Salantak interview; Rose Purzon interview, 21 Sept. 1978, Detroit, Mich.; Helen Piwkowska, joint interview with Cecelia Chromki, 21 Sept. 1978, Hamtramck, Mich.; Bureau of the Census, *Census of Population: 1900, Statistics of Women at Work*, p. 241. Rose Purzon was born in Detroit of Polish parents and began working as a buncher in 1923 when she was fifteen. Helen Piwkowska began working in the early 1920s when she was fourteen, shortly after her arrival from Poland in 1922. The war had disrupted the area where she lived and she migrated with her sister. With the exception of Frances Salantak, all five women whom I interviewed in Detroit began working in the 1920s. Since the industry there changed little between the pre- and post-World War I periods, this information, in my view, accurately reflects the period about which I am writing.

18. U.S. Congress, Senate, *Cost of Living in American Towns*, p. 180; *CMOJ*,

May 1910, p. 4; July 1915, pp. 10–11; Jan. 1916, p. 29; Harvey Whipple, "Cigar Manufacture in Detroit," *The Detroiter,* June 1911, p. 11; *Tobacco Leaf,* 16 July 1908, p. 11; Michigan State Department of Labor, *Annual Report, 1900* (Lansing, 1900, 1905), pp. 6–37; *1905,* p. 479; U.S. Bureau of Labor Statistics, Bulletin 135, *Rates of Wages in the Cigar and Clothing Industries, 1911 and 1912* (Washington, D.C., 1913), p. 22; Women's Bureau, "Publications Other than Bulletins, Michigan Study," Box 29, R.G. 86, NA.

19. *Report of the Michigan State Commission of Inquiry,* p. 430.

20. Salantak interview, *CMOJ,* July 1915, pp. 10–11; *Report of the Michigan State Commission of Inquiry,* p. 426.

21. *Tobacco Leaf,* 14 Dec. 1911, p. 4; *CMOJ,* July 1915, pp. 10–11; *Report of the Michigan State Commission of Inquiry,* p. 430.

22. *Tobacco Leaf,* 24 Sept. 1908, p. 18; 1 Oct. 1908, p. 24; U.S. Commissioner of Labor, *Eleventh Special Report,* "Regulation and Restriction of Output" (Washington, D.C., 1904), p. 568.

23. *CMOJ,* July 1915, pp. 10–11.

24. Ibid.; *Tobacco Leaf,* 3 Nov. 1910, p. 34.

25. *CMOJ,* May 1910, p. 4; Jan. 1916, p. 29; David S. Jones, *Sight Seeing in Detroit's Foreign District,* CMIU pamphlet, 1912, Vertical File, Labor Collection, Detroit Public Library, pp. 4–5.

26. *Report of the Michigan State Commission of Inquiry,* pp. 426–28.

27. *CMOJ,* Nov. 1911, pp. 3–4; Feb. 1913, p. 4; Michigan State Department of Labor, *Annual Report,* 1900–1916; *Detroit Labor News,* 18 Aug. 1916; A. L. Faulkner to William B. Wilson, 10 Oct. 1916, file 33/290, Federal Mediation and Conciliation Service, R.G. 280, NA; *Report of the Michigan State Commission of Inquiry,* p. 423.

28. *Detroit Labor News,* 10 July 1914; *CMOJ,* Dec. 1911, p. 3; *Report of the Michigan State Commission of Inquiry,* p. 424; Purzon interview; Natalie Nietupski interview, 19 Sept. 1978, Detroit, Mich. Natalie Nietupski was born in Poland and as a teenager learned to be a buncher in a Detroit cigar factory in 1921.

29. Willis N. Baer, *The Economic Development of the Cigar Industry in the United States* (Lancaster, Pa., 1933), pp. 55, 165–68; U.S. Industrial Commission, *Report of the Industrial Commission on the Relations and Conditions of Capital and Labor,* vol. 15 (Washington, D.C., 1901), p. 387; *York Daily Record,* 15 Nov. 1982.

30. U.S. Bureau of Corporations, Tobacco Investigation, R.G. 122, NA; *CMOJ,* Sept. 1892, p. 6; Walter E. Baum, *Two Hundred Years* (Sellersville, Pa., 1938), p. 101; *CMOJ,* Apr. 1903, p. 4; Sept. 1906, pp. 12–13; Oct. 1906, p. 8; May 1907, p. 10; Nov. 1909, p. 20; *Tobacco Leaf,* 9 Dec. 1903, p. 45; 7 Dec. 1904, p. 6; *U.S. Tobacco Journal,* 14 Jan. 1911, p. 9; City of Hanover, *Souvenir Program: Centennial of Centennial of Incorporation* (Hanover, Pa., 1915), p. 89; Grier Scheerz, "Tobacco and Its Cultivation in Bucks County," *A Collection of Papers Read before the Bucks County Historical Society,* vol. 5 (Bucks County Historical Society, 1924), p. 612.

31. U.S. Industrial Commission, *Report,* vol. 15, pp. 387–88; U.S. Bureau of Corporations, Tobacco Investigation, R.G. 122; Norman Wieand interview, 21

June 1984, Quakertown, Pa.; *Pennsylvania State Gazetteer and Business Directory, 1903–1904* (Detroit, 1903), p. 2531; Meyer Jacobstein, *The Tobacco Industry in the United States* (New York, 1968 [1907]), p. 89. A similar pattern developed in the stogie industry. See Eva Smill, "The Stogy Industry on the Hill in Pittsburgh, Pa." (M.A. thesis, Carnegie Institute, Pittsburgh, June 1920), p. 18.

32. *Pennsylvania Gazetteer,* pp. 2267, 2397, 1286, 582.

33. *Quakertown Free Press,* special 100th anniversary issue, 15 Aug. 1980; Baum, *Two Hundred Years,* pp. 89–101; James Bennett Nolan, ed., *Southeastern Pennsylvania: A History of the Counties of Berks, Bucks, Chester, Delaware, Montgomery, Philadelphia and Schuykill,* vol. 1 (Philadelphia, 1943), pp. 433, 443, 461.

34. Everett Alderfer, *The Montgomery County Story* (Norristown, Pa.), pp. 205, 230, 258; Clifton Hunsicker, *Montgomery County, Philadelphia: A History,* vol. 1 (New York, Chicago, 1923), pp. 112, 154–55, 262, 385; Guy C. Whidden, *Pennsylvania and Its Manifold Activities* (Phildelphia, 1912), p. 244; F. W. Balthaser, *The Story of Berks County, Pennsylvania,* (Reading, Pa., 1925), pp. 266, 271, 282; Cyrus T. Fox, *Reading and Berks County Pennsylvania, a History,* vol. 1 (New York, 1925), p. 353; Sidney Goldstein, *The Norristown Study: An Experiment in Interdisciplinary Research Training* (Philadelphia, 1961), pp. 26, 140; Howard W. Kriebal, *A Brief History of Montgomery County, Pennsylvania* (Norristown, Pa., 1923), p. 123; Theodore W. Bean, *History of Montgomery County, Pennsylvania* (Philadelphia, 1884), pp. 117, 586; Paul Chancellor, *A History of Pottstown, Pennsylvania* (Pottstown, Pa., 1953), p. 119; Pennsylvania, Department of Labor and Industry, *Third Annual Report of the Commissioner of Labor and Industry, 1916* (Harrisburg, Pa., 1918), p. 21.

35. Balthaser, *Story of Berks County,* pp. 118, 272, 282, 290–91, 304, 311, 332; Nolan, *Southeastern Pennsylvania,* pp. 138–59; Morton Montgomery, *History of Berks County* (Philadelphia, 1886), p. 726; Paul Golis, "Cigar Making in Berks County, to 1860," *Historical Review of Berks County,* 5 (Oct. 1939), 67–70; Arthur Graeff, *Industrial Berks County, 1748–1948* (Reading, Pa., 1948); Fox, *Reading and Berks County,* p. 357; Raymond Albright, *Two Centuries of Reading, Pa., 1748–1948: A History of the County Seat of Berks County* (Reading, Pa., 1948), pp. 242, 271; *CMOJ,* Apr. 1920, p. 40; Pennsylvania Department of Labor and Industry, *Third Industrial Directory of Pennsylvania, 1919* (Harrisburg, Pa., 1920), pp. 556–68.

36. City of Hanover, *Souvenir Program,* p. 89; *U.S. Tobacco Journal,* 21 Jan. 1911, p. 4; 4 Feb. 1911, p. 21; *Pictoral Souvenir: The Borough of Red Lion* (York, Pa., 1930), pp. 4, 5, 11, 50, 171–91; Richard E. Ritz, *Red Lion: The First One Hundred Years, 1880–1980* (York, Pa., 1980), p. 72; U.S. Office of Internal Revenue, *Annual Report of the Commissioner of Internal Revenue, 1910* (Washington, D.C., 1910), p. 127; Baer, *Economic Development of the Cigar Industry,* pp. 165–68; George Prowell, *History of York County,* vol. 1 (Chicago, 1907), p. 768; *Pennsylvania Gazetteer, 1900,* p. 786; *York Daily Record,* 15 Nov. 1982; Timothy J. Lockyer, "Rollers 'n Strippers, Twofers 'n Crooks: The Cigar Industry of Red Lion," *Pennsylvania Heritage,* Fall 1981, pp. 15–19.

37. Baum, *Two Hundred Years,* pp. 89, 101; Nolan, *Southeastern Pennsyl-*

vania, pp. 138–39, 433, 443, 461, 463; Chancellor, *History of Pottstown*, p. 57, 87, 171; Alderfer, *Montgomery County Story*, pp. 229–30, 205; Balthaser, *Story of Berks County*, pp. 118, 206, 271, 282, 290, 304, 332–37; Hunsicker, *Montgomery County*, pp. 112, 142, 155, 283, 299, 370–80; Kriebal, *Brief History of Montgomery County*, pp. 283–86; Albright, *Two Centuries*, pp. 2, 212, 256, 265, 271; Fox, *Reading and Berks County*, pp. 79, 195; Ritz, *Red Lion: The First One Hundred Years*, p. 34; *Seventy-fifth Anniversary of the Borough of Ephrata; Incorporated August 22, 1891; Anniversary Celebration Week June 19 to 25, 1966* (Albany, N.Y., 1966), pp. 18, 19, 21–22, 33, 85; D. R. Hertz, *History of Ephrata, Pennsylvania: Giving a Brief Sketch of the Settlement of the State and County; The Battle of Brandywine, The Cloister and Monument to be Erected at Mount Zion and the Borough of Ephrata* (Philadelphia, 1894), p. 44; John N. Zoob, *Historical and Pictorial Lititz* (Lititz, Pa., 1905), pp. 36, 38, 59, 60, 212, 216; Homer Tope Rosenberger, *The Pennsylvania Germans, 1891–1965* (Lancaster, 1966), pp. 25–33; Gladys Palmer, *Union Tactics and Economic Change* (New York, 1971 [1932]), p. 41; Ritz, *Red Lion: The First One Hundred Years*, p. 34; Emerson H. Loucks, *The Ku Klux Klan in Pennsylvania* (Harrisburg, Pa., 1936), pp. 29, 197; David M. Chalmers, *Hooded Americanism: The History of the Ku Klux Klan* (New York, 1981 [1965]), pp. 236–42; *CMOJ*, Aug. 1907, p. 9; June 1910, p. 10.

38. *East Greenville Borough Centennial, 1875–1975. East Greenville, Pa., June 14–21, 1975* (East Greenville, Pa., 1975), pp. 6–18, 21–22, 32, 34, 44, 49, 51, 58, 61; Hunsicker, *Montgomery County*, pp. 262, 283–86, 361.

39. Mervin Kaltreider interview, 16 June 1982, Red Lion, Pa. Mr. Kaltreider's family started in the cigar business at the turn of the century. Both his father and his uncle owned factories in Red Lion. Retired, he is a local historian in Red Lion.

40. Ritz, *Red Lion: The First One Hundred Years*, pp. 25–28, 34, 35, 40, 43; *Pennsylvania Gazetteer*, p. 2306; C. M. Ehehalt, *Pictorial Souvenir: The Borough of Red Lion, York County, Pennsylvania, Golden Jubilee, 1880–1930* (York, Pa., 1930), pp. 63–128; Lockyer, "Rollers 'n Strippers," p. 16; *Tobacco Leaf*, 18 June, 1902, p. 5.

41. Lockyer, "Roller 'n Strippers," pp. 15–19; *Quakertown Free Press*, 15 Aug. 1980; Scheerz, "Tobacco and Its Cultivation," pp. 612–15; Henry L. Freking, "Cigar Makers," *Bucks County Traveler*, June 1954, p. 35; July 1954, p. 34; Baum, *Two Hundred Years*, pp. 99–101; Bean, *History of Montgomery County*, p. 586; Hunsicker, *Montgomery County*, pp. 262, 370–80; *Official Souvenir Year Book 1927* (Red Lion, Pa., 1927), pp. 3, 41–42; Edward Thompson interview, 9 Jan. 1976, Red Lion, Pa.; Clarence Jacobs interview, 17 Dec. 1982, Red Lion, Pa.; Mary Berkheiser, interviewed by Red Lion oral history project, Kaltreider Memorial Library (KML), 21 Dec. 1979 and 24 Jan. 1980, Red Lion, Pa.; Margaret McDowell, interview by KML, 9 Jan. 1980, Red Lion, Pa.; CMOJ, Apr. 1903, p. 4; *Tobacco Leaf*, 9 Dec. 1903, p. 45; 7 Dec. 1904, p. 6; City of Hanover, *Souvenir Program*, p. 89; *U.S. Tobacco Journal*, 4 Feb. 1911, p. 23. Edward Thompson's father was a partner of T. E. Brooks of Red Lion and the family continued its association with the company until they sold the business during the 1970s. Clarence Jacobs was born in Yorkana in 1889 and started working in 1902 when he was

thirteen and learned the trade complete. Both of his parents were cigar makers.

42. *East Greenville Borough Centennial,* pp. 12–14; Hunsicker, *Montgomery County,* p. 262; Wieand interview; *Pennsylvania Gazetteer,* pp. 1286, 2267, 2397; Chancellor, *History of Pottstown,* p. 119.

43. Ehehalt, *Pictorial Souvenir,* pp. 55–56; Kaltreider interview; C. Mervin Kaltreider, "Cigar Manufacturing in Red Lion," typescript, KML; Pennsylvania Department of Labor and Industry, *Third Industrial Directory, 1919,* pp. 1099–1100; *Second Industrial Directory of Pennsylvania, 1916* (Harrisburg, Pa., 1916), pp. 1443–44; *Official Souvenir Yearbook 1927,* p. 42; Lockyer, "Rollers 'n Strippers," p. 16; *U.S. Tobacco Journal,* 4 Mar. 1911, p. 9.

44. *Official Souvenir Year book 1927,* p. 11, 49–50; Ehehalt, *Pictorial Souvenir,* pp. 171–86.

45. See n. 44 and papers of Edward Noll, manufacturer, private collection in the possession of Harry Thompson, York, Pa.

46. McDowell interview of KML.

47. U.S. Industrial Commission, *Report,* vol. 15, p. 387; Pauline Stauffer interview, 21 June 1977, Hanover, Pa.; Editha Mattingly interview, 21 June 1977, Hanover, Pa.; Raymond Markle interview, 26 Feb. 1977, Hanover, Pa.; Valetta Leiphart interview, 17 June 1982, Red Lion, Pa.; Neva Fake interview, 17 Dec. 1982, Windsor, Pa.; Jacobs interview; Catherine Groft, Rose Smith, Editha Mattingly, and Pauline Stauffer, Senior Citizen Center group interview, 25 Feb. 1977, Hanover, Pa. Pauline Stauffer was born in 1897 and began work as a teenager in Hanover and McSherrystown. Her mother stripped tobacco and her father had his own shop. He had formerly been a member of the CMIU. Editha Mattingly was born in Hanover and began working when she was twelve in 1914, although she had done some stemming at home before that time. Her father was a cigar packer and her mother a roller. Raymond Markle was born in 1892 in Pleasant Hill, Pennsylvania, where his father had his own factory until 1906, when he gave up the business and began working in cigar factories in the area. Markle started working when he was thirteen in Hanover cigar factories. He left the trade after World War I and went into business as a bricklayer. Valetta Leiphart grew up on a farm near Red Lion, learned to roll cigars nearby, and moved to Red Lion with her husband in the early 1920s. Born in 1899, Neva Fake began to roll cigars when she was sixteen. She boarded with her sister in Windsor, Pennsylvania, only a few miles from Red Lion. The group interview was conducted at the Senior Citizens Center in Hanover. No one in Smith's family had worked in the trade and she quit after only a few weeks because of the smell. Groft worked as a stemmer. Her mother had stemmed tobacco at home.

48. Pennsylvania State Department of Labor and Industry, *Third Annual Report,* p. 21; Wieand interview; Jane Hollenbach interview, 16 Mar. 1984, Sellersville, Pa.; Valeria Glatfelter interview, 15 December 1983, Sellersville, Pa.; Mary Diehl interview, 13 Jan. 1984, Quakertown, Pa.; *CMOJ,* Apr. 1912, p. 8. Hollenbach, Glatfelter, and Diehl are all ficticious names. All three women asked that they not be identified. Hollenbach was born in 1887 in a small town near Perkasie, Pennsylvania. She started bunching whe she was thirteen. In the 1920s

she and her husband opened a business selling eggs after many factories in the area closed. Valeria Glatfelter was born in 1889 in Hilltown, Pennsylvania, near Sellersville on a small farm. She began working when she was fourteen. Mary Diehl began working when she was fourteen, in 1907. Her father worked for a box factory in Quakertown. She learned both bunching and rolling.

49. Pennsylvania Department of Internal Affairs, *Report on Productive Industries of the Commonwealth of Pennsylvania for 1916–1917–1918–1919* (Harrisburg, Pa., 1920), pp. 214–511; "Cigar Manufacture in Philadelphia," Tobacco Investigation, R.G. 122, NA.

50. Baum, *Two Hundred Years,* p. 101; Hollenbach interview; Markle interview; Wiead interview; McDowell interview by KML; Jacobs interview; Glatfelter interview.

51. Fake interview; Diehl interview; Wiead interview; Markle interview; Stauffer interview; Mattingly interview; Agnes Mary Haddon Byrnes, *Industrial Home Work in Pennsylvania* (Harrisburg, Pa., 1922), pp. 39, 140–48.

52. Byrnes, *Industrial Home Work,* pp. 39–41; Markle interview; Mattingly interview; Stauffer interview; Jacobs interview; Kaltreider interview; Baum, *Two Hundred Years,* pp. 101–2; Berkheiser interview by KML. Fake's mother stripped tobacco at home. Byrnes also noted that women home workers dreaded the "regularity of factory life."

53. Diehl interview; Glatfelter interview; Hollenbach interview; Wiead interview.

54. *Quakertown Free Press,* special 100th anniversary issue, 15 Aug. 1980; Ehehalt, *Pictorial Souvenir,* p. 175; Kaltreider typescript, "Cigar Manufacturing in Red Lion," KML; Hollenbach interview; Fake interview; U.S. Industrial Commission, *Report,* vol. 15, p. 288.

55. Lockyer, "Rollers 'n Strippers," pp. 17–18; *CMOJ,* Feb. 1900, p. 3; Sept. 1905, pp. 12–13; Jan. 1907, p. 4; June 1907, p. 6; Apr. 1912, p. 33; "Investigation of Tobacco Industry in Lancaster, Pennsylvania," file 46/2-C, Department of Labor, R.G. 174, NA; *Tobacco Leaf,* 16 Nov. 1911, p. 24; Mattingly, Stauffer, Groft, Smith group interview; McDowell interview by KML; Kaltreider interview.

56. See n. 55 and Paul F. Brissenden, *Earnings of Factory Workers, 1899 to 1927: An Analysis of Payroll Statistics* (Washington, D.C., 1929), p. 124; Pennsylvania Department of Internal Affairs, *Report,* pp. 78, 197; William Frear, E. K. Hibshman, B. S. Olson, and Otto Olson, "The Cigar Industry in Pennsylvania," *Bulletin of the Pennsylvania Department of Agriculture,* 5 (Nov. 1922), 76–77; Markle interview; Glatfelter interview; McDowell interview; U.S. Industrial Commission, *Report,* vol. 15, pp. 287–88. Lockyer, "Rollers 'n Strippers," p. 18. Brissenden found that statewide incomes for cigar industry women in Pennsylvania averaged $218 in 1899 yearly to $236 in 1914 and jumped up to $510 in 1919.

57. U.S. Industrial Commission, *Report,* vol. 15, pp. 387–88; Kaltreider Memorial Library, *Rollers and Strippers, Twofers and Crooks,* typescript, KML, p. 4; Lockyer, "Rollers 'n Strippers," pp. 16–17; *CMOJ,* Sept. 1905, p. 8; Wiead interview; Jacobs interview; Markle interview; Kaltreider interview; Harry and

Edward Thompson, interview by KML, 21 Dec. 1979; Prowell, *History of York County*, p. 560.

58. Fake interview; Leiphart interview; Jacobs interview. In the early 1920s when large Philadelphia firms moved into Hanover, discipline grew more strict. Workers interviewed also tended to resent the fact that many of the supervisors and owners were Jewish.

"Independent as a Hog on Ice": Women's Work Culture

Gender powerfully shaped the work culture that women cigar makers created. It did so in part because of the system of subordination that women encountered in their daily lives. But that sexual hierarchy did not mean that women were passive victims, dependent on home and family and unwilling to or uninterested in challenging the conditions under which they worked. Instead, women cigar makers in very different settings developed a rich and vibrant work culture, one which asserted their values and protected their interests. Manufacturers would not find it much to their liking.

At first glance, women cigar makers seemed to suit the needs of those who hired them. Certainly they failed to join labor organizations in great numbers and the few organizing attempts were unstable and short-lived. In 1900, Daniel DeLeon's Socialist Trades and Labor Alliance in New York City organized some cigar makers, and it is likely that the unsuccessful Machine Hands Cigar Makers' Union was an outgrowth of that effort. The Industrial Workers of the World (IWW) had at least ten cigar locals around the country in 1906, and included some women members. The IWW publicly blasted the CMIU for failing to organize more women team workers, and the CMIU resorted to a full-page advertisement in the *CMOJ* to rebut the charges. The CMIU did engage in some organizing efforts among women during these years, but its attempts were neither systematic nor intensive. Not until 1915 when it adopted the Class A plan did the CMIU make a real effort to organize women, and even then it was less than enthusiastic.[1]

strategies related to U . mculer

Union figures for 1912 pegged women's representation in the CMIU a
10 percent of total membership. The largest locals were those in New York
State, such as a Binghamton team workers' union and a Bohemian local in
New York City which reputedly had a large contingent of women members. The CMIU barely organized any women in Pennsylvania or New
Jersey, however. In other locals where women belonged, they were "far
outnumbered" by men, according to one study of women and unions, and
had "no influence in shaping policy." Evidence suggests that a sizable proportion of the 10 percent was a fluctuating figure—rising during a particular strike and falling when the strike ended. While several locals, particularly 97 in Boston, heartily supported stemmers' unions, their position
on women members was ambiguous at best.[2]

Many factors reinforced unionists' distrust of women, particularly basic
economics. Male unionists feared that women would lower their own
wages or even turn them out of a job. They could cite a long list of examples such as the Lilies Cigar Company, where nonunion women replaced union men. Also, the condescension many union members felt toward the labor market in Pennsylvania, where so many women worked,
hampered recruitment—one CMIU member claimed he would not "dis-
grace" his travel card by depositing it in Pennsylvania. It is also possible
that the intensity of feeling against the region related to the fact that so
many women worked there. Organizing women was further complicated
by the fact that the union usually opposed team work. Chicago cigar
makers did not permit the system, they said, because it "increases the
manufacturers' profits and the workers' idleness and poverty." When the
CMIU organized the Jacob A. Mayer Company in Lancaster in 1907,
thirty women were fired because the union did not allow "this kind
of work."[3]

Such actions and attitudes understandably made many women wary of
the CMIU, and in most cases they were no more interested in the unions
than the unions were in them. First were the simple demographic differences between them. Male unionists tended to be older and they were
more likely to be married than women. Women generally came from more
recently arrived ethnic groups and many could not speak English. Male
unionists came from different ethnic backgrounds, particularly German,
and they were far more "Americanized" than women in the industry. A
majority of them conducted union business in English. Other practical
matters also made unions seem alien. Union dues were expensive consid-

ering women's wages and meetings were often held in the evenings when it was difficult for them to attend.[4]

Women's lack of presence in the CMIU, however, must be understood in broader terms. Male unionists were trying to redress the power imbalance they encountered within the industry and respond to the exploitative working conditions they found there. Unionists did not necessarily overtly aim at reducing the opportunities of others, but as this group of workers sought to use available resources for self-protection, they closed off opportunities to outsiders. Their collectivist consciousness led them to work as a group to assert their class interests vis-à-vis employers, but their ethic operated narrowly to preserve those gains and privileges for themselves without attempting to open them to all in the industry.[5]

Male and female work cultures also clashed over values and different conceptions of morality. Men in the CMIU created a loyal world of insiders and by definition those beyond these bounds seemed suspect and even dangerous. To maintain whatever gains they had won and some position of power relative to manufacturers they needed a loyal and disciplined membership, but they regarded women as weak and unreliable. They drew strength from their sense of pride and dignity, but that pride came in contrast to the work of others who permitted themselves to be exploited by manufacturers. Women then could hardly be manly. Because of general notions regarding women's inferiority, when women performed essentially the same work as men masculine culture interpreted it as degrading, undignified, and dishonorable. Unable to treat women as equals, male unionists often depicted them as needy, vulnerable, and victimized, suggesting that many women cigar makers were prostitutes because they needed the money. Such portrayals only offended women who were concerned about their own dignity and respectability. A group of women cigar makers in Philadelphia refused to affiliate with the CMIU in 1916 both because they distrusted the men's sincerity in organizing them and because the local met in a building which housed a saloon.[6] In their struggles with each other, men and women reflected often-divergent ways of interpreting life around them.

Women's lack of access to the CMIU meant that they were considerably more vulnerable as workers, which once again made them seem, on the surface, ideal employees. While it would be a tautology to argue that men had unions because they had the advantages of unions and women did not because they lacked the backing of unions, it is helpful to recognize their relative resources and privileges. Belonging to the union meant a financial cushion of benefits and strike payments. These, along with other union traditions, reinforced a sense of collective strength. Newcomers to the CMIU were initiated with stories of past struggles and a group history. Male unionists shared a tradition of geographic mobility which fostered a sense of belonging to a larger group. Cigar makers' tramping also gave them connections to each other and a better understanding of the structure and operation of the industry as a whole. Women had none of these supports and thus might be expected to have more difficulty viewing themselves collectively. Less mobile, they had no connections to each other beyond a particular factory or community. While "manhood" offered legitimacy for men to challenge managerial authority, cultural constructions of womanhood might work to undermine women's claims for justice.[7]

Despite such seeming disadvantages, however, women cigar makers forged a strong work culture. Like union men, they were concerned with their time, the condition of the tobacco, their wages, and their relationship to foremen. While there were important parallels, their occupational patterns were not simply mirror images, though. Women's work culture was shaped by many different things in their lives, but gender played a central role. Women drew on their values and socialization as women— their own women's culture—to interpret their experiences and formulate responses.

The very system of male domination which set women apart and created a "women's sphere" could permit a space in which to create some autonomy from men and to build a kind of solidarity among women. Historians have used the concept of women's culture to describe "the way women perceive and impose social order, construct family relationships, act out their own roles, socialize one another and acknowledge meaning in their lives."[8] This women's culture revolved around a myriad of women's traditional concerns including the daily tasks relating to family and children. But it was also rooted in certain specific values and accepted notions of woman's place in society. Women's culture did not imply a feminist consciousness and at times it could work to reinforce the "sex/gender" system, but it could also operate as a resource for women workers, providing them with some clear expectations about how they should be treated.[9]

As many scholars have begun to demonstrate, domestic concerns and obligations did not by themselves define working women's consciousness in the late nineteenth and early twentieth centuries. Women cigar makers were no exception. Their experience of work was central to their outlook and actions. While the workplace reproduced the patterns of inequality and gender hierarchy in the home for cigar makers as well as other workers, the shared experience of work could also transform these relations. The physical closeness and common experiences provided women workers with an opportunity to develop a group identity and a recognition of their collective interests. The very nature of the cigar-making work process drew women together in ways which paralleled the solidarity-building role of the CMIU for men and facilitated the development of a sense of mutuality and interdependence.[10]

Scholars have also recently begun to document a rich associational life among working-class women, a web of ties and networks which contrasted to the isolation of the home. For the women in this study, community and work intersected and often reinforced each other. In Detroit, women's Polishness and their opportunities to see each other outside the workplace strengthened their cohesiveness. In southeastern Pennsylvania, the specific details of everyday life may have differed greatly, but they too provided a backdrop for women's work culture. Certainly women saw themselves as daughters, mothers, and sisters, as well as members of ethnic and religious groups, but at the same time they had strong identities as women and as workers.[11]

The cigar factories which provided the immediate setting of women's work culture were less than pleasant environments. They were usually larger and cleaner than the shops in which most male unionists worked, but investigations in many cities found them universally dusty, poorly ventilated, and crowded. Toilets were often uncared for and cafeterias and first aid rooms (when they existed at all) were not always clean and sanitary.[12] Factories with welfare programs undoubtedly improved on these conditions, but most never adopted such amenities. In summer the factories could be "stinking hot. . . . You couldn't have the windows open," Lucille Speaker explained, since that would "dry the tobacco out and then you couldn't use it. It was terrible, it really was."[13]

The strong smell of the tobacco permeated the air and affected any newcomer to a cigar factory, union or nonunion. Jane Hollenbach recalled her first days of work in Perkasie: "I was just like a drunken person . . . and I would get sick." Those who "couldn't stand it" and get over their nausea had to quit. The work itself was dirty and required cigar makers to wear aprons because "there's quite a bit of dust," which was also "hard on your breathing." The tobacco smell lingered inside clothing long after the workday ended, a fact which some considered demeaning. Anna Bartasius, a Lithuanian cigar maker in Philadelphia, took the streetcar home each day and never doubted that fellow riders easily guessed where she worked. Stella Sutton, working in the Deisel-Wemmer factory in Lima, Ohio, remembered that "when you came out of there everybody turned up their nose at you. You stink! I used to take my apron . . . and roll it up in paper and take it home."[14]

While male unionists found piecework a blessing, under the team system it could serve as an instrument of coercion and "consent." It dictated an intense pressure to work steadily and quickly, which could "make a nervous wreck out of you," an Evansville, Indiana, cigar maker complained. After all, noted another maker, "the speed is where we made our money."[15] In Detroit in 1908, women could make as much as ten dollars a week, but only if they worked without interruption. There and elsewhere, the pressure to take home enough pay on Saturday meant that many women ate lunch in the workroom, rather than in the cafeteria or a nearby restaurant. Rose Purzon of Detroit and her friends brought their own lunches and only bought coffee at the factory. This way they took less time away from their work and spent less money than if they purchased meals "at cost" in the cafeteria. Despite the tobacco, "you ate right there where you were working," said Natalie Nietupski; "you got used to the smell of it so you never noticed it." Some took "no lunch hour." That way, explained Frances Salantak, she could earn "pretty good money." Another Detroit cigar maker remarked that "you didn't even have time to go to the bathroom because you were afraid that you were going to lose ten minutes and you were going to lose ten to fifteen cigars or twenty. But many times you just waited until you got home."[16] Valetta Leiphart in Red Lion recalled that women were in such a hurry that "you'd almost knock each other down" racing to get more tobacco. In Pittsburgh stogie factories, women could be fired for not making a certain quota of stogies; and while cigar factories did not have such stringent requirements, slower workers could not expect to keep their jobs. Piecework was a major cause of the worker "fatigue" that factory inspectors noted.[17]

Yet women did not always place maximum earnings as the first priority, and evidence suggests that many resisted such a feverish pace. Some cigar makers in the North Penn Valley, for example, often set an informal limit "among themselves" on the number of cigars they would make—"that much and no more." Pearl Hume in Lima set her goal at 800 a day on five-cent cigars and 550 to 600 on ten-cent brands. That way she "didn't have to be a nervous wreck." She also never skipped lunch: "I liked to get out from the place." Many Lima workers ate at a restaurant down the street from the factory, breaking up the day and continuing conversations from the morning. A 1913 Bureau of Labor study found that some workers preferred to "take things easy," rather than overstrain.[18]

Piecework operated as a form of exploitation, but, as in union factories, it could also have its advantages, permitting a degree of control and flexibility if hours were not too rigidly set. In Detroit, "you could leave anytime you wanted and you could stay home anytime you wanted," explained Frances Salantak. It was not necessary for them to explain their absences, though they might send word to the foreman via a friend. Because of the great labor needs there and elsewhere, even if a woman quit her job for several weeks she could expect to get it back. "You can always get a job," noted Philadelphian Anna Bartasius. "If not in this factory, then in another factory." Using this freedom, women could interrupt monotonous work schedules to make time for other activities, or they could simply assert their claim on their own time. Philadelphia manufacturers in 1900 complained when hundreds of women stayed home during the intense heat wave that summer. Also, if the Fourth of July fell on a Wednesday, manufacturers might have only half their work force during the entire week. In York County, Pennsylvania, cigar makers frequently abandoned work on spring and summer afternoons in order to attend local baseball games—in 1903, the large Kerbs, Wertheim and Schiffer factory in York resorted to discharging "a large number of hands" for consistently abandoning the bench for the games. Women's increased activities in summer made it "difficult to keep them at work, no matter how pressing the demands [for cigar orders] might be," sighed one industry observer in Binghamton, New York.[19] Religous holidays were especially important to women. In York and Lancaster counties, an observer noted in 1912, women took Ascension Thursday as a holiday, "some believing that it is a bad omen to work that day." In Detroit, women refused to work during the Polish holidays, so that the factories were "all compelled to shut down." When workers there refused to labor and stayed home during Holy Week (the week before Easter), *Tobacco Leaf* reported that "this is the nearest to a real strike the local cigar factories get."[20]

The flexibility also served as a strategy for combining work and home roles, something male unionists did not need to do. Stella Sutton continued to work at the factory in Lima once her children arrived. "I would go home and nurse them at noontime," she explained. A study of women cigar makers in Philadelphia in 1917 found that "it is the habit of some workers to come late in the mornings, to take extra time at the lunch period, and at times to leave early in the afternoons." In New Orleans, city factory inspectors found that many married women came in early and worked quickly so that they could leave work in time to meet their children when they came home from school. An investigation of Lancaster, Pennsylvania, factories found that women's hours were considerably more irregular than men's. The pattern of production in most factories employing women meant that mothers could stay home with sick children or single daughters could help out with household tasks. Women could also quit their jobs when children were born and return several months later in most factories, and manufacturers were always glad to rehire someone who was already trained. Thus women could use piecework and their skills in important ways to serve their own interests. While this could and did work at cross-purposes with manufacturers' requirements, it nevertheless satisfied and reinforced the needs of the patriarchal family by freeing some of women's time for household activities.[21]

Yet this flexibility was limited by the structure of the work process. The team system not only made training easier, permitted lower wages, and gave manufacturers more control over the production process, it obligated women for the most part to report for work punctually in the mornings. The team functioned as a unit and wages were calculated on the entire team's output, so "you were kind of dependent on each other."[22] Bunch makers needed to keep rollers supplied so that all kept working steadily and made as many cigars as possible. If a buncher left early, rollers had to make other "arrangements." If a buncher came in late in the morning, her two rollers had no work to do unless they could fill in for someone else. When the tardy cigar maker arrived, there might then be no opening available. She had no choice but "to go back home." As Lucille Speaker put it, "there was no advantage to being late, I'll tell you."[23]

This work process created tremendous potential for conflict, because if someone could not keep up the pace it hurt the whole team. A bad buncher or roller could "slow you down," a frustrating experience for one who was more proficient. One always wanted a fast roller or buncher because then "you make more money." Stella Sutton, a roller, noted that "if the bunch breaker didn't have nice smooth bunches, the roller could raise cain with her, but they done it between themselves." Buncher Pauline Stauffer pointed out that "the roller could make it bad for you if she wanted to." A roller could help because some "could do pretty good with the bunch if it wasn't just right. They could shape it. But other ones couldn't do it . . . and those were the picky ones."[24]

But the team system could just as easily operate in ways which drew workers together rather than split them apart. If a buncher "ran short" of tobacco, rollers waiting for bunches might "run up and get her stock or help her. Many times we used to help her," explained one roller. A Detroit buncher recalled that when she had bunched enough and had some time, she "helped the girls rolling cigars."[25] Lucille Speaker in Lima agreed that members of the team "helped one another. . . . If maybe you [got] through a little early and you could help them out a little bit . . . cause it only made it better for all of you, if you sort of worked together." Some women prided themselves on learning the other operation in addition to their own, though foremen did not necessarily like to see time wasted in this way. Also, women may have consciously tried to overcome the conflict inherent in the work in order to sustain their personal relationships with each other, connections which they valued highly. Pauline Stauffer, for example, recalled that differences in speed and skill had caused friction between her and another woman in Hanover, but eventually the two "worked it out. We got to be friends again."[26] Because foremen usually assigned the teams, discontent regarding their composition could well be focused on him, not just on each other. Women also had some leverage in requesting changes if they could demonstrate that an unbalanced team hindered production. In Perkasie and Sellersville, by contrast, cigar makers formed the teams "among ourselves, and if it was satisfactory, why the foreman wouldn't bother."[27] In this way women carved out an extra measure of authority for themselves.

Most important, the team system contributed to women workers' sense of the importance of group, rather than individual, concerns and reinforced the connective aspects of women's culture. The team reminded each cigar maker of the needs of the woman next to her, so that she worked not only for herself, but for her co-workers as well. This was an experience not duplicated in the isolated household. In Detroit, a buncher might come in a little earlier to begin making bunches for her rollers. They in turn stayed a little later in the day to finish up their work.[28] To gain control over time, women had to cooperate and arrange their schedules with each other, negotiating their comings and goings during the day. If partners in Bucks County agreed to "get home at three o'clock, they would get up and go." In Detroit, if anyone wanted to leave ahead of schedule, "you'd talk it over with your girls and you'd go home." In Lima, women had to "get permission" in order to leave, but in Detroit and the country districts women did not have to consult foremen before leaving, so their arrangements were final. With the welfare of the whole team in mind, a buncher who anticipated being late the following morning stayed late the night before and made several extra bunches, so rollers would not have to wait idly for her arrival. "It was the partnership or nothing," said Rose Purzon. The team system promoted a sense of interdependence and cooperation.[29]

Because of turnover, the composition of a team might not remain the same for long periods, although teams also "worked for quite a few years together." Stella Sutton preferred a stable team "because you know just exactly what they was going to do and they knew what you were going to do. You got to know each other that well. It was almost just like being married." In Hanover, Pauline Stauffer worked for several years with two sisters and always got along well. In some cases, women who knew they could depend on each other's skills applied for jobs together. Mary Diehl explained that she and her girlfriend "traveled together" to the factories in town. Turnover, on the other hand, provided women with a chance to meet new people and widen circles of acquaintances.[30]

Women cigar makers had several concerns in making the day go well. They needed to devote great attention and care to their work, making sure that the bunches were uniform, had the correct thickness and length, and had no "holes," as Detroit women termed the soft spots. The buncher took filler leaves and broke them off to the proper size and thickness, squeezing them in her left hand and arranging them with her right. Although this system was less demanding than all-hand work, women still needed skills similar to those of union men. "You have to feel in your hand," one described the process. Jane Hollenbach explained that one had to "shape it in your hand. . . . You would know when you had a bunch." Sometimes a less-experienced woman used the mold as a measure for the amount of tobacco and the shape and thickness of the bunch, but the experienced worker knew just how much to use. Then, after completing the operation, she quickly and without looking up placed the bunch in the mold propped up in front of her. Women viewed this work as skilled: "You had to know just what you were doing."[31]

Rollers removed the bunches from the mold and cut the wrappers into the proper shape, judging how much leaf to use and how to cut around its imperfections. Stock "full of holes" made the job difficult if not impossible. "You can't work with that," lamented Pearl Hume. Ironically the cigars for which women were paid the least, since they were the cheapest, also tended to be made using the worst stock and therefore required the

most skill. Summer heat made work more difficult since it dried out the
tobacco quicker and made it harder to handle.[32] The roller might spend a
few minutes mending or shaping the bunch if needed. When applying the
wrapper she had to make sure that the tuck and the head were formed
and smoothed properly. "Oh, there was an awful lot to it." Once finished,
she placed it in the "bundler," the wire rack on the shelf in front of her. At
each step, something could complicate the process. "If things went well—
if your wrappers wasn't too bad and your bunch breaker could keep after
you and when you got what you thought you could roll, then that was a
good day."[33]

Inspections came both during the day and again when cigar makers
brought up completed cigars for credit to their accounts. If the cigars
were faulty, "we have to replace them," and "that was just lost time"
noted two Lima workers.[34] "You don't make it right," warned Anna Bartasius, "you don't get paid."[35] In Detroit, where cigars were inspected
systematically at the end of each day, a foreman could remove any he
deemed substandard and subtract the number from the team's total. For
every cigar removed, a woman had to return to her table to get other
cigars for replacement. The CMIU argued that this practice meant that
women were making several cigars a day for free as a part of company policy. In 1914, the *Detroit Labor News* estimated that a team could lose as
many as forty cigars a week. And the cigar makers knew that the cigars
were not discarded. "They [the manufacturers] were selling those cigars
that they took away from us as seconds," said one woman worker.[36]

Management's careful monitoring of tobacco usage was also on each
cigar maker's mind as she rolled or bunched cigars. One could be fired or
temporarily laid off for wasting tobacco. In the stockroom, one or two employees dispensed stock and punched cigar makers' cards according to the
amounts of preweighed packages of binder and wrapper leaves they received. "They just made [up] their mind that we had to make one hundred cigars out of the pack that they gave you," noted Piwkowska. Detroit
women who failed to meet the quotas were fined and lost anywhere from
twenty-five cents to three dollars from their weekly pay envelopes.[37] Although fines were less common elsewhere, management seemed no less
serious about the issue. A foreman in Lima, Ohio, explained that "if you'd
catch a girl getting one wrapper out of that where she could get two,
you're supposed to get on her," and a Lima cigar maker recalled that "you
really got the dickens" for not making a high enough average. "I used to
get bawled out a lot." Jane Hollenbach in Perkasie argued that "You didn't

San Telmo Cigar factory, Detroit, circa 1916. Photo courtesy of the Burton Historical Collection of the Detroit Public Library.

W. C. Frutiger factory, Red Lion, Pa., 1927[?]. Photograph courtesy of Mary Berkheiser and the Kaltreider Memorial Library, Red Lion, Pa.

waste it, but they didn't give you enough. . . . If you didn't get that much out, why you were short and then at the end of the week . . . you'd catch cain for going short. But you can't make something out of nothing."[38] When the stock was bad, as it often was, especially on cheap cigars, the problems of working quickly and using as little tobacco as possible were intensified.

Although women lacked the rules and protections unionism might have afforded, like their union counterparts they developed ways to appear to reach acceptable averages without actually doing so. While men established formal procedures for masking individual use of tobacco, women relied informally on their friendships and ties inside the shop. When "the company wasn't looking," women quietly shared tobacco with each other. "You didn't say nothing about that," Lucille Speaker cautioned. Pearl Hume noted that in Lima women maintained "what they call a bank." Those with extra tobacco put it aside for use in the bank. "Then if you'd be short," those with tobacco to spare would "give it to you." In Windsor, Pennsylvania, Neva Fake recalled that "close" wrapper cutters gave to those who were not, but unfortunately for her the ones who sat near her "were as bad as I was."[39] In addition to sharing, women sometimes set an average among themselves. Hume aimed in the middle range, "not too low or not too high." In Lima, shop mates called down a woman who consistently had a higher average than everyone else. "She made it harder for everybody. . . . A lot of them was really mean to her."[40]

Cigar makers adjusted the work process in other ways to better accommodate themselves. Several shortcuts added to speed, but they too had to be concealed from the foreman's glance. One might quickly lick the flag at the end of the cigar instead of reaching for the paste cup, for example. Biting off the ends of the tobacco instead of taking time to use the knife shaved off several seconds as well.[41]

Labor shortages and turnover predictably gave women additional levers in the work place. The expense of training newcomers and the expansion of cigar production created a demand for women cigar makers, which in turn enabled women to win some concessions. In 1900, when many Pennsylvania male cigar makers left the area to take the jobs of strikers in New York and Philadelphia, women cigar makers who remained behind were able to win wage increases through scattered strikes in York County because of the labor shortages. In 1909, a labor shortage developed in Lancaster that lasted more than a year and a half and forced manufacturers to raise wages to attract more workers.[42]

Turnover even operated as a form of protest. A survey of New Orleans manufacturers suggested that only 36 percent of their women workers left because of unsatisfactory working conditions, and that 50 percent left for personal reasons. The responses of women cigar makers in the city, however, showed that 64 percent of those who had recently left jobs in tobacco did so because they found conditions unsatisfactory. When conditions were unacceptable, women left and applied for work elsewhere. "Most of the time women, they just quit in one place and they went to the other place," said Natalie Nietupski of Detroit. If a cigar maker suspected her imminent dismissal—"they were maybe watching you too much or something so you just quit."[43] Another Detroit worker noted that "if anything got too bad in one place, you know like the tobacco wouldn't be just right or something—they tried to save money on that—you tell them to go to hell and go someplace else. Like I said, you could get a job today and start working tomorrow. They were always desperate for help." Sometimes several factors combined to augment women's power. In 1910 a strike in Tampa caused Detroit orders to reach record highs. An industry spokesman complained derisively that "all the available girls were employed and they are as independent as a hog on ice, refusing to work if they don't feel like it because they know they can get as good a job at a moment's notice at another factory."[44]

Resistance to manufacturers and expressions of aloofness from them could be expressed in a variety of ways, some of them quite subtle. In Lima, cigar makers worked sitting on wooden boxes rather than chairs. They clearly defined this space as their own, not employers'. Inside they stored personal belongings "and all kinds of things. Our box. That was private property."[45] More obvious was women's sense of entitlement to some of the cigars they made. Manufacturers liked to boast that hiring women eliminated the "free-smoker nuisance," but cigar makers apparently did not see matters in the same light. In Detroit, women removed cigars from the factories for their boyfriends, fathers, and husbands. To escape detection, they carefully concealed the cigar so "no one could see it."[46] In Quakertown, Mary Diehl recalled that only if one had enough extra tobacco could she successfully make her own smokers and take them home. Even then, "you didn't tell that to the boss." In Perkasie, women felt entitled to the "imperfects," Jane Hollenbach explained, and while one "wasn't supposed to take any home," most did so. Lucille Speaker related that the company "wouldn't give you nothing," so some women "used to steal cigars." Such petty pilfering was undoubtedly common, but one woman in New York City took the practice rather too far. She was caught leaving the factory with 250 cigars concealed in her bloomers.[47] Women then were unwilling to be deprived of something they saw as rightfully theirs, even if it meant stealing. What was a right for men became a crime for women.

While their attitude toward smokers revealed both a sense of entitlement and a feeling of opposition to company interests, it also highlighted a sometimes ambiguous relationship with foremen. Himself an employee, the foreman did not always identify with the company. "If you had a good foreman," noted Pearl Hume, "he'd say 'Now you can have them, but be careful they [higher officials] don't see you.'" A foreman at Deisel-Wemmer in Lima recounted that a woman had left a purse at the shop and when he checked inside to see who owned it, "she had five cigars in there." She was a "good worker . . . so I just took those cigars and never let anyone know, but I told her about it. I said, 'God Almighty, watch yourself on that, cause somebody else is going to pick that pocketbook up sometime.' Stuff like that, I always try to cover up for the girls." In Perkasie, one foreman "was on our side in a way," Jane Hollenbach observed. He "used to go downstairs somewhere before they'd go home. If he was asked . . . no, he didn't see any. And he could swear he didn't because he was out of the way. It was all a trick." Others pointed out that "higher-up" bosses were more strict and that their immediate foremen were sympathetic to them.[48]

Relationships with foremen, however, could also be quite adversarial. Cigar makers resented favoritism—"a lot of them had their pick people"[49] —which also created divisions among workers. Many were offended by the uncivil way some foremen spoke to them. Pearl Hume recalled one foreman who had been especially "terrible. And he'd bawl you out. You could hear him all over the shop." Another Lima cigar maker remarked bitterly, "they treated us like dogs." Pauline Stauffer complained about those who were "sarcastic," while Valetta Leiphart remembered ones "that would curse you." When a cigar maker failed to get enough cigars out of the tobacco, Stella Sutton explained, the foreman "would chew you out . . . and the second time they get a little bit rougher. And you better not do it a third time." While one might not get fired immediately, "they would walk all over you. And when they walked, they walked heavy."[50] Sexual harassment, such as flirting and other unwanted advances, created additional pressures for women especially, one worker argued, for "some of them that . . . was married."[51]

Their responses to foremen and to unfavorable working conditions often expressed a mood of resignation, even fatalism. "They give hell to you," noted Anna Bartasius. "Do better." A woman might not like this treatment, but feelings "don't matter. . . . You want to work, you have to take it." The yelling was embarrassing, noted Stella Sutton, but "we all took it. . . . You didn't say anything." If the stock was poor, "you pretty much took what they gave you." One simply "made the best you could out of it." As Neva Fake explained: "There was nothing you could do . . . you got what you got." If a foreman "would scold you, you would just take it. That was all. Tried to do the best you can." Although women were familiar with submissiveness and intimidation because of gender roles, such attitudes may have illustrated further some of the psychological injuries of women's subordination.[52]

Yet these sentiments also may have reflected a "clear-sighted appraisal"[53] of their actual economic vulnerability. Fear of dismissal was ever present. "Sure," nodded Anna Bartasius, "you don't do it right, they fire you anytime." Valetta Leiphart explained that cigar makers might complain to a foreman in Red Lion about something which was unfair, but "if you went too much then you were out of a job." Many women interviewed commented that certain employers were "nice to work for,"[54] which meant a lot, considering the exploitative conditions under which many labored. Given their vulnerable position in the labor market, they were grateful to have a job and to have a "decent" employer, but this did not signify their complete surrender nor did it preclude an oppositional work culture or even militant strikes. While one woman in Lima never questioned men's higher wages ("he has to take care of his family"), another found it "pretty hard to take."[55] In 1922, the wage differential would become a major cause of a strike there. Jane Hollenbach in Perkasie resented feeling "so tired all the time. Cause you tried to do your best, but they ask more than you can do." Then, "you get cross." On her first day of work, Hume recalled being warned: "'If you don't have to stay here, don't stay.' A lot of people didn't like it."[56]

Women collectively acted to protect and separate themselves from managerial intrusion. Nicknames served to "mark" a foreman. An especially strict boss in Red Lion was known as "the street walker." Some names were used deliberately to demean or diminish him. Cigar makers in Lima nicknamed the superintendent at one factory the "Booger Man" because he "used to pick his nose."[57] When a foreman or owner began inspection rounds, word quickly spread through the shop as a warning.

Dora Rosenzweig in Chicago recounted that their foreman, Fritz, "could be as mean as the devil. There would be an underground signal: Fritz is coming. We stopped whatever we were doing and shut up." One cigar maker in Lima recalled that when women worked past lunch on Saturday, they got hungry and liked to nibble while working—forbidden by company policy. Someone kept a lookout for the foreman and when she spotted his shadow against the glass partition on his approach, she would "alert the rest. And you should have seen those sandwiches disappear."[58] When Henry Deisel, the short, pudgy, co-owner of the Deisel-Wemmer Company in Lima, decided to inspect his own plant, the cigar makers were usually ready. They spread the word and then "tried to keep shiners [their best cigars] ahead of him" for display.[59]

Although men's and women's work cultures both acted to distance workers from employers, the two had different approaches to the authority structure. A woman's relationship to a foreman would be affected by gender difference. This might be revealed in her deference and resignation or her real fears of harassment. All of these were aspects of the power imbalance on the shop floor that male unionists simply did not face. To cope with this form of domination, women either took advantage of paternalistic attitudes of foremen or united in opposition to them.

Attitudes toward the job were usually framed by the pressures and company rules that accompanied the actual work process. "When things didn't go right, why it was a terrible job," concluded Stella Sutton of Lima. "When everything was going all right, it was good." Yet interviews generally revealed a positive view of intrinsic aspects of the work itself and a pleasure and pride in doing the job well. Rita Amadee, a black cigar maker in New Orleans, learned the trade from a buckeye manufacturer who was at times "rough" on his pupils. Yet in the end she appreciated his approach because "he made good craftsmen out of us, you see."[60] In Lima cigar makers spoke positively of the work: "I enjoyed making cigars," or "I really liked it." Some aspects were frustrating. One roller complained that after taking such care to make the head perfect she was disappointed that "the first thing a man does is bite that head off." Although some women in Hanover jokingly referred to cigars as "railroad spikes" and "monkey wrenches," and to themselves as "bug pushers," Pauline Stauffer remembered her disappointment when a foreman told her that her bunches looked like a "sack of potatoes," because she took pride in making them well. Stella Sutton recalled that foremen came through the factory several times a day to spot-check their work. "They would tell you if you weren't doing it right," but she always wished that the foreman would also compliment a job well done.[61]

Breaks during the workday, especially lunch, also helped make the job more pleasant. Cigar makers in the country districts who lived near work frequently walked home for the noonday meal, even if it meant working longer at night.[62] Many cigar makers, like Pearl Hume in Lima, Ohio, went out for lunch for a change of scenery. In East Greenville, Charles Conway ran a restaurant across the street from the Eisenlohr factory and was known for the "oyster soup and ice cream" he served (not together!) to the cigar makers who crowded into his place at noon.[63] In Red Lion, local restaurants sent employees to the factories during the day to peddle light snacks. Another opportunity to pause came when cigar makers had to stop to get their own tobacco and to take up the finished cigars in bundles of fifty or one hundred for inspection. The occasional walk broke the monotony of steady work and gave women a chance to speak to friends on the other side of the room.[64]

Indeed, the warm social ties among cigar makers and the enjoyable, friendly atmosphere on the shop floor were very much a part of women's work culture. Cigar making was quiet and women sat in rows facing each other, an arrangement which facilitated conversation. "We were all talkers," recalled Natalie Nietupski of Detroit. Topics covered "anything and everything," from front-page headlines to boyfriends, matters of concern to women, sometimes serious, sometimes humorous. Pearl Hume recalled one discussion of women's honeymoons. A friend asked her "Pearl, where did you go?" "And I said, 'I went out west.' And she said, 'Where did you go?'" Hume's answer, "to Delphos," a town fourteen miles west of Lima, made her shop mates break out in laughter. Certain factories did have boundaries on what could be said and definitions of appropriate female behavior. Pauline Stauffer noted, for example, that in Hanover it was permissible for women to swear "if something didn't go right," but not in nearby Catholic McSherrystown. Usually people talked to those sitting closest, although "once in a while they'd holler back and forth."[65]

There were some limits on these discussions. In Lima and Red Lion, for example, cigar makers had to keep their voices low or "you'd hear a foreman bellowing, 'You people are too loud.'" Pearl Hume noted that in Lima the foremen tried to keep the volume down because "they were afraid the higher-ups would come in, see? They'd say, 'Cool it. Cool it.'" Nationality and language differences sometimes created barriers. Valeria Glatfelter struggled to learn Pennsylvania German so she could participate. "I just listened and tried to make use of everything and learned it."[66] Anna Bartasius noted that in the large factories where she had worked in Philadelphia, many different nationalities were "mixed" together. Since there were fewer Lithuanians than other groups, and since talking caused her to make mistakes, she rarely joined in. A few kept apart because "the more you talked, the less you earned."[67]

In addition to talking, women workers liked to try their voices in song. "Some of the girls would sing," recalled Editha Mattingly of Hanover. "Oh my glory, yes." In many towns of southeastern Pennsylvania, cigar makers sang hymns since everyone knew the words.[68] Observers often interpreted women's singing as a sign of their satisfaction. One health inspector in Philadelphia wrote that women's attitude was "universally one of contentment and cheerfulness, and it was not uncommon in our tours of investigation to walk into a department where the operatives were singing in chorus or loudly laughing and talking as they proceed with their work." A Delphos, Ohio, factory had a piano and cigar makers danced at noon, while in Trumbauersville, Pennsylvania, a local musician and his two sons from town "went around to the cigar factories . . . [with] two violins and a harp."[69] Although it was apparently not common in the early twentieth century, Raymond Markle recalled a reader of sorts in one Hanover factory where women, as usual, outnumbered men. For a short time, the cigar makers had someone read evangelist Billy Sunday's column from the Baltimore paper which arrived at the factory around 11 A.M. each morning. Manufacturers could not have been too perturbed by the conservative, antilabor comments of Sunday, a contrast to the radical tracts being read in Tampa. In some factories women celebrated birthdays and special occasions by bringing in food—women's own version of a congenial and supportive work environment—although some companies forbade food in the work area. Jokes and pranks relieved boredom as well. In McSherrystown, for example, every year at Halloween, some of the cigar makers at one factory stole the outhouse.[70]

The camaraderie of the shop floor and the spirit of mutual aid which the team system helped to foster nourished their developing solidarity. Rose Purzon explained that what she liked best about the cigar factory was "the friendliness." "At the cigar factory it was like you were going home." Friends at work were often friends and neighbors outside the factory. "You were always in a bunch," she continued. "It was like a family. Not only that you knew them, but your family knew them too." Lucille Speaker agreed. "That's where I had a lot of good friends, really, when I worked in the cigar factory. . . . Especially in a town like Delphos, you knew about everybody. . . . Maybe your mother and father is friends with their mothers and fathers." In Sellersville, Valeria Glatfelter "knew everybody that worked there. . . . It was just like one big family. They may have their little spats, but they always would stick together anyway."[71] Friendships were fundamental to women's culture, but rather than inhibiting collective consciousness, as some have argued, they helped to cement bonds and instill in the participants a strong sense of themselves as a group.

The ties and networks among women at work and in the community intertwined and joined together in workplace culture. Job recruitment often came through friends and relatives, and friendships often overlapped in the two seemingly separate arenas. In Detroit, women's community life focused around the parish church and various social organizations. Attached to the church were numerous women's religious societies. Fraternal and cultural clubs abounded on the east and west sides of the city; many of them had women's auxiliaries. A branch of the Polish Women's Alliance was organized there in 1911. During the late nineteenth and early twentieth centuries, various halls were constructed as gathering places for such groups. Dom Polski (Polish House), for example, was built in 1912 at Forest and Chene. All of these created opportunities for women to meet outside work as both women and members of the Polish community. In addition, many walked to work together: Gratiot Avenue was "alive with people" by 7 A.M. and women cigar makers might share the journey to or from the factory or stop together at a corner store to pick up items for the evening meal.[72]

Throughout the country districts of Pennsylvania women cigar makers formed networks within and beyond factory walls which affected their work culture and were in turn influenced by their experiences at work. To an observer from the Pennsylvania Department of Labor and Industry in 1916, the Perkiomen Valley district had "a woeful lack of amusements and little opportunity for recreations."[73] Yet cigar makers there and throughout the area spent time together away from the workplace. Churches sponsored picnics and other opportunities for meeting. In Sellersville, the local fire company held a carnival each summer. Valeria Glatfelter might spend Saturday night at the local theater or movie house. More commonly she and her girlfriend would simply go "up the street for a walk." The towns were small and people usually knew everyone at work and almost everyone in town as well.[74] Editha Mattingly of Hanover recalled that she and her friends tended to "stick together" after work. They rode the trolley to a nearby town, attended baseball games and movies, or simply went to the drugstore for a soda. On "Saturday we'd take hikes."[75] Few women interviewed were highly active in community affairs, although several belonged to women's branches of fraternal groups. Margaret McDowell of Red Lion twice served as president of the local Ladies Aid Society and was active in the Daughters of Liberty lodge and the Ladies Auxiliary of the fire company. Most towns, including Red Lion, Perkasie, and East Greenville had bands which played in the local park on Saturday nights, where there was also dancing. In the winter there were skating parties and indoor fairs.[76] In Lima, churches were rarely social, but cigar makers joined up after work to attend the circus, Chautauqua sessions, dances at Hoover Park, or band concerts in the town square.[77]

Yet work and nonwork patterns might also be compartmentalized. Stella Sutton of Lima recalled that naturally not all of the women who worked together were friends outside of work. These women were "nice to each other" at work, but did not get together until "we went back to work again." In New Orleans, Rita Amadee noted that workers were often friendly with each other at work, but she and her friends did not generally socialize with their mostly Cuban and Spanish co-workers once they left the factory. By contrast she and her friends frequently met to play bridge or go to the lake for picnics in the summer. Shy Anna Bartasius seldom met with women from work since she did not live near them and few were Lithuanian.[78]

Gender defined a common experience among women cigar makers whether from the paternalism of employers, the concerns of women's shop-floor conversation, or a sense of sexual solidarity vis-à-vis male managers. This was particularly true in terms of women's dual roles as workers and as women, for after the factory closed a second job remained to be done. Rose Purzon in Detroit explained that "you were never in that big of a hurry to get home. Because you knew what was waiting . . . wash clothes and do all the work at home." She tried to do the week's baking on Sunday. Yet she never recalled questioning her busy schedule: "You had to do it so what else? . . . We didn't think nothing of it." Pearl Hume in Lima considered herself lucky. She left the cigar factory and reached home by 5:30, but her husband did not get back until 7. "So I had time to get dinner." She stopped at a grocery near the factory on her way home. She also learned to use the weekend wisely. "Sometimes on Friday night I'd do all my cleaning, dusting, and mopping, the kitchen." She did the wash on

Saturday morning and ironed on Monday nights. Her husband, a barber, "had to have a white shirt every day." The laborious work had been difficult, "but I lived through it." Neva Fake helped her sister with the housework and cooking in Windsor since her brother-in-law did not do any of these tasks. In Red Lion, the exceptionally long hours meant something different for men and women because of household duties. "I don't know how we did [it]," Margaret McDowell remarked of her double day, "but we managed." Her own grandmother had done much the same thing— home at 6 to make dinner, then back to the factory until 8 or 9 at night. Anna Bartasius had "run home" each day to begin preparing dinner for her family. Doing both jobs had been hard work, but "when you're young you don't mind. European people more strong because we don't have it sweet." In Detroit, Philadelphia, and the country districts, women also raised vegetables and possibly a few chickens in their small yards. Unless husbands assisted, as they sometimes did, this just added on more time to an already long day.[79]

Women learned from each other how to organize and lighten housework; this was one way that paid work affected their lives at home. Stella Sutton, for example, recalled that she had painstakingly ironed even her dish towels when she first married, but in talking with co-workers, she found that they did not. "I never ironed another towel after that." Lucille Speaker gave herself some extra time by paying her mother to do her wash.[80]

Thus work culture captured women's several identities and operated on the shop floor to create both solidarity and a collective resistance to the prerogatives of employers. This did not mean that it was without weaknesses or that women challenged employers at every juncture. Unquestionably women identified with employers at points and accommodated to their goals. Resistance and consent were at times bound up with each other. Both men's and women's work culture reflected, to borrow a term from George Rudé, an "inherent ideology,"[81] one which grew out of direct experience and might contain contradictions and even reactionary elements within an oppositional consciousness.

Aspects of work could have contradictory effects. In shops where all the workers were women and all the managers were men, the sexual division could simply reinforce male dominance, yet it could also bond women together in their own form of sexual solidarity. Piecework might cause rushing, or the team system might create the potential for conflict, but in many ways women manifested a will to overcome these exploitative characteristics and assert their own version of satisfying work. They claimed their own time, resisted the pace, took smokers, poked fun at foremen, shared tobacco, quit, and maintained strong associations with each other. In scores of ways they acted to see that the day's events worked to their own benefit, not men's and not bosses'.

Notes

1. *Tobacco,* 22 *June 1900, p. 7; CMOJ,* May 1906, p. 9; Nov. 1906, p. 9; Nov. 1906, p. 5; *U.S. Tobacco Journal,* 30 June 1906, p. 11. After the introduction of Class A membership in 1915, organizing efforts quickened and female membership rose from 4,756 in 1912 to 7,038 in 1920. The 1920 figures, however, do not represent a steady increase in the number of women, but a temporary increase resulting from wartime strikes. The union had 3,976 Class A members in 1916 and 1,365 in 1918. (*CMOJ,* Apr. 1920, p. 59.) On the IWW, see also *U.S. Tobacco Journal,* 15 June 1912, p. 6.

2. *CMOJ,* Sept. 1912, p. 14; Belva Mary Herron, "The Progress of Labor Organization among Women, Together with Some Considerations concerning Their Place in Industry," *University Studies,* 1 (May 1905), pp. 46–49.

3. Edith Abbott, *Women in Industry: A Study in American Economic History* (New York, 1913), p. 208; U.S. Congress, Senate, *Report on Condition of Woman and Child Wage-Earners,* vol. 9, *History of Women in Industry in the United States,* by Helen Sumner, 1911, pp. 199–204, and vol. 10, *History of Women in Trade Unions,* by John B. Andrews and W. D. P. Bliss, 1911, pp. 92–94, S. Doc. 645, 61st Cong., 2d sess.; Ann Schofield, "The Rise of the Pig-Headed Girl: An Analysis of the American Labor Press for Their Attitudes towards Women, 1877–1920" (Ph.D. dissertation, State University of New York at Binghamton, 1980), pp. 54–60; *CMOJ,* Oct. 1900, p. 3; Oct. 1901, p. 3; Nov. 1903, p. 12; Jan. 1907, p. 4; June 1912, p. 9; May 1915, p. 7; *Tobacco Leaf,* 22 May 1907, p. 7; 11 Oct. 1915, pp. 27–28.

4. See Alice Kessler-Harris, "Where Are the Organized Women Workers?" *Feminist Studies,* 3 (Fall 1975), 92–109.

5. Frank Parkin, *Marxism and Class Theory: A Bourgeois Critique* (New York, 1979), pp. 44–119.

6. *CMOJ,* July 1900, p. 4; Oct. 1900, pp. 3, 6; May 1902, pp. 8, 9; Oct. 1906, p. 4; Nov. 1906, p. 16; Jan. 1907, p. 4; May 1910, p. 8; June 1912, p. 9; Oct. 1916, p. 19. See also Schofield, "Rise of the Pig-Headed Girl."

7. Temma Kaplan has demonstrated the utility of cultural constructions of womanhood or "female consciousness" to women initiating collective action in Barcelona in the early twentieth century. See Temma Kaplan, "Female Consciousness and Collective Action: The Case of Barcelona, 1910–1918," *Signs,* 7 (Spring 1982), 545–66. For an emphasis on how these traditional roles undermined women's collective action, see Leslie Tentler, *Wage-Earning Women: Industrial Work and Family Life in the United States, 1900–1930* (New York, 1979), and

John Sharpless and John Rury, "The Political Economy of Women's Work, 1900–1920," *Social Science History*, 4 (Aug. 1980), 317–46.

8. Alice Kessler-Harris, "Problems of Coalition-Building: Women and Trade Unions in the 1920s," in Ruth Milkman, ed., *Women, Work and Protest: A Century of U.S. Women's Labor History* (Boston, 1985), pp. 110–38.

9. Gerda Lerner et al., "Politics and Culture in Women's History: A Symposium," *Feminist Studies*, 6 (Spring 1980), 49–54; Kaplan, "Female Consciousness and Collective Action," pp. 545–66; Susan Porter Benson, *Counter Cultures: Saleswomen, Managers, and Customers in American Department Stores, 1890–1940* (Urbana, Ill., 1986), esp. chap. 5; Cynthia Costello, "Working Women's Consciousness and Collective Action: The Case of the Strike at the Wisconsin Educational Association Insurance Trust," paper presented at the meetings of the American Sociological Society, Aug. 1983, Detroit, Mich., pp. 3, 4; Ardis Cameron, "Bread and Roses Revisited: Women's Culture and Working Class Activism in the Lawrence Strike of 1912," in Ruth Milkman, ed., *Women, Work and Protest*, pp. 42–61; Judy Smith, "Our Own Kind: Family and Community Networks in Providence," in Nancy Cott and Elizabeth Pleck, eds., *A Heritage of Her Own: Toward a New Social History of American Women* (New York, 1979), pp. 393–411. Kaplan refers to women's culture as "solidarity built around networks" (p. 547).

10. In my view, Tentler's book, *Wage-Earning Women*, errs in emphasizing the debilitating effects of women's traditional roles. For another approach which supports her view, see Sharpless and Rury, "Political Economy of Women's Work." Other research presents a very different picture. See, for example, Kessler-Harris, "Problems of Coalition-Building"; Benson, *Counter Cultures;* Barbara Melosh, *"The Physician's Hand": Work Culture and Conflict in American Nursing* (Philadelphia, 1982); Sara Eisenstein, *Give Us Bread but Give Us Roses: Working Women's Consciousness in the United States, 1890 to the First World War* (London, 1983); Thomas Dublin, *Women at Work: The Transformation of Work and Community in Lowell, Massachusetts, 1826–1860* (New York, 1979); Evelyn Nakano Glenn and Roslyn L. Feldberg, "Male and Female, Job versus Gender Models in the Sociology of Work," *Social Problems*, 26 (June 1979), 524–38. Certainly, as Benson has pointed out, it would be a mistake to assume that the labor process alone determines workers' consciousness, but Louise Tilly has made a strong argument for the importance of the context of work and the nature of the work process in predicting women's likelihood of engaging in collective action. Indeed, she found that French tobacco workers were particularly strike-prone because of the nature of the work process. See Louise A. Tilly, "Paths of Proletarianization: Organization of Production, Sexual Division of Labor, and Women's Collective Action," *Signs*, 7 (Winter 1981), 400–417.

11. Gayle Rubin, "The Traffic in Women: Notes on the 'Political Economy' of Sex," in Rayne Reiter, ed., *Towards an Anthropology of Women* (New York, 1975), pp. 157–210; Dolores Janiewski, *Sisterhood Denied: Race, Gender and Class in a New South Community* (Philadelphia, 1985); Judy Smith, "Our Own Kind," pp. 393–411; Cameron, "Bread and Roses Revisisted," pp. 42–61. Susan Porter Benson carefully lays out these various identities in her study of saleswomen, *Counter Cultures*.

12. Catherine Groft, Senior Citizens Center group interview with Rose Smith, Editha Mattingly, and Pauline Stauffer, 25 Feb. 1977, Hanover, Pa.; U.S. Congress, Senate, *Report on Condition of Woman and Child Wage-Earners in the United States,* vol. 18, *Employment of Women and Children in Selected Industries,* S. Doc. 645, 61st Cong., 2d sess., 1913, p. 95; New Orleans Factory Inspection Department, *Report* (New Orleans, 1912), p. 2; Annelle Mann, *Women Workers in Factories: A Study of Working Conditions in 275 Industrial Establishments in Cincinnati and Adjoining Towns* (New York, 1974 [1918]), p. 22; Kansas Board of Public Welfare, Bureau of Labor Statistics, *Report on the Wage-Earning Women of Kansas City* (Kansas City, 1913), p. 25; Jane Robbins, "The Bohemian Women of New York," *Charities,* Dec. 1904, p. 195; T. Grier Miller and Henry F. Smyth, "Health Hazards of Cigar Manufacturing," *Pennsylvania Medical Journal,* 21 (Mar. 1918) 360–63; "Survey of Tobacco Factories," p. 10, Employment folder, Young Women's Christian Association Papers, Tulane University, New Orleans, La.; U.S. Public Health Service, Bulletin 73, *Tuberculosis among Industrial Workers: Report of Investigation Made in Cincinnati with Special Reference to Predisposing Causes* (Washington, D.C. 1915), p. 131; Frances Salantak interview, 20 Sept. 1978, Detroit, Mich.; *Report of the Michigan State Commission of Inquiry into Wages and the Conditions of Labor for Women and the Advisability of Establishing a Minimum Wage* (Lansing, 1915), p. 422.

13. Lucille Speaker interview, 22 Aug. 1982, Lima, Ohio. Lucille Speaker was born on a farm and moved to the small town of Delphos, Ohio, in 1910 when she was nine years old. She began making cigars for Deisel-Wemmer in 1917.

14. Jane Hollenbach interview, 16 Mar. 1984, Sellersville, Pa.; Stella Sutton interview, 19 Aug. 1982, Lima, Ohio; Pearl Hume interview, 23 Aug. 1982, Lima, Ohio; Speaker interview; Anna Bartasius interview, 31 Mar. 1982, Philadelphia. Stella Sutton was born in 1892 and grew up in Indiana, where her father worked on a farm. When she was seventeen she came to Lima and lived with an uncle and began working for Deisel-Wemmer with her cousins. Pearl Hume's parents also farmed, but they sold their Celina, Ohio, farm in 1900 when their daughter was five and moved to Lima. Her father worked in a locomotive factory and her mother raised ten children. Hume began working in 1912 at the Deisel-Wemmer plant where her four sisters already worked. Anna Bartasius was born in Lithuania in 1892. Her parents farmed a small plot of land. Her brother and sister emigrated first and in 1912 Bartasius arrived in Baltimore. Pinned to her dress, since she knew no English, were instructions and her brother's address in Philadelphia. She immediately started working in a cigar factory, preferring it to a sewing factory job, and married in Oct. 1913.

15. Agnes White interview, 4 Feb. 1982, Evansville, Ind., conducted by Glenda Morrison for the Indiana State University-Evansville, Indiana Labor History Project (ILHP); Sutton interview.

16. Rose Purzon interview, 21 Sept. 1978, Detroit, Mich.; Natalie Nietupski interview, 19 Sept. 1978; Salantak interview; Helen Piwkowska interview, 21 Sept. 1978, Hamtramck, Mich. Pennsylvania interviewees echoed similar sentiments, though none had cafeterias where they worked. I use the term "consent"

as discussed in Michael Burawoy, *Manufacturing Consent: Changes in the Labor Process under Monopoly Capitalism* (Chicago, 1979).

17. Valetta Leiphart interview, 17 June 1982, Red Lion, Pa.; Valeria Glatfelter, interview, 15 Dec. 1983, Sellersville, Pa.; Elizabeth Butler, *Women and the Trades, Pittsburgh, 1907–1908* (New York; 1909), p. 86; Mann, *Women Workers in Factories*, p. 22.

18. Norman Wieand interview, 21 June 1984, Quakertown, Pa.; Hume interview; U.S. Congress, Senate, *Report on Condition of Woman and Child Wage-Earners*, vol. 18, p. 93.

19. Salantak interview; Bartasius interview; *Tobacco Leaf*, 20 July 1900, p. 7; 10 June 1903, p. 26; *Tobacco*, 6 July 1900, p. 8; 13 July 1900, p. 6.

20. *Tobacco Leaf*, 29 Aug. 1906, p. 46; 27 Mar. 1907, p. 28; *U.S. Tobacco Journal*, 5 May 1912, p. 27; 29 Mar. 1913, p. 8.

21. Sutton interview; T. Grier Miller, "A Sociologic and Medical Study of Four Hundred Cigar Workers in Philadelphia," *American Journal of the Medical Sciences*, 155 (Feb. 1918), 165; New Orleans Factory Inspection Department, *Report* (New Orleans, 1923), p. 2; "Investigation of Tobacco Industry in Lancaster, Pennsylvania," file 46/2-C, Department of Labor, Record Group (R.G.) 174, National Archives (NA); Glenda Morrison, "Cigar-making as Woman's Work," unpublished paper for the Indiana Labor History Project; Bartasius interview; Hume interview; U.S. Department of Labor, Women's Bureau, Bulletin 74, *The Immigrant Woman and Her Job*, by Caroline Manning (Washington, D.C., 1930), pp. 14, 17.

22. Speaker interview.

23. Hume interview; Sutton interview; Speaker interview.

24. Speaker interview; Sutton interview; Pauline Stauffer interview, 21 June 1977, Hanover, Pa.

25. Piwkowska interview; Salantak interview.

26. Speaker interview; Stauffer interview. See also Ken Kusterer, *Know-How on the Job: The Important Working Knowledge of "Unskilled" Workers* (Boulder, Colo., 1978), p. 59; Stauffer interview.

27. Sutton interview; Mary Diehl interview; 12 Jan. 1984, Quakertown, Pa.; Hollenbach interview.

28. Nietupski interview; Cecelia Chromki, joint interview with Helen Piwkowska, 21 Sept. 1978, Hamtramck, Mich.; Purzon interview; *Report of the Michigan State Commission of Inquiry*, p. 422.

29. See n. 28; Wieand interview; Sutton interview; Hume interview; *Report of the Michigan State Commission of Inquiry*, p. 422; Purzon interview.

30. Nietupski interview; Salantak interview; Sutton interview; Stauffer interview; Stauffer in group interview; Diehl interview.

31. U.S. Bureau of Labor Statistics, Bulletin 135, *Rates of Wages in the Cigar and Clothing Industries, 1911 and 1912* (Washington, D.C., 1913), p. 10; Piwkowska interview; Hollenbach interview; Sutton interview; Purzon interview.

32. *Report of the Michigan State Commission of Inquiry*; Speaker interview.

33. Mary McDowell interview, 9 Jan. 1980. Red Lion, Pa., by Red Lion Oral History Project, Kaltreider Memorial Library (KML); Bartasius interview; Hume

interview; Speaker interview; Rita Johnson Amadee interview, 20 June 1978, New Orleans, La. Amadee learned the trade in a buckeye shortly before World War I. In 1918 she moved to a larger factory, A. Falk. In 1922 the Trellis company began hiring blacks and she started working there.

34. Neva Fake interview, 17 Dec. 1982, Windsor, Pa.

35. Speaker interview; Sutton interview; Bartasius interview.

36. Piwkowska interview; *Detroit Labor News*, 10 July 1914; Salantak interview.

37. Piwkowska interview; Purzon interview; Salantak interview; *CMOJ*, Dec. 1911, p. 3; *Detroit Labor News*, 10 July 1914; 14 July 1916; *Report of the Michigan State Commission of Inquiry*, p. 424.

38. Lima foreman interview, 24 Aug. 1982, Lima, Ohio; Speaker interview; Hollenbach interview. The Lima foreman I interviewed preferred that his name not be used.

39. Wieand interview; Clarence Jacobs interview, 17 Dec. 1982, Red Lion, Pa.; Speaker interview; Sutton interview; Hume interview; Fake interview; Leiphart interview.

40. Hume interview.

41. Bartasius interview; Jacobs interview; Mary Berkheiser interview, 21 Dec. 1979 and 24 Jan. 1980, by KML. Almost every description of cigar factory work mentions these shortcuts. Indeed long-time cigar makers often had worn teeth from biting off the tobacco. These practices were forbidden in most factories, although some manufacturers paid more attention to it than others.

42. *Tobacco Leaf*, 1 Nov. 1905, p. 58; 21 Jan. 1909, p. 40; Oct. 1910, p. 28; *Tobacco*, 6 Apr. 1900, p. 5.

43. U.S. Council on National Defense, Committee on Women's Defense Work, Louisiana Division, Women in Industry Committee, *Conditions of Women's Labor in Louisiana* (New Orleans, 1919), p. 125; Nietupski interview; Purzon interview.

44. Purzon interview; *Tobacco Leaf*, 3 Nov. 1910, p. 34.

45. Sutton interview.

46. *Tobacco*, 8 Nov. 1906, p. 22; *Tobacco Leaf*, 23 July 1908, p. 18; Salantak interview.

47. Diehl interview; Hollenbach interview; Speaker interview; *Tobacco Leaf*, 7 Jan. 1903, p. 12.

48. Hume interview; Speaker interview; Lima foreman interview; Hollenbach interview.

49. Fake interview.

50. Hume interview; Lima cigar maker interview; Stauffer interview; Leiphart interview; Sutton interview. I have chosen not to reveal the interviewee in Lima since her former employers still live in the city.

51. Hume interview. Two interviewees in Lima spoke to me about sexual harassment. I have chosen not to reveal their names.

52. Bartasius interview; Sutton interview; Speaker interview; Hollenbach interview; Fake interview; Leiphart interview. See also *CMOJ*, Aug. 1901, p. 2, where a union organizer commented on women who "say they are satisfied."

53. Dolores Janiewski, "Subversive Sisterhood: Black Women and Unions in the Southern Tobacco Industry," paper presented at the meetings of the Berkshire Conference in Women's History, June 1984.

54. Elizabeth Cohen to author, May 1982.

55. Hollenbach interview; Sutton interview; Speaker interview; Hume interview. Women interviewed frequently noted if a particular company was a "nice" place to work.

56. Hollenbach interview; Hume interview.

57. Leiphart interview; Hume interview.

58. Studs Terkel, *American Dreams: Lost and Found* (New York, 1980), pp. 118–19; Bessie Ray Henry interview, 21 Aug. 1982, Lima, Ohio.

59. Lima foreman interview.

60. Sutton interview; Amadee interview.

61. Hume interview; Speaker interview; Stauffer interview; Raymond Markle interview, 26 Feb. 1977, Hanover, Pa.; Sutton telephone call, 21 Aug. 1982; Speaker interview.

62. Everyone I interviewed in Pennsylvania indicated that if possible people liked to walk home for lunch.

63. Hume interview; *East Greenville Borough Centennial, 1875–1975. East Greenville, Pa., June 14–21, 1975* (East Greenville, Pa., 1975), pp. 16–18; Wieand interview.

64. Leiphart interview; *Report of the Michigan State Commission of Inquiry*, p. 424; Henry F. Smyth and T. Grier Miller, "A Hygienic Survey of Cigar Manufacturing in Philadelphia," *Medicine and Surgery*, 1 (Sept. 1917), 717; Purzon interview.

65. Salantak interview; Nietupski interview; Sutton interview; Hume interview; Stauffer interview; Fake interview.

66. Hume interview; Wieand interview; Speaker interview; Glatfelter interview.

67. Bartasius interview; Women's Bureau, Bulletin 74, *Immigrant Woman and Her Job*, p. 106; Diehl interview.

68. Editha Mattingly interview, 21 June 1977, Hanover, Pa.; Leiphart interview; Jacobs interview; Hollenbach interview.

69. Miller and Smyth, "Health Hazards of Cigar Manufacturing," p. 360; Speaker interview; Wieand interview.

70. Markle interview; Berkheiser interview; McDowell interview; Sutton interview; Stauffer interview; Mattingly interview.

71. Purzon interview; Speaker interview; Glatfelter interview. The Diehl, Salantak, and Bartasius interviews were the only three which did not make a special point of the feeling of friendship on the shop floor. It may be that this spirit did not exist where they worked or that they for whatever reasons did not participate in it.

72. Olivier Zunz, *The Changing Face of Inequality: Urbanization, Industrial Development, and Immigrants in Detroit, 1880–1920* (Chicago, 1982), pp. 187–92; Lawrence D. Orton, *Polish Detroit and the Kolasinski Affair* (Detroit, 1981), pp. 163–94; Sister Mary Napolska, *The Polish Immigrant in Detroit in 1914* (Chi-

cago, 1946), pp. 63–85; Salantak interview; Nietupski interview; Purzon interview.

73. Pennsylvania Department of Labor and Industry, *Third Annual Report of the Commissioner of Labor and Industry, 1916* (Harrisburg, Pa., 1918), p. 21.

74. Leiphart interview; Jacobs interview; Glatfelter interview.

75. Mattingly interview; Stauffer interview; Markle interview; Stauffer in group interview.

76. McDowell interview; Glatfelter interview; Wieand interview; Jacobs interview; Richard E. Ritz, *Red Lion: The First One Hundred Years, 1880–1980,* pp. 28, 43.

77. Speaker interview; Sutton interview.

78. Sutton interview; Amadee interview; Bartasius interview; Diehl interview.

79. Fake interview; McDowell interview; Bartasius interview; Napolska, *Polish Immigrant in Detroit,* p. 44; Hume interview; Sutton interview; Purzon interview; Fake interview; McDowell interview; Bartasius interview.

80. Sutton interview; Speaker interview.

81. George Rudé, *Ideology and Popular Protest* (New York, 1980), pp. 15–40.

CHAPTER

9

A "Spirit of Unrest"

During the first sixteen years of the twentieth century, the team system had become the dominant form of cigar making. Nonunion manufacturers during the period had contained labor costs while increasing production, and had placed the CMIU on the defensive. Still, nonunion manufacturers had not achieved the labor conditions they had envisioned. Women's lack of participation in unions did not reflect passivity or submissive natures; they too shared an active work culture. While operating within powerful constraints imposed both by manufacturers and by their position as female wage earners, women's work culture offered them ways to influence at least some of the conditions of their work. At times they took their grievances to the point of open resistance and militant strikes. Throughout the period a "spirit of unrest"[1] persisted among women cigar makers, which raised doubts in the minds of some manufacturers about the efficacy of using women to solve their labor problems. Highly visible events in 1916 confirmed these misgivings on a national scale.

While the precise dimensions of women's strike activity are unknown, the trade press, the *Cigar Makers' Official Journal*, and various investigations of the tobacco industry suggest that it was considerable in the years before World War I. The Bureau of Labor provided only aggregate statistics on strikes in the United States, but some states collected more specific information. The New Jersey Bureau of Labor compiled a yearly "labor chronology" beginning in the 1890s and running through 1917. These reports provide an outline of women's strike activity in a state that was central to the "cigar belt" of female employment in the industry. Table 8 reveals strike patterns in New Jersey from 1901 to 1917.

Between 1901 and the spring of 1917 at least twenty-four strikes of

247

Table 8. Strikes of Women Cigar Makers in New Jersey, 1901–17

Date	Place	Number of Workers	Duration	Demand	Result
1. Apr. 20, 1901	Passaic	100	2 weeks	increase wages	lost
2. May 9, 1901	Elizabeth	unknown	2 days	reinstate foreman	lost
3. Aug. 1901	Trenton	200	unknown	hour for lunch Sat. half-holiday	lost
4. July 1906	Newark	unknown	unknown	no wage cut	won
5. Aug. 1906	Elizabeth	150	unknown	wages	lost
6. May 1907	Perth Amboy	700	8 working days	increase wages	lost
7. Aug. 3, 1908	Newark	465W 5M	2 months	reinstatement of fired worker	lost
8. Aug. 25, 1909	Elizabeth	unknown	unknown	reinstatement of foreman	compromise
9. Oct. 23, 1909	New Brunswick	500	3 weeks	increase wages, better stock	lost
10. June 8, 1912	Perth Amboy	1,300	36 days	increase wages,	lost

		10M		worker	
12. June 19, 1915	Perth Amboy	150	3 days	reinstate foreman	lost
13. June 23, 1915	South River	300	5 days	increase wages	lost
14. Oct. 1, 1915	Elizabeth	158	1 week	increase wages	lost
15. Jan. 11, 1916	Newark	150	9 weeks	increase wages	lost
16. Jan. 19, 1916	Newark	140	14 days	increase wages	lost
17. Jan. 25, 1916	New Brunswick	500	10 days	increase wages	won
18. Feb. 17, 1916	Camden	150	10 days	increase wages	won
19. Apr. 8, 1916	Perth Amboy	20	1 day	stock	unknown
20. Apr. 12, 1916	Chrome	130	16 days	increase wages	won
21. Aug. 21, 1916	New Brunswick	300	10 working days	increase wages	won
22. Aug. 28, 1916	New Brunswick	150	4 days	increase wages	won
23. Feb. 17, 1917	Newark	300	4 days	increase wages	won
24. Mar. 12, 1917	Chrome	175	14 days	feared wage cut	lost

Source: New Jersey Bureau of Statistics of Labor and Industries, *Annual Report* (Camden, 1900–1917).

women cigar makers took place in New Jersey, while the state's male cigar
makers during the same period struck only three times. The frequency of
strikes rose after 1914, reflecting national strike trends.[2] Of the twenty-
four strikes, seven were at least partially successful. In most cases, the
strikes lasted only a few days, although two continued for two months,
and they generally occurred during the warmer months from April to
September. The reasons given for strikes in New Jersey resembled those
of cigar makers elsewhere, both men and women, union and nonunion. In
fifteen of the New Jersey confrontations women demanded wage increases.
In two strikes they feared a wage cut resulting from changes in their work.
In three strikes women wanted the reinstatement of a foreman; and in two
others the strike resulted from the discharge of fellow employees. The
rest related to fines, hours, work rules, and poor stock.

Many disputes arose over wages. Women in York County won a strike
for higher pay in 1903, because of a shortage of cigar makers there at the
time. Even the American Cigar Company, with its preventive policy of
voluntarily raising wages in some plants to prevent strikes, was not im-
mune that year.[3] A long strike took place in Cincinnati in 1910 when
women at the L. Newberger and Bros. factory walked out to demand increases of forty-five to sixty cents for rolling. Striking in January, the workers returned in March when they reached an agreement with the company, but then struck again. This time the male workers in the factory
joined the women, because a new system of work introduced after the
first strike made it "impossible" for workers to earn more than $1.11 a
day, according to the union. The strike lasted until June when both male
and female workers returned to their jobs in defeat.[4]

Most strikes against changes in methods of work developed because
workers feared their wages would be cut. In 1900 workers in New York
City struck over their opposition to the increased use of suction tables. In
1902 the American Cigar Company plant in Binghamton, New York,
changed the method of work and *Tobacco* reported that women went out
on strike because they felt "affronted at being asked to make cigars after a
fashion hitherto unpracticed." The manufacturers fired all of the strikers
and hired more agreeable workers in their places. In June 1912, United
Cigar Manufacturers in Lancaster introduced a new cigar shape, but
offered only $6.50 per thousand for making it. One hundred and forty-one
women walked off the job, claiming that the offer amounted to a wage cut.
After a lengthy lockout they lost the strike.[5]

Strikes for higher wages also indicated that in some cases women were able to compare their own wages with those in other factories. A cigar strike took place in South River, New Jersey, in June 1915, when Hungarian women working for the South River Cigar Company learned that their own wages were two cents per hundred less than those paid to workers in a nearby Perth Amboy factory owned by the same firm. The women stayed off the job for five days and returned to work only when given proof that the wage rates in the two factories were identical.[6]

Dismissals of foremen and subsequent employee protest indicate that manufacturers may have realized that foremen were not always acting in their best interests. Without the benefit of a union, women workers dealt directly with foremen in matters of tobacco stock, work assignments, and removal of unacceptable cigars. By cultivating this relationship, women created yet another way to exercise some authority over work, as the case of smokers illustrated. Losing an educated foreman could make a tremendous difference in the workday, while enduring a hated one could be intolerable. Either could be well worth fighting over. On November 22, 1900, 250 women cigar makers struck the Seidenberg Company in New York City because of the "tyranny of their foreman." The company investigated their complaint and fired the foreman, after which the women returned to work. In Albany, New York, in 1902, 150 women struck the American Cigar Company to have a new manager fired and his predecessor rehired.[7] Women at the Brown Brothers factory in Detroit struck in 1902 when the American Cigar Company, which had purchased the factory, broke its promise and fired the general manager. In 1912, 350 women cigar makers at one Lancaster factory of United Cigar Manufacturers walked out when the company fired a superintendent and foreman and let it be known they were moving the workers to an old cotton-mill building. The workers demanded reinstatement of the fired managers and refused to work in the new quarters.[8]

Poor stock also precipitated strikes. Women working at the Eisenlohr factory in Lancaster, Pennsylvania, in early 1916 began talking at lunch one day in March at a restaurant near the factory. A few drafted a note on a piece of brown paper. "Notice: Cigarmakers, are we going to continue working these small wrappers? Do you know the result? Nervous and physical wreck is the result. Are we going to continue, cigarmakers? Let us all say no. Therefore at 3 o'clock let us all go to the stock counter and demand more wrappers. Remember the time." The note circulated in the shop after lunch and at the appointed hour all but three went to the counter with the demand. The superintendent promised to take the matter up with management, but the company soon announced that the branch factory would close.[9]

Ethnic divisions among women, which precluded solidarity during strikes, revealed tensions and contradictions within their work culture and, once again, the ways in which it expressed several identities, not just one. In at least two strikes in New Jersey where women of different ethnic backgrounds worked together in the same factories, strike activity broke down along ethnic lines. In both cases the strikers were Hungarians, while Polish, Italian, and some "American" women kept aloof. However, several nationalities participated in the Newark strike in 1916, including "Jewish, Polish and Italian" workers.[10] In a 1908 strike in Newark, a state report commented on women's solidarity across ethnic lines. "An interesting circumstance in connection with this strike is, that practically all the women and girls employed in other manufactures of cigars in and about the city of Newark have contributed regularly every week a certain percentage of their earnings to assist the strikers."[11]

Occasionally women used tactics involving sabotage and physical force in their strikes. During the New York City strike in 1900, women left water faucets running before they walked out of one factory. Strikers in Kingston, New York, in 1903 were angry when the company refused to pay them their back wages after they had struck. They broke into the factory and attacked fifty workers who had remained at work, and then walked through the plant "shouting defiance." The company summoned the police, who were unable to clear the building for several hours. The strikers argued that they had a right to occupy the building until the company paid the back wages owed to them.[12] A 1907 strike involving women at the Rosenthal Bros. factory in New York City saw several women strikers arrested for assaulting women who continued to work, and for violating an injunction against picketing. In a 1909 strike in New Brunswick, New Jersey, strikers threw rocks at women who crossed the picket line. During the 1915 South River walkout, strikers appeared at the factory the day after the strike began as if they were ready to return to work. Once inside they made a "furious" attack on those women who continued to work. Police arrived and emptied the factory in half an hour. In several other New Jersey strikes, manufacturers also resorted to summoning the police, according to state investigators.[13]

Although in many strikes the CMIU tried to help and after 1914 often attempted to organize unions among women team workers, using the new Class A membership plan, women themselves occasionally formed their own organizations. In August 1908, *Tobacco Leaf* reported a strike of women at the large I. Lewis Company in Newark, noting that the strike had started when the company fired an employee for ignoring orders and "doing generally as she pleased, and setting a bad example for the other girls." What the trade journal failed to add was that the woman had been an outspoken defender of a two-year-old labor organization to which many of the women belonged. In 1906, when the I. Lewis Company proposed a wage cut, the predominantly Jewish women workers formed a United Ladies Protective Association and successfully fended off the attempt. They elected a president, vice-president, recording secretary, financial secretary, sergeant-at-arms, and treasurer. In two years they collected nearly $2,000 in dues. In August 1908, I. Lewis Company management fired Sadie Silberman, the vice-president of the group, and sparked the strike. Publicly the firm claimed that Silberman's personal characteristics, not her union activity, had been responsible for her dismissal. Hyman Lewis, superintendent of the company, stated that "the discharge of Miss Silberman was essential to the discipline of the factory." Since the protective association was formed, she had been "a disturbing element among the employees" and had been "insubordinate to a superintendent." The workers responded that "Miss Silberman was not treated by the superintendent as we think a lady ought to be treated." While it is not possible to penetrate further into the thoughts of these strikers, the comment suggests that they had very concrete and clear norms regarding acceptable treatment of women and that these expectations formed the basis for their actions. The CMIU local in Newark, along with the Essex Trades Council and the Women's Trade Union League, all provided assistance to the strikers, but the manufacturers held out and the women were compelled to return to work.[14]

There were other independent women's labor organizations, but they left little record of their history and activity. Women in Cincinnati in 1910 formed a short-lived union during a strike, but the organization died when the strike was broken. In 1916 there was a Philadelphia Cigar Makers' Protective Association, which apparently organized women, but its fate is unknown. It may have been affiliated with the most successful independent union having large numbers of women members, the Cigar Makers' Progressive Union. Organized in 1908 by Jake Billow, a former member of the CMIU and a socialist, the Progressive organized women team workers in some of the largest shops in Chicago, including one controlled by the American Tobacco Company. By 1912 it claimed seven hundred members, a majority of whom apparently were women. In 1919 David Saposs, who was then an economic research associate at the University of Wisconsin, estimated that 65 percent of the members were Jewish, while the rest were Bohemian, Polish, and Irish. Leadership seems to have remained in the hands of men, however. The union joined the CMIU under the Class A plan in 1916 as Local 527, but disaffiliated in September 1920. While little evidence regarding this union remains, one member, interviewed by Studs Terkel, explained that the bad working conditions first brought her into the union. There she met other women like herself. "Most of the cigar makers where I worked wanted a better life, they were looking for culture, going to lectures, going to night school. . . . There was something in the air that affected all of us."[15]

While they may not have been cigar makers, even stogie workers in Pittsburgh forged an organization and conducted a remarkable strike, completing the chain of labor militancy from the makers of the grandest (the Havanas) to the makers of the meanest. While men dominated the hand stogie-making jobs, women claimed the positions of bunching and rolling. The CMIU refused to organize Pittsburgh's stogie workers and in 1912 a number of them affiliated with the IWW, despite their socialist sensibilities and opposition to much of Wobbly ideology, especially sabotage. They staged a strike for better pay and conditions and won that year. Emboldened, workers targeted a large stogie company in July 1913 and asked for an increase. The rest of the city's employers promptly declared a lockout and while the new union might have folded, it staunchly fought employers and in the end won an increase. Patrick Lynch, the historian of this struggle, has noted that the strike remained confined to Pittsburgh's Hill District, which was primarily Jewish, and argued that "it was the support by the Jewish community in the Hill District that gave the stogie workers' local its strength." Lynch noted that women belonged to the union, but rarely served as strike leaders.[16]

The CMIU may not have initiated strikes of women cigar makers, but it frequently offered financial and other assistance once a strike had begun. Particularly after 1915, CMIU locals also tried to form unions from the ranks of women strikers. As unionists the men felt bound to aid other workers on strike, but their ambivalence and hostility toward women complicated their efforts at assistance. In February 1916 an AFL organizer wrote Samuel Gompers that he had gone to a meeting of two hundred striking cigar makers in Baltimore—women bunchers, rollers, machine, and suction table workers who were demanding a wage increase.

The CMIU local there, however, made little effort to organize them into a Class A local and the union secretary was "very emphatic in relation to hands off." When locals did respond they used the *CMOJ* to appeal for money to support women's strikes with reminders that all strikes should be supported: "Now respond as liberally as you can, which cigar makers are known for—never to allow a union to be annihilated by capital." Yet some appeals actually contributed to the gap between men and women cigar makers by depicting women as unable to defend themselves. Although they might also be described as "loyal and brave," the "lady strikers" remained outsiders. Organizers had difficulty masking their attitudes: that women should be home tending children or, worse, many of the women were prostitutes.[17]

Another barrier to union members' willingness to aid women strikers was their feeling that women were losers. Male cigar makers recognized the significance of employers' power, but they also blamed women themselves for losing strikes so frequently: too often they returned to work under old conditions. Allowing such indignities was unmanly. Members who made this argument would always point to the New York strike of 1900 for proof. The 1900 strike in New York City had been the largest strike of women there since 1877. Strategically, it was significant because of the importance of New York as a cigar-making center at the turn of the century. The strike had begun spontaneously in March in the Kerbs, Wertheim and Schiffer factories, where women opposed the further introduction of machinery and complained that the company cut wages in order to spend more money on advertising. Within a few days the strike had spread to include perhaps as many as seven thousand women, mostly Bohemians.[18]

Shortly after the women walked out, the CMIU's Joint Advisory Board injected its presence into the strike and took almost complete control over running it, from organizing pickets to raising and distributing money for the strikers. The CMIU had hoped to organize New York more thoroughly, and the women's strike seemed to present the perfect opportunity. Once the union was committed, winning became important in terms of the entire future of organizing efforts. Losing the strike, organizers worried, would seriously "demoralize" the union in New York for decades. The union was also worried about the use of new immigrant groups in the cigar industry. Manufacturers wanted "to drive out of the cigar trade every intelligent male or female cigar maker and to replace them with boys and girls from the slums of Italy or the offspring of the refugees of

Poland and Russia." Urged to contribute because the union needed a victory in New York more than in any "other battle that we have ever had," New York CMIU locals raised $91,428, and cigar makers nationally contributed another $80,000. Boston's Local 97 alone donated $14,000. Other labor organizations raised $20,000. Thus, the CMIU raised a total of $212,000 for the struggle.[19]

The strike began with enthusiasm, but as it wore on spirits started to flag. The courts issued an injunction which prohibited all picketing, and by the time it was lifted the damage had been done. Worst of all, manufacturers began establishing branch factories outside the city. The Hilson Company opened a factory in Elizabeth, New Jersey; Hirschorn and Mack moved to New Brunswick; Harburger-Homan moved to Philadelphia; and Kerbs opened branches in Lancaster and York.[20] Those manufacturers who remained in New York used strikebreakers to get their production back into gear. By September the *CMOJ* carried little information on the progress of the strike.

Bitterness followed in its wake. Many male union members, disregarding women's hard-fought efforts and stressing only the loss of a major strike, drew the conclusion that the women strikers were simply not worth helping. In the future, suggested one disgruntled member, the union should only aid strikes composed of "strictly union men." The New York strike had drained union finances and brought no tangible changes. The new union members gained were "mostly women and children who later on go back to work for these same people." The New York episode and what unionists chose to read into it clearly affected the CMIU's aid to subsequent women's strikes, although there were numerous efforts on the local level to assist women strikers during these years. Efforts quickened in 1916, however, when many union members noticed a "pronounced sense of unrest" among women cigar makers, and when they had a way to bring them into union membership, the Class A plan.[21]

For their part, manufacturers had sensed an attitude of discontent among women workers in New York in 1900, made more frightening by the efforts of the CMIU to organize them. Because the manufacturers feared that women strikers might join the union, they took a particularly tough stand against the strike, refusing "to be dictated to in regard to the management of their business." They assailed the "rule or ruin" tactics of the union. *Tobacco Leaf* editorialized that owners could not afford to "place themselves in the hands of the union, and surrender for good all their legal and natural rights to their own factories." As strikes broke out in Dayton, Philadelphia, and Camden, manufacturers worried that "some occult manner" was relaying the "spirit of unrest" in the East to the Midwest as well.[22]

At first New York manufacturers could not believe that the strike was actually happening. Women could not be protesting on their own; they must have been misled by the union, factory owners thought. "It was simply a case of letting other people do your thinking for you," *Tobacco* argued. Other manufacturers believed that their own workers would stand beside them because they had always treated them so fairly. "I am always willing to listen to anything they have to say, and always treat them with consideration," wrote one manufacturer. "I am sure they all appreciate this." They believed that those workers who joined the union had done so only "on the impulse of the moment."[23]

Once the strike had subsided and the manufacturers had won, they recognized that the CMIU had been ineffective in trying to organize nonunion workers, and would probably be unable to make such a push again for some time. Manufacturers showed less anxiety in the trade journals about the possibility of organizing women and in the coming years the trade press rarely reported extensively on cigar strikes. Because operations were increasingly dispersed into several different branch factories, the large employers of women workers did not have to fear strikes to such a great degree since they could shift production to the annex plants. The companies' public relations material stressed how happy and contented the women workers were. One observer noted in 1905 that women cigar makers in Detroit were quite satisfied with their lot. "This is proven by the fact that strikes are very infrequent."[24]

Detroit manufacturers had certainly presented a model public image of clean and modern factories and happy and healthy employees. The local press treated the industry favorably, although not extensively, and the Chamber of Commerce's publication, the *Detroiter*, boosted the local cigar industry. In a 1911 piece the *Detroiter* remarked that the cigar factories "very quietly and without ostentation" had "given the employees of the enterprise a 'square deal' and a large measure of comfort in employment, with clean, airy factories, modern and accessible—which makes not only happier workers but insures better products."[25] Nationally the trade press portrayed Detroit as a showcase for what could be accomplished with team work.

Only a few ripples of labor unrest had ever appeared in Detroit. There had been a small strike involving about one hundred women in the George

Moebs shop in 1900. They won. Two years later women workers at the American Cigar Company factory briefly formed a "protective associa-tion" and went on strike over the dismissal of the old superintendent and the introduction of suction tables.[26] In the summer of 1913, eighteen women working at the Hemmeter Cigar Company quit and crossed the river to work in Windsor, Canada, where a former Hemmeter foreman now worked. Hemmeter took out an injunction against the Canadian com-pany for hiring the women, but the American courts lacked jurisdiction. There were also signs that the industry was not as healthy and happy as it had proclaimed. In September 1913 the Detroit *News-Tribune* published a small article describing child labor in the cigar factories in critical terms, tarnishing the industry's image. The CMIU was also printing ar-ticles detailing conditions in the Detroit factories and calling for a boycott of Detroit cigars. Union pamphlets pointed to "slavery in the cigar indus-try," "Detroit's Shame," and manufacturers' "insane Madness for Gold." The union accused the manufacturers of hiring "poor, half-grown girl la-borers." David A. Jones, a member of Local 22, led this publicity cam-paign during 1912 and 1913. However, a 1915 governor's report on the conditions of women workers in Michigan presented a positive picture of Detroit's cigar factories, counteracting much of Jones's effort.[27]

In January 1915 *Tobacco Leaf* featured the San Telmo Company in De-troit, much to the pleasure of the company's owner, Oscar Rosenberger. His San Telmo Company had been responsible for providing money to build many of the homes in the Polish neighborhood, the article ex-plained. His factories had provided excellent work opportunities for young Polish girls, at wages far and above what they "could hope to re-ceive elsewhere." These women were fortunate because "only the hum-blest employment at very small wages was their lot until the cigar facto-ries had provided a service through these wages," and the factory system had also filled the Polish women with the "spirit of Americanism." The San Telmo factory was a "model of its kind." There one could hear the "constant babble of conversation and laughter. Every one is happy." These were "bright, rose-faced girls, filled with the joy of youth who seem to regard their daily labor more in the nature of play than a task."[28]

It came as a shock to the industry, therefore, when just over a year later the women of the San Telmo factory walked out on strike in the summer of 1916. The Detroit strike—one of the biggest explosions in the history of cigar making in the United States—began in Lilies Factory No. 1, the company which eight years earlier had moved to Detroit to solve its "labor problems." Four hundred and fifty women walked out of the factory on Thursday afternoon, June 29, in the midst of a heat wave. They struck spontaneously, and were led solely by women. They demanded an increase of one dollar per thousand on all cigars, a uniform wage scale for all cigar makers, and an end to the docking system. Women also complained of "disrespectful remarks" which the foreman had made to the workers. Each day more women left work. Strikes broke out at Lilies's other shop, and at San Telmo, Wayne Cigar, William Tegge, American Cigar, Hemmeter Cigar, Alexander Gordon, Stephan Cigar, Mazer Cigar, City of Straits, Superia, and Comas. Banner Cigar locked its workers out before they could strike. Thus, within only a few days, six thousand cigar makers had left their benches and shut down all of the city's large cigar factories.[29]

Wages appeared to have been the underlying cause of the 1916 strike. The subject was not unfamiliar to Detroit's industrial labor force, especially after Henry Ford's five-dollar-day plan for auto workers, which he announced in 1914. A more immediate cause, however, was the wage increase which union cigar makers had recently won. On June 26 the men secured an increase of from one dollar to two dollars in their bill of prices without a strike. This meant that union men were earning at least double the rates that women made on many of the same cigars. Women workers became angry over the piece rate differentials, and they knew that the companies were then extremely busy with orders.[30]

Women workers at the Lilies factory contacted the officers of Local 22 of the CMIU in Detroit to ask for assistance. Despite the rocky relationship between the union and women, the CMIU lost no time in getting involved in the strike. Within days they set up Class A Local 528, and began enrolling members and collecting dues. By the time all factories had been struck, the CMIU had taken almost complete charge of the strike. President Perkins hired one of the strike organizers, Emelia Weiss, as a general organizer, and sent in three other organizers from the International office. David Jones acted as the primary representative for Local 22, and American Federation of Labor president Samuel Gompers sent in AFL organizer Mary Scully. Scully was an exception, and not the rule, since the AFL placed only a limited emphasis on organizing women workers at the time. She was a former member of the Women's Trade Union League, and had worked successfully in organizing Connecticut women and getting eight-hour agreements, thus her nickname, "Eight-Hour Scully."[31]

Women cigar makers picketed the factories, which were mostly located in their neighborhoods, and each day they held mass meetings at Schiller Hall. Although local papers printed almost no information about the strike, the *Detroit Labor News,* the city's only labor paper, covered it fully, and several women began selling the *Labor News* on the picket line. The trade press downplayed the strike. *Tobacco Leaf* reported that Mazer Cigar Company would still hold its annual outing for employees, taking the steamer *Toledo* to Sugar Island. But the event never took place. Feelings on both sides were stronger than observers realized, and the conflict moved into July with no change. The factories remained closed and the strikers picketed daily. Manufacturers ignored the CMIU organizers' efforts to open negotiations all through the month. In the meantime, hundreds of strikers had joined the union, with one organizer estimating that as many as 70 percent of the strikers were union members by the end of June.[32]

Strikers objected to the wage differential with male unionists, and they also resented the arbitrary nature of the wage scales where they worked. Scales were not posted and a woman might think she was making a certain dollar amount for a cigar, but would receive her wages based on a lower scale. Strikers also opposed the foreman's power to reject and remove cigars from their benches. They called for better sanitation inside the factories, and complained that they were required to work longer than the state's fifty-four-hour law allowed. They referred to sexual harassment by listing "improper conduct toward girls on the part of foremen" as a grievance. Manufacturers refused to have anything to do with the strikers. *Tobacco Leaf* reported that the manufacturers felt they could only raise wages if they raised prices, and they were not ready to do so.[33]

Locally and nationally the CMIU provided enormous support for the strike. The union raised and distributed money, organized relief, and helped with the picket lines. In early August the AFL executive council sent out a circular to all affiliated unions calling for voluntary contributions. Nevertheless, barriers between the men and women remained, and if they did not seriously impair the strike, they damaged chances for a permanent organization of women in Detroit under the auspices of the CMIU. The men continued to view women paternalistically as "half-grown girls" and "little unfortunates." A Local 22 flyer on the strike noted that women's wages were insufficient for them to live or "retain their virtue." One *Detroit Labor News* article pictured the women as "helpless and unprotected" until the CMIU and organized labor in Detroit had come "nobly to the rescue." The CMIU also noted that the women's hard fight in the strike had placed them on a "pedestal of honor."[34]

Problems in the conduct of the strike also stemmed from the different views of local and national union leaders. The men agreed that it should rest primarily in their hands. This situation made Mary Scully's role a difficult one—so much so that Gompers telegraphed impatiently to Perkins in early August. One of the problems with the strike, Gompers noted, was the "failure of comprehensive policy pursued by organizers there. Will you please direct that International Union's Organizers hold conference and decide as to which course should be pursued and then have it followed, rather than each expressing individual judgment leading nowhere. Federation Organizer Mrs. Scully will cooperate upon any given line decided but she cannot act upon individual options, particularly when they conflict. Please telegraph answer." Scully also complained about the lack of publicity for the strike in the city. Perkins disputed all of Scully's criticisms and noted that the local press deliberately ignored the strike. The policy his lieutenants had pursued thus far had been successful enough and there was little cause for changing their approach.[35]

Although the union insisted on running the strike, several women emerged as strike leaders, chief among them Emelia Weiss. Weiss listed her address as Joseph Campau Street, where Sophia Wisiecki, also a cigar maker, lived. Weiss apparently spoke English and Polish well, and was instrumental in spreading the strike to all the factories. In fact, AFL organizer Mary Scully complained to Gompers that the strikers showed stronger allegiance to Weiss than to her. CMIU president Perkins, however, argued that Weiss was the strikers' own leader. He had not chosen Weiss, "her own personality, reputation, and standing among these girls made her the logical leader, and the strikers made her such." The strikers were Polish and had no previous experience with any labor group. "Hence, we have had by force of these circumstances to keep Miss Emelia Weiss the organizer . . . always to the front," Perkins wrote to Gompers. "These women worship her and will follow her. This we cannot change if we would and for strategic reasons are not trying to do so." Other Polish women strike leaders included Celia Okroy and Anna Swiezkowska.[36]

During the last days of July, rumors spread through Detroit that the manufacturers might soon give in, or that at least some would break ranks and settle separately. Some companies hired Burns detectives to find out which among them might break first. The *Detroit Labor News* reported on the manufacturers' growing unhappiness, and on the success of several hundred women in finding jobs across the river in Canada. Manufacturers began making threats to move out of the city to Pennsylvania and Cincinnati if the strike did not end soon. Union victories in other strikes in Chicago, New York City, and Tampa encouraged the Detroit women and the CMIU.[37]

Near the end of July, the manufacturers made a desperate move to end the strike by sending notes to the homes of women workers announcing that on August 8 the factories would reopen. Anyone who wished would be allowed to return to work. But if the manufacturers expected many of the women to take up their offer, they were disappointed. Cigar makers adopted mass picketing and turned out in full force to form almost a human belt around the factories (this practice had first been developed at the textile strike in Lawrence in 1912). No incidents arose during the day, but that evening ten women were arrested for throwing bricks at a cigar factory and trying to intimidate strikebreakers as they left work. The next night violence accelerated and twenty-one women were arrested for rioting near the factories. Several policemen were hurt when women tried to storm the Lilies Cigar plant on Porter Street. On Thursday afternoon, mounted police rode into the crowds of women near several factories. That night the most serious confrontation took place at Wayne Cigar in Hamtramck, where demonstrators broke every window in the factory with rocks and bricks. A crowd of over 10,000 had gathered at the factory. Many women brought their children with them, and small boys gathered up stones to provide ammunition. It took firemen using streams of pressurized water to drive them away.[38] Union officials pointed out that strikers had been provoked when police on horseback "brutally attacked" strikers, who had responded by throwing bricks. They referred to the police as "Detroit's Cossacks" and tools of the manufacturers. Twenty-three people were arrested that night. Two other women, Nettie Swickowski, age sixteen, and Rose Pinnki, age nineteen, were arrested for stoning the house of a strikebreaker.[39]

Violence subsided after a Wayne County circuit judge issued an injunction prohibiting strikers or members of the CMIU from any activity to influence those who wished to work. The injunction made picketing impossible and Perkins noted that it was so broad that it kept strikers "from doing anything practically except breathing." Even walking and singing near the factories were prohibited. Violence in a strike of pattern makers at the same time, followed by injunctions and arrests, added further legitimacy to police and court actions. The strikers continued their daily meetings, but moved to Dom Polski Hall and in Hamtramck to Alpine Hall.[40]

Throughout August more women returned to work, especially after the manufacturers offered a five-dollar weekly bonus to those who came back. Perkins received information that priests were encouraging girls to return to work because some of the parishes owned stock in the cigar companies. Whether that was a rumor or not, certainly the clergy had traditionally distrusted unions. State mediator Frank L. Dodge became active in efforts to intervene during the month, and received permission from Governor Woodbridge Ferris to conduct an investigation of the conditions leading up to the strike. Dodge interviewed at least sixty strikers and his subsequent report substantiated many of their claims. Dodge's report met with antipathy from the manufacturers, who pointed to the 1915 investigation as proof that the strikers' claims were unfounded. Women from the Detroit Federation of Women's Clubs visited the factories to talk with the strikers, but predictably they refused to endorse the strike.[41]

Local press coverage had increased during the various riots. The papers alternately portrayed the women as "fighting Amazons" and childlike girls who were "laughing, laughing, laughing" while taunting the police, their faces gleaming with "mischief." The *Detroit News* commented on how "sassy" many of the women strikers had become and expressed amazement that some women brought their children to strike gatherings. *Tobacco Leaf* still did not devote much space to the strike. In one article, a response to a query, the reporter (a Detroit tobacco dealer) concluded that "outside labor agitators" had caused all the trouble. "It is alleged that they hired ringleaders to do the dirty work, threatened girls who were willing to work and forced the factories to close down to prevent violence."[42]

The striking women held dances and bazaars to raise funds, and accepted voluntary contributions from workers in Detroit and CMIU locals around the country, but things were not going well. In September several Polish organizations attempted a settlement, but the manufacturers rebuffed their efforts. When a committee of strikers appealed to Governor Ferris to intervene, *Tobacco Leaf* commented that the move showed the strikers had "lost hope" of winning. Women continued to return to work, and there were several arrests of strikers for violating the injunction.[43] During September the San Telmo and Lilies companies set up annex factories in areas outside of Detroit, including York, Pennsylvania, Cincinnati, Evansville, Bay City, and Lansing, the Detroit industry's first branch factories. Late in the month six women strikers were found guilty of contempt of court and sentenced to fifteen to thirty days in jail.[44]

In early October, Secretary of Labor William B. Wilson dispatched a federal mediator, A. L. Faulkner, to Detroit, at the request of Samuel Gompers. After investigating the situation, Faulkner became convinced that the strikers' cause was "a just one," and noted that because manufacturers had recently raised the wholesale prices of their cigars they could probably afford to increase the women's wages. Faulkner arranged a meeting with the employers and state mediator Frank Dodge, minus the strikers, since the owners refused to have any dealings with them. The strikers authorized Dodge and Faulkner to drop all demands except for a wage increase, but even this the manufacturers rejected. At the same time, AFL organizers reported to Gompers that they had made no progress in the strike. Between five hundred and seven hundred women had returned to work and the manufacturers remained "obdurate." Efforts to settle seemed futile since the manufacturers had said they would give "not one penny increase."[45]

Federal mediator Faulkner continued his efforts, but he became convinced that the strike would drag on for a long time, since "the employees and employers are still full of the fighting spirit which has dominated the situation from the very beginning." Although the strikers' enthusiasm was still high, manufacturers were now running their factories at about 25 percent capacity, and they expected further increases in their labor force. The courts and the Detroit Employers' Association fully backed the cigar manufacturers. Faulkner attributed his failure to settle the strike "wholly to the unreasonable and unyielding attitude of the employers." Although the Detroit pattern makers' strike was successfully arbitrated in mid-October, it did not set precedent for the cigar makers' strike.[46]

By early November the manufacturers had become convinced that they had won. About one-third of the workers had returned to the factories. The jailing of the three women for contempt had been a hard blow to the strikers, and as funds became harder to raise, strike resources dwindled. Tallies of CMIU contributions indicated that while a few unions had given generously, the great majority had not. Local 22 chided fellow cigar makers for not giving more money, and noted the "antipathy to the Class A plan" among many members. They cited the readiness of many male union members "to condemn it without a fair trial, but we distinctly recall the vociferations of the 'so-called progressive element' in our union for a broader form of representation. We adopted it, and without solicitation in Detroit the opportunity knocked loudly at our door. . . . Must we now sacrifice that chance of victory and deal a death blow to the onward march of our organization for lack of co-operation and financial support?" If the strike were lost, the local concluded, "the blame will rest on the heads of those unions that were able, yet failed, to respond, and not on the form of organization."[47]

All efforts to arbitrate the strike, even by the Detroit police commissioner, failed. Manufacturers stopped dealing with state mediator Dodge, and not long after made it clear to federal mediator Faulkner that he was no longer welcome. Faulkner withdrew from Detroit in late January, saying that his mission had failed because of the manufacturers' "inconsistent spirit and . . . uncompromising attitude." In February 1917 the striking cigar makers declared a "truce," and although they refused to declare the strike over they did not continue it. Many workers had left the trade, others had found employment in Windsor, but the majority returned to their old jobs. Membership in the local dropped to 1,093 in April and by the next year only 79 members were left. Soon after, the women's local disbanded.[48]

For the manufacturers the lesson of the strike had been not to "keep all their eggs in one basket." To insure against future strikes crippling them as this one had, almost all Detroit manufacturers by the end of the strike had opened branch factories outside of the city. The strike's devastating impact was apparent, but no one knew just how permanent the damage might be. In early May, Alexander Gordon filed for bankruptcy. In 1918 Oscar Rosenberger sold San Telmo to Haas Brothers and before the war ended both men had died. Wayne Cigar passed into the hands of American Cigar Company in 1918. From the strikers' perspective, the strike had not been completely in vain. In February 1917 manufacturers raised wages by fifty cents in all the Detroit factories.[49] The Detroit strike had also boldly and visibly demonstrated to the entire industry that women team workers were not necessarily "easy to handle" and "orderly." The Detroit strike failed to close the door on labor militancy; it was only a beginning.

Considering the obstacles to women's organizing, it was significant that the Detroit strikes had taken place at all. Yet a closer look reveals several factors working in their favor. Louise Tilly has recently attempted to draw some conclusions about the conditions which historically have facilitated women workers' collective action: women associate with each other and can structure this association formally; they have resources upon which to draw; their employers are dependent on them; the economic climate is favorable and their own position not extremely vulnerable; the general climate is supportive; they have the opportunity to act autonomously. Tilly also argued that women who lived with parents and whose families claimed "their wages and loyalty" would normally be less likely to strike.[50] While Detroit women had such family connections, in other ways their lives reflected many of the elements on Tilly's list. The labor shortage heightened manufacturers' dependence on these women workers, who were neighbors and friends inside and outside of the factories. Their bonds and networks threaded through home and work and sustained them in a drawn-out strike. Their shop-floor culture had grown out of their work experiences, though linked to their identities as Polish women. They learned the importance of interdependence and sisterhood, and they developed a strong group identity. Work culture had emphasized the need to control time and work and the desire to delimit the authority of employers. With the strike of 1916, it stretched to include overt opposition to management in the factories.

Notes

1. U.S. Commissioner of Labor, *Twenty-First Annual Report, 1906, Strikes and Lockouts* (Washington, D.C., 1907); U.S. Department of Labor, Bulletin 651, *Strikes in the United States, 1880–1936*, by Florence Peterson (Washington, D.C., 1938).

2. David Montgomery, "The 'New Unionism' and the Transformation of Workers' Consciousness in America, 1909–22," in *Workers' Control in America: Studies in the History of Work, Technology, and Labor Struggles* (Cambridge, 1979), pp. 91–112.

3. *Tobacco Leaf*, 19 June 1903, p. 24; 7 Oct. 1903, p. 30; 4 Nov. 1903, p. 20.

4. *Tobacco Leaf*, 24 June 1903, p. 18; 3 Feb. 1910, p. 26; 28 July 1910, p. 28.

5. *Tobacco*, 6 Feb. 1902, p. 3; 25 Apr. 1902, p. 8; *Tobacco Leaf*, 19 Mar. 1902, p. 40; *CMOJ*, June 1912, p. 9.

6. New Jersey Bureau of Statistics of Labor and Industries, *Annual Report, 1915* (Camden, 1916), p. 264. See also *Tobacco*, 25 Apr. 1902, p. 8; *Tobacco Leaf*, 20 May 1903, p. 44; *CMOJ*, Mar. 1906, p. 3; Jan. 1917, p. 19.

7. New York State Board of Mediation and Arbitration, *Annual Report* (Albany, 1901), p. 125; *Tobacco Leaf*, 14 May 1902, p. 30; 21 May 1902, p. 30; 4 June 1902, p. 26; 17 Dec. 1902, p. 3; David Montgomery, "New Unionism," p. 98.

8. *Tobacco Leaf*, 28 May 1902, p. 25; *CMOJ*, June 1902, p. 11; June 1912, p. 9.

9. *CMOJ*, Feb. 1917, p. 10.

10. *Tobacco Leaf*, Nov. 1909, p. 8; New Jersey Bureau of Statistics, *Report*,

1908, pp. 258–59; 1915, p. 264; Henry Hilfers to Samuel Gompers, 24 Jan. 1916, and Frank Morrison to Hugh Frayne, 25 Jan. 1916, Papers of the American Federation of Labor, "Cigar Makers, 1901–1937," Reel 36, American Federation of Labor Records: The Samuel Gompers Era (Sanford, N.C., 1979).

11. New Jersey Bureau of Statistics, Report, 1908, p. 348.

12. Tobacco, 18 May 1900, p. 7; 25 May 1900, p. 4; Tobacco Leaf, 24 June 1903, p. 18.

13. Tobacco Leaf, 27 Mar. 1907, p. 5; CMOJ, Nov. 1909, p. 8; New Jersey Bureau of Statistics, Report, 1915, p. 264; Newark Evening News, 5 Aug. 1908, p. 1. See "Labor Chronology" in New Jersey Bureau of Statistics, Report, 1900–1917.

14. Tobacco Leaf, 6 Aug. 1908, p. 9; Newark Star, 5 Aug. 1908; Newark Evening News, 3 Oct. 1908; New Jersey Bureau of Statistics, Report, 1908, p. 348; newspaper clipping on the strike, undated, National Trade Union League Papers, Schlesinger Library, Radcliffe College, Cambridge, Mass. My thanks to Dr. Edward James, editor of the NWTUL microfilm project, for passing this along to me.

15. Tobacco Leaf, 3 Feb. 1910, p. 26; 28 July 1910, p. 28; U.S. Tobacco Journal, 20 Apr. 1908, p. 20; 4 May 1908, p. 14; John R. Ograin interview, 11 Aug. 1976 and 15 Sept. 1978, Chicago, and by telephone; CMOJ, Jan. 1916, p. 43; Feb. 1916, p. 20; Chicago Daily Socialist, 5 Nov. 1909; 23 Jan. 1912; "Interview with R. Youkelson, Financial Secretary Progressive Local 527 Cigar Makers, Chicago, Ill. January 14, 1919," Box 21, folder 16, David Saposs Papers, State Historical Society of Wisconsin, Madison (SHSW); Studs Terkel, American Dreams: Lost and Found (New York, 1980), pp. 118–19. See CMOJ, 15 July 1921, p. 2, for an account which suggests that Billow later collaborated with employers and informed to a detective agency. My thanks to Steve Sapolsky for the Saposs reference and to Bill Pretzer for calling my attention to Terkel.

16. Patrick Lynch, "Pittsburgh, the I.W.W., and the Stogie Workers," in Joseph Conlin, ed., At the Point of Production: The Local History of the I.W.W. (Westport, Conn., 1981), pp. 79–94.

17. CMOJ, July 1900, p. 4; Oct. 1900, p. 6; May 1902, pp. 8, 9; Oct. 1906, p. 4; Nov. 1906, p. 16: David S. Jones, Sight Seeing in Detroit's Foreign District, CMIU pamphlet, 1912, Vertical File, Labor Collection, Detroit Public Library. One section of Jones's pamphlet is entitled "Reasons Why Many Young Girls Are Going Wrong Today."

18. New York Tribune, 16 Apr. 1900; Tobacco Leaf, 11 Apr. 1900, p. 4; Tobacco, 18 May 1900, p. 7; New York State Bureau of Labor Statistics, "Strike and Lockout of the New York City Cigar Makers," Bulletin of the Bureau of Labor Statistics, no. 5 (June 1900), pp. 112–23.

19. CMOJ, June 1900, p. 9; Sept. 1900, p. 6; Oct. 1900, p. 4; Financial Statement of the JAB of Cigarmakers' Unions of New York and Vicinity, Relating to the Defense Fund of the Striking and Locked Out Cigarmakers of New York City, 1900–1901, 1901, U.S. Department of Labor Library (USDL), Washington, D.C.

20. CMOJ, May 1900, p. 8.

21. CMOJ, June 1900, p. 4; July 1901, p. 3; Aug. 1901, p. 2; Mar. 1906, p. 3; Oct. 1906, p. 4; Jan. 1908, p. 3; Feb. 1916, p. 2; Tobacco, 16 July 1903, p. 7.

22. *Tobacco Leaf,* 7 Mar. 1900, p. 3; 14 Mar. 1900, p. 6; 21 Mar. 1900, p. 7; *Tobacco,* 16 Mar. 1900, p. 4.

23. *Tobacco,* 27 Apr. 1900, p. 1; 29 June 1900, p. 8; *Tobacco Leaf,* 4 April 1900, p. 4.

24. *Tobacco Leaf,* 6 Sept. 1905, p. 38.

25. Harvey Whipple, "Cigar Manufacture in Detroit," *The Detroiter,* June 1911, p. 13.

26. Michigan State Department of Labor, *Annual Report, 1901* (Lansing, 1901), p. 27; *Tobacco Leaf,* 4 Apr. 1900, p. 9; 4 June 1902, p. 18; 11 June 1902, p. 39.

27. *CMOJ,* July 1917, pp. 9–10; *Detroit Labor News,* 10 July 1914; *Detroit News-Tribune,* 7 Sept. 1913; Jones, "Sight Seeing in Detroit's Foreign District," p. 1; *Report of the Michigan State Commission of Inquiry into Wages and the Conditions of Labor for Women and the Advisability of Establishing a Minimum Wage* (Lansing, 1915), passim.

28. *Tobacco Leaf,* 14 Jan. 1915, p. 18.

29. A. L. Faulkner to William B. Wilson, 10 Oct. 1916, file 33/290, Federal Mediation and Conciliation Service (FMCS), Record Group (R.G.) 280, National Archives (NA); *Detroit News,* 7 July 1916. There is some possibility that Local 527 was involved in the Detroit strikes. See Saposs's interview with Youkelson, Saposs Papers.

30. *Detroit Labor News,* 7 July 1916. See also Harry Braverman, *Labor and Monopoly Capital: The Degradation of Work in the Twentieth Century* (New York, 1974), p. 149.

31. *Detroit Labor News,* 24 July 1916; James Kenneally, *Women in American Trade Unions* (St. Albans, Vt., 1978), p. 87.

32. Detroit Labor News, 21 July 1916; 28 July 1916; *Tobacco Leaf,* 15 July 1916, p. 34; "Preliminary Report of Commissioner of Conciliation," 16 Sept. 1916; Circular, CMIU Local 22 to Organized Labor, 1 Aug. 1916, file 33/290, FMCS, R.G. 280, NA; Faulkner to Wilson, 10 Oct. 1916, file 33/290, FMCS, R.G. 280, NA.

33. *Detroit Labor News,* 21 July 1916; *Tobacco Leaf,* 20 July 1916, p. 47; Faulkner to Wilson, 10 Oct. 1916, file 33/290, FMCS, R.G. 280, NA.

34. Circular, CMIU Local 22 to Organized Labor, 1 Aug. 1916, file 33/290, FMCS, R.G. 280, NA; "SAFETY FIRST! Beware of Your American Rights," flyer, ca. 1916, attached to Louis F. Post to David S. Jones, 18 Jan. 1918, file 68/1–a, Office of the Chief Clerk, U.S. Department of Labor, R.G. 174, NA; *Detroit Labor News,* 4 Aug. 1916, 6 Oct. 1916; *CMOJ,* Oct. 1916, p. 19; May 1910, p. 8; Jones, "Sight Seeing in Detroit's Foreign District," pp. 1–2.

35. Samuel Gompers to George W. Perkins, 11 Aug. 1916, Reel 211, no. 482, Samuel Gompers Papers, microfilm, Library of Congress (LC), Washington, D.C.; George Perkins to Frank Morrison, 19 July 1916, and Perkins to Gompers, 16 Aug. 1916, *American Federation of Labor Records.*

36. *Detroit City Directory,* 1916; Circular, CMIU Local 22 to Organized Labor, 1 Aug. 1916, file 33/290, FMCS, R.G. 280, NA; *Detroit Labor News,* 14 July

1916; *CMOJ,* July 1916, p. 18; George W. Perkins to Morrison, 19 July 1916, *American Federation of Labor Records*. Most of the women mentioned in newspapers or circulars were not listed in the city directory. Weiss herself was not. Some undoubtedly anglicized their names for the press. One leader, Celia Okroy, lived at home with her parents on Florence Street. Her father was a laborer. The family is listed as Okroj. It would be interesting to know if Weiss was Jewish.

37. *Detroit Labor News,* 28 July 1916; 4 Aug. 1916.

38. *Detroit Labor News,* 4 Aug. 1916; 10 Aug. 1916; 11 Aug. 1916; *Detroit Free Press,* 11 Aug. 1916; *CMOJ,* Aug. 1916, pp. 2, 33.

39. *Detroit Labor News,* 11 Aug. 1916; 12 Aug. 1916; 16 Aug. 1916; *Tobacco Leaf,* 17 Aug. 1916, p. 8; Perkins to Gompers, 14 Aug. 1916, *American Federation of Labor Records; CMOJ,* Sept. 1916, p. 17; Michigan Board of Mediation and Conciliation, *First Annual Report* (Lansing, 1916), pp. 13–14.

40. *Detroit Labor News,* 15 Sept. 1916; Perkins to Morrison, 11 Aug. 1916, *American Federation of Labor Records*. Perkins noted that Burns detectives had been hired by the companies to help keep order and that "the police are openly against the people." For arrests see *Detroit Labor News,* 25 Aug. 1916; Mazer Cigar Manufacturing Company, Lilies Cigar, San Telmo, Wayne Cigar v. CMIU Local 22, R. S. Sexton, R. B. Stickley, William McCabe, Mrs. Mary B. Scully, Miss Emelia Weiss, David S. Jones et al., Chancery Calendars, Index Docket no. 55487, Wayne County Circuit Court, Detroit, Mich.

41. *Detroit Labor News,* 12 Aug. 1916; 15 Sept. 1916; Perkins to Gompers, 16 Aug. 1916, *American Federation of Labor Records;* Faulkner to Wilson, 10 Oct. 1916, file 33/290, FMCS, R.G. 280, NA; *Detroit News,* 13 Aug. 1916; Sister Mary Napolska, *The Polish Immigrant in Detroit to 1914* (Chicago, 1946), p. 39.

42. *Detroit News,* 11 Aug. 1916; *Detroit Free Press,* 11 Aug. 1916; 22 Aug. 1916; *Detroit Labor News,* 18 Aug. 1916; *Tobacco Leaf,* 2 Nov. 1916, p. 3.

43. *Detroit Labor News,* 18 Aug. 1916; 1 Sept. 1916; Faulkner to Wilson, 10 Oct. 1916 and 23 Oct. 1916, file 33/290, FMCS, R.G. 280; NA; Mazer Co. v. CMIU Local 22, Docket no. 55487, Wayne County Circuit Court; *Tobacco Leaf,* 7 Sept. 1916, p. 4.

44. *Tobacco Leaf,* 14 Sept. 1916, p. 36; *CMOJ,* Oct. 1916, p. 6; *Detroit Labor News,* 20 Sept. 1916; 25 Sept. 1916.

45. Faulkner to William B. Wilson, 10 Oct. 1916, file 33/290 FMCS, R.G. 280, NA; Stickley and Sexton to Gompers, 7 Oct. 1916, *American Federation of Labor Records*.

46. Faulkner to Wilson, 10 Oct. 1916, 17 Nov. 1916, and 24 Nov. 1916, file 33/290, FMCS, R.G. 280, NA.

47. *Detroit Labor News,* 10 Nov. 1916; 24 Nov. 1916; 22 Dec. 1916; Faulkner to Wilson, 24 Nov. 1916, file 33/290, FMCS, R.G. 280, NA; *CMOJ,* Dec. 1916, p. 7.

48. Faulkner to Wilson, 22 Jan. 1917, file 33/290, FMCS, R.G. 280, NA; *CMOJ,* Apr. 1917, p. 66; Apr. 1918, p. 60.

49. *Tobacco Leaf,* 22 Feb. 1917, pp. 13, 16; 3 May 1917, p. 4; 22 Nov. 1917,

p. 47; 16 May 1918, p. 26; 18 July 1918, p. 3; *CMOJ*, Mar. 1917, p. 13; Aug. 1918, p. 12.

50. Louise A. Tilly, "Paths of Proletarianization: Organization of Production, Sexual Division of Labor, and Women's Collective Action," *Signs*, 7 (Winter 1981), 400–417.

10

War in the Cigar Industry, 1917–19

Between 1917 and 1919, the cigar industry was shaken both by the war in Europe and an internal war. A wave of labor militancy began in 1917, gathered force the next year, and crashed wide open in 1919. Cigar makers, union and nonunion, male and female, made temporary alliances and participated in bold strikes on a scale never before attempted in the industry. At the heart of these strikes stood workers' assertion of the right to control the conditions of their work. The strikes marked a major departure for workers in the industry in terms of both militancy and labor unity. The extent of their strike activity undermined manufacturers' traditional strategies for enforcing labor discipline and for minimizing the impact of local strikes. In response, manufacturers manifested their superior power by introducing far-reaching changes which would spell the end of a competitive, decentralized, handcraft stage of production, and would fundamentally alter the work cultures of the cigar makers.

Each group caught in the strike movement of the war years saw the struggle from a different perspective. For their part, manufacturers experienced rising costs of production and a labor shortage. They viewed the massive strike movement as a serious development because it momentarily united union and nonunion workers and spread so widely that it made farming out work to branch factories impossible. CMIU president George W. Perkins also feared the militancy of the strikes because they posed a threat to his and Gompers' authority among cigar makers and threatened to heighten ideological differences which could fragment the CMIU. Too many strikes would weaken locals and strain a dwindling union treasury. While union leadership hesitated, rank-and-file cigar makers seized the opportunity provided by wartime conditions, particularly the acute labor shortage, to make explicit demands for higher wages and more shop-floor autonomy.

Across the country in early 1917, cigar manufacturers watched international events anxiously, wondering what effects the war might have on them. By late May, some seven weeks after the American declaration of war, a *Tobacco Leaf* editorial stated that the industry faced the "greatest crisis in its history." Tobacco prices—particularly on imported Sumatra wrapper leaf—the cost of boxes, labels, and glue had all risen dramatically. While business remained brisk, manufacturers in Detroit and elsewhere complained as the year progressed that their profits were flagging because of recent wage increases and higher cost of materials. The war also brought revenue tax raises of 10 to 35 percent, which only squeezed manufacturers further. To conserve paper and wood, many companies dropped much of the ornamentation on boxes for the fall rush season in 1917.[1]

In the view of some of the industry, raising prices afforded the only solution to the problem of escalating costs, but the traditional rigidity of the retail price scale made such a move difficult to contemplate. Manufacturers worried that consumers would not tolerate the advance from a nickel to six cents, especially given the spreading popularity of cigarettes. No one wanted to be first and risk losing business to manufacturers who did not follow suit. The Tobacco Merchants Association, formed in 1915 to represent the tobacco trade's interests, and *Tobacco Leaf* together took the lead in pressuring manufacturers to forget their rivalries by "restandardizing prices." By the end of the year, despite uneasiness, several major manufacturers, including Eisenlohr, Bayuk, Bobrow's, Cressman Cigar, and General Cigar announced price increases to six cents.[2] Costs continued to rise, however, and the trade press urged further price increases. By early 1919, what had cost five cents when the U.S. entered the war now sold for eight cents. Stogie prices likewise rose to five cents. Ballooning demand created additional strains which were only exacerbated when the wartime Fuel Administration called for closing factories an extra day a week in early 1918, making it even more difficult to fill orders.[3]

The United States government never added tobacco manufacture to its list of "essential" industries and significant numbers of male cigar makers deserted the factories to avoid military service and to earn higher wages in war-related jobs. This shift plus the loss of draftees created a serious labor shortage in the industry. Nationally manufacturers complained that they were "losing hands every day."[4] In Detroit it was "impossible to keep enough cigar makers owing to the large demand for girls in other lines," and in York and Lancaster, Pennsylvania, manufacturers reported that "many cigar makers are leaving the factories to accept work elsewhere at higher wages, the munition plants having made a heavy toll of workmen in the cigar factories." The severe flu epidemic that hit in the fall of 1918 further depleted the ranks of the cigar makers despite some workers' claims that the tobacco protected them from the illness. By August 1918, the shortage, editorialized *Tobacco Leaf*, had made the labor situation "precarious."[5]

The scarcity of labor provided workers with some advantages. Companies often raised wages to compete with each other for labor. Even Pittsburgh stogie workers found their meager wages going up between 1917 and 1919. Others, such as the Deisel-Wemmer Company in Lima, tried to attract new workers through advertisements: "Those who are attentive as well as industrious endure little difficulty acquiring the knowledge necessary to increase their earning power." Problems with shortages of labor grew worse when a number of union and nonunion strikes broke out during the year, so that fewer factories tried to meet a growing volume of orders. A union strike in Hartford, Connecticut, ended in May leaving manufacturers "in a bad way" because of "defections from the ranks" during the three-week strike. Some had taken war jobs while others had left the city to work elsewhere. One manufacturer complained that he had lost 60 percent of his men. Not only were the cigar makers hard to replace, but "some of the girl strippers also found work in local shops and munition factories during the progress of the strike, and thus far have refused to return to their former employers."[6]

Doubtless many manufacturers hoped that the war would usher in a period of labor peace as cigar makers and other factory workers rallied patriotically to support the war effort. However, many cigar makers recognized that the labor shortages gave them a strategic edge. Strikes erupted intermittently throughout 1917 and 1918 among union and nonunion workers alike, who gained confidence in airing their grievances in an atmosphere suddenly more conducive to success. The CMIU attempted to use the situation to advance its position and launched organizing campaigns in Cincinnati, Lima, and Wellston, Ohio, as well as in Evansville, Indiana. Amid scattered strikes in Lancaster, York, Bucks, and Berks counties, where less than a quarter of cigar makers belonged to the CMIU, locals began organizing drives aimed at eventually setting up Class

A locals in the country districts. To counter possible interest in these campaigns, some manufacturers gave fifty-cent wage increases and told workers that the companies could take better care of cigar makers than unions could.[7] In March 1917, a number of unionists met in Reading to discuss a possible general strike of Pennsylvania cigar makers, union and nonunion, in the spring. Plans were eventually cancelled, but scattered strikes broke out anyway. Many manufacturers threatened to close factories should cigar makers strike and others temporarily shut down plants at the end of May as a warning. A few acceded to demands without any strikes, and by the year's end, many companies in southeastern Pennsylvania had granted fifty-cent to one-dollar increases without work stoppages. However, no new unions emerged from the effort.[8]

Strikes of union members broke out all over the country in nearly every cigar-making center. In 1917, Louisville, Denver, New Haven, and Hartford cigar makers won wage increases.[9] Manufacturers in St. Louis consented to raise wages by one dollar and accept a new bill, but opposed several "technical points" in the bill such as giving the local executive board final say over the dismissal of employees. Los Angeles cigar makers struck in October not for an increase in wages, but for a new bill which required manufacturers to furnish clean cuspidors daily and to allow cigar makers to smoke as many cigars during work hours as they wished, in addition to the "customary number of smokers." Between January and August 1917 more than thirteen thousand CMIU members went on strike, and the number grew in the fall. In Boston, cigar makers walked out of Waitt and Bond "over the tone of voice of the new foreman." According to a *Tobacco Leaf* report, the foreman "corrected four of the men working on cigars" and cigar makers resented not his criticism, but his "personal manner." The strike ended quickly when the foreman in question resigned. In November, Boston cigar makers voted to demand a one-dollar increase on ten-cent cigars and a fifty-cent raise on nickel cigars, in the midst of the holiday rush. At the end of December manufacturers granted all demands and the cigar makers returned to work.[10]

The number of strikes swelled early in 1918 as cigar makers recognized that the usual January-February lull and accompanying layoffs had never materialized. Unionists struck in many areas, including New Haven, New Orleans, Cincinnati, St. Louis, Cleveland, Chicago, and San Francisco. Boston cigar makers walked out in January for three weeks without union sanction, and again in July they struck, asking for a two-dollar increase on all work and double pay for overtime. They won a partial increase. By early June, 9,155 CMIU members had already been involved in strikes, losing two, winning nineteen, and compromising five, with six pending at the time of the report. Twenty-five thousand other members had won increases without striking.[11] While the majority of strikes in the industry were conducted by members of the union, many nonunionists stopped work as well. Tampa workers, about half of whom belonged to the CMIU, struck in the spring of 1918 and asked only for a modest 8 percent increase, which they won. The CMIU tried to capitalize on such strikes for organizing purposes, especially in Tampa and in southeastern Pennsylvania. In most cases strikers demanded wage increases and, since manufacturers were using cheaper stock to cut production costs, workers also called for better-quality tobacco. As soon as one strike ended, noted the *U.S. Tobacco Journal*, another one began.[12]

George W. Perkins viewed the unusual circumstances of the war with misgivings. The CMIU faced serious problems. The general fund fell below the constitutional minimum during 1917, but members voted down the dues hike needed to shore up union finances. Strikes drained union funds, but so did demographics. A segment of the membership had so advanced in age that for several years the death benefit had consumed a larger and larger portion of union money. In the fall of 1917, Perkins used his constitutional power to assess each member to replenish the general fund beginning with a one-dollar levy on all but Class A members, who paid fifty cents. Between January and August of the following year, Perkins levied three more one dollar assessments, but still the general fund dipped lower. Prohibition threatened to pass, cutting off the union's foremost retail outlet. In August the executive board of the CMIU met together—the first such meeting since 1884—to discuss the various threats the union faced. Wages had risen and strikes had been successful, but CMIU officers lamented that strikers in high-wage areas had been more eager to strike than those in low-wage areas and that the wage gap among various regions had only widened.[13]

Strikes particularly alarmed Perkins. He made his views known to the membership primarily through circulars from International headquarters in Chicago, preferring this medium for discussing the progress of strikes because he felt that using the *CMOJ* would provide manufacturers with too much information. During the fall of 1917, he began cautioning members about hasty strikes and spontaneous walkouts, warning them that their power was temporary, and that they would be vulnerable to retaliation once the war ended. He admitted that "the vast majority of applications to increase bills have proved successful, chiefly because trade is good." However, these were abnormal times and conditions. "I strongly advise that unions with fairly good or topnotch bills take into considera- tion that there is to be a tomorrow, that the abnormal conditions now existing will not last after the war is over, and that as it continues and taxes go up there is bound to be a saving in the average man's expenditures." Care should be taken "not to destroy good union towns and good union shops."[14]

As part of his effort to jolt members into a more conservative mood with regard to strikes, Perkins presented disquieting information in the *CMOJ*. The number of cigar factories had declined sharply in the previous ten years, he wrote, although overall employment had risen. The trend indi- cated the increasing importance and domination of large shops, which members knew full well were unlikely to be organized. Although he did not mention it, he might also have pointed to the fact that several new, large companies had incorporated in 1917 and 1918, such as the General Cigar Company (formerly United Cigar Manufacturers), while the old- style manufacturers of another day were beginning to pass from the scene. Frank R. Rice, the popular owner of the F. R. Rice Company in St. Louis, died in June 1917 and one year later Roger Sullivan died suddenly in Manchester at the age of sixty. Over one thousand Sullivan employees attended the funeral and stores across the city closed for the day.[15] These deaths symbolized the changing of the guard in the cigar industry and the unsettled conditions which troubled Perkins. A new generation of men was coming into its own, leading the industry into the future. In late 1917, Perkins even printed a notice of a patent on a cigar machine. In the past he had not deemed such rumors worthy of mentioning, but perhaps this time he hoped to shake any complacency on such matters.[16]

Despite these dark forebodings, cigar makers' attention remained fixed on the dramatic strikes taking place in the industry throughout the war years. Women cigar makers at Henry Offterdinger's Washington, D.C., factory struck in early 1918, just ten years after Offterdinger had fired striking men, adopted the team system and the open shop, and started hiring women. On March 18, over 80 of the 110 women and all of the 6 men working in the factory walked out, demanding that women be paid at the same rates as men, that all wages be raised, that dressing rooms be provided for women, and that sanitary conditions in the factory be im- proved. The strike drew the attention of several local luminaries includ- ing Cornelia Bryce Pinchot (married to Gifford Pinchot), head of the

Pickets at the Offterdinger factory, Washington, D.C., 1918. Photo courtesy of the Library of Congress.

Washington, D.C., chapter of the National Women's Trade Union League (WTUL). CMIU Local 110 also took an interest and encouraged the strikers, who had formed an independent union, to affiliate with the CMIU. Through the offices of these parties, the strike reached the National War Labor Board, the first case in the country to be submitted to the newly formed body. The board sent it on to the Conciliation Service in the Labor Department. On May 11, Offterdinger agreed to raise wages, equalize them, improve sanitary conditions inside the factory, and affirm the right of strikers to organize. Yet the victory proved fleeting, as a "sequel" report issued by the WTUL in 1921 revealed. A "woman spy, planted in the factory by a Baltimore agency, succeeded in 'framing up'" the woman who had led the strike, on a charge of theft. "The victim was driven from her job, and the girls' organization eventually disrupted."[17]

Men and women working in New York City for the Havana-American Cigar Company (owned by American Cigar) struck in August 1917, demanding wage increases equivalent to the company's wage rates in Chicago. Shortly thereafter, cigar makers at the company in Chicago, many of whom belonged to Local 527 of the CMIU led by Jake Billow and Charles Winfield, voted to support the New York workers and strike in sympathy. Their work stoppage was officially sanctioned and they received benefits, but no settlement was reached with the company. Other strikes in New York City in 1917 increased the number of union shops and advanced wages in yearlong agreements.[18]

Yet the Havana-American situation continued to simmer. In May 1918, New York workers struck the company again and Chicago workers a second time walked out in sympathy and also demanded a wage increase. After three weeks, New York cigar makers returned to work, and in July Chicago strikers won an agreement recognizing Local 527 and allowing the union to collect dues during work hours. In December, however, the company reneged on the agreement, and the men and women belonging to 527 struck on December 21, when the company fired all shop collectors.[19] Department of Labor conciliator Oscar Nelson reported his own efforts to bring the two sides together but concluded that the company had made the order and fired workers "with deliberate intent to develop the issue and if possible disperse the Union during the slack season following the holidays." The strike continued into 1919, even after manufacturers offered five dollars a day in wages to anyone who came back. Although the Chicago Federation of Labor supported the protest, cigar makers found themelves confronted by an injunction, arrests with high bond, and a company threat to leave the city unless they returned to their jobs. Still, they held out into the spring of 1919.[20]

The situations in New York and Chicago were, however, more complicated still, and threatened to disrupt the union in Chicago. Tempers there flared over the wording of the agreement which had admitted Jake Billow's dual union of team workers into the CMIU as Local 527, about half of whose members, according to one estimate, were women. Some members of the joint unions, particularly those in Local 14, argued that the agreement prohibited Class A members from voting on Joint Advisory Board (JAB) officers. Local 527's members, supported by many from locals 15 and 383, the Spanish union, argued that the agreement technically permitted the newcomers to vote. The controversy polarized Chicago unions, especially when Perkins denied 527's appeal against the Chicago JAB and the executive board sustained his decision. The matter did not reach the general membership for a vote until August, a delay Local 527 supporters charged only suited the purposes of Perkins, who hoped to defeat it. When the vote tallies came in, they heavily supported the board's position, according to official results published in the *CMOJ*. Angry cigar makers in Chicago suspected, however, that Perkins had somehow tampered with the vote.[21]

Perkins found himself in the middle of a growing controversy within the CMIU over the Class A plan. He explained to Gompers in early 1918 that he had initially devised Class A only to "avert" the dual union movement taking shape in Chicago and to prevent insurgents from going to the public and claiming that the CMIU refused to admit all workers. In a letter to the executive board, Perkins noted that he had always conceived of the Class A plan as "simply a stepping-stone to full fellowship and membership in the International Union." He assumed it would ultimately be phased out, although members would have to drop the optional clause in order for the union to continue organizing team workers.[22]

Union members disagreed on Class A. On one extreme stood the segment of the membership who clung to the craft aspects of work culture, with its inherent exclusivity, and who were unmoved by either appeals of class solidarity or even sheer expediency. On the other were those who supported the idea of organizing all cigar makers and were increasingly attracted to the concept of industrial organization within the tobacco industry—a strategy to unite workers on the basis of class rather than craft. Some in this group hoped to win control of the CMIU through taking over a few locals, which would serve as a base for forging a more class-conscious unionism.[23]

Essentially the complex configuration of alliances and divisions within the CMIU as a whole regarding strikes and organization broke into three factions: traditional craft unionists who wanted no changes in union structure but supported better conditions for themselves; Perkins and his allies; and those, including many socialists, who supported labor militancy and more fundamental change. These ideological ruptures within the CMIU intensified during the course of the war, and the calls for industrial organization grew louder. Local 97 argued that stemmers should be able to affiliate directly with the CMIU, and elsewhere the idea of organizing others in the factories attracted adherents. Those on the left within the CMIU stressed the identical class position of all who worked in cigar factories, but their analysis lacked any particular interest in the situation of women workers.[24]

Events in New York City in the spring of 1918 heightened the growing conflicts involving workers and leaders inside and outside the union. A movement for dual organization took shape early in the new year and on February 17, at the Manhattan Lyceum, from five hundred to fifteen hundred workers met and formed the Cigarmakers' Council. The council issued the CMIU an ultimatum, threatening to form a dual union unless the International changed its strike laws to permit strikes in any shop at any time without permission. The council also directed demands to the manufacturers on various shop conditions, the most important being that every shop be allowed to form a grievance committee of five employees elected by the workers in each shop, "whose duty shall be to decide, arbitrate and adjust every question pertaining to stock, workmanship and shop conditions, the same decision to be brought up for the approval of the people of that shop." The grievance committee had no real precedent among workers in the industry. CMIU members had shop collectors and/ or committees whose functions were to handle grievances of workers, but the grievance committee the council proposed would have real power over shop management. The council circulated demands throughout the city and sent a letter to Perkins demanding an immediate reply. Characteristically Perkins loudly blasted the insurgents in the *CMOJ* and ignored their deadline.[25]

Two men, Adolph Sussman and Louis Feinstein, served as spokesmen for the Cigarmakers' Council, which was led by syndicalist cigar makers in the city bitterly opposed to the CMIU. They reported a membership of about two thousand but claimed a following of seventeen thousand, which included a six thousand-member Spanish Auxiliary of Cuban and Spanish cigar makers. Workers in the city were attracted to this movement for various reasons. Some were nonunionists who had never joined the CMIU out of principle; others belonged to the union but felt ideologically closer to the new movement. Many simply found the militant style and approach of the council appealing, especially given workers' improved bargaining position. The New York *Call* noted the divisions among socialist leaders in the CMIU and tried to explain the schism. Longtime socialist members opposed their union's policies, but they also opposed a dual union movement and wanted to avoid "disruption in the ranks." The "radicals," on the other hand, were, according to the *Call* and to JAB secretary David Lenz, "young men," Austrian and Jewish immigrants—many of the latter recently from Russia for whom the Bolshevik revolution brought a message of hope and promise. They demanded immediate, militant action and opposed the older socialists in the CMIU, who came from the ranks of German, Jewish, and Bohemian immigrants of an earlier day.[26]

After a "fiery" meeting on March 25, the council formalized the split. Over the next few weeks, in actions reminiscent of the New York schism of the 1880s, the council struck seven union label shops to supplant the International, ultimately winning three, and called over twenty-five other strikes in the city as well. *Tobacco Leaf* viewed the situation gravely because some manufacturers with government contracts had settled quickly with the council, and its ability to win big wage increases had only attracted more cigar makers into its camp. The grievance committee was particularly disturbing because it practically amounted "to turning over the factory to the cigarmakers to run."[27] Manufacturers should not be lulled into thinking they could handle the situation individually; they should instead organize to combat the "bolsheviks." "The cigar manufacturing industry in this city will do well to remember what happened in Detroit a year or two ago. If the local situation is not handled promptly and methodically, the consequences may prove disastrous." Labor "unrest" had been building for some time, particularly among the "Russian" cigar makers. The strikers did not represent the CMIU, *Tobacco Leaf* reminded readers, and the new organization had broken several trade agreements from the previous year. The council was composed of Bolsheviks, "fanatics," and "rabble," who led other cigar makers "like sheep."[28] In May, a company official mailed to the Military Intelligence Division of the War Department a list of names of all leaders in the Cigarmakers' Council. He was a little late. JAB secretary Lenz had sent a longer list in April to the Justice Department, which had forwarded it to the chief of Military Intelligence. Just to be sure that the government had the names of the "principals in the New York Cigar Matter . . . the ones that are active in the Bolsheviki movement in the cigar makers," Samuel Gompers sent an abbreviated list to a federal agent in Atlantic City in July.

Thus it was not surprising that Perkins denounced the council in terms similar to those of the manufacturers and that he went so far as to ask Gompers privately whether someone could "hint" to manufacturers under siege in New York that they seek injunctions against the strikers. The idea was not so outrageous, he explained, because "this is war." Further fueling Perkins's apprehensiveness, word came that a group of Chicago cigar makers had sent the council a $1,500 donation.[29]

The strikes only affected about fourteen hundred cigar makers, but the council succeeded in attracting a wider group of supporters because of its eagerness to organize everyone and its tough stance on wages and conditions. Many New York cigar makers viewed the CMIU as exclusive and conservative. Such lessons were not lost on the socialist leadership in the CMIU in New York, most of whom sympathized with the goals of the council. The New York *Call* reported on various efforts at unity, but noted that "bitter personal antagonism which has been aroused between the leaders of the two factions has complicated the situation." Other voices called for restraint, and by June the atmosphere had changed: the clash was dormant and strikes at an end.[30]

When the armistice was signed in November 1918, manufacturers hoped that life could return to normal in the cigar industry, and the trade press reported an increase in the labor supply in several cities. *Tobacco Leaf* noted that the year had been "fraught with grave industrial difficulties . . . rife with new and strange experiences," but still the message was positive: "Cheer Up, Friends! The Worst Is Over for the Tobacco Trade—Peace, Power and Prosperity Are Just Around the Corner." A sort of calm descended on the industry and the only event of any consequence was a report that *Tobacco Leaf* lifted from the *New York American* that the American Tobacco Company had developed an automatic machine which could make cigars in a continuous process. The American Cigar Company denied the report: just another rumor in the mill.[31]

The New Year began quietly enough. The trade journals initiated discussion of ways workers and employers could cooperate better and make unions unnecessary. *Tobacco Leaf* noted how successful the New York Cigar Manufacturers' Association had been during the labor troubles there in 1917 and 1918 and extolled the virtues of dealing "fairly" with labor. It was true, of course, "that the class of labor employed in the cigar manufacturing industry has a reputation for actions erratic and demands unreasonable." The journal also included a cartoon picturing labor and the manufacturers' association shaking hands and smiling. A *Tobacco* article remarked on the pleasant atmosphere at one of the new General Cigar factories in Shenandoah, Pennsylvania, northwest of Reading. "Sing and work, and work while you sing," such was the policy at the company for several thousand women making cigars. Between three and four each afternoon, a paid performer began piano playing and workers sang along. During that hour "the work room resembles a social gathering more than an industrial establishment." A few factories in York and Lancaster, Pennsylvania, gave voluntary wage increases and in early March labor conditions in Philadelphia were described as "serene."[32]

Although hopes for a return to "normalcy" abounded, no one could turn back the clock. Manufacturers eulogized the five-cent cigar: "the old-time nickel cigar is an unperformable trick—it simply can't be done." The campaign to convince the public of the fact was not helped by an off-hand remark made by Vice-President Thomas Marshall during a Senate debate on the needs of the country: "What this country needs is a good five-cent cigar." The public agreed and the remark became enshrined in American folklore. The trend toward centralization in the industry became more apparent as statistics revealed that the number of cigar factories had dropped from 20,555 in 1913 to 13,217 in 1918. Consolidated Cigar Corporation, formed in Delaware during 1919, combined a total of forty factories across the country once the merger of several smaller firms was complete. Other large companies such as General Cigar continued to eliminate many of their various brands and concentrated instead on only a handful.[33] Ratification of the prohibition amendment seemed certain, and while the prospect alarmed many unionists and small producers, the large cigar companies hardly seemed to mind. *Tobacco Leaf* even suggested the impact might be positive and might increase cigar consumption. Rumors flew that the large firms secretly contributed to the Anti-Saloon League thinking that Prohibition would eliminate competition from smaller independent firms.[34]

Perkins hoped that, given these realities, union strike activity had mercifully taken a rest and warned members against "hasty or ill-advised tendencies."[35] But soon he was faced with the crest of the wave of labor militancy, which had been building in the cigar industry since the 1916 strike in Detroit. Nationally in 1919, over four million U.S. workers, almost one-quarter of the entire labor force, participated in strikes. Estimates suggested that at least one hundred thousand cigar makers struck over the course of the year. While a majority of cigar strikes during the war had been conducted by unionists, in 1919 more nonunionists, particularly women, joined their ranks. As in the case of strikes in many other trades during the year, high employment and relative labor shortage helped embolden workers. The language and style of wartime patriotic appeals provided another resource in workers' challenge to authority in 1919. The "industrial despot and autocrat" replaced the German one as an object worthy of battle.[36]

Throughout the year, Perkins and his followers had little influence, much less control, over the strikes in the cigar industry. The largest and most significant union strikes went unsanctioned by the International because, like nonunionists', they stressed industrial unionism, direct action, and workers' shop-floor control over the conditions of work. Internally the CMIU was in tumult by the spring of 1919. The Boston, Chicago, New York, and Philadelphia unions were now in open revolt against CMIU leadership and while a majority of other locals did not overtly join them, they too struck in droves, much to Perkins's dismay. In January, members agreed to change the strike laws of the organization, removing the old seasonal barriers to striking and inserting instead a limit which only forbade members from asking for wage increases between December 15 and January 15 each year. Significantly, union leaders in the largest strike centers more often than not appealed directly to cigar makers elsewhere, thus circumventing lengthy union procedures.[37]

Nonunionists also struck. On April 8 about six hundred nonunion women in Trenton walked out of the Seidenberg Cigar Company. They were soon joined by women in another Seidenberg plant in the city. They demanded an eight-hour day, improved sanitation, better stock, higher allowances on tobacco, and "more respectful treatment" from management. The results were limited, but important. With the aid of the CMIU local there, they won a nine-hour day (down from ten).[38]

Just as the number of union strike applications began to swell, members of Local 97 in Boston voted on March 14 in favor of a resolution which they presented to the CMIU membership in a circular. It reflected a syndicalist spirit which attracted a growing segment of the membership, although the document itself went further than most were actually willing to follow. Still it alarmed Perkins as nothing had since the dual union movements in Chicago and New York. Local 97's resolution argued that cigar makers did not receive a fair share of the profits of manufacturers. Only reorganizing society "to make the Trade Union State the State of the Nation as a whole could end this crime." It called for the conscription of all property, workplaces, and utilities into the control of the AFL. All people over age eighteen would have the right to work, but no more than six hours a day. The war itself was used to add to the argument for viewing society differently. "We have seen the governing power of this country enact legislation by conscripting millions of young working men for fields of battle, and their pay was $1.00 a day, to further war and ruin." In the same way the working class should "conscript the land and workshops in the interest of all the people." Enough locals sanctioned the resolution to put it to a general vote of the membership.[39]

Perkins responded by issuing a stinging attack on the amendment, adding that it should be called "An Act to Establish the Bolshevik or Soviet Form of Government." The resolution, he lectured readers, was "no joke." The figures Local 97 used to calculate labor's true share of wealth disturbed Perkins most. "If the entire profit of the manufacturing industry were equally divided among all the people engaged in that industry," he believed, "there would be . . . little above a fair wage to divide." While many supported the spirit of the proposal, fewer stood ready to back it seriously, and it lost by a vote of 2,366 to 5,630. At the same time, Perkins asked Secretary of Labor William B. Wilson to undertake a study of conditions in the cigar industry. In his mind, "ignorance of economic facts is a prolific cause for unrest and radicalism." Although such a study was already in motion when he wrote, work on it halted in the face of a rising tide of strikes.[40]

In March, Boston cigar makers applied for permission to strike for higher wages. They wanted a 10 percent increase on all work and guaranteed good stock. In addition, foremen were too frequently finding "frivolous faults" with workers, "making our members nervous wrecks." Cigar makers also demanded the formation of a grievance committee composed of workers to reach decisions on shop grievances. Ironically the new bill continued to prohibit team work within 97's jurisdiction. Perkins sent out the strike application warning members that eight thousand members already were involved in strikes and that the situation was "grave and potentially extremely serious." The application was defeated by a vote of the membership and 97's members blamed Perkins, whom they said had "jug-gled the facts" and "misled the membership." In a circular to all mem-bers, 97 challenged Perkins's authority. "Members are asking the ques-tion, 'why pay dues and assessments to an organization, whose officers use such underhanded methods to defeat them in their efforts to better their conditions?'"[41]

Nothing Perkins could have done would have forestalled the tidal wave of discontent and militancy which surged through the cigar industry dur-ing the summer and early fall of 1919. Perhaps any tremor might have set events in motion, although the specific one related to the long-running conflict between cigar makers and the Havana-American Company in New York and Chicago. The Chicago strike, precipitated in December when the company prohibited collection of union dues at work, dragged on without resolution, but in June the two thousand workers at the New York City plant struck once again in sympathy. At about the same time scattered strikes broke out in Tampa and Puerto Rico.[42]

The labor situation in New York quickly focused attention there as a mood of resistance spread throughout the city's cigar factories in the wake of the Havana-American walkout. Leaders of the Cigarmakers' Council and its affiliate, the Spanish Auxiliary, began cooperating on a plan to call strikes in all trust (chain) shops in the two cities. Despite the rancor of the year before, the goal of organizing New York cigar makers helped the vari-ous factions in the city submerge their differences. The New York Joint Advisory Board supported the strike action and soon seven thousand cigar makers left work. The Cigarmakers' Council, the Spanish Auxiliary, and the CMIU jointly held a mass "inter-shop" meeting in late June with rep-resentatives of nearly every cigar factory in the city, organized and unor-ganized. Some who attended wanted to join together all cigar makers in the city in one organization; unionists may have feared for the CMIU, but hoped to extend use of the label; and still others had no stake in the spe-cific nature of the factions, but hoped to use the opportunity to win more favorable conditions in the shops they represented. Unity served every-one's immediate purpose, however, and all three factions evenly shared conducting the meeting. In action which recalled the great 1877 cigar strike, delegates voted to call a general strike in New York of all cigar mak-ers, packers, stemmers, and cigar factory workers to begin July 1, 1919.[43]

The demands sketched out at the meeting aimed at appealing to all cigar makers in the New York City area: a forty-four-hour week, a 50 per-cent increase in wages, the right to organize, and recognition of a grievance committee. The last proposal called for workers to elect a committee of three to five members who would have the authority to act on all matters of concern within the shop. Their decision would be final. No one could be dismissed from any factory without the grievance committee's approval. Such a proposal was not peculiar to cigar makers during these years. Shop committees in many other industries had been growing in popularity in the years before the war, but between 1917 and 1919 they reached a peak of importance. Often, as with the cigar makers, they arose independently of and unbeholden to traditional union leadership and structure. For "radical" cigar makers, the grievance committee represented a first step toward making workers' organization the governing apparatus of the country. For the majority of workers, however, the committee specifically addressed the question of control over work and formed common ground for what had heretofore been two very different work cultures. The importance of the strike demands lay in their attraction to workers both inside and outside the CMIU.[44] Cigar makers further demanded the equalization of wages to effect a citywide scale, an end to U.S. interference in Russia, and freedom for Tom Mooney, a California labor radical accused of bombing a 1916 Preparedness Day parade. Thousands walked out on July 1, and on the Fourth, the JAB officially joined the movement without waiting for CMIU approval.[45]

While events in New York claimed center stage, women cigar makers in Newark, Perth Amboy, Trenton, and New Brunswick had already begun strikes of their own demanding wage increases. The movement started on June 23 at Bayuk Brothers in New Brunswick. The next morning women working at Gans Cigar and General Cigar in the city also walked out. The Lipschutz Company raised wages immediately by $1.50, momentarily averting a strike of women there, but on July 2 they struck as well. The stoppages spread to other New Jersey cities as strikers persuaded workers at the same company in different locations to join the walkout. Strikes in the Lehigh Valley of Pennsylvania began in Bethlehem July 2, moved to Allentown by the next week, and broke out in Northhampton and Coplay on July 14. They too began in factories already struck elsewhere, such as General Cigar, Bayuk, Consolidated, and Allen R. Cressman. They spread by company rather than by city and were led by women. Strikes started in Philadelphia during the second week of July. A CMIU organizer in Pennsylvania who attempted to assist the grass-roots effort declared that "the showing made by these women and girls has never been equaled." As of early July, according to one estimate, at least four thousand cigar makers in Pennsylvania and about the same number in New Jersey were out on strike.[46]

Jake Melhado, head of the New York JAB, reported in early July that the New York strike included 18,000 to 20,000 people. At its peak later in the month, the strike numbered 24,500, according to the state Industrial Commission. Early reporting on the strike, particularly in the New York *Call*, initially treated strikers as though they were all men, but soon observers recognized that at least 60 percent of the strikers were women. With thousands on strike, manufacturers were unable to round up strikebreakers. The spread of the strike to so many other areas challenged manufacturers' traditional methods for dealing with isolated strikes through the branch factory system. The strike committee noted that "[c]losing down in New York and reopening in some small shop elsewhere will no longer avail them."[47]

Individual shops held meetings during the week and mass meetings of strikers were held weekly. These included speeches in English, Spanish, Bohemian, Yiddish, and Italian. Many of the speakers were women, and on at least one occasion, former Knights of Labor and WTUL organizer Leonora O'Reilly left retirement long enough to address the crowd. Mass picketing took place on Mondays, although the committee encountered some problems getting enough pickets each time. Strikers maintained two strike headquarters in Manhattan and one in Brooklyn. To quell rumors of splits within the ranks and provide accurate strike reports, the general committee set up an information bureau. A number of small manufacturers wanted to settle immediately, but the strike committee took several days to draft a citywide bill of prices along with instructions for settling. Strikers raised money by holding music concerts and appealing to unions and shops in the city.[48]

New York manufacturers denounced strikers for walking out and leaving the day's tobacco behind to spoil when the strike began. They argued that they could not possibly afford to grant the wage demands, but the general committee replied that employers were only "whining and seeking sympathy." Manufacturers found the demand for a grievance committee most disturbing and asked for further clarification of its proposed function. Trade journals pronounced in headlines that "Striking Cigar Makers Demand Practical Control of Factories," and articles equated striking with various forms of radicalism, such as the IWW and Bolshevism. In response, the strike committee replied that "if endeavoring to live like a human being is Bolshevism, then we are for it heart and soul."[49]

On July 7 about twenty-five hundred Boston cigar makers began an unsanctioned strike for a wage increase of 13⁷⁄₁₁ percent, a fairer share of company profits, they stated. The *Boston Evening Transcript* reported that Boston manufacturers had rejected union demands for wage increases and a shop committee. Recently, cigar makers had prohibited the weighing of any tobacco in the Boston shops and manufacturers claimed that the practice had cost them a good deal of money. When manufacturers offered in late July to accept all demands except the grievance committee, members rejected the move and continued the strike in order not to "break one link in the chain" of the larger strike movement. Within hours of the Boston strike, Manchester cigar makers also left their benches for a wage increase at R. G. Sullivan. At the end of the month, unionists in St. Louis began their second strike of the year.[50]

Strikes continued to spread to nonunion workers throughout July and observers in New York expressed surprise at the enthusiastic response from cigar makers elsewhere who had previously been thought "unassailable." The number of factories out continued to grow as strikes spread to factories in Chrome and Jersey City, New Jersey, and several places in Pennsylvania. GHP Cigar Company factories in Perth Amboy, Hanover, and Lancaster joined the list by the end of the month. By mid to late July most of the factories of General Cigar, Bayuk, Klorfein, and Gans in New Jersey and Pennsylvania were under siege. Strikes in Baltimore, Poughkeepsie, and several places in Ohio were reported in the *Call*.[51] Around July 14, cigar strikes in Philadelphia gained momentum and within two weeks all factories in the city were closed "tight as a drum." About 80 percent of the strikers in Philadelphia were women. Women team workers in Binghamton, New York, struck against the largest companies there, including American Cigar, asking for wage increases of $1.50 per thousand. Philip Wagaman, a cigar maker and seventh vice-president of the Pennsylvania Federation of Labor, remarked that "anyone predicting a strike of this magnitude even as late as six months ago, would have been deemed an idiot." The national strike encompassed "every language and dialect under the sun," he marvelled. Some rallies needed six interpreters to speak to the audience. The strike was the largest the industry had ever known. By any measure, the proportions of the strike were becoming astounding.[52]

Although strikes seemed to spread by communities, they actually traveled within each company as strikers urged workers in branch factories elsewhere to join them. Representatives thus traveled to different communities in adjacent areas where their firms had branches. For example, cigar makers striking against the Seidenberg Company in Philadelphia (owned by American Cigar) crossed the river to Camden, New Jersey, and made their way to that Seidenberg factory, urging women there to strike. Although manufacturers had voluntarily given a wage increase of fifty cents three weeks earlier, the one thousand factory workers at the plant all left their jobs. Indeed, the *Reading Labor Advocate* pointed out, manufacturers had customarily broken strikes by shifting production to a branch factory, but the current movement would make it "impossible to play this hide and seek game." Strikers regarded manufacturers' threats to move with some "merriment," another *Advocate* article explained. "They cannot figure out where the bosses will move their shops except to the planet Mars as every centre of the United States is already involved in the strike." [53]

Many strikes began with only wage demands, but most strikers eventually adopted the general format of the New York movement, including a grievance committee, shortened hours, a 50 percent or so increase in wages, and/or equalization of wages in a given city or area. Stressing that the CMIU did not control or direct the strike movement, the *Advocate* termed the strike a "rank and file" effort which included cigar makers, packers, strippers, and all other factory labor. [54]

Strikes hit every major cigar center in July and August, but those in rural Pennsylvania were perhaps the most intriguing and surprising. The *Call* commented that the "spirit of revolt" in the "country districts" in particular was a development one would "never believe . . . was possible." According to one estimate, about 17,000 Pennsylvania cigar workers were out on strike in mid-August. Strikes swept factories in Allentown, Emaus, Coplay, and South Bethlehem in the Lehigh Valley; Perkasie, Quakertown, and Sellersville in Bucks Country; Boyertown, Sinking Springs, Womelsdorf, Hamburg, and Reading in Berks County; East Greenville, Gilbertsville, Pennsburg, Red Hill, Green Lane, Sumneytown, Pottstown, and Norristown in Montgomery County; Ephrata, Denver, Lititz, Manheim, and Lancaster City in Lancaster County. Workers in several York and Harrisburg factories also left work. In Philadelphia the industry had already shut down completely. [55]

Before late July, Pennsylvania strikes had been numerous, but relatively uncoordinated. CMIU officials met in Ephrata on July 27 and hosted a statewide meeting in Reading on August 3. Representatives from striking factories, primarily in the First and Ninth Internal Revenue districts where the strike was centered, formed a general strike committee (composed entirely of men, not all of whom were unionists) to coordinate the strike and agreed to adopt the New York strike demands. The next day the committee declared a general strike of cigar workers in Pennsylvania and the state CMIU Blue Label League handled distributing a list of demands to all manufacturers, "whether they be individuals, partnerships or corporations." In addition to the 50 percent wage increase, the shortened workday, and the right to a shop committee, strikers demanded good stock, "a sufficient amount of wrappers and binder" for making the required number of cigars, the "equalization" of work in slack times, and the payment of all wages weekly in cash. The committee also began publishing the *Cigarmakers' Bulletin* to provide information on the progress of the strikes in each town. The first issue appeared on August 6 and reported that in East Greenville "we are still 90% out at Eisenlohr's, 100% at American Tobacco Corp. and at Pennsburg Eisenlohr, 11 out of 72 went in this morning. At Klorfein they are going out at 10 o'clock; what percentage is going out we will let you know tomorrow." In Philadelphia, cigar makers issued demands on August 4 (although all factories had already been closed for ten days) which repeated those of New York and elsewhere. A federal mediator intervened on August 15, but he reported that Philadelphia "manufacturers manifest no disposition to meet and confer with representatives of the men and women on strike, nor will they give me anything in the way of a counter proposal to submit to them." Throughout the state, local chapters of the WTUL assisted in conducting the strike.[56]

The once-quiet towns of Perkasie, Sellersville, and Quakertown, like so many other communities, were now scenes of intense activity. The first few weeks of July, when life seemed to proceed normally, had been deceptive. The yearly religious camp meeting opened in Perkasie on July 14 at the local park as always, but just ten days later cigar makers from the entire North Penn district met in Quakertown to discuss the strike in Pennsylvania and New York. On Saturday, July 28, Perkasie cigar makers began a walkout which spread to Sellersville and Quakertown. Not every factory in Sellersville joined the strike, and Mary Diehl recalled her foreman forbidding women to go to the windows to watch the parade of strikers and warning those who wanted to join the strike that "your jobs will not be open when you come back." Nevertheless, by the end of the week operations throughout the North Penn Valley were "practically at a standstill," according to the *Doylestown Daily Intelligencer.* "For the first time in the history of Quakertown," the front-page story continued, "practically every cigar factory of consequence is tied up."[57]

Throughout the counties of the country districts, the strikes proceeded along similar lines, and each locale shared information in the *Bulletin*. Public rallies were held at least weekly and meetings of strikers by town or by shop occurred more frequently. In Red Hill, for example, a spokesman reported that "we have meetings every morning." In addition, to raise funds for "those in need," strikers in each area sponsored ball games (Perkasie played Quakertown on August 5), picnics, dances, and band concerts. Cigar makers in Green Lane even held an "ice cream party" at the Red Men's Hall in town. The method of spreading the strike continued the general company-based pattern, with General Cigar and Eisenlohr seemingly serving as the focus of activity, but cigar makers in the country districts added a new twist. Parades of strikers moved from branch to branch, town to town, accompanied by town marching bands or a fife and drum corps. As they approached each factory where a few cigarmakers were still at work, "funeral dirges were played." In some cases they marched on foot, in others they rounded up automobiles to carry them forward. When East Greenville strikers heard a rumor on August 8, that Klorfein workers in Pennsburg were considering coming out, they hastily assembled a parade and marched to the nearby town. The Klorfein cigar workers, related one of the marchers, "joined us and we marched back to the hall and held another meeting and organized the necessary committee and appointed pickets."[58]

One of the biggest demonstrations was held in Quakertown on August 12. Over three hundred strikers from the Perkiomen Valley squeezed into some fifty automobiles and traveled to Quakertown. There they joined with the thirty-member East Greenville fife and drum corps and cigar makers from North Penn in marching through the streets of Quakertown. Estimates of the crowd ranged from one thousand to eighteen hundred, "of which very many were women." Twenty carloads of strikers journeyed to the General Cigar factory in Trumbauersville carrying banners emblazoned with "Your Last Chance," "The Longer You Stay In The Longer We Must Stay Out," "We Ask a Working Wage," and "America United We Stand." Workers at the Eisenlohr factory had joined the strike the day before. By evening the strikers returned for another parade and rally at Lulu Park.[59]

If the North Penn area was typical, then strikers may have enjoyed significant local support and sympathy. Local businessmen in Quakertown aided strikers and contributed money from the outset. At public meetings there and in Perkasie, local leaders spoke and encouraged the workers and at least one clergyman addressed a Quakertown crowd, urging it "to conduct a clean, open fight." Bystanders cheered and waved handkerchiefs when "several hundred strikers" marched to band music between Perkasie and Sellersville on August 15, and the *Bulletin* reported enthusiastic public support for the strikes in the whole region. Local sympathy may have been based on a general recognition that wartime living costs and cigar prices had risen, but wages had not. The *Doylestown Daily Intelligencer* continuously reported the strike sympathetically, noting in one story that "it is a fact that many families . . . were hardly able any longer to meet honest debts." The paper also noted that "the principal factories at Quakertown are operated by New York and Philadelphia concerns." Thus another possible explanation of local sentiment was the feeling that the firms were outsiders in contrast to workers, who were local people.[60]

The general strike committee based in Reading oversaw the strike and acted as a clearinghouse, but it was not controlled by the CMIU. Certainly the union organized locals and took an active part in the strike, but the CMIU did not direct it, and *Bulletin* reports only occasionally mentioned the union. Most locals in the state joined the movement and gave it money, but neither they nor Perkins seem to have played a leading role in it. The *York Dispatch* remarked that while few strikers belonged to the CMIU, they were so well coordinated "in spirit and action" that they were "acting as one organization."[61]

While local strike committees appeared to have been composed primarily of men, notices of meetings included women speakers, both from Philadelphia and from the local area. The *Bulletin* gradually included more mention of "the women and girls" who not only dominated the strikes of the Lehigh Valley, but who were clearly visible in the country districts. Initially the Doylestown newspaper's account of the strike included no mention of gender, but soon noted that "many women, who compose the majority of the strikers, are taking an active part on committees, as well as picketing and soliciting funds, and are handling their end of the strike in a very creditable manner." The belated recognition was not without irony, but suggested that labor militancy was not confined to the male sex.[62]

While workers in most cigar-making towns in Bucks, Berks, Montgomery, and Lancaster counties struck, the strike movement encountered less success in York County. Most cigar workers at General Cigar in York City had walked out, but they represented only about a quarter of the town's cigar workers. The company offered a one dollar increase and an additional one dollar bonus for those who returned to work and brought someone else with them, but General Cigar workers remained firm. They were not, however, joined by fellow workers in the city. Even more complacent were the cigar makers of Red Lion. Not a single strike was reported in the town during the entire upheaval.[63]

Just why cigar makers to the east struck enthusiastically while Red Lion workers remained at their benches invites explanation. Perhaps the movement simply lost momentum as it moved westward. Also, the gender ratio in the two areas differed: women outnumbered men to a greater extent in Red Lion and York County than they did to the east. Yet women were the majority of workers in other strike centers, particularly in nearby Lehigh Valley, so sex ratios reveal little. A more likely explanation lay in the very structure of the industry and the workplace in the two regions. In all of the counties save York, cigar manufacturing was dominated by "New York and Philadelphia concerns," and had been so for many years. Eisenlohr, Lipshutz, Klorfein, Gans, General, Roig and Lansdorf, Theobald and Oppenheimer—these were the names familiar to cigar makers throughout the region. While these companies employed local help, the upper management came from outside the area. In Red Lion, by contrast, the heart of the industry was conducted by local businessmen who had started the industry and built it up. Red Lion did not have an Eisenlohr factory until 1917, the same year that San Telmo opened a branch factory in the town. I. Lewis of New Jersey opened a factory there in 1919, but these large firms arrived late and were in a distinct minority in Red Lion. Cigar makers and even the general community in the eastern counties might more easily see employers in oppositional terms, while in Red Lion, local elites dominated the cigar business. Opposition to them automatically had less legitimacy than elsewhere. Too, the strike tended to spread by branches, rather than from town to town. Red Lion was simply not a branch factory town. Work process itself may have reinforced this general pattern. Red Lion cigar makers did not work under the team system, while those in the other counties did, a fact which may have facilitated their recognition of common interest.[64]

Strikes continued elsewhere in August. Chicago cigar makers in Local 527, led by Jake Billow, decided to strike beginning August 4, and while Perkins dutifully circulated their strike petition, he tried to discourage the application and it was defeated. From twenty-five hundred to four thousand Chicago cigar makers struck anyway, demanding an overall 5(percent increase, an extra dollar an hour for working bad stock or having to wait for tobacco, and a grievance committee. Although numerous small manufacturers settled fairly quickly, the large firms resisted the demands.[65]

The strike committee cautioned cigar makers that various manufacturers were offering "false promises" in order to get them back to work. In Jersey City, New Jersey, strikers complained that manufacturers spread rumors that the strike had ended as a ruse to break it. New strikes in Newark, Elizabethport, and Greenville, New Jersey, lengthened the list of walkouts in the state, however, and those which had begun earlier continued. Several factories in Baltimore, Milwaukee, and Evansville closed as cigar makers there joined the ranks of the strikers. At the same time, the number of authorized union strikes climbed. Union cigar makers in Westfield, Massachusetts, demanded that manufacturers provide free ice water from July through October each year and insisted that no sweeping could take place in the factory during working hours. Various estimates of the extent of strike activity by mid-August ranged from 90,000 to over 120,000. Perkins remarked that there were so many strikes of unionists by August that the only way he could manage the files was to assign them numbers.[66]

Women working in every major five-cent cigar center joined the strike except those in Detroit. Unionists struck in that city in August, but women failed to venture forth this time, likely recalling their own struggle and defeat three years earlier. Local CMIU members chided women in the pages of the *Detroit Labor News* for not moving to do something about their "sorry" conditions.[67]

Strikers frequently confronted police, particularly when injunctions prohibited picketing. Arrests of both men and women took place in New Brunswick, New York City, Philadelphia, Norristown, Poughkeepsie, and elsewhere in August. In Binghamton, women cigar makers painted some of the houses of those who had not struck and several "daubed" workers "with grease and syrup."[68] Workers also frequently invoked the values for which the recent war had been fought. One of the rallying cries of the strike, for example, was: "An American Standard of Living—44 Hours a week." Strikers protested "Kaiserism" and "un-American conditions," and termed manufacturers' refusal to deal with workers and their demands as "un-American." Cigar makers had supported the "just fight against Autocracy," but had received nothing in return. Using wartime symbolism to justify and legitimate their fight, male cigar makers in Pennsylvania wore army uniforms while picketing and marching and parades of strikers carried the American flag.[69]

George Perkins would have given almost anything to stop or contain the strike wave. He feared its radicalism and worried about whether the strike could possibly serve the union's interests. He agreed that cigar makers had justifiable reasons for striking, but the current movement could be successful only if "kept within reasonable bounds and guided by men of experience." He attacked the "revolutionary" leaders who challenged his authority, denounced "bolshevik" tendencies, and decried unauthorized strikes. Current conditions presented opportunities to organize the unorganized, but "hasty, ill-timed action" only wasted the chance. He labeled the cigar makers who had struck without first working up stock or presenting any demands as "irresponsible." Members turned down another bid to raise dues and union finances remained shaky. Perkins warned those who had not yet struck that if too many tried to collect benefits at one time he would have to levy heavier assessments.[70]

Manufacturers denounced the strikes as the work of Bolsheviks or the IWW, and bitterly attacked the idea of the grievance committee. *Tobacco* editorialized that "the manufacturers see in the shop committee a menace which will place the factory completely in the power of the employees." The *U.S. Tobacco Journal* concurred: the shop committee aimed at "practical control of the factories." As a group, cigar makers were known to be difficult, unpredictable, and particularly prone to striking. Indeed, their actions invited mechanization as a possible solution. "Cigar labor has been for years whimsical, where it has not been dictatorial in the extreme." Labor "demands too much," and forced manufacturers to look elsewhere for relief. Strikes had occurred almost weekly for two years, the *Tobacco Leaf* noted, "yet rarely, if ever, do we hear of labor trouble in the cigarette business. . . . Eventually machinery will solve the cigar-making problem just as it solved the cigarette-making problem."[71]

The strike had reached unbelievable proportions by August, uniting workers from diverse areas and backgrounds and launching the greatest strike movement in the history of the cigar industry. Yet by early August, a distinct uneasiness prevailed among cigar makers in the country's most secure union city, Boston. Rumors had spread that one of the leading companies there had opened branch factories elsewhere. Soon the awful word came. Waitt and Bond was operating two strike factories in Newark, New Jersey, under the name of Park Cigar Company, but worse, the cigars were being made by automatic machines run by unskilled women. Henry

Hilfers, CMIU secretary in Newark, watched the machines in operation and grimly confirmed the reports to Perkins. After years of rumor and threat, the dreaded machine had finally been perfected.[72]

The American Machine and Foundry Company (AMF), former subsidiary of Duke's American Tobacco Company, had invested several million dollars and eighteen years of effort, but had ultimately succeeded in designing a machine to make cigars "complete." No one doubted the opportunity the new machine provided to replace the old labor force with a new one and AMF carefully instructed prospective users that only young women, new to the industry, should be hired. "Cigar makers are too particular," the company explained. "Hire green hands and break them in." The device took four operators. The first fed tobacco filler leaves into an "endless feed belt," while the machine cut the filler to size and pressed it together. At the same time a second operator spread a binder leaf out on a suction plate. The machine rolled the filler into the binder and carried the bunch to the wrapper layer, who stretched the wrapper leaf on another suction plate. The machine rolled the cigar, finished the head, and sent it on to the fourth operator, who inspected it. The experimental machines in Newark could produce from six thousand to eight thousand cigars a day.[73]

Hints about improved machinery had surfaced all year. Even advertisements in the trade press seemed to prepare for changes in the methods of production. "The old 'Strictly Hand-Made' slogan" had been handed down through families, one ad began, but in the future, manufacturers would need to think about machinery. With a machine "a mere hand worker becomes the controller of a mechanism that does his work. . . . There is something to stir his imagination . . . and a feeling inside the man that he has moved upward several rungs on the ladder of his life's accomplishments." Trade journal articles throughout the year had frequently linked the use of machinery with the outbreak of so many strikes. No amount of clues, however, could have eased the shock that Waitt and Bond, one of the nation's foremost blue label factories, had been the first to adopt machinery and had done so to break a strike. By the end of the month, Waitt and Bond had closed its Boston factory and two other companies, Breslin and Campbell and CCA Cigar, also left the city.[74]

In front of the Park Cigar Company factories in Newark, union cigar makers conducted intensive picketing. Inevitably, their anger and sense of betrayal produced several public disturbances, especially when the company asked for and temporarily got an injunction against the pickets.

Courtroom testimony revealed that Waitt and Bond had actually operated the Newark factories since January. Back in Boston demoralized cigar makers agreed to compromise conditions. They dropped the grievance committee, accepted a 7 percent wage increase, and permitted the weighing of all tobacco. Members of the strike committee resigned in protest.[75]

The last days of August brought depressing news from many corners. In Chicago the largest manufacturers were pulling out of the city altogether. Within two weeks forty-two new buckeyes took out licenses as cigar makers staved off unemployment by opening their own shops.[76] Reports from New York and Pennsylvania indicated that some strikers were returning to work. The Binghamton walkout ended with only a few concessions from manufacturers, and women there complained about a lack of support from male unionists. The Manchester strike ended more happily than the one in Boston, although cigar makers got one dollar less than they had demanded. Perkins wearily answered a letter from AFL secretary Frank Morrison: "Replying to yours of recent date in which you state I am evidently having my troubles. I want to say that you are more than right."[77]

In early September both Perkins and Gompers finally gave the New York strike a public endorsement and Gompers sent a circular to all affiliated locals requesting donations. Yet the strike movement had already started to unravel there as well as in Pennsylvania. Federal mediator Elmer Greenawalt, formerly a cigar maker, did not reach the Philadelphia area until the end of August, when manufacturers "declined both collectively and individually" to accept his services. The tone of the *Bulletin* began flagging by late August as more cigar makers headed back to the factories, although as of August 27, the general strike committee counted 9,322 Pennsylvania cigar makers still out on strike. The strike committee reorganized on September 12, but workers increasingly returned to their jobs as "manufacturers started to make compromise offers." At a September 28 meeting in Reading, the strike committee agreed to encourage strikers to settle with independents on the "best terms possible." At first the committee pledged to continue the fight against chain factories, but when the latter offered concessions, strikers began accepting. Pennsylvania wage settlements ranged from 10 to 25 percent, but rights to organize or have grievance committees were not recognized. Jane Hollenbach explained that strikers felt forced to return to work. They "couldn't afford to stay out too long because they had their home and we wasn't rich." The resentment toward those who had not gone out was intense and had resulted in scattered incidents throughout the strike. Once workers re-

turned to work in Perkasie, with only a small increase, "it was kind of in-
sulting to us, because they [strikebreakers] got the same price and didn't
lose any money, and we did, fighting for it. They were babies and didn't
fight for it." Wage increases in New Jersey ranged from $1.50 up and
CMIU organizers there commented that few had returned to work before
agreements were reached.[78]

In New York the strikes followed a similar pattern although the process
stretched further into the fall. Some smaller firms began settling in September, putting about four thousand back to work. Gradually others
settled without the sanction of the strike committee. A conference between strikers and the manufacturers association reached no agreement
on September 18, but piecemeal settlements continued. Finally in early
October the committee reached a general compromise agreement with a
number of independent manufacturers, on increases of 10 to 15 percent,
and many workers returned to their benches on October 25. The trust
began offering wage increases of about 10 percent and by late November
most New York factories were busy filling Christmas orders. Perkins noted
at the end of the year that "practically every nonunionist in the country"
and most union members had received wage increases of one to two dollars per thousand during the year.[79]

The strike movement achieved wage increases for thousands of cigar
makers, but it signified much more. For the first time union and nonunion
workers, encouraged by wartime conditions, particularly the labor shortage, had joined together to challenge manufacturers' power in the industry. For years craft unionism had been unable to bridge the gap between
union men and nonunion women. The CMIU had been forged and shaped
out of one work culture and was ill suited for another. Despite the differences in traditions and practices of the two work cultures, they held important elements in common. Both drew on a sense of community and
cooperation and both asserted, albeit in different degrees and forms, collective control over the conditions of work. The demands of the strike
movement and its militant tone centered on control in the workplace. By
speaking directly to both cultures, the movement galvanized large numbers of cigar makers into action. The demands for shorter hours, higher
wages, and worker self-management in the shape of a grievance committee, pulled cigar makers into an unusual alliance and suggested potential
for a new form of organization.[80]

But the convergence of the two groups of cigar makers and their victories were fleeting. Some pieces of evidence suggest that their united

movement was undermined in part by internal differences. Jane Hollenbach from Perkasie recalled the intense hostility many women workers
there felt toward the CMIU. In the midst of the strike it had organized a
local, which they felt had taken their money unfairly. Women in New
Brunswick, New Jersey, retained bitter memories of the CMIU for at least
ten years and refused in 1929 to affiliate with the union during a strike
there, recalling that the union had collected their dues and had not given
them anything in return.[81]

Yet the most powerful forces of containment and disruption came from
the state and employers. Both the Justice Department's Bureau of Investigation and the Intelligence Division of the War Department kept tabs
on cigar makers and their strikes after 1917. Spies attended and reported
on meetings and pried into the affairs of leaders. The Bureau of Investigation described Jake Billow as advocating the "soviet idea applied to the
cigar industry," and in this he was aided by "Henry Abrahams of Boston,
J. M. Barnes in Philadelphia, and I. Sommerfeld in Chicago." Barnes,
"strong" in his "Socialistic tendencies," was of particular interest to the
bureau and agents reported on his activities and movements throughout
1917 and 1918. Reports for both agencies were filed on various other leaders of the strike movement. A State Department memo passed to Gompers and Perkins via the Military Intelligence Division of the War Department claimed that "bolshevist leaders (IWW) are concentrating their
energy in the U.S. among the Cigar Makers." Gompers did not attempt to
dispute the claim, but explained to agents that his enemies were intent
upon fully discrediting him. The "instigators" were "Russians and Jews
and . . . they are well known to him," the federal agents reported.[82]

Of particular interest were Boston, New York, Tampa, Philadelphia,
and Chicago. Local 527 was reported to be "infested with an unusual
number of radicals," and military intelligence officers reported on the
"radical literature" being read in Tampa and Key West factories. Often
these reports were sloppy. One in 1919 related with complete seriousness
that the AFL and its affiliates had engaged in "bayonet practice" in meetings. A military intelligence report on the CMIU in Tampa referred to the
union's president as Charles W. Perkins and seemed gratified to report that
the organization had branches in "Boston, Mass.; New York City, Milwaukee, Wisconsin," but was "most numerous" in the latter city. It concluded with the peculiar remark that "while the Key West branch of this
organization is controlled from Tampa, the Tampa branch is controlled
from Chicago." Agents also reported that Tampa cigar makers in May

1919 were anticipating a strike in August and that all efforts "are made to lessen the productivity in order that the manufacturers might not be allowed to obtain a surplus in their storehouses and vaults." In New York City, Local 90 was seen to be "radical-connected," while investigators in Boston identified Local 97 officers as the "inner ring" who framed the infamous resolution in the spring.[83]

Manufacturers found the strike movement intolerable. "It is a regrettable fact that cigar makers have mishandled the striking privilege more than any other body of workers," said *Tobacco Leaf*. "The records show that cigar makers are in the habit of striking on extremely short notice; indeed not infrequently they have struck first, and given their reasons for striking afterwards."[84] Manufacturers by early 1920 referred to 1919 as a "nightmare," and named labor as the number one problem in the industry. Too many manufacturers had given in to wage increases which had encouraged irresponsible labor leaders to become "emboldened" by this success, and beginning in July 1919 these leaders had "attempted a coup" in the industry. The movement had been "virulently infected" with the "Russian theory of soviet government." Strikers' demands had contemplated "the confiscation of the entire investment of the industry for the benefit of those who would term themselves 'the working class.'" Cigar makers had, during the strike, been "repeatedly held up by their employees and forced to agree to an undeservedly large remuneration, under the threat of not being able to manufacture cigars at all."[85]

To meet the challenge, manufacturers had stiffly resisted strikes during the summer and by offering compromises had helped to dampen the wave by late August. Undercover, however, some companies had attempted to disrupt the movement. Charles Winfield, one of the leaders of Local 527, was apparently employed by the American Cigar Company, and sent reports not only to the company, but to the Military Intelligence Division as well. Although the records are inconclusive, evidence surfaced in 1921 which suggested that Billow, who in 1920 led Local 527 out of the CMIU, had been working for a detective agency, and the accusation completely discredited him in the eyes of Chicago cigar makers. Companies in New York began relocating elsewhere, and by the fall of 1919 hardly a large firm remained in Chicago. Sam Paley moved his Congress Cigar Company to Philadelphia in early September.[86]

Employers had already begun to see the machine as a powerful instrument of control and intimidation. "Cigar makers . . . are ill-advised if they create conditions now that cause manufacturers to take thought concerning cigar machinery," warned *Tobacco*. In another article the journal advised that "if hand labor becomes too unreasonable and costly that it cannot be employed except at constant loss, the manufacturer may see what he can do with machinery." John W. Merriam, whose New York factory had been a target in the recent strike, declared in an interview with *Tobacco Leaf* that the cigar makers had only themselves to blame. They had "by their arrogant attitude and impossible demands during the present preposterous strike" triggered the introduction of machinery. He predicted in the *U.S. Tobacco Journal* that "the time is not distant when the machine will almost entirely replace hand labor in the cigar making business."[87]

The strategy of simultaneous strikes posed a challenge to the evolving structure of the industry—large firms with many branches. It foiled the manufacturers' usual tactic of shifting work from a strike site to another location. Manufacturers also found the movement chilling because it raised the specter of a united labor force. The size of the strikes, their mood, the nature of their demands, and the break with traditional unionism made them a significant moment in the working lives of cigar makers and a clear threat to manufacturers.

The threat was short-lived. Employer intimidation, government surveillance, worker poverty, and postwar reconversion defined the final battle lines in the industry's war. The cigar machine was the manufacturers' ultimate weapon. On the eve of technological revolution in the industry, cigar makers converged into a massive strike movement, but their combined strength proved no match for the forces arrayed against them.

Notes

1. *Tobacco Leaf*, 18 May 1917, pp. 3, 5; 24 May 1917, p. 3; 14 June 1917, pp. 3, 7; 19 July 1917, p. 6; 4 Oct. 1917, p. 22; 18 Oct. 1917, p. 3; 23 Nov. 1917, p. 20; 29 Nov. 1917, p. 30; 20 Dec. 1917, p. 9.

2. *Tobacco Leaf*, 4 Jan. 1917, pp. 5, 6; 1 Mar. 1917, p. 3; 24 May 1917, p. 6; 31 May 1917, p. 6; 28 June 1917, p. 3; 16 Aug. 1917, p. 40; 6 Sept. 1917, p. 29; 18 Oct. 1917, p. 42; 25 Oct. 1917, p. 3; 8 Nov. 1917, p. 3. General Cigar became the new name of United Cigar Manufacturers in December 1916. The change was made because of confusion with United Cigar Stores, the retail chain of the trust. See *Tobacco Leaf*, 1 Mar. 1917, p. 4.

3. *Tobacco Leaf*, 24 Jan. 1918, p. 5; 31 Jan. 1918, p. 34; 14 Feb. 1918, p. 14; 28 Mar. 1918, p. 3; 16 May 1918, p. 3; 1 Aug. 1918, p. 4; 26 Sept. 1918, p. 32; *U.S. Tobacco Journal*, 4 May 1918, p. 12.

4. *Tobacco Leaf*, 23 Feb. 1917, p. 45; 29 Mar. 1917, p. 16; 17 May 1917, p. 5; 5 July 1917, p. 39; 26 July 1917, p. 5; 6 Sept. 1917, p. 39; 1 Nov. 1917, p. 3.

5. *Tobacco Leaf*, 21 Feb. 1918, p. 40; 7 Mar. 1918, p. 35; 23 June 1918, p. 38; 1 Aug. 1918, p. 4; 3 Oct. 1918, p. 5; 10 Oct. 1918, p. 38; 17 Oct. 1918, pp. 9–10; Deferred Classification, General Correspondence, file 8–A1, Labor Division, War Industries Board, Record Group (R.G.) 61, National Archives (NA), Washington, D.C.

6. *Tobacco Leaf*, 8 Mar. 1917, p. 43; 8 May 1917, p. 24; 24 May 1917, pp. 24, 42.

7. *Tobacco Leaf*, 11 Jan. 1917, p. 5; 21 June 1917, p. 7; *CMOJ*, Feb. 1917, p. 17; July 1917, pp. 15–16.

8. *CMOJ*, May 1917, p. 16; June 1917, pp. 16, 17; Dec. 1917, p. 21; *Tobacco Leaf*, 29 Mar. 1917, p. 8; 24 May 1917, p. 38; 31 May 1917, p. 26; 7 June 1917, p. 34.

9. *CMOJ*, Jan. 1917, p. 19; *Tobacco Leaf*, 17 May 1917, pp. 45–46; 24 May 1917, p. 26; 31 May 1917, p. 46.

10. *Tobacco Leaf*, 31 May 1917, p. 49; 14 June 1917, p. 30; 12 July 1917, p. 20; 19 July 1917, p. 8; 13 Dec. 1917, p. 20; 27 Dec. 1917, pp. 24, 28; CMIU circular, 31 Oct. 1917, Box 2, folder 7, Papers of Local 162, State Historical Society of Wisconsin (SHSW).

11. "Report of the Executive Council of the American Federation of Labor," 18 Apr. 1918, Box 1, Cornelia Pinchot Papers, Library of Congress (LC); *CMOJ*, Jan. 1918, p. 16; Feb. 1918, p. 9; *U.S. Tobacco Journal*, 20 Apr. 1918, p. 20; 6 June 1918, p. 5; 20 June 1918, p. 11; *Tobacco Leaf*, 23 May 1918, p. 32; 4 July 1918, p. 20; 25 July 1918, p. 18; 31 Oct. 1918, p. 44.

12. *Tobacco Leaf*, 21 Feb. 1918, pp. 3, 6; *U.S. Tobacco Journal*, 27 Apr. 1918, pp. 4, 16; 4 May 1918, p. 5.

13. *CMOJ*, Apr. 1917, p. 6; June 1917, pp. 10–11; July 1917, p. 27; Aug. 1917, p. 9; Oct. 1917, p. 23; *Tobacco Leaf*, 26 July 1917, p. 14; Jan. 1918, p. 2; Aug. 1918, pp. 4, 6.

14. CMIU circular, 2 Nov. 1917, Box 2, folder 1, Papers of Local 162, SHSW.

15. *Tobacco Leaf*, 28 June 1917, p. 44; 25 July 1918, p. 18; *U.S. Tobacco Journal*, 20 Mar. 1920, p. 3. As Sullivan's funeral procession moved past the Amoskeag mills, it paused briefly as textile mill workers filed out along the sidewalk to watch the cortege pass.

16. *CMOJ*, Mar. 1917, p. 2; Aug. 1917, p. 7; Sept. 1917, p. 3.

17. *Washington Post*, 12 May 1918; Emma Steghagen to Executive Board Members, 18 Apr. 1918, Reel 2, National Women's Trade Union League Papers, LC; *CMOJ*, May 1918, p. 13; Cornelia Pinchot to Miss Guggenheimer, 7 Apr. 1918, Box 1, Cornelia Pinchot Papers, LC; Ethel M. Smith, "Low Wages Send Cigar Makers on Strike," *Life and Labor*, 8 (1918), 92–93; Case no. 1, War Labor Board, R.G. 2, NA; *Tobacco Leaf*, 4 Apr. 1918, p. 18; Offterdinger strike, file 33/1357, Federal Mediation and Conciliation Service (FMCS), R.G. 280, NA; Ethel M. Smith, "In the Dooryard of the World's Largest Employer," *Life and Labor*, 11 (1921), 179.

18. *CMOJ*, Oct. 1917, p. 16; CMIU circular, 15 Aug. 1917, Box 2, folder 1, and 11 Sept. 1917, Box 1, folder 4, Cigar Makers' International Union of America, Papers of Cigar Makers' Local 162, Green Bay, Wis., SHSW; *Tobacco Leaf,* 21 Feb. 1918, p. 3.

19. Joint Unions of Chicago to the Officers and Members of Local Unions, CMIU circular, 4 Jan. 1919, Box 1, folder 4, Cigar Makers' Joint Unions of Chicago; Bulletin no. 2, 1 Apr. 1919, Box 1, folder 4; Perkins to the Officers and Members of Local Unions, 27 June 1918, Box 2, folder 2, Papers of Local 162, SHSW.

20. Circular, "Strike Bulletin No. 1," Joint Unions of Chicago to All Cigar Makers, 30 Jan. 1919; Circular, "Statement about the Locked-Out Cigar Makers of the 'La Preferencia' Cigar Co.," 8 Apr. 1919, Box 1, folder 4, Papers of Local 162, SHSW; Joint Advisory Board to Perkins, 16 Aug. 1919, Reel 36, *American Federation of Labor Records: The Samuel Gompers Era* (Sanford, N.C., 1979). On the Tampa strike, see Durward Long, "The Open-Closed Shop Battle in Tampa's Cigar Industry," *Florida Historical Quarterly,* 67 (1968), 101–21.

21. S. J. Butler to I. Sommerfeld, 27 Mar. 1918, Papers of the American Federation of Labor, "Cigar Makers, 1901–1937," Reed 36, *American Federation of Labor Records; CMOJ,* Sept. 1917, pp. 18, 26.

22. Perkins to Samuel Gompers, 19 Jan. 1918; Perkins to Executive Board, 27 Mar. 1918, Reel 36, *American Federation of Labor Records.*

23. *CMOJ*, Jan. 1917, p. 27; "Preliminary Report of Conditions," 6 Apr. 1917, file 33/332, FMCS, R.G. 280, NA. Members also disagreed over the constitutional minimum for a bill of prices. They did agree on changing the constitution to allow members serving overseas to collect death benefits. Locals also campaigned to urge the government to purchase union label cigars for American troops. See *CMOJ,* Sept. 1917, p. 22 and Labor Division, file 8-A1, folder 75, War Industries Board, R.G. 61, NA.

24. *Call,* New York, 17, 19 Feb. 1919; *Tobacco Leaf,* 21 Feb. 1918, pp. 3, 6, 7; "What Do the Cigar Makers of New York City Want?" flyer, Strikes, Unions, Labor Troubles file, Tobacco Merchants Association Library (TMA), New York; *CMOJ,* Mar. 1918, p. 2. The demands were printed in English, Czech, Spanish, and Hebrew.

25. *Call,* 19 Feb. 1918; 2 Mar. 1918; 26 Mar. 1918; *CMOJ,* May 1918, p. 6; New York strike, file 33/568, FMCS, R.G. 280, NA. Census data and figures compiled by Lucy Winsor Killough suggest that there were perhaps only 17,000 cigar makers in the entire New York City area, including parts of New Jersey. Killough, *The Tobacco Products Industry in New York and Its Environs: Present Trends and Probable Future Developments,* Regional Plan of New York and Its Environs, Monograph no. 5 (New York, 1924), p. 25; David Lenz to Alexander Bruck Bielaski, Chief of Division of Investigation, Department of Justice, 10 Apr. 1918, file 10110–920, R.G. 165, Military Intelligence Division, War Department, NA.

26. *Call,* 2 Mar. 1918; 26 Mar. 1918; Lincoln Bros. Cigar Co. to Perkins, 4 May 1918; Perkins to Lincoln Bros., 7 May 1918; Perkins to Gompers, 7 May 1918, Reel 36, *American Federation of Labor Records; Tobacco Leaf,* 4 Apr. 1918, p. 3.

27. *Tobacco Leaf,* 21 Feb. 1918, pp. 3, 6; 9 May 1918, p. 6; 23 May 1918, p. 7; R. M. C. Glenn to Office Depot Quartermaster, 28 May 1918, files 10634–101,

R.G. 165, NA; Lenz to Bielaski, 10 Apr. 1918, file 10110–920, R.G. 165, NA; report of J. F. McDevitt, 30 July 1918, file 146772, R.G. 165, NA

28. Perkins to Gompers, 14 May 1918, Reel 36, *American Federation of Labor Records;* Memo, 28 July 1918, Chicago Staff, Military Intelligence Division, Records of the War Department General and Special Staffs, R.G. 165, NA; *CMOJ*, May 1918, p. 6. My thanks to Sara Dunlap Jackson at the National Historical Records and Publications Commission for calling my attention to Military Intelligence records. There was sympathy for the New York movement in Philadelphia as well.

29. *U.S. Tobacco Journal*, 11 May 1918, p. 6; *Call*, 12 Apr. 1918; 14 Apr. 1918; *CMOJ*, June 1918, p. 9.

30. *Tobacco Leaf*, 3 Oct. 1918, p. 4; 21 Nov. 1918, p. 3; 28 Nov. 1918, p. 36; 12 Dec. 1918, p. 3; 19 Dec. 1918, p. 5; 26 Dec. 1918, p. 3.

31. *Tobacco World*, 15 Jan. 1919, p. 11; *Tobacco Leaf*, 9 Jan. 1919, p. 4; 13 Mar. 1919, p. 10; *Tobacco*, 2 Jan. 1919, p. 33; *CMOJ*, Jan. 1919, p. 9.

32. *Tobacco*, 27 Mar. 1919, pp. 3, 4, 13; *CMOJ*, Jan. 1919, p. 7; June 1919, p. 5; Dec. 1919, p. 8; *New York Times*, 17 May 1919. Marshall's remark was made to John Crockett, chief clerk of the Senate.

33. *Tobacco Leaf*, 23 Jan. 1919, pp. 3, 4; 6 Mar. 1919, p. 9; 17 Apr. 1919, p. 4; Ograin interview, 8 July 1977, Chicago.

34. *CMOJ*, Jan. 1919, pp. 2, 4, 7; Apr. 1919, p. 3.

35. U.S. Department of Labor, *Strikes in the United States, 1880–1936*, by Florence Peterson (Washington, D.C., 1938), p. 39; *CMOJ*, Mar. 1919, p. 2.

36. *CMOJ*, Jan. 1919, p. 18.

37. *CMOJ*, Jan. 1919, p. 8; Mar. 1919, pp. 3, 4; *Tobacco*, 6 Mar. 1919, p. 16; *Tobacco Leaf*, 6 Mar. 1919, p. 32; (Trenton, N.J.) *Trades Union Advocate*, 11 Apr. 1919, 18 Apr. 1919, Reel P70–1661, Tamiment Institute, Bobst Library, New York University, New York; Fort Wayne, Indiana, strike, file 170/250, 3 June 1919, Report of the Commissioner, file 170/422, FMCS, R.G. 280, NA.

38. "Resolution Adopted by Boston Union 97," 14 Mar. 1919, Box 1, folder 4, Papers of Local 162, SHSW.

39. *CMOJ*, May 1919, pp. 2–3; June 1919, pp. 17–19; Aug. 1919, pp. 8–9; Perkins to Matthew Woll, 26 May 1919; Perkins to William B. Wilson, 26 Mar. 1919; Perkins to Woll, 26 May 1919, file 165/32, FMCS, R.G. 280, NA.

40. Circular to "All Officers and Members of Local Unions," 19 Mar. 1919, Box 2, folder 3; circular from Local 97 to "Fellow Members," Box 1, folder 4, Papers of Local 162, SHSW; Report of Intelligence officer, 9 June 1919, interview with Henry Abrahams, file 389913, R.G. 165, NA.

41. Circular, "Strike Bulletin No. 1," Joint Unions of Chicago to All Cigar Makers, 30 Jan. 1919; circular, "Statement about the Locked-Out Cigar Makers of the 'La Preferencia' Cigar Co.," 8 Apr. 1919, Box 1, folder 4, Papers of Local 162, SHSW; Joint Advisory Board to Perkins, 16 Aug. 1919, Reel 36, *American Federation of Labor Records; New Majority* (Chicago), 11 Jan. 1919, p. 12; 22 Feb. 1919, p. 13. On the Tampa strike, see Long, "Open-Closed Shop Battle in Tampa's Cigar Industry," pp. 101–21.

42. *Call*, 23 June 1919; 25 June 1919; 29 June 1919; Circular, JAB of New York

to Sirs and Brothers, "New York Cigarmakers End Their Slumbers," 10 July 1919, Box 1, folder 4, Papers of Local 162, SHSW. Unaffiliated cigar makers were represented at the meeting, but apparently did not have a role in conducting it. While the meeting endorsed the principle of industrial unionism, which theoretically would have to include women, the organizations involved were run by male cigar makers only.

43. *Call*, 30 June 1919. The council claimed there were twenty to twenty-five thousand cigar makers in New York City, but these figures are hard to substantiate. Doubtless census figures underestimated the number in the city. The general area probably had 20,000 and Manhattan alone probably had about 10,000 to 12,000. See David Montgomery, "New Tendencies in Union Struggles and Strategies in Europe and the United States, 1916–1922," in James E. Cronin and Carmen Siriani, eds., *Work, Community and Power: The Experience of Labor in Europe and America, 1900–1925* (New York, 1984), pp. 104–6. See also on wartime strikes, Cecelia F. Bucki, "Dilution and Craft Tradition: Bridgeport, Connecticut, Munitions Workers, 1915–1919," *Social Science History*, 4 (Winter 1980), 105–24.

44. See n. 43 and James Hinton, *The First Shop Stewards Movement* (London, 1973).

45. *Call*, 30 June 1919; 2 July 1919; 9 July 1919; *CMOJ*, July 1919, p. 2; Oct. 1919, pp. 10–11; *Tobacco*, 17 July 1919, p. 5; Perkins to AFL secretary Frank Morrison, 30 June 1919, Reel 36, *American Federation of Labor Records; Cigarmakers' Bulletin, Issued by General Strike-Committee of Pennsylvania*, no. 7, 14 Aug. 1919, U.S. Dept. of Labor Library (USDL), Washington, D.C.

46. *Call*, 2, 10, 17, 18 July 1919; New York State Industrial Commission, *Annual Report*, 1920 (Albany, 1921), p. 162.

47. *Call*, 3, 4, 6, 11, 15, 22 July 1919; 5, 7 Aug. 1919; Judith O'Sullivan and Rosemary Gallick, *Workers and Allies: Female Participation in the American Trade Union Movement, 1824–1976* (Washington, D.C., 1976), p. 73.

48. *Call*, 18 July 1919 and 5 Aug. 1919; *U.S. Tobacco Journal*, 4 July 1919, p. 3; 12 July 1919, p. 3.

49. *Call*, 11, 12 July 1919; *Boston Evening Transcript*, 24 July 1919; *U.S. Tobacco Journal*, 5 July 1919, p. 8; 12 July 1919, p. 8; 2 Aug. 1919, p. 2; *Tobacco*, 24 July 1919, p. 12; Circular, 5 Aug. 1919, Box 1, folder 3, SHSW; Circular to Members of Local Unions, 16 Aug. 1919, Box 2, folder 3, Papers of Local 162, SHSW.

50. *Call*, 9, 10, 12, 15, 20, 28 July 1919; *Tobacco*, 31 July 1919, p. 21.

51. *Tobacco*, 31 July 1919, p. 20; *Call*, 17, 22 July 1919; *Progressive Labor World*, 7 Aug. 1919; *U.S. Tobacco Journal*, 26 July 1919, p. 10; 2 Aug. 1919, p. 7; *Binghamton (N.Y.) Sun*, 21 Aug. 1919; *Cigarmakers' Bulletin*, no. 10, 21 Aug. 1919.

52. *U.S. Tobacco Journal*, 2 Aug. 1919, p. 7; *Call*, 25 July 1919; *York (Pa.) Labor Advocate*, 18 July 1919; *Reading Labor Advocate*, 9, 16 Aug. 1919.

53. *U.S. Tobacco Journal*, 26 July 1919, p. 10; *Tobacco*, 31 July 1919, pp. 4, 20; *Call*, 22, 23, 27 July 1919; 16 Aug. 1919; *Reading Labor Advocate*, 9 Aug. 1919.

54. *Call*, 17, 22, 23, 27 July 1919; 16 Aug. 1919; *Cigarmakers' Bulletin*, no. 5, 12 Aug. 1919; *York Gazette and Daily*, 16, 17, 19, 22, 28 July 1919; 2, 5–8, 11–16,

19–26 Aug. 1919; *Tobacco*, 31 July 1919, p. 20; *Progressive Labor World*, 7 Aug. 1919; *U.S. Tobacco Journal*, 26 July 1919, p. 10; 2 Aug. 1919, p. 7.

55. *Reading Labor Advocate*, 2 Aug. 1919; *York Gazette and Daily*, 2 Aug. 1919; *Cigarmakers' Bulletin*, no. 1, 6 Aug. 1919.

56. *Cigarmakers' Bulletin*, nos. 1 and 7, 6, 14 Aug. 1919, USDL; Preliminary Report of Elmer E. Greenawalt, 9 Sept. 1919, file 170/698, FMCS, R.G. 280, NA; *York Labor Advocate*, 22 Aug. 1919.

57. *Doylestown Daily Intelligencer*, 3, 9, 16, 24, 28, 30, 31 July 1919; Mary Diehl interview, 12 Jan. 1984, Quakertown, Pa.

58. *Cigarmakers' Bulletin*, nos. 1–11, 6–23 Aug. 1919; *Call*, 3, 13 Aug. 1919; Jane Hollenbach interview, 16 Mar. 1984, Sellersville, Pa.; *Doylestown Daily Intelligencer*, 31 July 1919.

59. *Cigarmakers' Bulletin*, no. 3, 9 Aug. 1919; no. 7, 14 Aug. 1919; *York Gazette and Daily*, 13 Aug. 1919; *Doylestown Daily Intelligencer*, 13 Aug. 1919.

60. *Doylestown Daily Intelligencer*, 30, 31 July 1919; 16 Aug. 1919; *Cigarmakers' Bulletin*, no. 2, 8 Aug. 1919.

61. *Cigarmakers' Bulletin*, nos. 1–11, 6–23 Aug. 1919; *Doylestown Daily Intelligencer*, 31 July 1919; *York Gazette and Daily*, 31 July and 11 Aug., 1919.

62. *York Gazette and Daily*, 11 Aug. 1919; *Cigarmakers' Bulletin*, no. 7, 14 Aug. 1919; *Doylestown Daily Intelligencer*, 31 July 1919.

63. *York Gazette and Daily*, 28 July 1919; 6, 7, 8, 11, 14, 19, 22, 26 Aug. 1919; *York Labor Advocate*, 22 Aug. 1919; *Cigarmakers' Bulletin*, no. 11, 23 Aug. 1919.

64. York County, *City Directories*, 1915, 1917, 1919. My thanks to Phyllis Frey at the Kaltreider Memorial Library in Red Lion for tracking down these directories for me. There are some hints in several of my interviews that anti-Semitism helped to forge this negative attitude towards the outsiders from Philadelphia since many of these upper-level managers were Jewish. Herbert Gutman found similar patterns of hometown support for strikers. See *Work, Culture, and Society in Industrializing America: Essays in Working-Class and Social History* (New York, 1977).

65. Ograin interviews, 8 July 1977 and 19 May 1979; circular, JAB Chicago, n.d. and 2 Aug. 1919, Box 1, folder 6; *The Vindicator: Published in the Interest of the Striking Cigarmakers of Chicago*, Box 1, folder 5, Papers of Local 162, SHSW; *Call*, 1, 15 Aug. 1919.

66. AFL circular, 5 Sept. 1919; Gompers to Ralph Easley, 5 Sept. 1919, Reel 36, *American Federation of Labor Records*; *Call*, 1, 3–5, 7, 8, 16, 17, 19 Aug. 1919; *CMOJ*, Aug. 1919, p. 13.

67. *Detroit Labor News*, 1, 8, 22 Aug. 1919; *CMOJ*, Mar. 1919, p. 9.

68. *Call*, 10, 20, 24 Aug. 1919; *Tobacco Leaf*, 4 Sept. 1919, p. 3; *Tobacco*, 28 Aug. 1919, p. 20; *Binghamton (N.Y.) Sun*, 21 Aug. 1919.

69. *Call*, 18 Aug. 1919; 8 Sept. 1919; L. Hernfeld to William B. Wilson, 13 Aug. 1919, file 170/698, FMCS, R.G. 280, NA; Regis Chauvenet to A. Mitchell, n.d., Central File, 16–128, Justice Department, R.G. 60, NA.

70. *CMOJ*, July 1919, pp. 4, 12; Circular, 25 July 1919, Box 2, folder 3, Papers of Local 162, SHSW.

71. *Tobacco,* 17 July 1919, p. 20; 7 Aug. 1919, pp. 6, 22; *U.S. Tobacco Journal,* 5 July 1919, p. 4; 12 July, 1919, p. 3; 2 Aug. 1919, p. 3; *Tobacco Leaf,* 26 June 1919, p. 4.

72. Circular, 5 Aug. 1919, Box 1, folder 3; Circular to Members of Local Unions, 16 Aug. 1919, Box 2, folder 3, Papers of Local 162, SHSW.

73. Ograin interview, 8 July 1977;U.S. Bureau of Labor Statistics, "Technological Changes in the Cigar Industry and Their Effects on Labor," *Monthly Labor Review,* 33 (Dec. 1931), 12; "Rufus Lenoir Patterson's Cigar Machine," *Fortune,* June 1930, p. 58; "When Gears and Levers Replace the Cigar Maker's Adept Fingers," *Scientific American,* Nov. 1922, pp. 311–36.

74. *Tobacco Leaf,* 16 Jan. 1919, p. 6; 24 Apr. 1919, pp. 32–33; *Tobacco World,* 15 July 1919, p. 11.

75. *Call,* 6 Aug. 1919; Henry Hilfers to Gompers, 29 Aug. 1919; "The Cigar Makers' General Strike of 1919 or Who Spilt the Beans," typescript, undated, Boston, Reel 36, *American Federation of Labor Records;* Roy Dickinson, "When Labor Goes Too Far," *Printer's Ink,* 20 May 1920, pp. 3, 4, 8, 166, 169. Boston cigar makers, however, did not just fade away. In 1923 they held another strike over some of the same issues. See R. A. Brown to Hugh Kerwin, 10 Aug. 1923, file 170/2154, FMCS, R.G. 280, NA.

76. Carroll Lawrence Christenson, *Collective Bargaining in Chicago, 1929–1930, a Study of the Economic Significance of the Industrial Location of Trade Unionism* (Chicago, 1933), p. 4; *Tobacco,* 28 Aug. 1919, p. 24; 18 Sept. 1919, p. 16; Ograin interview, 11 Aug. 1976 and 19 May 1979. Included in the exodus was the Congress Cigar Company, makers of the La Palina cigar, owned by Sam Paley. Paley moved to Philadelphia because of the "labor problems"in Chicago. In Philadelphia, Paley purchased the radio station that did his advertising. See Robert Metz, *CBS: Reflections in a Bloodshot Eye* (New York, 1975), p. 10; *Tobacco,* 4 Sept. 1919, p. 23.

77. *Binghamton (N.Y.) Press,* 20 Aug. 1919; *Boston Advertiser,* 31 Aug. 1919; *Manchester (N.H.) Leader,* 2 Sept. 1919; Perkins to Morrison, 12 Aug. 1919, Reel 36, *American Federation of Labor Records.*

78. *Call,* 8, 11 Sept. 1919; Gompers to Ralph M. Easely, 5 Sept. 1919; Henry Steinecker to Frank Morrison, 7 Nov. 1919, Reel 36, *American Federation of Labor Records; York Labor Advocate,* 12 Sept. 1919; *Tobacco,* 4 Sept. 1919, p. 22; 11 Sept. 1919, pp. 12, 22; 18 Sept. 1919, p. 33; E. E. Greenawalt to Director of Conciliation Service, 31 Oct. 1919, file 170/698, FMCS, R.G. 280, NA; *Cigarmakers' Bulletin,* nos. 16, 17; *CMOJ,* Nov. 1919, pp. 9–11; E. E. Greenawalt to Director, Division of Conciliation, Department of Labor, 31 Oct. 1919, R.G. 280, NA; Hollenbach interview.

79. *Call,* 9, 23, 30, 31 Sept. 1919; *Tobacco,* 30 Oct. 1919, p. 6; *CMOJ,* Nov. 1919, p. 2.

80. David Montgomery discusses the syndicalist tendencies of the 1919 strike wave and notes that demands for shop committees were not uncommon. See also on wartime strikes, David Montgomery, "The 'New Unionism' and the Transformation of Workers' Consciousness in America, 1909–22," in *Workers' Control in America: Studies in the History of Work, Technology and Labor Struggles* (Cam-

bridge, 1979), pp. 99–108; Bucki, "Dilution and Craft Tradition," pp. 105–24; Maurine Weiner Greenwald, *Women, War and Work: The Impact of World War I on Women Workers in the United States* (Westport, Conn., 1980).

81. Hollenbach interview; Elizabeth Christman to Members of the Executive Board, National Women's Trade Union League, 2 Oct. 1929, National Women's Trade Union League Papers, Schlesinger Library, Radcliffe College, Cambridge, Mass.

82. Report, 1 June 1917, file B.S. 48–33, R.G. 60, Department of Justice, Bureau of Investigation, NA; report by C. V. Mallet, 19 Nov. 1917, OG 10573, R.G. 60, Bureau of Investigation, NA; report, 12 Sept. 1919, file 10110–1958, R.G. 165, Military Intelligence Division, War Department, NA: report, J. P. McDevitt, 5 July 1918, file 10110–857, R.G. 165, Military Intelligence, NA; reports in LG 2325, R.G. 60, Bureau of Investigation, NA.

83. Report, 27 May 1920, file 10110–1584–115, R.G. 165, Military Intelligence, NA; R. W. Clark to Intelligence Officer, 28 Nov. 1919, file 10110–1239, R.G. 165, Military Intelligence, NA; Assistant Director and Chief to George F. Lamb, 14 Oct. 1919, OG 2325, R.G. 60, Bureau of Investigation, NA; Raymond Sheldon to Director, Military Intelligence Division, 31 July 1920, file 10110–2026, R.G. 165, Military Intelligence, NA: Arthur C. Tuteur to Director, Military Intelligence, 5 May 1919, file 10110–1239, R.G. 165, Military Intelligence, NA; report on the Communist Labor Party, 1920, files 379535 and 389913, R.G. 165, Military Intelligence, NA.

84. *Tobacco Leaf,* 30 Oct. 1919, p. 4.

85. *U.S. Tobacco Journal,* 3 Jan. 1920, p. 4; 10 Jan. 1920, p. 35; 17 Apr. 1920, p. 4; 6 Nov. 1920, p. 22.

86. *CMOJ,* July 1921, pp. 2–3, report of C. J. Scully, 23 Sept. 1919, regarding Charles Winfield, file 146772, R.G. 165, Military Intelligence, NA; report, 17 Nov. 1920, file BS 48–33, R.G. 60, Bureau of Investigation, NA; *Tobacco,* 4 Sept. 1919, p. 23; 28 Aug. 1919, p. 24; *U.S. Tobacco Journal,* 10 Jan. 1920, p. 4.

87. *Tobacco,* 14 Aug. 1919, pp. 5, 6; 4 Sept. 1919, p. 5; *Tobacco Leaf,* 4 Sept. 1919, p. 11; *U.S. Tobacco Journal,* 6 Nov. 1920, p. 22.

11

Always a Cigar Maker

As the new decade opened, workers like José Santana worried about the cigar machine, but remained skeptical about its powers. He simply could not believe that anything mechanical could actually produce what it had taken him years to master—a fine cigar. Manufacturers hoped the experiment would prove successful, but remained focused on the immediate problem of the "tyranny of labor." Both views proved to be simplistic.

Changes set in motion during the war soon transformed the industry and altered the nature of labor relations forever. Over the course of the 1920s, large, fully mechanized firms came to dominate the cigar-making landscape and made the delicate skills of the handworker increasingly obsolete. At the same time, cigar manufacturing slid into serious decline as smokers, in step with the fashion of the flapper decade, switched to cheaper, slimmer, quicker smokes—cigarettes—and relegated the cigar to a bygone era. Production plummeted from eight billion in 1920 to four billion by 1933. The increasing size of firms, the use of machinery, and the continued relocation of industry boosted the level of female employment—by 1940 women were 81.3 percent of the labor force. Caught in the squeeze of tumbling production and mechanization, some cigar makers now wondered whether they would have a job at all.[1]

To arrest the immediate postwar deterioration of the market in cigars, some manufacturers proposed a simple solution—find a way to meet Vice-President Thomas Marshall's challenge and produce a good quality five-cent cigar. Skeptics argued that that was quite frankly "an unperformable trick," but in 1923 the General Cigar Company introduced the William Penn, the first serious nickel smoke since the war and the beginning of national brand names in the industry. Other companies followed suit and by 1929, 55 percent of U.S. cigar output retailed for five cents or less.

Within a decade the proportion had reached nearly 90 percent. The magic ingredient in this seeming sorcery was, quite simply, the cigar machine. In 1926, 18 percent of U.S. production was machine-made; by 1936, the figure was at 75 percent and still rising.[2]

The return of the five-cent cigar and the spread of mechanization combined to mean much more, however. By every indicator cigar making was a declining industry after 1920, yet the largest firms posted record profits, not losses, throughout the postwar decade. The depression in the cigar industry in the 1920s had provided them with an opportunity, a chance to consolidate control of the industry and eliminate competition. In the bitter contest for survival in a shrinking market, large manufacturers using AMF machines had a powerful advantage. In most cases, nickel cigars could not be produced at a profit without mechanization and only the largest firms could afford to lease and operate the expensive machinery. For one hundred machines, a manufacturer needed about $380,000 for installation and then from $50,000 to $100,000 a year for rental. The lowered unit cost of production achieved through economies of scale and reduced labor cost (paying lower wages to less skilled women workers) now accelerated forces at work since the turn of the century, and the industry became increasingly concentrated in the hands of a few giant companies. In 1930 the ten largest firms—American Cigar, Consolidated, General, P. Lorillard, Bayuk, Deisel-Wemmer-Gilbert, Webster-Eisenlohr, Mazer-Cressman, Congress Cigar, and the Porto Rican American Tobacco Company—together accounted for more than half of all U.S. production. To reduce overhead and cut costs further, these corporations now closed branch factories and consolidated operations in one or two huge plants. This move, combined with the bankruptcy of thousands of smaller operations, meant a drastic drop in the number of factories— down from 14,578 in 1921 to 5,292 in 1936.[3]

Not incidentally, using AMF cigar machines bestowed many advantages. Mechanization helped eliminate the competition, and it provided increased control over the manufacturing process itself, permitting manufacturers to set the production rate precisely and regulate tobacco usage much more closely. A roller had only a few seconds to stretch out the wrapper leaf on the metal die and had little chance to deviate from the preset course, "since it is not left to his [*sic*] judgement as to how much work he should do or how little, all of this having been skillfully worked out by the engineer who designed the system."[4]

As the slump killed off their competitors, larger firms with machines and greater financial resources could make a bad situation work to their advantage. Prohibition spelled disaster for smaller, independent manufacturers who depended on the saloon for a retail outlet. This was especially true for those using the blue union label. But for large firms which never relied on these local outlets, the Volstead Act could even be viewed as a blessing. Indeed, there were rumors, but no concrete evidence, that a number of them had donated liberally to the Anti-Saloon League hoping thereby to cut out small-time competition. Many of these same firms also had preferential agreements with national drugstore chains, another important retail outlet for cigars, which put smaller competitors at a disadvantage. Several large companies also bought out regional jobbers and took over distribution activities themselves, a move which seriously disrupted the distribution networks of smaller firms. Too, the big ten used their sales volume, generated in part by national advertising, to push remaining jobbers into handling their products on a mutually exclusive basis: to secure the right to sell the national brand the jobber had to agree to refuse to handle brands of others. Smaller-sized manufacturers were also hurt by changes in the leaf business. Integrating vertically, several of the big ten set up their own tobacco warehouses and began dealing directly with growers. Independent dealers had a weaker bargaining position and were increasingly unable to give their clients a reasonable deal on tobacco prices.[5]

Even the infamous "spit" campaign worked to the advantage of the large, mechanized manufacturers. Fearful of adverse consumer reaction, most of them had delicately avoided mentioning machine methods of production. But the American Cigar Company broke the taboo in 1929 and ran ads in major U.S. newspapers emblazoned with the headline: "Spit is a horrid word, but it's worse if on the end of your cigar," implying that handmade cigars were unsanitary. Cremo cigars were, by contrast, made by machine under modern, sanitary conditions. Sales skyrocketed: Americans would no longer be wedded to the notion that handmade is better. The smaller companies, struggling to survive amid relentless decline in consumption, thus bore a disproportionate burden of the industry's crisis.[6]

The Depression intensified earlier trends. Thousands of cigar makers who had managed to hang on were now thrown out of business. Even the large companies suffered. Profits fell sharply between 1930 and 1933 and most firms responded with price cutting. Many eliminated or cut dividends to shareholders, but all continued to operate in the black and by the late 1930s, they were recording profits once again. The big ten drafted the code of fair competition under the National Recovery Act and, not surprisingly, designed it to best serve their interests. The code resulted in further concentration of the industry. In 1935, 5,100 small companies, about 90 percent of the total, produced 5 percent of U.S. output, while the largest fifteen firms, less than 1 percent of the industry, accounted for 66 percent of production. By the end of the decade, five-cent cigars, made by women workers on automatic machines, were just over 80 percent of total U.S. production. The transformation from handcraft to mass production, from men to women workers, was virtually complete.[7]

Mechanization and the new structure and policies of the industry resulted from conscious decisions on the part of corporate managers. For many workers the resulting changes spelled disaster and despair. Between 1921 and 1935 average wages dropped nearly 30 percent and over fifty-six thousand jobs in the industry were completely eliminated. Many more cigar makers were out of work, however, because manufacturers tended to replace former employees, male and female, with a new group of women workers with no previous experience in the industry, a policy that AMF strongly recommended. Perhaps the CMIU was the most visible casualty. "The cigar makers' union, once one of the most powerful of organized labor groups," crowed a *Barron's* article in 1931, "is today almost history." This time the epitaph made sense. Union members, fearful of the threats to their jobs, closed ranks behind CMIU president Perkins, who did not retire until 1927. The following year, members finally agreed to organize machine workers and permit the label on their goods, but by then it was too late and the label had little value anyway. CMIU membership dropped from forty thousand in 1919 to fifteen thousand in 1933. Few entered the trade to replace those who died or had to leave it, and the average age of a union member in 1928 was sixty-four.[8]

A weakened CMIU could provide little cushion for members who lost their jobs or found their earnings, now lower than those of semiskilled machine operators, insufficient for a living. Members voted to drop the traveling system in 1928 and wipe out the debt of thousands of dollars in outstanding loans. "What the heck [was] the use of carrying it over on the books?" asked John Ograin. "Most of them were dead." The union had to curtail other benefits that year and in 1931 members had no choice but to eliminate the death benefit altogether.[9]

The CMIU and independent companies united briefly to protest the NRA codes which favored the more powerful corporations, but the C found itself in an awkward position since the smaller firms also petit to pay lower wages than the code permitted. The CMIU had little success in organizing machine workers during the 1930s and competed for a time with the CIO Cannery Workers union for members. Gradually cigar makers in Tampa, facing mechanization themselves, came to dominate their old enemy, the CMIU.[10]

Some cigar makers left the bench, as did William Theisen, who began working in a furniture store in the early 1920s. John Ograin took a job with the International union. When Chicago factories in the late 1920s placed union men on a "limit," José Santana found he needed to supplement his income in order to support his wife and daughters. Finally in 1930 and 1931 he worked as a census enumerator and saved enough money to open his own shop. His success enabled him to offer employment to former shop mates who had lost their jobs.[11] In Manchester, New Hampshire, the R. G. Sullivan Company raised the question of machinery each year, and time after time cigar makers voted to take a wage cut rather than permit mechanization. In 1930, however, they quit trying. The first "iron cigar makers" began to arrive and foreman Frank Shea notified the men one by one that they would no longer be needed. Reorienting production moved him from the third floor back down to the second, where he had begun as a stock boy years before: "Only it was machines this time, not men." Many of the laid-off cigar makers opened buckeyes, but six years later, 64 percent of the fired men were still unemployed. Theresa Shea, formerly a tobacco stemmer, took a machine job and recalled the tragic consequences for the hand craftsmen she knew. "A lot of the men died after that . . . a lot of the old-timers. They were just heartbroken. They couldn't work."[12]

Union men were not alone. Many women team workers also lost their jobs because many manufacturers adopted a policy of hiring a new group of women workers for machine jobs. Even where manufacturers encouraged their conversion to machine work, as in Lima, Ohio, there were not enough places for everyone. Also, scores of branch factories in Pennsylvania, Ohio, New York, and New Jersey were closed as companies consolidated operations into one plant during the 1920s. Thousands of workers, most of them women, lost their jobs. When factories halted operations in East Greenville, Perkasie, Norristown, or Lancaster in southeastern Pennsylvania, some women looked for other jobs locally, while others commuted longer distances to nearby towns to work in remaining factories until they too closed their doors. Recalling the bitter strikes of 1919, many firms dared not announce a shutdown in advance for fear of sabotage or violence. In most cases, a Women's Bureau study reported, the closings occurred without notice just after a Fourth of July or Thanksgiving holiday.[13]

There were exceptions and variations, of course. York County did not mechanize until the early 1930s, and while numerous factories closed there, enough remained to provide continued employment for many, including Editha Mattingly and Pauline Stauffer. Detroit manufacturers, for the most part, also waited until the 1930s to use machines as did Tampa's Clear Havana manufacturers. As late as the 1950s, union cigar makers in scattered smaller communities, especially in Connecticut, continued to work by hand as before. For those who found jobs in the industry for the first time, machine cigar making offered an opportunity. New to the trade, they had little with which to compare the conditions they encountered.

Despite this massive transformation, workers renewed their labor militancy, especially in the 1930s. Cigar makers in Tampa, Florida, Richmond, Virginia, Jacksonville, Florida, and elsewhere engaged in huge strikes early in the decade. In 1934, cigar makers in Red Lion, Pennsylvania, made headlines when they rioted in front of factory gates on Pine Street in the midst of a strike there. (Within a year, Red Lion manufacturers had adopted machinery.) The most sensational strike, however, took place in Detroit, where women workers staged a massive sit-down strike in 1937.[14]

Although the cigar industry temporarily revived during World War II, it quickly resumed its downward spiral. More and more companies closed and the industry disappeared from Boston, Chicago, New York City, Detroit, Denver, New Orleans, and most of the cigar centers in Pennsylvania. By the 1960s, the only remaining cigar factories of any consequence were to be found in Tampa, Jacksonville, and the small towns of York County. The largest companies outlived the rest either as subsidiaries of still larger firms or as independents, diversifying into other products. Many moved their plants outside of the continental U.S., particularly to Central and South America. General Cigar became Puerto Rico's largest single employer during the 1950s and early 1960s and won giant tax breaks for locating there. "Operation Bootstrap"[15] was hailed as a way to bring needed revenue to the island, but before long it became clear that few jobs would be created and profits would be spent elsewhere. The CMIU continued to dwindle. In 1974, with only two thousand members, the Cigar Makers' International Union of America ended its 110-year history and merged with the Retail, Wholesale and Department Store Union.

The last two members of Local 14 in Chicago, José Santana and John Ograin, voted in 1964 to dissolve their union and retire their cards. But for Santana, life did not really change very much. He still rose each morning at 4 A.M., brewed a pot of strong coffee, carried a cup of it down to his basement shop, and, lighting one of his own smokes, sat down to roll cigars. He kept to this ritual until only a few weeks before his death at the age of eighty-nine in April 1980. He could hardly have done otherwise—after all, "Once a cigar maker, always a cigar maker."

Notes

1. Roy Dickinson, "When Labor Goes Too Far," *Printer's Ink*, 20 May 1920, pp. 3–4, 8, 166,169; *U.S. Tobacco Journal*, 5 July 1919, p. 4; 12 July 1919, p. 3; 2 Aug. 1919, p. 3; 5 Mar. 1921, p. 4; 1 Jan. 1926, p. 2; *Tobacco*, 17 July 1919, p. 20; 7 Aug. 1919, pp. 6, 22; 14 Aug. 1919, pp. 5, 6; 4 Sept. 1919, p. 5; *Tobacco Leaf*, 26 June 1919, p. 4; 4 Sept. 1919, p. 11; Jack J. Gottsegen, *Tobacco: A Study of Its Consumption in the United States* (New York, 1940), p. 14.

2. *U.S. Tobacco Journal*, 5 Mar. 1921, pp. 4, 6; 30 Apr. 1921, p. 4; 25 June 1921, p. 18; 16 July 1921, p. 4; 21 Jan. 1922, p. 4; 18 Mar. 1922, p. 4; 9 Aug. 1924, p. 4; 17 Jan. 1925, p. 8; 27 Feb. 1926, p. 4; 12 June 1926, p. 5; "Smokers Set Advertising Theme of the 5-Cent Cigar," *Printer's Ink*, 9 Mar. 1933, p. 6; "Competition in Cigar Machinery," *Barron's*, 12 May 1931, p. 20; J. H. McMullen, "Machinery Brings Back the Five-Cent Cigar," *Commerce and Finance*, 26 Jan. 1927, pp. 217–18; "Net of American Machine and Foundry up 85%," *Barron's*, 5 May 1930, p. 10; "When Gears and Levers Replace the Cigar Maker's Adept Fingers," *Scientific American*, Nov. 1922, pp. 312, 336.

3. *U.S. Tobacco Journal*, 3 Dec. 1921, p. 39; 3 Jan. 1925, p. 8; "Technological Changes in the Cigar Industry and Their Effects on Labor," *Monthly Labor Review*, 33 (Dec. 1931), 1275; Lucy Winsor Killough, *The Tobacco Products Industry in New York and Its Environs: Present Trends and Probable Future Developments*, Regional Plan of New York and Its Environs, Monograph no. 5 (New York, 1924), p. 118; Reavis Cox, *Competition in the Tobacco Industry, 1911–1932: A Study of the Effects of the Partition of the American Tobacco Company by the United States Supreme Court* (New York, 1933), pp. 90–91, 135; "Tobacco Prospers," *Business Week*, 2 Feb. 1935, p. 12; *U.S. Tobacco Journal*, 10 Jan. 1925, p. 5; 22 Jan. 1921, p. 12; Joseph C. Robert, *The Story of Tobacco in America* (New York, 1952), p. 227; "Costs Dropped and Sales Increased When We Cut 152 Brands to 5," *Sales Management*, 6 Aug. 1927, pp. 201–2; Charles D. Barney, *The Tobacco Industry: Annual Review* (New York, 1927), pp. 5, 18–25; "General Cigar Company Maintains Its Strength despite Decline in Industry," *Magazine of Wall Street*, 18 Feb. 1933, p. 491.

4. *U.S. Tobacco Journal*, 13 May 1922, p. 32; *Tobacco Leaf*, 3 Aug. 1929, p. 13; McMullen, "Machinery Brings Back Five-Cent Cigar," pp. 217–18.

5. Cox, *Competition in Tobacco Industry*, pp. 110–11, 135; "Bucking the Cigar

Industry's Trend," *Barron's*, 14 Aug. 1939, p. 13; "Concentrating on One Brand Builds Volume for This Jobber," *Sales Management*, 3 Apr. 1926, p. 515; Raymond Steber interview, 24 July 1978, Warren, Pa.

6. "'Cremo' Picked for Sustained Campaign in Cigar Field," *Printer's Ink*, 20 June 1929, p. 102; *Tobacco Leaf*, 29 June 1929, p. 7; 28 Sept. 1929, pp. 30–31; Cox, *Competition in Tobacco Industry*, p. 237.

7. "Some Cigar Companies May Cut Dividends," *Barron's*, 16 June 1930, p. 27; "Cigars, a Classic Ten-Center Becomes a Nickel Cigar," *Business Week*, 25 Jan. 1933, p. 9; "1930 Burned up Fewer Cigars; Burned out More Cigar Makers," *Business Week*, 11 Feb. 1932, p. 10; U.S. Bureau of Labor Statistics, Bulletin 660, *Mechanization and Productivity of Labor in the Cigar Manufacturing Industry*, by Wilmoth D. Evans (Washington, D.C., 1939), pp. 1–4, 43–64; *Barron's*, 14 Aug. 1939, p. 13; *Barron's*, 20 July 1931, p. 18; Joseph Newman, "Competitive Copy Not Needed Here," *Printer's Ink*, 29 June 1933, p. 34; "The Cigar Attempts a Comeback; Advertising Budgets Increase," *Sales Management*, 22 Feb. 1930, p. 350; "Five-Cent Cigar Increases Lead," *Barron's*, 5 May 1930, p. 26; *Moody's Industrials*, 1930–39; "Transcript of Hearings," Cigar Industry Code, 7225, Record Group (R.G.) 9, National Recovery Administration, National Archives (NA), Washington, D.C.

8. U.S. Department of Labor, Women's Bureau, Bulletin 100, *The Effects on Women of Changing Conditions in the Cigar and Cigarette Industries*, by Caroline Manning and Harriet Byrne (Washington, D.C., 1932), pp. 11–20, 27–129; Willis Baer, *The Economic Development of the Cigar Industry in the United States* (Lancaster, Pa., 1933), pp. 216, 258; U.S. Bureau of Labor Statistics, *Mechanization and Productivity of Labor*, pp. 1–4, 43–64; McMullen, "Machinery Brings Back the Five-Cent Cigar," pp. 217–18; "Competition in Cigar Machinery," p. 20; J. H. Korson, "The Technological Development of the Cigar Manufacturing Industry: A Study in Social Change" (Ph.D. dissertation, Yale University, 1947); Russell Mack, *The Cigar Manufacturing Industry* (Philadelphia, 1933), p. 77; George W. Perkins, "Women in the Cigar Industry," *American Federationist*, 32 (Sept. 1925), 808–10; John P. Troxell, "Machinery and the Cigarmakers," *Quarterly Journal of Economics*, 48 (Feb. 1934), 338–47.

9. See n. 8 and David J. Saposs, *Left Wing Unionism: A Study of Radical Policies and Tactics* (New York, 1926), pp. 104–9, 155; Marion Savage, *Industrial Unionism in America* (New York, 1971 [1922]), pp. 289–93; Troxell, "Machinery and the Cigarmakers," p. 343; Sumner H. Slichter, *Union Policies and Industrial Management* (New York, 1968 [1941]), pp. 218–22.

10. U.S. Department of Labor, Wage and Hour Division, *The Cigar Industry*, (Washington, D.C., 1941), p. 37; "Transcript of Hearings," Cigar Industry Code, 7225, R.G. 9, NA, "Minutes," 13 Mar. 1937, Webster-Eisenlohr folder, Series II, Box 16, Cigar Makers' International Union of America Collection, McKeldin Library University of Maryland, College Park.

11. William Theisen interview, 17 Aug. 1979, Denver, Colo.; John R. Ograin interviews, 1976–80, Chicago; and José Santana interviews, 1976–80, Chicago.

12. U.S. Works Progress Administration, National Research Project, *Cigar Makers—After the Lay-Off: A Case Study of the Effects of Mechanization on Em-*

ployment of Hand Cigar Makers, by Daniel Creamer and Gladys V. Swackhamer (Philadelphia, 1937), pp. 51–57; T. Frank Shea interview, 26 June 1979, Manchester, N.H.; Theresa Shea interview, 28 June 1979, Manchester, N.H.

13. Women's Bureau, *Effects on Women,* pp. 27–129; Editha Mattingly interview and Pauline Stauffer interview, 21 June 1977, Hanover, Pa.

14. Regarding these strikes, see Federal Mediation and Conciliation Service, case files 176–1246, 182/1813, 199/51, 199/442, 176/117, 182/2233, 199/917, R.G. 280, N.A.; *York Gazette and Daily,* 27–31 July 1934; *Detroit News,* 18 Feb. 1937; Maurice Sugar Papers, clipping files, Walter Reuther Labor Archives, Wayne State University, Detroit, Mich. Cigar makers had been relatively quiescent since 1922. For some thoughts about why workers are militant in one period and silent in another, see Yves Lequin, "Social Structures and Shared Beliefs: Four Worker Communities in the 'Second Industrialization,'" *International Labor and Working Class History,* 22 (Fall 1982), pp. 1–17.

15. *United States Tobacco Journal,* 18/25 Dec. 1975, p. 26.

Conclusion

Comparing men and women in the cigar industry during these years has yielded a number of useful and sometimes rather puzzling insights. I expected to find separate spheres and scores of dualities.[1] Certainly men and women experienced work differently and developed contrasting work cultures. Gender tragically divided cigar makers from each other and limited their ability to resist and transcend their respective subordinated positions. But they also shared much, and it is equally important to stake out and name this common ground. A final look at these work cultures and the relations between male unionists and women team workers will help sharpen some of these issues and tie up a few still-loose ends.

The cigar industry was in transition during the early twentieth century. The five-cent cigar, once lowly and cheap, now came into its own. As the five-cent branch grew, the union, which had long concentrated in medium-priced cigars, increasingly found itself in retreat. The manufacturers of nickel cigars tended to operate large firms with many branches, and consciously chose to divide the labor process and pay low wages to young, single immigrant women who they hoped would prove docile and easy to manage. Elementary machinery for the bunching and rolling processes was available, but cigar makers throughout the country still essentially worked with their hands using a considerable degree of skill. While the industry itself remained competitive, economic power within the trade was gradually shifting into the hands of the large female-employing firms and by the end of the period a small cluster of companies, all makers of five-cent cigars, now came to dominate the industry.

Still, cigar makers throughout the country experienced many of the same general material conditions of work. While a few manufacturers adopted welfare measures for their employees, most cigar makers worked in less than healthful environments amid dust, fumes, and grit. Team work

319

using molds and machinery was less skilled than unionists' out and out hand or mold work, but all cigar making required training, attention, care, knowledge, and ability. The work itself was paid by the piece, which gave workers some adaptability in the workday and focused their attention on output, rather than hours. Every cigar maker worried about the quality of the tobacco, the ratio of cigars made to tobacco used and the authority of those who employed them. Untouched by scientific management or elaborate rationalization schemes, cigar makers negotiated their positions amid relatively traditional styles of management by a foreman and company owners. Thus while the life of any cigar maker, male or female, was economically limited and insecure, the handcraft nature of the trade and its informal operations afforded workers a degree of flexibility and autonomy many other industrial workers no longer had.

Their positions in the industry, however, were unequal. Men may have worked in smaller, older factories, but they always made higher wages than women and the benefits their union offered cushioned them financially. Women workers more acutely experienced low piece rates, intense work, and a division of labor. The piece rate differential meant both that women had to work much longer hours than unionists in order to sustain an adequate income and that men had more freedom to come and go during the day. Yet all workers used the piece system to give themselves more control over time and demonstrated that earnings were not always a first priority even for the lowest-paid workers.

The work cultures cigar makers developed and sustained, which revealed the values they respected most, have many parallels. Women and men shared the human potential to act, and the desire to make claims based on their own needs, not those of their employers. Their work cultures operated subversively to undermine the strength of the power relationship inherent in their wage work. Analysis of work culture reveals limitations and accommodations, but it also uncovers a good bit of courage, pride, and dignity.

In every factory, cigar makers confronted an authority structure which defined the conditions of work and disciplined workers. Union members tried to regulate formally foremen's conduct and demeanor toward the men. Women team workers often revealed an air of resignation and powerlessness in challenging a manager's abusive behavior toward them. Union rules and customs dictated no hint of collusion or association with employers. Women's frequent complaint of boss's favoritism suggests their concern with this same issue, but less success in dealing with it. Yet women adopted strategies to constrain their supervisors as well. They called each other down for producing too many cigars for the tobacco allotted just as men did. They might mark a foreman with a deprecating name and warned each other of his approach. The specific practices may have looked different, but men and women both drew important distinctions between themselves and those with power over them and sought openings to limit and divert that power.

Cigar makers had distinct ideas regarding fair and unfair uses of their labor. Most cigar makers appear to have recognized that working purely for oneself, striving to make as many cigars as possible from the tobacco given, might benefit the individual in the short run, but hurt everyone in the end. Unionists tried to control the allowances set on use of tobacco to make them as liberal as possible and both unionists and team workers acted informally to limit output relative to tobacco usage. Women created a bank so that they could share tobacco with each other out of the foreman's sight and help everyone meet the quota, which reflected a collective, rather than individual, approach to shop-floor discipline.

Neither unionists nor women team workers regarded work as sacred and both defined conditions under which they would refuse to perform it. Male unionists might withold labor individually or collectively if they perceived an insult or found tobacco unworkable. Women too claimed their own time. In Detroit they quit in one place and got a job in another to find better conditions. Manufacturers had to suspend operations during weeks with religious holidays there and in southeastern Pennsylvania an afternoon ball game might lure most of the force away. Men's and women's reasons for not being at work might have differed, especially with regard to women's home duties, but in varying degrees workers expressed some sense of owning their own time.

A feeling of entitlement extended to other matters in addition to time. Women cigar makers in Lima, for example, sat on wooden boxes they regarded as personal property, not to be invaded. But the most obvious case in point was smokers. Unionists insisted on their right to take home three free cigars a day and this unwritten rule could hardly be violated without serious consequences. Women could not make such an open claim. Yet they believed in their right to a share in the product they had made, and simply took what they felt was their due.

Cigar makers had clear notions of what constituted proper treatment on the shop floor. This might relate to many identities they brought with them to work, including their internalized definitions of what it meant to be a man or a woman. Manliness carried with it "connotations of dignity, respectibility, defiant egalitarianism and patriarchal male supremacy."[2] Cigar makers expected to act in manly ways and demanded that they be treated as men. At first glance conventional notions of womanhood might not seem much of a basis for similar claims for women. Women's role might dictate submissiveness, the importance of obeying men, serving others, and placing the needs of others first, but the cultural definitions of being a woman could and did act as a resource in women's shop-floor struggles with manufacturers. The women who went out on strike in Newark, New Jersey, in 1906 protested that they were not being treated as ladies, and in 1916 women strikers in Detroit objected to improper behavior on the part of foremen. In both cases their expectations regarding their rights and roles as women formed a basis for their protest.

Both men and women fiercely protected their dignity, but their concepts of it at times might look different. Clothes expressed a union man's respectability and equality with the boss. While I never talked with a woman who regarded clothes the same way, some women commented on the indignity of smelling like a cigar factory even if one took care to wrap her work apron in newspaper before making the trip home at night. Unionists stressed their refusal to compromise principle or submit to exploitation or abusive language and asserted the right to practice their craft under honorable and self-respecting conditions. Women may have felt they had to endure harsh comments from foremen, but they affirmed their own worth by making fun of him or taking smokers, or even resisting to the point of striking. While theirs was not a consciously feminist vision (no one I interviewed had been actively interested in or supportive of suffrage, for example), they had a sense that being a woman should guarantee some level of respectful treatment. They wanted to work and be women too. At some point they drew a line beyond which they felt offended or misused. The males who owned and managed the firms where women worked could possibly just reinforce the hierarchy of gender found outside the factory and women were perhaps unpracticed in setting the terms for relationships with men. Yet women cigar makers repeatedly stood their ground and found ways to resist their male employers both covertly and openly in the form of strikes.

Their gendered work cultures were obvious from the very style each adopted. Unionists clustered, for example, at the saloon after work. Members had to prove themselves to the group and they relished telling their own tramping stories and exploits. Travel also captured their emphasis on masculine independence. Women did not perhaps see independence in the same way, but they did assert their freedom of movement by changing jobs and quitting when they felt like it. The practice had prompted one Detroit observer to remark that they were "independent as a hog on ice." Female culture included their ties to each other at work. They brought in food, traded information about the operation of a household, and discussed their families, boyfriends, and marriages. They shared even the tobacco they used in sisterly efforts to circumvent the rules and protect each other.

It is not surprising that men and women had somewhat different attitudes toward their work. While both may have assumed they would work as adults, male unionists saw themselves as lifelong workers, primary breadwinners, and practiced craftsmen. Women interviewed recognized their contributions to their families' incomes or to their own support, but they did not for the most part see themselves as tradesmen or the permanent chief providers for the household. At the same time they saw themselves as part of a continuous community of working people, and work became an important part of their identities just as other aspects of their lives were. The strength and diversity of their work cultures testifies to the substantive place work held in their lives. Both men and women drew pride and pleasure from the work itself. A sense of confidence in the ability to do the job well offered a source of self-worth and accomplishment to cigar makers regardless of how self-consciously they thought about it. For a unionist this might mean disdaining the use of the label on inferior quality goods; for a woman team worker it might mean wishing the foreman would compliment her cigars or feeling wounded when her wares were compared to a sack of potatoes.

Self-esteem for unionists also came from their union. It gave them some power in the workplace, provided a source of security, and validated their resistance to managerial prerogatives. Nor could one overlook that one of their members headed the American Federation of Labor. Union affiliation and geographic mobility drew them together into a circle which cut across the divisions of distance, region, ethnicity, and religion. It provided them with a measure of economic security, but also a sense of collective identity and fellowship. Women lacked this kind of institutional backing, but despite its absence, sources of cohesion and unity were evident in their work cultures as well. This sense might come in part from the neighborhood and community—their Polishness in Detroit, or their kin and networks in the towns and hamlets of southeastern Pennsylvania.

Most important in terms of this study, however, it sprang from the shared experience of paid work. The work process itself demanded their cooperation and mutual dependence, and the cultures they forged reinforced their sense of belonging together, a feeling some likened to family ties.

Yet internal conflict and fragmentation could undercut these sources of unity and cohesion. Unionists battled with each other over socialism, admission of new workers, leadership, control of the organization, and the use of funds and dues. While union work culture had traditionally embraced a degree of internal conflict, these internal fissures grew more divisive as the union's position in the industry came more visibly under siege. The record hints at examples of discord among women too, as in New Jersey in 1908–9 where ethnicity divided workers during a strike or as in the strike movement of 1919 when some workers stayed at their benches. The team system itself could fan dissension because workers were so dependent on each other's proficiency for their earnings.

Conflict with employers, however, was at the very heart of both work cultures and labor militancy came to be associated with cigar making whether in Tampa, the union factories from Boston to San Francisco, the nonunion firms in Detroit, New Jersey, or Pennsylvania, or the stogie shops of Pittsburgh. When one also considers that Louise Tilly found women cigar makers to be some of the most militant of French working women, it seems possible that there might be something to the notion that there was something *in* the tobacco . . .

Resisting that temptation, however, requires a few brief and more plausible explanations regarding labor militancy in the industry. Evidence in this study offers no firm models for predicting labor militancy, but it does suggest that work process is a powerful determinant. The content of workers' daily lives, the customs and habits they practiced, the languages they spoke, the gender roles they filled, and the places in which they lived and worked may have been different, but in work, in making cigars, they shared some common territory. They knew the trade, its skills and pitfalls. They shared a similar position vis-à-vis manufacturers and a keen desire to take control of their own lives in whatever ways they could see to do so. These were not always consciously stated goals, but they were values and concerns embedded in every aspect of work culture. Recognition of this joint outlook emerged in the brief alliance of workers during the war and especially in 1919. For the first time cigar makers collected their grievances and concerns and voiced them through a militant, even vaguely syndicalist, strike movement. (Here they joined the ranks of thousands of other workers with comparable concerns out on strike in other industries.) No union led the way. Rather cigar makers operated outside union structure and forged their own mass movement.

Women's militant strike action and their active work cultures laid to rest suppositions about their passivity and lack of ambition. But were women's strikes different from men's? Certainly men and women seem to have struck for many of the same reasons—to improve bad stock, to fire or restore a foreman, to increase wages, or to stop a change in the system of work. On other levels, however, there appear to have been differences. Styles of striking, for example, look somewhat gendered. Women in Detroit brought their children to picketing and rioting outside the factories in 1916, and elsewhere women often engaged in spirited demonstrations such as occupying buildings, attacking scabs physically, or sabotaging factory operations, methods which were absent from the record of union men. Most important, while men and women valued dignity and respect and would strike to preserve both, the meanings of these values could differ. A woman's perception of dignity might be related to her conception of how a woman should be treated, while unionists often defined it in terms of manliness and a refusal to cower. Cultural differences, then, qualified the surface appearance of similarity.[3]

Gender divided men and women in very concrete and unambivalent ways. There are hints in the record that it impaired and fractured the strike movement of 1919. Most visibly, it had a great deal to do with why the CMIU and its members were unable to open their doors to the expanding force of women in the industry. The male work culture that unionists created, which was codified and reflected in nearly every aspect of union organization, strengthened this group of craftsmen in their struggles with employers and enabled them to play a leading role in the labor movement as a whole. At the same time, however, it contained inherent contradictions that unionists never overcame. It sealed an attitude of exclusivity which prevented them from organizing women or saving their own skins in the midst of a changing industry. Work culture and its traditions drew them together into a community, but a select and ultimately narrow one. A small minority did continue to argue for the organization of the whole craft, but the majority remained recalcitrant. Such exclusivity, I hasten to add, was not the unique province of male unionists. Communities of women defined by race and class have historically oppressed and excluded their sisters from their own circles. By dissecting the CMIU's relationship to team workers, however, we reach a fuller understanding of the meaning of craft unionism and the crisis it faced in the early twentieth century, and we expose the dynamics of gender relations in the industry.[4]

Why did the CMIU fail to admit women team workers on any significant scale? After all, some unions such as the Amalgamated Clothing Workers and the International Ladies Garment Workers did so, although not without difficulty and acrimony. There were certain obvious differences between the CMIU and these clothing unions, however. Both the Amalgamated and the ILGWU were newer unions in the early twentieth century, fighting and replacing an older craft union, the United Garment Workers, whereas the CMIU itself was one of the oldest craft unions in the country. Frequently men and women in the garment industry worked in the same locations and plants, while a majority of cigar makers worked in largely sex-segregated settings. The women who made five-cent cigars in Detroit worked as teams in large factories totally removed from union shops in the city and the two groups were unlikely to have any contact. Unionists tended to make ten-cent cigars, often in smaller shops. For a long time unionists could convince themselves that they did not need to organize women since the two types of cigars seemed to cater to two separate markets. But Perkins warned against such folly. Unionists' sense of security proved false because the improvements in the nickel smoke threw it into direct competition with union products. The new industry leaders who headed the five-cent firms made choices and set policy: they hired women, used a division of labor and sometimes machinery, and established branch factories. All of these gradually challenged the Seed and Havana niche that unionists believed they had secured for themselves.

The issue of organizing women, however, was not a new one. Through good times and bad, the CMIU had continued to grapple with the question of whom to organize. They had never simply slammed the doors shut and cut off the debate entirely. In an abstract sense, they supported the organization of all in the craft and said so in the union journal. There were also countless examples of union men coming to the aid of nonunion strikers, whether male or female, and spending thousands of dollars in clashes they had not initiated. Detroit in 1916 was no isolated case and the strike movement of 1919 suggested the possibility of men and women creating a united front. Still, the CMIU remained undeniably a man's union and the formal attempt to bring team workers into its ranks proved a colossal failure.

Many obstacles stood in the way of a united labor force. To start, unionists and nonunion women were simply very different people. Young, often single, immigrant women had little in common with older men, more likely to be married, who represented different ethnic groups—often those which had immigrated much earlier. Union reluctance to organize team workers had a good deal of logic behind it too. Union cigar makers may have been privileged with regard to women in the trade, but their working lives were still uncertain and unhealthful. These were no grand aristocrats. Many members at the turn of the century could recall being paid in truck or having to pay for oil in their lamps at work. Others such as José Santana had worked in nonunion shops where they had been treated, as he phrased it, "like dogs." Many unionists were all too aware of their essentially precarious position. The team system and women workers did undermine them. In many towns and cities unionists had watched manufacturers fire union men, change the system of work, and hire women. By organizing the team system they would in effect condone it and open the way for their own labor to be divided. If the blue label could appear on team-made goods, what incentive would manufacturers have for continuing out and out handwork? Their own wages would be cut and they would have had little or no recourse. If craft unionism served as a strategy for protecting workers from such degradation then the economic logic of craft unionism dictated exclusivity. For survival they needed to protect the ground they had managed to carve out.

But economic logic does not explain enough. Cigar makers under the team system would make only half a cigar. This might have meant lower wages, but it also insulted the craftsman. A key source of union cigar makers' self-esteem and feelings of value and worth came from making quality cigars. Pride in his work was one of José Santana's chief motors as a human being, at the very core of his sense of self-respect. If cigar makers wanted to argue for economic reasons that out-and-out work was needed, they also had to argue that other systems of work were inferior. But unionists truly believed in these distinctions, this ranking of occupations, flawed as their thinking may have been. Their self-confidence as individuals came in part from their jobs as craftsmen making quality goods. Women team workers might subvert the label in economic terms, but they would by virtue of their inferior work subvert the quality of the cigar too. That mattered very much to these men.

Here we begin to close in on the heart of matters. The work culture that men created, which reinforced their feelings of dignity and self-worth and which operated to strengthen them in their daily conflict with employers, was inherently restrictive. A true union man had to prove his loyalty, which was essential to the collective strength of the union. Clovis Gallaud knew this only too well when he reassured members that his new recruits in New Orleans were learning to love the union. Cigar makers acknowledged it when they worried about those who became members only because their bosses wanted the blue label. Their caution was also revealed in their suspicions of "mushroom membership" which swelled at the height of a strike only to disappear once it was over. If a man joined the union only so that he could travel west for his health, he was suspect. Most important, he could be dangerous. He could weaken the union and undermine its ability to bargain effectively with employers. Unionists could wonder whether they might risk everything they had built and achieved if they permitted the uncommitted and the weak to enter their organization.

It was not simply their jobs, however, but their whole culture which was at stake. Team workers were not just any outsiders. The vast majority of them were women and this complicated the duality of exclusivity and solidarity by introducing the complex meanings of gender into an already volatile mixture. Fundamentally union cigar makers had created a male preserve. Nothing could have lessened the shock of women's intrusion there. Unionists drew strength from their masculine culture and sexual solidarity, built as they were on a respect for manliness. Men's abstract definition of womanhood made women doubtful unionists. Women were submissive, weak, and in need of protection. While the record might clearly show that women cigar makers struck their employers with force and tenacity on many occasions and while union men in their own families might have experienced women's less than submissive natures, the ideology remained powerful. Men saw women as potential losers. Aware of their own statistics they knew that unionists rarely lost their strikes, but all too often they had watched women return and submit. Just as significant, unionists did not want women in their union because basically they were not like men. They were somehow alien. Their own imagery depicted women as victims and prostitutes and their statements often lumped them with mutes and the disabled, which carried the implicit message that somehow women were not quite whole human beings. This unstated perception was neatly captured in the Class A membership plan: women were not full members either. Their weakness threatened the union and their differences fundamentally challenged male culture. The catch was, of course, that the more unionists needed to bring women into the fold, the more they had to fear from potentially weak members who could undermine their deteriorating bargaining position still further.[5]

The CMIU was a reflection of a male work culture, one which stressed mutuality, brotherhood, loyalty, and solidarity. The traveling fraternity bound them together across great distances and helped to strengthen their national culture. Their strength, however, proved to be the very source of their downfall. Their work culture insulated and isolated them as it merged manhood with male supremacy and solidarity with exclusivity. It helped to create and make attractive a strata of nonunion workers. Thus unionists' unwillingness to organize women played right into the hands of manufacturers, who had once noted in self-satisfied tones that the divisions among workers in the industry had made the possibility of "one great union" thankfully "outside the pale of practical effort." Union men could not bend to save the very work culture they so jealously protected: few of them ever recognized the irony.

In the end, the history of cigar making is not simply the chronicle of failure and missed opportunity. Rather, it is a complex story of arrogance and pride, of fragmentation and unity, of privilege and equality, of resignation and resistance. Its true message is one of hope and possibility for the future.

Notes

1. On the notion of gender and dualities, see the excellent piece by Carole Turbin, "Beyond Conventional Wisdom: Interdependence in Mid-19th Century Working Class Families," paper delivered at the Social Science History Association, Nov. 1985, Chicago.

2. David Montgomery, *Workers' Control in America: Studies in the History of Work, Technology and Labor Struggles* (Cambridge, 1979), p. 13.

3. See Alice Kessler-Harris, "Problems of Coalition-Building: Women and Trade Unions in the 1920s," in Ruth Milkman, ed., *Women, Work and Protest: A Century of U.S. Women's Labor History* (Boston, 1985), pp. 110–38.

4. See Nancy Hewitt's fine review essay, "Beyond the Search for Sisterhood: American Women's History in the 1980s," *Social History*, 10 (Oct. 1985), 229–321.

5. Kessler-Harris, "Problems of Coalition-Building," pp. 110–38.

A Note on Sources

In 1975 the papers of the Cigar Makers' International Union were deposited at the University of Maryland where Stuart Kaufman, my advisor, was editing the Samuel Gompers Papers. Starting with the CMIU collection, I began the task of uncovering and interpreting the work culture of cigar makers. Soon I discovered that the collection's richness lay in the period after 1927, though by then the CMIU really was on its knees. To understand the causes of its decline and to capture the work lives of both men and women in the industry before mechanization, I had to begin at an earlier period, when the union still held the dominant position in the industry. I chose 1900 because it was the mid-point of the union's height of success, a period between 1890 and about 1906, and because of a strike in New York City in 1900 in which unionists and women briefly cooperated. Nineteen nineteen was an appropriate ending because the events of that year, a massive strike movement and the introduction of machinery, marked the end of the competitive, decentralized, and largely handcraft stage of production.

Although the CMIU papers provided little assistance, information on union men has survived in several other forms. These include copies of printed local constitutions, price lists, and bylaws which I found primarily at the State Historical Society of Wisconsin and the U.S. Department of Labor Library, the *Cigar Makers' Official Journal*, which I used at the Library of Congress, and the papers of Local 165 of McSherrystown, Pennsylvania, at the Adams County Historical Society (Gettysburg, Pennsylvania), Local 162 of Green Bay, Wisconsin, at the State Historical Society of Wisconsin, and Local 208 of Kalamazoo, Michigan, at Western Michigan University in Kalamazoo. Records for Reading, Pennsylvania, Local 236 at Pennsylvania State University covered a later period, but were still helpful. Federal labor records were invaluable, particularly the

331

raw data from the U.S. Bureau of Corporations, the U.S. Department of Labor, the U.S. Women's Bureau, and the Federal Mediation and Conciliation Service. Materials for the last chapter came from both Military Intelligence and Federal Bureau of Investigation files. All of these records were available at the National Archives in Washington, D.C., but I found them only through the efforts of many skilled archivists there. Published studies by the federal government were also invaluable, particularly the *Report on Condition of Woman and Child Wage-Earners in the United States*, the U.S. Industrial Commission hearings, the reports of the Immigration Commission, and published reports of the U.S. Bureau of the Census. Published data on labor and working conditions from the various states proved extremely helpful, particularly with regard to women workers. Glenn Westfall first introduced me to the industry's trade journals and I benefited most from *Tobacco Leaf* and the *U.S. Tobacco Journal*, available at the Library of Congress and the Tobacco Merchants Association in New York City. I always hoped to find company records, but was invariably told that records had been destroyed. Some may have actually survived, but perhaps my difficulty in gaining access to them is attributable to the business community's unfavorable impression of historical research that Ida Tarbell helped create eighty years ago.

These traditional sources revealed much about workers' culture, but oral history, an approach I had not initially considered, yielded some of the richest material. In the course of related research, I met José Santana, an eighty-five-year-old cigar maker from Chicago. Santana had worked and traveled throughout the United States and Canada between 1909 and 1917. He in turn put me in touch with John Ograin, who learned the trade in Salt Lake City and moved to Chicago in 1911. I interviewed them both over a four-year period from early 1976 through early 1980. They each called my attention to many aspects of union work culture, particularly the importance of geographic mobility. These interviews and those with other union men were completed first, and by about 1979 I had begun to interview women, primarily in southeastern Pennsylvania and Detroit. After completion of the dissertation, I interviewed women cigar makers and a foreman in Lima, Ohio, who had worked for the Deisel-Wemmer Cigar Company there and in 1982 and 1983 I returned to Pennsylvania to interview workers in several small towns in the cigar belt. Locating cigar makers in general was no easy task. I used newspaper ads and letters to libraries and historical societies, nursing homes, senior citizen centers, and cigar companies. I also combed through the CMIU papers and the *CMOJ* looking for names and tracking them through current city directories. My quest took me to sixteen states.

Oral historians, of course, use a rather skewed and unrepresentative sample—people who are still alive. Many places, people, and circumstances remain in the shadows in this study because of the nature of the sources and timing of interviews. I could not easily return for follow-up sessions, for example. I was also unable to locate many nonunion men, nor did I find any women who had been union members. I interviewed only two Tampa cigar makers, who are not quoted in this study, because I decided not to include Tampa as a focus. While bearing in mind these limitations and the problems of human memory and interpretation, I view oral history as an invaluable tool for the historian. It provided information not otherwise obtainable and pointed to the complexity of issues or topics which I had not initially perceived as important. I have attempted to match and weigh recollections against each other and the documentary evidence to gain a sense of their reliability. In using and quoting both oral and written documents, I have tried to retain their original meaning and context. There are significant subjective elements in oral history interviewing. The race, sex, and class background of the interviewer and the interviewee distinctively shape and define the nature of the interaction. I was either working for a Ph.D. or writing a book, and that set me apart in no uncertain terms. While I acknowledge that these factors are crucial, I obviously believe that they did not seriously impair or distort the information I gathered. In several cases I used pseudonyms at the request of interviewees. The tapes and transcripts are at this writing in my possession, although I hope eventually to place them in a university library. The research was funded in part by a doctoral dissertation grant from the Department of Labor's Employment and Training Administration.

I have handled information about men and women in this study very differently and one might at a glance wonder whether it does not fall into the trap Evelyn Glenn and Rosalyn Feldberg pointed out several years ago. They complained that scholars tended to view men in terms of work and women in terms of family. While I agree with their conclusions that both men and women must be viewed in both contexts, I have not practiced them faithfully here for several reasons. Inspired by Harry Braverman's *Labor and Monopoly Capital*, I began my study with a concern about the long-term trend toward craft and skill destruction in America.

My initial focus and early interviews were entirely on the workplace. Because I wanted to stress their national work culture and sense of community and because of the nature of available source material, I decided to focus on men nationally. Only in Boston could I have used manuscript census data to locate more information about cigar makers' lives outside the factory (since it was the only city where being a cigar maker was the same thing as being a union member), yet conditions there were so unique they offered no guide to the lives of most union members. While I asked male respondents generally about their families and home responsibilities, few were very interested in talking about these matters. They were completely at ease in discussing their work and in presenting themselves in a public way, and had no trouble conceiving of these as important and worthy of study. Most with whom I talked had been in the trade as young single men. What they chose to narrate to me was their work and their participation in their union.

When I turned to women workers I found it much more logical to treat them in particular places in part because of the nature of the sources, but also because it seemed most appropriate to their work culture. It was easier to place women in one location than it had been men and the women I found and interviewed were deeply rooted in their communities and families. They had little sense of connection to women elsewhere. It also enabled me to provide more information on the links between home and work roles for women, although that never became a focus of the study. I easily found information on women in Detroit and southeastern Pennsylvania, in part because both had been such homogeneous communities. What I learned might have been different if I had had more success in locating information on women in more heterogeneous settings.

Women were almost always puzzled by my interest in them and their work. Apologetically they explained that they knew little that could be of any use. Where union men needed little prompting to describe work processes in extensive detail, women briskly and without embellishment described their jobs and assumed the interview was over. Once it became clear that I took their work seriously, they willingly provided fuller descriptions. Women interviewees also blurred the lines between work, home, and community while the men I interviewed compartmentalized their lives more, separating work and home into distinctly different realms. By the time I had noticed some of these patterns and wanted to reinterview union men, many of them had died and I was unsuccessful in relocat-

ing others. I decided then to present them here largely as they had presented themselves to me. While it would be instructive to know more
about the nonwork lives of men, the structure of this story reveals something, I think, about the way gender shapes the experiences of all of us
and the ways we view the world and our place in it.

Oral Histories

Amadee, Rita. Interview, 20 June 1978, New Orleans, La.

Bartasius, Anna. Interview, 31 Mar. 1982, Philadelphia, Pa.

Bates, Frederick. Interview, 27 June 1979, Manchester, N.H.

Baust, Herman. Interview, 24 Mar. 1977, North Haven, Conn.

**Berkheiser, Mary. Interview, 21 Dec. 1979 and 24 Jan. 1980. Conducted by the Red Lion oral history project, Kaltreider Memorial Library (KML), Red Lion, Pa.

Brinkman, Fred. Interview, 24 Aug. 1982, Lima, Ohio.

*Diehl, Mary. Interview, 13 Jan. 1984, Quakertown, Pa.

Durso, James. Interview, 24 Mar. 1977, New Haven, Conn.

Fake, Neva. Interview, 17 Dec. 1982, Windsor, Pa.

*Glatfelter, Valeria. Interview, 15 Dec. 1983, Sellersville, Pa.

Groft, Catherine; Smith, Rose; Mattingly, Editha; Stauffer, Pauline. Group interview, 25 Feb. 1977, Hanover, Pa.

Henry, Bessie Ray. Interview, 21 Aug. 1982, Lima, Ohio.

*Hollenbach, Jane. Interview, 16 Mar. 1984, Sellersville, Pa.

Hume, Pearl. Interview, 23 Aug. 1982, Lima, Ohio.

Jacobs, Clarence. Interview, 17 Dec. 1982, Red Lion, Pa.

Kaltreider, Mervin. Interview, 16 June 1982, Red Lion, Pa.

Kehm, Margaret. Interview, 25 July 1978, Warren, Pa.

Kramasz, Jennie. Interview, 27 June 1979, Manchester, N.H.

Lima foreman. Interview, 24 Aug. 1982, Lima, Ohio.

Leiphart, Valetta. Interview, 17 June 1982, Red Lion, Pa.

**McDowell, Margaret. Interview, 9 Jan. 1980, Red Lion, Pa. Conducted by KML.

Markle, Raymond. Interview, 26 Feb. 1977, Hanover, Pa. Letter to author, 22 Feb. 1977.

Mattingly, Editha. Interview, 21 June 1977, Hanover, Pa.

Nietupski, Natalie. Interview, 19 Sept. 1978, Detroit, Mich.

Ograin, John R. Interviews, 11 Aug. 1976, 8 July 1977, 15 Sept. 1978, 19 May 1979, 17 May 1980, Chicago, Ill. Letters to author, 15 Jan. 1976, 29 Sept. 1979.

Piwkowski, Helen, and Chromki, Cecelia. Joint interview, 21 Sept. 1978, Hamtramck, Mich.

Purzon, Rose. Interview, 21 Sept. 1978, Detroit, Mich.

Rogiers, Leon. Interview, 27 June 1979, Manchester, N.H.

Salantak, Frances. Interview, 20 Sept. 1978, Detroit, Mich.

Santana, José. Interviews, 11 Jan., 13–16 Aug. 1976, 6–11 July 1977, 15–17 Sept. 1978, 16–18, 20 May 1979, Chicago, Ill. Telephone conversations and letters are too numerous to list separately.

Shea, T. Frank. Interview, 26 June 1979, Manchester, N.H.

Shea, Theresa. Interview, 28 June 1979, Manchester, N.H.

Sodekson, Julius. Interview, 29 June 1979, Roslindale, Mass.

Speaker, Lucille. Interview, 22 Aug. 1982, Lima, Ohio.

Stauffer, Pauline. Interview, 21 June 1977, Hanover, Pa.

Steber, Raymond W. Interview, 24 July 1978, Warren, Pa.

Sutton, Stella. Interview, 19 Aug. 1982 and telephone call, 21 Aug. 1982, Lima, Ohio.

Theisen, William J. Interview, 17 Aug. 1979, Denver, Colo.

Thompson, Edward. Interview, 9 Jan. 1976, Red Lion, Pa.

Thompson, Harry. Interview, 16 June 1982, Red Lion, Pa.

**Thompson, Harry and Edward. Interview, 21 Dec. 1979, Red Lion, Pa. Conducted by KML.

**White, Agnes. Interview, 4 Feb. 1982, Evansville, Ind. Conducted by Glenda Morrison for the Indiana State University-Evansville, Indiana Labor History Project (ILHP).

Wieand, Norman. Interview, 21 June 1984, Quakertown, Pa.

*pseudonyms
**not interviewed by the author

Index

A Note on the Author

Patricia Cooper received her Ph. D. in history from the University of Maryland and is a member of the history and politics faculty of Drexel University. She has published articles in *Labor History,* the *Journal of Social History,* and in Charles Stephenson and Robert Asher, eds., *Life and Labor* (New York, 1986). She is currently writing about workers in Philadelphia between 1930 and 1960.